I0643848

Kohlhammer

Praktische Theologie heute

Edited by
Stefan Altmeyer
Christian Bauer
Kristian Fechtner
Thomas Klie
Helga Kohler-Spiegel
Benedikt Kranemann
Isabelle Noth
Birgit Weyel

Volume 168

Ottmar Fuchs

Committed Spirituality

Verlag W. Kohlhammer

1. Edition 2020

Production: W. Kohlhammer GmbH, Stuttgart

Print:
ISBN 978-3-17-037549-9

E-Book:
pdf: ISBN 978-3-17-037550-5

Contents

Foreword

The texts collected here come from different periods of my teaching and research at the Universities of Bamberg and Tübingen. In this and in their thematic classification they represent the result of my pastoral theological and practical theological work, especially what is important to me to this day. This English volume will not have an analogous German volume.

The theme of this book suggests that it is always about the connection between faith and commitment, spirituality and social practice. Spirituality will be recognized in the fruits; spirituality will be the source of solidarity. Again and again, the dynamic of this theme is emphasised and with it also the associated turn of the Second Vatican Council from word to deed, from faith to experience, unfolds.

In one of his last speeches at a conference with Greek scientists and trade union representatives in Athens in May 2001, Pierre Bourdieu, the French sociologist of culture, made it clear how dangerous knowledge, reduced to performance and application, is when it is linked to the processes of globalisation policy. The knowing person then becomes the accomplice to a development against which they would actually have to stand if he or she combined their knowledge with the commitment to more justice. Bourdieu therefore qualifies the dichotomy in the knowing minds between knowledge and commitment as disastrous and demands knowledge that cannot be put to service for anything, but which, with all its professionalism, never ignores the horizon of justice. However, this commitment side of knowledge can only emerge and live if it is anchored in and networks with the corresponding social movements and organisations. What this means for the relationship between social educational institutions and the pastoral mission of the Church must be spelled out accordingly, especially in the field of pastoral work.

Sometimes the original context comes to light in the essays, such as the discussion about the Women's World Day of Prayer in 1995 on the question of whether Palestinian Christian women are allowed to pray the Jewish lamentation prayers of the Bible. This sense of occasion does not prevent, but rather encourages the transfer of the discussion to other and current contexts, such as the forthcoming World Day of Prayer in 2024, which will again come from the experiences of Palestinian women.

The translations are mostly pre-translations, not in the sense that they are not complete translations, i.e., raw translations, because they are complete, but they were also always correctable and made precise against the background of theological meanings and ideas. Some texts I translated first and then had corrected. This is especially true for the sermon attempts at the end of the book.

I thank all those who have taken the trouble to translate, understand and edit my texts with all my heart. I would particularly like to thank Mrs Margaret Lampe, who has examined the entire text for its English compatibility, so that the English language is not overly injured by the permanent temptation to Germanise it. I would like to thank her for her patient, prudent, interested and often difficult clarification of the English text. Many thanks also to Mrs Andrea Töcker for doing the typesetting.

Since I have worked on the English text to the end, supplemented it and changed it, all mistakes and clumsiness are at my expense. The respective translators have no liability in this respect. In the appendix at the end of the book the translators are named as far as I know them. Since the division of the chapters does not always coincide with the published articles, there are overlaps in the translation parts as well, i.e., they are insertions and changes that I have first translated and then inserted myself.

I would like to thank the editors of the publishing house, Mr Sebastian Weigert and Mr Florian Specker, for their kind support of the project and the editors of the series "Praktische Theologie heute" for inclusion in the series. I think back fondly on more than 25 years of our work and our meetings in this circle, especially on the fascinating colleagues with whom I was allowed to work.

The deeper motive for this publication is also emotionally anchored. The very idea that I will be able to give this book away on my next visits to England and Ireland to people I am very fond of fills me with joy; I am also looking forward to sending this book to my colleagues and friends in the countries where I was invited. I was invited to give guest lectures or have guest professorships at Pretoria at the Unisa (I am thinking in particular of Henny Pieterse and Jaco Dreyer), at Augustin College in Johannesburg as well as in Chicago at Loyola University and at Theological Union College (with Robert Schreiter). Before that I learned and participated in a training course for catechists at the Lumko Institute in Johannesburg.

It's been 50 years since I came to England for the first time. Many trips followed, almost always also to Buxton, sometimes with different company, in 1973 as chaplain with my youth group from the parish of St. Michael in Nuremberg, several times also with my sister Irene and with Brigitte Fastenmeier and Ulrike Bechmann. My Anglophilia began in 1969, while I was still a student, with a working stay at the Spastic Society Residential Centre in Buxton, in the High Peak District south of Manchester. After many subsequent stays in Buxton, this city became something like my English home.

I dedicate this book to all those whom I have learned to appreciate and love in these contexts:

To the deceased in grateful memory:
Biddy McCarthy and her father John, with whom I lived in 1971 in my diaconate internship in Buxton. Janice Baker, the other dear colleague in care. Gerry Collins, the priest in Buxton, later Ashbourne. For several years I was allowed to spend two to three weeks each in his parish so that he could go on vacation. Fr. Dennis Higgins, Buxton as well. We were connected by an intense friendship and deep spiritual understanding. I am also thinking here of my school friends Hans-Günther Nievelle and Erwin Meiler, who accompanied me to England several times. They also died far too early.

To the living in friendly affection:
In Buxton Pat McDonald and her family, to whom I am very much indebted until today. Sr. Bernardette Doherty from Presentation Convent and her hospitable family in Ireland, Sue and Mike Hardman and their family, thank you again for a long and cordial friendship. I have wonderful memories of the hikes to Solomon's Temple and through the Goyt Valley. Martin and Nicki Ott and their family near Lincoln, for whom I was allowed to conduct the marriage ritual in the village church of Holton le Moor.

A. Realisations of the Good News

I. Basics of the Church

1. *In the Beginning: Word and Deed*

1.1 The Experience of Meaning

I would like to begin with some socio-linguistic deliberations or "grassroots" concerning the relationship between word and meaning. When a young child learns to say "mama", then this happens in the context of a certain particular encounter where the mother behaves in a certain way with the child and gives this process a name, "mama". Therefore, from the beginning, the meaning of a word is defined in the context of certain experiences by actions with which it is used and learnt. Even when in advanced stages of learning vocabulary and of linguistic structures, the power of abstract thinking increases to connect the same words with different concrete individuals (other children also have mamas and they all look different); the child does not lose the deep-rooted "case history" of his or her unique own mother and the linked learning process for this term (with all its ambivalent power). How mothers with other children are and look is learnt in encounters with these themselves.

The enormous achievement in learning a language lies in the combination of the abstract and the concrete; the term "mama" can be used for all mothers, even when they are all different and even contradictory. For the mothers of other children there is no separate word in the linguistic system because the term "mother" means all women with a child or children. The term "mother" on its own does not go into details concerning which mother is meant, a liberating or a suppressing one. To which particular mother this term relates is not defined by the word, but, for example, by an additional pointing phrase such as my mother or John's mother, etc. The speaker refers to a particular person and evokes the corresponding concrete experience.

These simple considerations already make clear that there are two definitions of a word: the lexical meaning within a language system (mother is a woman who has a child or children) and the referential definition that refers to a particular mother "outside" of the language system. The meaning is only unequivocal, unambiguous in practice, when the speaker combines the word with a concrete person or real facts. The latter case can happen in two ways: in the connection of the word with a story about the concrete person or in connection of the word with realty itself, for example, with reference to a personal or actual process that is happening in direct experience. The latter happens relatively rarely unless one happens to have a photograph or film in one's pocket. In linguistic communication we mostly have to rely on naming the actual subject in speech itself, namely through description or narration. This involves a high power of differentiation, namely between the one and the other realisation of the same word. This happens for the benefit of communication and creates understanding and a connection to reality.

The relationship described above between word and reality is applicable to all areas and levels. Such great words as justice and freedom, which are used by everyone, are only defined by the reality connected with these words. The freedom of which dictators speak is different from the freedom that is used in a situation of democracy. Although such words have a quality of automatic agreement (everyone is in favour of them), they do not express much if their universality is not reduced by the fact that the speaker can convincingly enough describe and relate that which she or he actually supports.

A term not only attains its meaning by the fact that its quality is abstracted and defined in our thoughts, but also by the fact that one can refer to a reality or an action and can say, "Look how I do it and how the others do it or what the conditions are and how the relationships are structurally controlled; that's what I mean when I talk of freedom or peace!" Only then do the differences and contradictions of the discussion partner become apparent. And only then does one no longer argue about "fictitious" phenomena ("ideologies") but about the formation of real existing relationships. To understand a term, one must reduce it to its material or communicative components. Only when I can say that and how a word is linked with a particular action does the word achieve a dimension of meaning that describes the praxis.

To avoid possible misunderstandings, I wish to make clear at this point that the use of the term "action" here does not exclusively mean active behaviour but refers to human intentional actions as a whole,[1] also, for example, to being silent and waiting. The latter is integrated into the term "action" because I understand it as an action of and between human beings where not only speaking and giving have a place, but also silence and receiving, not only activity but also suffering.

We have now reached a brief anthropological background to understand the following more clearly: especially how the Bible deals with the word "God".

---

1 Cf. J. Habermas, Zur Logik der Sozialwissenschaften (Frankfurt a. M. 3/1973) pp. 138–164.

1.2 Biblical Stories of God

If we consider the experiences with God in the Old Testament, then in the very first revelation of the name YHWH we see something unusual and at the same time characteristic. This name "I am who I am or who I will be" (cf. Ex 3:14) contains no general or abstract quality that could be used to name God (by, for example, superlatives such as "all-bountiful", "omnipotent" or "omniscient"). The name says "only" that God is and will be there. It describes in this form a personal existence that cannot be obviously determined on a level detached from the concrete and real experience. In this respect, the name is "empty" or rather it is open for a meaning that still has to be experienced. This is concurrent with the Old Testament commandment that one should not make for oneself a graven image of God (cf. Ex 20:4; Dtr 5:8).

In the Bible the name of God only achieves meaning because it is told and discovered in connection with very specific encounters and experiences. The name "YHWH", for example, becomes meaningful in connection with the remembrance of the Exodus story or with other experiences of God's people: God is known through these stories and experiences and moreover as someone who stands on the side of the people and does not withdraw his trust and frees them from sin and oppression. The name YHWH in Israel is thus not determined by a summary of abstract qualities and titles full of authority (although these also exist, they are always in the context of or as a result of concrete experiences, in particular in the use of the psalms in prayer). God achieves moreover meaningful contours by the fact that God can be related with reference to real experiences in dynamic verbs, that is, in the dimensions of encounters and actions. (The verbal-structure of the Hebrew language is indeed the fitting linguistic medium for that purpose.) Otherwise, there is no longer a connection with the biblical God.

This process is always concerned with unique, very different stories which cannot be copied and which are very different, which, however, always "illustrate" the same in their differentiated situations and people: this very same is the liberating devotion of God in the history of humankind. The experience with God illuminates the fragments of human life like the light in a prism with contrasting colours, which are due to the possibilities and impossibilities, the richness and limitation of real people. Of course, there is nothing to be said against theologians who with logic argumentatively and speculatively consider how one may reflect on God and what one may further say about God. This "systematic theology", however, should not lose its contact with its basis of stories and experiences, in which the decisive and unique interpersonal encounters take place between God and humankind, which are thereby made possible for future experiences. Only an illustration of the term God through such memories redeems and releases us from having to produce God ourselves in our thoughts or to subordinate God to our argumentative or even magical access.

It is clear here that the biblical personality of God maintains the secret of God for, although one can name God in such unique stories of encounters, God does not become generally definable. The Old Testament, which is always accused of being too anthropomorphic and of referring too much to God in human terms, here displays itself as a critical stronghold against a theology that wants to ensnare God in thoughts and seize him by means of systematic connections. Inasmuch as this theology wants to possess something of God, it is more anthropomorphic than to tell of God in the context of concrete interpersonal stories because these stories remain open in their uniqueness of the you and I/we relationship for new stories in the present and the future in which God enters into new and unique encounters with new people. In this way God's promise made in the memory of the old stories will be realised once again in a different way than it can be calculated and foreseen by us humans.

Already in the written word, differing, in part contradictory human stories of experiences of the same God come together, so that neither unity nor a freedom from contradiction is characteristic for the presence of God in such stories, of which there are many, even contradictory ones because they all only come from individual people, however general they claim their thoughts to be. The answer to the justified question as to the "unity" of a definition of God in the creed cannot be given in a theological system of thought which requires the agreement of all believers, mostly in the form of structural subordination. The unity exists rather in the fact that the different stories are rooted in the same God and supplement each other as unique stories in their untouched individuality as well as in their ability and need for mutual interchange.

Moreover, the stories of YHWH contain a characteristic double structure, which is discussed in theology in the relationship between the indicative of God's mercy and the imperative of human behaviour, between given talents and using these talents. God is experienced as a liberating and helping companion in one's own distress. God provokes a particular interpersonal relationship and allows and enables us to act in a just, helping and liberating way with other people. Both dimensions related to the presence of God in the history of the people are given in special stories; Israel remembers the Exodus story from the viewpoint of the liberation of God; Israel remembers individual stories of the prophets which never arbitrarily referred to the will of YHWH but made perfectly clear that the belief in YHWH and his word are only compatible with a definite spiritual, social and political praxis. That these texts which thematise human behaviour are quite different in character and exist in tension with each other is apparent because of the differences between the people and situations and because of the different radicalness or compromise necessary or possible in a special context. Here also we see the mutual ability and need for interchange so that throughout the history of many stories one may experience what it means to organise one's life and act according to the will of God.

1.3 Jesus's Practical References to God

The embodiment of God that began in the Old Testament achieves its deepest foundation and realisation in Jesus of Nazareth. God becomes human through Jesus and takes the responsibility for his own practical "historical" and unique definition. The presence of God in history is then determined from that point onwards by the remembrance of the story of Jesus Christ. God does not "come from on high" in the form of ruling knowledge for humankind and does not appear before humankind in a showy overbearing display, dispensing redemption as a decree: "Because I am love, you are all redeemed!" She rather risks herself to show that she is love; he himself risks a story in which he appears and in which he realises himself in the words and deeds of a particular human being. God shows this love in the detail of a single man. To explain himself, God points at his only beloved son, as is told and illustrated in the story of the baptism of Jesus: "And when Jesus... was praying, the heaven was opened ... and a voice came from heaven, 'thou art my beloved son; with thee I am well pleased'" (Lk 3:21ff.). God shows us the real human being Jesus: look at him, then you will know who has a relationship to God; then you will know what the Kingdom of God means. Who God is as well as what humankind could and should be is given its meaning by the actions of this man and his relationship to God and humankind.

Let us now also consider the story of the transfiguration of Jesus on Mount Tabor. Here God also points to Jesus and refers to his words and actions: "That is my son, my chosen, listen to him!" (Lk 9:28–36, here 35). Those involved must once again descend to the ground level of humankind and the transfiguration has no value of its own but shows itself to be the "enthronement" of the human life of Jesus of Nazareth and his way to the cross, which he risked for the sake of love and as a result of the necessarily connected criticism of the inhumanity of those in power. To deal with God has to be a very earthly thing. Only as such it is heavenly enough.

Accordingly, Jesus himself does not speak of God outside of concrete healing and participating actions, outside redeeming and saving encounters. In doing so, he stands in the tradition of the prophets of Israel who claimed that humankind behaves in the way God has behaved with them, in that humankind works for justice for all and for mercifulness towards everyone and does not hide injustice and mercilessness by pious words. He speaks of and demonstrates the Kingdom of God when he carries out his mission of mercy and salvation in liberating encounters with the poor, the stigmatised and the weak or when he forgives in God's name those who have sinned. He also speaks of the Kingdom of God when in his stories and parables he shows solidarity with the poor and suffering. "When I heal with my finger on my hand, drive out terrible alienation and speak and act against the marginalisation of the suffering and the excluded then the Kingdom of God has reached you!" In his realised as well as related stories, the term "God" is endowed with an unmistakable practical unambiguity. These stories do not exclude the suffering and/or different people but incorporate them and relate the effect of God amongst the people in it. The effect of God is such that it always concentrates on the basic contradiction between those who create suffering and those who fight against suffering and risk themselves in this contradiction.

Jesus thus demonstrates (Lk 11:4–5) the "truth" of his Gospel and his sending in answer to John the Baptist in that he allows his healing deeds to be related with reference to Isaiah: "The blind receive their sight, the lame walk, lepers are cleansed, the deaf hear ... the poor have good news preached to them." The coming Lord will thus ask us if we have given the hungry food or if we have welcomed strangers and have visited the sick in his name (cf. Mt 25:31–46). Strangely enough, the Lord will obviously not question what we have believed. The religious outsider in the Samaritan story is the justified one because he helped the suffering man and the priest who was hurrying to the temple to serve God did not understand anything (cf. Lk 10:25–37). And Peter's verbal acceptance of Christ and his flight from following the suffering Messiah also belong here: Peter is blessed for his profession of faith as the "rock" of the Church and is called Satan for his flight from the real imitation of the surrendering and powerless Messiah for the sake of others.

These are the details by which the Kingdom of God becomes reality in the history of humankind. The criteria are explicitly of a practical nature! The conflicts with those who, although they also talk of YHWH, show counter-effective behaviour and conduct (namely, they cheat people of their rights and freedom) are predetermined. The deadly conflict explodes because of the irreconcilable contradictory deeds of the adversaries that they associate with the definition of God.

Let us now bridge nearly two thousand years and proceed to the Second Vatican Council. Here we will find a theological method that reinstalls what we realised in the Biblical Revelation.

2. *Christian Belief within Redeeming and Liberating Experience*

2.1 The Benefitting Church

I would like to start with a particular text that may serve as a preamble. The text is from Pope John XXIII who spoke these words a few days before his death. I understand these words as his legacy in the context of our subject: “In the presence of my colleagues, I am spontaneously moved to renew the act of belief. This is a proper thing for us priests, as we have to deal with the highest of matters for the good of the whole world, and therefore we must allow ourselves to be led by the will of God. We are orientated more than ever today, certainly more than in the last centuries, to serve humankind as such and not only the Catholics and are orientated in the first instance and above all to defend the rights of humankind and not only those of the Catholic church. The present situation, the challenge of the last fifty years and a deeper understanding of belief have confronted us with a new reality, as I said in my speech opening the Council. It is not the Gospel which has changed; no, we are the ones who are just beginning to understand it better. When one has had a long life and has seen oneself confronted with the new tasks of a social engagement at the start of this century and when one has spent twenty years in the Orient and eight in France as I have done and as a result is able to compare different cultures, then one knows that the moment has come where we must recognize the signs of the times, where we must seize the possibilities offered and look to the future.”[2]

I would like to underline the following sections of this text as I repeat them in the following summary: The act of belief, its renewal and dealing with the highest of matters have as their aim the well-being of the whole world. Therefore, we are orientated today to serve humankind as such and not only the Catholics and are orientated in the first instance and above all to defend the rights of humankind and not only those of the Catholic church. In my opinion, these comments express in a highly concentrated form the basic intention of Vatican Council II.

Thus, the issue is not only to “win” people for the Church, but also to question what the Church does with those people that it has already “won” for itself. Does it want to bring them into a ghetto-like church that only carries out the salvation of its own institution or does the Church want to enable the people to humanise their environments because they are supported by a church that realises itself for a more humane world and thereby for the Kingdom of

---

2 Cf. Orientierung no. 52, 10 (1988) p. 109.

God (with all the fragmented quality and partiality of these attempts by Christians and the Church to create as much reality as possible for the Kingdom of God)? The knowledge of the Good News is therefore not to be spread in a privileged know-all manner or as a ruling knowledge, but as a knowledge in our faith that should be for the benefit not only of ourselves, but also of as many people and cultures as possible. Thus, it is not primarily a question of acquiring competence and authority for the most effective application of strategies; it is rather a question of for what purpose both are to be employed.

One can, for example, read and teach the biblical text in a competent way, from the perspective of knowledge and method, but still basically misunderstand the critical background of evangelising, if one does not read the text principally and practically from the perspective of mercifulness and at least longed-for justice. When one does not approach biblical texts from the perspective of such practical hermeneutics for the benefit of humankind and particularly the suffering, then one will all too easily functionalise them for that which one wants to achieve (in particular for herself or for the benefit of a strong church). It is my concern therefore that we reach the basis of our identity and ask why we, as Christians and as the Church, are there and are called to be such in the world.

In the theology of Vatican Council II, a theological basis is given that can no longer be circumvented to disarm dispensing with much that in the long term has a destructive effect on us and others and to look what is possible for us and what is necessary according to the Gospel. Then, however, we must tackle that and act. However, nothing should be understood in terms of "doing still more" and progressive excessive demands, which rightly provoke defensive reactions. It is more probable that we should not do some of the activities that are at present taking place and should devote this energy to those places that are more necessary according to the Gospel and those affected. It is possible to do less but to do that then with more courage to stand up for one's belief and courage to take up our position and to show solidarity with those who need mercifulness and justice.

Vatican Council II places the authentic unity of belief and life, dogma and pastoral (the whole of actions and non-actions in certain contexts), teaching and praxis in the centre of its statements. It is here that we see in effect the dogmatic progress of this Council[3]. In the present strategy of forgetting and removing the importance of the Second Council, it is repeatedly said that the council did not announce any new dogma on the semantic level, that is, in the area of words, and for this reason it is not so binding. Such a conclusion is misleading. Of course, it is simply not correct, because the dogmatic progress of the Second Vatican Council, which is decisive for all church dogmata, lies in

---

3 Cf. E. Klinger, Der Glaube des Konzils. Ein dogmatischer Fortschritt. In: id./K. Wittstadt (ed.), Glaube im Prozeß (Freiburg 1984) pp. 615–626.

the fact that the dimension of experience and praxis of the Church's teaching and thus of all its dogmata is questioned. (Of course, the Council's texts should be read in its deeper intention and not just on the surface where, in its formulation for the sake of compromise and achieving working majorities, it can be used and quoted for completely differing positions). We have many dogmata for which the corresponding confessional agreement is demanded. At the same time, there is an enormous deficit regarding their existential meaning concerning the people's daily life, that is, their relevance to human existence. Which experience and design of human life do the Church's teachings challenge, offer and develop? Behind this is the unspoken idea that the treasures of our belief have been too little discovered to date for the communicative and liberating praxis of humankind and for the formation of social structures.

2.2 The Practical Meaning of the Teaching

This basic intention begins already with extreme consistency in the Dogmatic Constitution on Liturgy. In it, the teaching of the sacrament concerning the Holy Mass and what it has to do with the teaching of the Church in the context of apologetic and/or catechetical inculcations is not only renewed and impressed upon us, but the universal question is how the Holy Mass must be altered and conducted so that the believers may experience what the Church means by it in its teaching. The question of experience has changed the liturgical praxis to date. In this way, the text is aware of the "signs of the time", which themselves have a theological quality. For this reason, there is the extension of the service in word, the stress of the simplicity of symbols and above all the introduction of the vernacular.

This basic intention of the question of how that which has been collected and "secured" in the teaching of the Church for a long time finally develops its practical meaning for the people is inherent in all the texts of the Vatican Council, above all in the Dogmatic Constitutions *"Lumen gentium"* and *"Gaudium et spes"*. The question that dominates the latter text is: If what the Church claims of itself in its teaching is true, namely that it is here for the salvation of the world and can be termed at least in an analogous sense as "sacramentum mundi", how must the Church realise itself and be amenable to the world? Furthermore, how must it deal with the world so that it can be really experienced as that what it claims to be, namely, as salvation and liberation for the world in terms of the biblical message of God. In fact, quite a few systematic theologians have worked out that the Pastoral Constitution has to be regarded as the key text in order to understand Vatican Council II as a whole, for in this text the Church assesses itself from the outside perspective of itself. The meaning of the Church is the response it elicits.

In the Constitution on the Church, the same question is posed "towards the inside": How must the Church develop itself so that its own members experience their existence in the Church as a redeeming enrichment of their lives? For this reason, you find the basic importance of placing the people of God before the hierarchy and the basic importance of the charismata of all (cf. Lumen Gentium No. 12).

Even the very heart of the matter, the Dogmatic Constitution on the Revelation, links the Revelation of God strictly to the experience of the biblical authors. Without their vocations in their characteristic qualities as well as in their one-sidedness and in their own particular historical situation, the revelation would not have been possible.[4] Revelation and the content of the teaching can never attain historical meaning and reality through humankind without the influence of humankind upon them. Reality can only be obtained in the unbreakable connection with human experience and lives as well as with their diversity amongst each other, which can even go so far as being contradictory. The biblical revelation shows, in correspondence to it, not only a *variety* of vivid events, but often also different stories that are *contrary* to each other. For example: You can hardly compare the fashion of belief (or better "non-belief"?) of Qoheleth (Ecclesiastes) with such a highly developed faith as you find in Deutero-Isaiah. The same happens between the first letters of St. Paul and the so-called Pastoral letters concerning the church structures. The lack of contradiction is none of the God's names in either the revelation (which was once real life) or real life.

This is the exciting, revolutionary aspect of Vatican Council II: namely, that in its texts, which are called the "Dogmatic Constitutions", the question of praxis is approached. Thus, at the latest since the Council, pastoral theology can no longer be interpreted, for strict theological reasons, as an applied science of dogmatics or of fundamental theology. Praxis belongs moreover to the dogmatic teaching of the Church itself. The question as to the praxis of the Church and Christians is not an application of dogma but is an integral part of it. This is precisely the dogmatic progress of Vatican Council II; God's gift of redemption and human deeds of liberation belong together.

And here is also where the nail is hit squarely on the head, bringing up a painful subject for our church and for being a Christian! This is what educational theory calls "paradoxical communication", which is manifested, for example, in the combination of noble words with in part extremely despicable deeds. For many people, the credibility of the self-realisation of the Church is determined by the question: What is the praxis of the Church like in the Church itself and in its environment compared with its message of the redeeming and loving God? Where the meaningful connection of this talk of God is at odds with the praxis claimed by it, the Church reveals itself to be hardly attrac-

4 Cf. Dogmatic Constitution on the Divine Revelation No. 11.

tive as a social offering of the Good News, which would be its authentic identity.

We arrive at a further basic intention of Vatican Council II without which the term "evangelising" in the Catholic understanding cannot be understood and that also is connected in essence with the aforementioned intention. If the question as to the human praxis and ability to be experienced is itself a part of the dogma, then the question as to each individual believer and his or her meaning for the Church now becomes vitally important. For this reason, the Pastoral Constitution concerns itself extensively with the *calling of Christians.*

Thus, the relationship between word and deed is linked with a very specific theology of the vocation of the Christians. The texts of Vatican Council II give prominence to the calling of people in an amazing way. The Pastoral Constitution takes up its whole first section with this subject (sections 1–57). It thus agrees with the People of God Theology of the Church Constitution. "Belief illuminates everything in a new light, it reveals the divine decision with regard to the integral calling of mankind and orientates the spirit towards really humane solutions" (Gaudium et Spes No. 11). The council thus made "the calling of the people to the focal point of faith".[5]

For example, baptism is therefore not only the fulfilment of the Church's obligation to spread the Good News (through word and sacrament), but it is also simultaneously the advance payment for the duty corresponding to a Christian life and social behaviour; not only as the duty of the individual Christian to make something for humankind and society out of her or his calling in the following of Jesus, but also as a duty for the Church and its representatives to believe in the vocation of the baptised. The gift in the sacrament and the evoked duty return at the same time as the social responsibility to the person responsible for preaching this sacrament. This responsibility is to realise this reality, which is presented in the sacrament, in their communicative behaviour to the receivers of baptism. That which the Church preaches and spreads as a gift of mercy not only has consequences for the lives of those receiving it, but also for those conveying it and for the social organisation of the Church. Those are thus both of the basic orientations of the council texts: namely, first, the unity of belief and life on the basis of the second aspect, the importance and responsibility of all those baptised and confirmed. The latter (and here I can only be brief) happens principally through the de-monopolising of the term "vocation", which, up to now, has been mainly reserved for clerics and members of religious orders, but which is now expanded for the whole of God's people. I emphasise this important double structure of the basic intentions of the Council for the reason that this hermeneutic key function for all texts is mostly not sufficiently acknowledged. It is my opinion that the great "miracle"

5 Cf. E. Klinger, Der Glaube an den Menschen—eine dogmatische Aufgabe. In: Theologie und Glaube 78 (1985) pp. 229–238, p. 230.

of Vatican Council II lies in the fact that the self-deprivation of power is being carried out in the centre of power of the institution itself and that the responsibility for the formation of the Church is being shared through communal responsibility and the involvement of all.

With such a "fundamental synodalisation" of the Church based on a new theology of vocation, the Council again raises another painful subject that is of decisive meaning for diaconia, namely, the fact that there are many people who are wounded by and afraid of the Church for the precise reason that inside the Church the importance of the individual for the establishment of social structures of the Church, as well as the responsibility of the individual for the belief of the Church (in particular in differences of opinion and in cases of conflict), is too seldom accepted and called for. I remind us here of the fitting sentence that Paul VI wrote a decade later in his Encyclica "*Evangelii nuntiandi*": that the different vocations of the believers "make up the richness and beauty of the evangelisation" (that is, of the Church!).

2.3 The Unarbitrary Nature of Praxis

I would like to make clear what the praxis- and person-orientated theology of Vatican Council II stands for by means of a brief example concerning the sacrament of confirmation. This example has the advantage that both intentions explain and need each other, for the connecting and unifying of practical experience with the teaching of the confirmation is at the same time identical with the importance of taking the charismata seriously for the formation of the Church. The sacrament of confirmation is as a rule administered in the context of an impressive liturgical scenario. The young people are told with great insistence, already in the preparation as well as in the administering of the liturgical service of the sacrament, that they have the Spirit of God and that they should believe that they are carriers of this Spirit. The problem is, however, that many administers and quite a number of priests, although they themselves believe in the confirmation (as far as what the teaching says about the sacrament of confirmation), have massive difficulties with the praxis that is necessarily connected with it: namely, when it comes to the practical test, to believe their word, when it is really necessary to trust in the confirmed young people and to deal with them according to the positive prejudice that the confirmation theologically intends for them, which means to expect important statements from the people, which are possibly enriching and indispensable for the building up of the community. To believe in confirmation is one thing. It is another to introduce the potential value of life (which the confirmation and every sacrament, every dogma, every piece of creed contain) into the real communication of the Church and, on this basis of the importance of all charismata, to organise the social forms of the Church, which belongs to the appropriate recognition of Vatican Council II, not only to encourage the people to accept and believe the teachings of the Church, but above all to always question and look for the real meaning of a certain teaching as far as the experience, social praxis and pastoral aspects are concerned. However, demands of belief are often made by those who do not realise the praxis that should be connected with their demands. Is it possible here that Jesus's word that one should observe and practise what the ministers tell you, but not what they do (cf. Mk 23:3 and Lk 11:46), applies to the officials of the Church? This criticism is, of course, true for all Christians. I am convinced that the more we Christians concern ourselves with the praxis of that which we believe, the less we will have to worry about the continued existence of the Church and the less we will have to reckon with approval from the false side (that is, from directions that think that they can use the Christian view of the world for a praxis that is contrary to the Kingdom of God).

The theology of Jesus, or rather his theopraxy, is directed towards a mentality within the Church in which the question of praxis is dealt with a good deal more arbitrarily and in a more egalitarian way than the unambiguity of faith in the field of the correct profession of belief. If, for example, a catechetic teacher has openly admitted problems with the dogma of the virgin birth, then he or she will not easily be spared difficulties relating to their employment. If, however, the teacher deals with the pupils for years on end in a despising way, then as a rule she or he will have no problems as far as their employment is concerned. Characteristically, the term "heresy" is more established on the level of the consensus of belief than on praxis, which is connected with belief (to avoid misunderstanding here, I do not wish to introduce the term "heresy" also on the level of praxis, but only to make the reduction of the term "faith" significant with this example).[6]

6 Cf. H. Dietzfelbinger, Diakonie als Dimension der Kirche. In: H.-H. Ulrich (ed.), Diakonie in den Spannungsfeldem der Gegenwart (Stuttgart 1978) pp. 112–118.

II. Church as Evangelisation

1. *Evangelisation*

1.1 Integral Belief

I would now like to move from the Council to the document "Evangelii nuntiandi", which Paul VI published at the end of 1975. In this document, the quintessence of Vatican Council II, as outlined above, is incorporated, more precisely defined and linked to the term of *"evangelisation"* as the appropriate *"terminus technicus"*. I would like to stress that the Catholic understanding of "evangelisation" is quite different from the many different meanings this term has acquired in the denominations and in particular movements in the churches. For example, it must not be confused with this term as it is understood within charismatic (in the special sense) or evangelical groups.

The term "evangelisation" occurs already in the Council texts, but in different contexts and in any case not in this characterised terminology. For this reason, it is incorrect to suggest, as is often done in a defensive manner, that the term "evangelisation" is imported from the theology of liberation and comes from South America. Evangelisation is moreover a term authorised by the Church's teaching itself, which reconstructs the decisive dogmatic progress of Vatican Council II and which is unthinkable without not only the experiences of the churches in Africa and South America, but also without the European history of enlightenment within theology and of particular movements in the West European church before the Council took place.

The dogmatic term "evangelisation", as it occurs in EN, concentrates the findings of the Council regarding the Gospel in teaching *and* acting on the basis of the Church as the people of God. The self-fulfilment of the Church is precisely at this point.

The South American Bishops Conference in Puebla made this paper, with the special agreement of John Paul II,[1] the basic document of their discussions and results, whilst in European countries it has remained relatively unnoticed. According to "*Evangelii nuntiandi*" (EN), one must understand the meaning of the Gospel in its entirety: evangelisation not only takes place verbally or in the sacrament, but also in actions of the personal and political sphere of the Christian and the community. Nothing can be removed from the evangelising effect

---

1 Cf. John Paul II., Predigten und Ansprachen (Dominikanische Republik/Mexiko 1979) ed. Deutsche Bischofskonferenz (Bonn 1979) p. 49.

of the Church. "Evangelizing means for the church carrying the Good News to all areas of mankind and to change them by its influence from inside and to renew mankind itself...it would thus be most correct to say; the church evangelizes when it concerns itself, through the divine power of the message which it preaches, at the same time with the change of the personal and collective consciousness of mankind, the activity in which they are involved, their real life and present environment ..." (EN no. 18). "Evangelization has to reach life ..." (EN no. 47). The whole world belongs to the target area of evangelisation, in particular regarding the "righteous edification of the human community" and the "salvation of the human personality".[2] Exactly here lies the identity of the Church: "Evangelization is indeed the grace and the essential, the actual calling and vocation of the church, its deepest identity" (EN no. 14).

In this statement, the identity of the Church is defined by means of a purposeful process and thereby the hierarchical structural dimension and manifestation are no longer (at least, not primarily) claimed to be the absolute criteria of truth for the authenticity of the Church. Here, in a criteriological process, is determined what and where the Church is, which cannot be understood in any other way than that the hierarchy is subordinated to this criterion and has to be measured by it. However, true not only for the hierarchy, but also for the whole Church, is the following: "the church, as the carrier of evangelization, is beginning to evangelize itself...The Second Vatican Council reminded us and the Synod of 1974 took up with vigour this subject of the church which evangelizes itself by constant change and renewal to evangelize the world in a believable way" (no. 15).

Of decisive importance is the view that the concept of evangelisation is not thought of as the identity of the Church solely within itself, for the Church has to realise itself as an evangelising body by realising itself from the inside *to the outside*, for the meaning of evangelisation is nothing other than the service of the Church to humankind and this service is no other than the one which it realises within itself. And only when it acts evangelically in word and deed in the way of Jesus Christ does it reach theological self-awareness of being the sacrament of salvation for the world and humankind as concrete salvation and redemption in their concrete circumstances or with the necessary changes in these circumstances. Evangelisation is thus not identical to the term Christianisation, which presupposes the Christianity of the Church as the producer of Christianity and the deficit of Christianity and the need for it among the people who do not belong to the Church. Evangelisation, on the other hand, presupposes that Christians and the Church are constantly in need of it themselves and therefore only in this process can they encounter the need of humankind for healing participation and liberation. The term evangelisation thus means an identity of the Church that is not restricted outwardly or inwardly, but in

---

2 Thus already in *Gaudium et spes* no. 3, 43 and 45.

which it gives itself for the salvation of all people and by this finds the way to its own identity.

1.2 Orientation to the Incarnation

The Church finds its identity in being a sign and reality of the redemption and liberation for the world because "a merging of the earthly and heavenly community"[3] exists. The reason for this has a Christological nature, as "God's word, through which all is created, became flesh itself to rescue all in complete humanity and to unite the universe". E. Klinger accordingly defines this more precisely; "In evangelization, the basic formula of Christianity, the formula of the Council of Chalcedon, the inconfuse-indivise (unmixed and undivided) becomes a principle of the solution of the problem of politics. This pastoral extension of Christology into sociology, in my opinion, points the way and is unfortunately still unknown in Europe".[4] The Gospel and humankind belong together, unmixed and undivided in their social and worldly contexts.

Evangelisation is therefore *solidarity* for humankind and for the world and is therein (and never divided from it) the *preaching* of salvation. Furthermore, in its relationship to God and in the promise of the Kingdom of God, the preaching of salvation transcends the real service to humankind and the world in two directions (it is thus not simply mixed with this service): as a release from the immense pressure of having to create the Kingdom of God themselves (which mostly leads to resignation or to violence) and also as a release from hopelessness in failure and at the same time as a dynamic to never relinquish the service and liberation (with an orientation to Jesus, that is, in following him). Thereby the believed transcendence becomes deed in one's own willingness to transcend the existing situation in the changing action of renewal.[5]

The Church community or parish thus always involves itself in the preaching of salvation *as* the servant of the world and in the service of the world *as* the preacher of salvation. This takes place whenever the Church is the place where people believe in the Gospel and strengthen each other in this belief *and* where people help and encourage one another to determine and notice the places (instead of repressing and keeping them quiet) where appropriate action is necessary.

It is also where Christians realise the appropriate processes of action by diaconia and liberation according to their hope. The processes of change in evangelisation are not only discussed but are also dealt with. In an accurate interpretation of the Christological context of reality, they have an incarnate

---

3 Cf. *Gaudium et spes* no. 40.

4 E. Klinger, Politik und Theologie. In: Theologie und Glaube 71(1981) 2 pp. 184–207, p. 185.

5 Cf. John Paul II. 'Ansprachen' p. 64.

quality, inasmuch as the word becomes flesh in the "body of Christ living on in the church" through this evangelisation process.

Dogmatic truths are thus not only maintained and argumentatively claimed in the spoken word but are experienced as principles of human existence and communication. Thus, the message of redemption in the Christological dogma of Chalcedon is proved true as liberation. Theology then possesses "being in this life" as it "exposes the horizons of liberation in everyday life" as the praxis of liberating and healing solidarity for humankind and the world.[6]

This can also be formulated in terms of the Kingdom-of-God theology. The decisive duty of the Church lies in the preaching of the Kingdom of God and, with the help of God, to create a real existence of this Kingdom in history. According to the spoken action of Jesus: when I liberate people from their conditions of oppression with the finger of my hand, when I heal their illnesses, when I show solidarity with them; when I remove their burden of guilt in the name of God and tell them of God's hope, then this is all connected with the Kingdom of God. God's reality comes to the fore in such mercifulness and justice. The Church is then the symbolic (in word and sacrament) and social (in the community and solidarity to the outside and inside) means for preaching and partial realisation of the liberating "dominion" of a humane God amongst humankind. The Kingdom of God means the gift of belief in a God who values all people in their personal and structural fragmentation, who loves them unconditionally and does not desert them, even, and particularly, in death. The Kingdom of God thus means the facilitating power to live, work and fight in one's individual historical and social situation for justice and solidarity.

That which the Church is able to call the Kingdom of God because of the biblical revelation in a way which gives hope and inspiration goes further than the Church in its factual presence. And this not only in the actions of love and justice of many people but also in many religious transcendent and non-religious symbolisations (in works of art, in the context of meditation, in poetry, in music, etc.) that maintain hope in many hopeless situations, also in the ever-threatening suspicion of senselessness in the risk of practically representing justice, freedom and love in this world.

In the background of this briefly mentioned Kingdom-of-God theology, evangelisation is then that process in which the Church not only believes in the presence of the Kingdom of God within itself, but also discovers, supports and provokes it in other forms, previously unknown to the Church, in people, cultures and societies. In addition, it gives the message that humanity and solidarity are not to be understood as mere laws which lead to despair or vio-

6 Cf. E. Klinger, Theologie im Horizont der Politik. In: S. Castillo et al. (ed.), Herausforderung. Die dritte Welt und die Christen Europas Regensburg 1980) pp. 47–63, p. 53.

lence, but as a blessing which also sustains in loss and failure because there is a God who shows solidarity with those also showing it and who gives with his help a new beginning to those who fail or are guilty in consolation without end.

The crucial difference in the image of the Church that stands to debate can perhaps be concentrated in two questions: do the people belong to the Church, or is the Church with the people? Is the Church realised as an end in itself in that the boundaries of the Kingdom of God are reduced to the boundaries of the Church and the membership of the Kingdom of God is strictly limited to the membership in the Church? After this church-integrated and integrating model the traditional sentence would still be valid; outside the Church, there is no redemption (also not beyond death). Then people who are still frightened by this can only subject themselves to the pressure of self-integration to take part in the reward.

There lies the fundamentalist attitude that one's own fundaments (belief, church, culture, view of life) represent as a matter of course good or at least the better, whilst other cultural and social areas are subject to the principal proviso of being bad or worse. If one views for example the relationship between Church and world in such a dualistic black and white view, then the Church can only produce good and the world bad. Everything which is not Church can only become good or better if it commits itself to the Church. The Church is regarded as identical to the Kingdom of God. Missionary work presents itself as a one-sided activity of the believers towards the godless. And as the "world" does not possess anything of value itself, the world can be used and exploited for the aims of the Church. In the instrumental use of that which the world has to offer in the way of human intelligence, energy, technology and media, one no longer needs to be petty. But such an instrumental use (better, misuse) of the "world" merely for the sake of the Church and its powerful influence is counter-effective to the service of the Church for the sake of the world, destroying the possibility to communicate with the world in a dialogical and appreciating way.

1.3 The Competence of the Basis ("Basis Communities")

If one can describe the identity of the Church in this way as a *process* of evangelisation, then preaching can no longer be reduced to the "authorised" preaching of the ministers in word and sacrament, although this is still indispensable (naturally in the communicative exchange with all Christians and charismata). When the "underdogs" of society are themselves the location of the presence of the "above" (of the Gospel of the Son of God), then this has consequences for a new definition of those responsible for this evangelisation.

The Church cannot take it for granted "that its message is restricted only to the religious area by not interesting itself for the current problems of mankind" (EN No. 34). Thus, one cannot be told often and expressly enough that evangelisation does not stop with preaching and the explanation of teaching. For evangelisation must reach life, the individual and social life; only then does this life reach the horizon of the Gospel and it will be opened in itself for the supernatural life, which is not the negation, but the transfiguration and intensification of natural life (c£ EN No. 47). Thus, it is true to say: "the whole church is therefore called to evangelization and thus there are different tasks within it which are to be fulfilled in the service of the conveying of belief" (EN No. 66).

Decisive statements from the Council are thus included in the precise context of the term "evangelisation". Here one has to consider particularly the inclusion of the theology of the *charismata* in the ecclesiological conception of the church as the holy people of God, *as* well as the Christological determination and simultaneous integration of the *service* for the preaching of redemption (and for believing in it) *and* for the humanisation of the world (where both of the latter occur in the Council documents unfortunately as relatively independent next to one another, sometimes divided between the preaching services of the ministers and the "worldly" services of the lay people).[7]

Accordingly, evangelisation is a *communal* duty of both lay people and ministers (and here not divided anymore between service for the world and service for the redemption). Only the whole parish can be the basis of this reality-orientated preaching, inasmuch as it has a social relevance for both the edification of the parish and for the improvement of the social environment. Those who wish to realise that "new way of life, of communal life which the Gospel opens up" form a community "which is itself a sign of change, a sign of new life; the church, the visible sacrament of salvation" (EN No. 23). Therefore, "out of the need to experience the life of the church more intensively, or out of the wish or the search for a personal atmosphere which the large parishes cannot offer" smaller church communities form, in which the individual life and the life with the Church and society are discussed amongst themselves based on the Gospel and in prayer to God (cf. EN no. 58).

All believers are principally theologically indispensable with their specific charismata for the processes of evangelisation as well as being indispensable in the self-experience of the parish as responsible and necessary participants:

First, the believers need each other to perceive adequately what is going on, to communicate with one another and to analytically comprehend the *reality*. They need each other, second, to discuss the revelation in the written word and tradition as the source of their hope, their solidarity and their

---

7 Compare for example *Lumen Gentium* no. 12 and no. 33 with no. 31.

change in praxis and in such *remembrance* to allow their individual charismata to be realised for the explanation of biblical and theological sources. Third, the believers need each other to talk together about the *change* in their ways, to conceive it in the various stages, to organise corresponding action and thus become, in the area of their situation for themselves and others, a place of humanity and salvation. For these *three steps of solidarity* (which, of course, often occur within each other and mixed up together) of seeing, judging and acting on the horizon of a Gospel which is collectively remembered and is realised in change, an ecclesiology can only be valid in which the charismata of all are required (also in their one-sidedness and thus in their individual abilities) and which forms the Church in unity and supplementation with one another.

Two *abilities* will have particularly to contact with one another within the "*seeing*" of diaconia: *first*, perception accompanied with mercifulness and, *second*, analysis orientated to social justice, so that individual help does not become stabilising therapy of the political or social system and so that, conversely, the structural criticism does not lose sight of the suffering and treats them without compassion. Christian diaconia should never come under suspicion of perpetuating the structural conditions through its abstinence in the field of political diaconia, by treating the problems and therapising them only caritatively. In this context, one must reflect more exactly on the specific processes of diaconal action, between actions of help on the one hand *and* social or economic criticism on the other, in their mutual relationship and support.

One could provisionally envisage these two *steps* of diaconia (concerning seeing and doing under the guidance of the Gospel):

1. the direct perception of human need *and* the analysis of its individual and structural existence and origins (seeing);
2. liberating actual and long-term action of help (with lasting patience) for the suffering (which improves their individual and structural situation now) *and* at the same time socio-political involvement which takes sides with appropriate social as well as political competence (doing).

Options based on social factors are to be defined in this sense individually and structurally. The term "option" pertains to the Latin American Theology of Liberation and means in no way something that is optional, but precisely the opposite. "Option" means decisive priorities, which have to be understood hermeneutically in the sense of the Magnificat, especially: "He has exalted these of low degree ... He has filled the hungry with good things" (Lk 1:52–53) and: "He has regarded the low estate of his handmaiden" (Lk 1:48). This means: all who enjoy no priorities at all, but are disadvantaged and below, are the hermeneutical and real basis in finding options in order to become "exalted". This is according to the will of God. Whoever, however, gives priorities to the ones who enjoy them already, so that they become even richer and more powerful at the expense of the poor, decides for options that are against God's will, who is going to send the rich away empty and to degrade the mighty.

The most crucial problem in this context is, however, how the competence of the supposed incompetent, how the importance of the unimportant people is guaranteed structurally. Which institutions have to be established so that the disadvantaged get their advantage to speak up? If we do not change the corresponding structures, then nothing will happen.

I would like to display this problem in the field of church ministry. The ministers of the church have their power for the sake of the powerless. It is their duty therefore to care for the structural possibilities that suffering people have something to say in the Church. They should not only speak instead of them or merely advocate for them, but they have to provide the institutional facilities in which the disadvantaged people can speak about their lives and needs. It is an integral part of the official ministry of teaching and preaching that the ministers know that there are two *sources* of Christian preaching the Gospel: first, not to forget the stories of revelation in the past, in the tradition, especially of course in the Bible. And, second, not to forget the people in the present, who are suffering and who are deprived of rights, for the real encounter with them is the condition of the possibility to understand the stories of the past as stories of victims themselves and to discover that the Kingdom of God is especially for them and has to reach them by means of the Church: following the most important victim according to the Christian belief, Jesus himself, who became a victim because he had shown solidarity with victims.

The decision towards an option in the highly complex processes of industrialised and computerised societies is not an easy one, especially if concrete situations are concerned. One cannot always formulate an option in general terms (as for a whole country, for example), but often only in contact with specific experiences of need in the place itself (with the unemployed, where their number is particularly increasing, with young people, where they are particularly in danger of drug abuse, with the refugees, etc.). Only based on such partially recognised social problems can interregional options be discussed. The social contradictions have to be discovered in a particular place and in detail, and they are easily distorted or even hidden by the global view of a society. Of course, conversely, structural analyses of interregional and global contexts must be applied to experiences of need that are confined to one area.

1.4 From the Many Words to the Decisive Deed

Maybe it is true that words are the Church's weakest resource. How does the great arsenal of words (both in the area of the Church's teaching and in the texts of the Jewish-Christian tradition) come into the realm of deed? For that which is the decisive action in the respective situation and for which we have the necessary competence and energy, there are, of course, too many verbal statements than that which we are able and have to put into action in the course of our lives. We are already limited by our corporeality and the limitation of presence forced on us by it, but also by the limitation of the length of our life and by our specific possibilities and impossibilities. The recognition of this limitation also belongs to our existence as human beings, if we do not want to play at being gods. Thus, the relationship of word and deed in individual people, but also in groups of Christians, in the parish and in the religious communities cannot be imagined in any other way than in the image of a funnel, through which only a small amount of the many words can reach their practical realisation as they pass down the tapered section of it. If the contact of word and deed happens in our life, then we are forced to make it in limited actions and limited places. It is important in the life of Christians, of the parish and of the religious orders to set one's own priorities in this process because one cannot do everything to see the chosen action through with the necessary consistency.

In the concept of evangelisation such a decisiveness in the goal of a person or of a community has to be called an "option" again. Therefore, this term must not be misunderstood as an oversized and excessive term of achievement but takes the reality and the limitation of the charismata seriously, as it also responds to definite challenges of the personal and social situation and at the same time concentrates itself on them. With reference to Jesus, we see that he allowed himself in his options to be determined especially by the situation of the oppressed, the disadvantaged and the suffering. Without doubt, the experiences of need of those affected have an outstanding prerogative to provoke the charismata of Christians and to be brought into contact with them. Thus, an option combines in a humane way the indicative of the personal and communal possibilities and the imperative of the situational and historical challenges. Necessary exertion in praxis and the necessary limitation in engagement need each other, so that, at least in one area, sometimes like a drop in the ocean, word becomes deed. The term "option" also combines eschatologically the tension and release (from total demands of the super-ego) of the "Yes, already" and the "Not yet" of the Kingdom of God within our history.

When the biblical prophets speak out, they never speak in an arbitrary way (concerning praxis) of the will of YHWH; rather they say unmistakably that the belief in YHWH and his choice of Israel and his word are only compatible with a specific religious, social and political praxis. It becomes clear that the prophetic process is sparked off at the moment when the determination of options occurs in the concept of evangelisation. Within evangelisation, the option determines that which is the concrete precision and unyielding nature of the biblical prophecy; prophecy, in the sense if this prophetic process within evangelisation, represents an inalienable characteristic of the Church's identity and existence, for the decision of priority is mentioned within it where in view of the position and time (of the individual, community, town, country, part of the world) an urgency of a specific action exists of a type which allows no deviation. Other matters become of secondary importance but not absolutely so, as in other situations and times they too may enter the horizon of priority.

The term "option" is therefore a term of criticism against any pastoral care of an "all around" nature, which wants to achieve and pursue everything possible, but does not tackle that which is decisive in a particular situation (in particular, in situations of need). This insight relieves us from the ever-present pressure of quantity, which is in our hearts and minds and replaces it with quality through limited quantity. Christians will not be able to do more in this present "eon" (age) if they *really* believe that the complete Kingdom of God can only penetrate our history with the coming of Jesus Christ. Our quantitative ideas of the super-ego have nothing to do with evangelisation. I believe that this is a completely redeeming and liberating message for all those responsible within the Church.

The term "option" is often accused of unduly narrowing the "fullness" and "universality" of the revelation, in that it reduces the *"free"* or "neutral" reception of the Gospel by a preliminary decision. The "option for the poor" is accused therefore of being a pauperism because the rich no longer appear as the target group of the revelation. Didn't Jesus die for all and hasn't he redeemed everyone? The latter is of course correct but does not include the fact that everyone may read and receive the Bible as he or she wants. Precisely when the Gospel is applicable for all (and not in general terms, but concrete), then their different situations must integrate into the communication with the revelation and must be made clear in it, so that they can be really reached as they are. The poor and the rich will be allowed or will have to identify themselves in the biblical texts with those as they occur there (for example, as the poor referred to in the first Beatitude or as the rich in the story of the rich young man). From this viewpoint, the option for the poor corresponds exactly to the "option for the rich", that the latter accept the Gospel when they follow Jesus in his message of change for the benefit of the poor and thus free themselves from their fear concerning their possessions and power (that is from their "spiritual poverty").

Options are from this perspective the discovery of situations and people of the present in the stories and figures of the Bible in order to activate the relationships between people and God or among people that are related and shown favourably there for a concretely defined and often also innovative recalling of the message. The options for the reception of biblical models (but also of dogmata) are thereby neither unlimited nor arbitrary. After all, the important issue for the determination of options is a decisive goal that does not make the Church's other areas of praxis redundant, but also realises itself in these and takes its power from them (particularly in the service in prayers for the suffering and to obtain the power to help them and bear the risks of solidarity). Always, you have to decide about non-optional options in living communities.

2. *The Service of God and the Service of Humankind*

2.1 Essential Realisations of the Church

A more precise definition of the three basic functions of the Church[8] (*koinonia, martyria* and *diakonia*; community, preaching and service) as well as their relation to each other is given from the perspective of evangelisation. This concern for the basic functions of the Church *identifies* the areas of action of the Church in the *theological* concept of evangelisation as well as in its systematic principles and practical consequences. In such a deeper definition, the reference to biblical terminology and events seems to be theologically more legitimate. The principal determination of the relationship between *diakonia* and *martyria* on the horizon of evangelisation also allows *koinonia* to appear more differentiated.

Although the basic functions are three or four dimensional (with liturgy), *martyria* (as verbal and sacramental preaching of the love of God) and *diaconia* (as the love of one's neighbour through justice and mercy) epitomise Christological qualities of evangelisation in a different way than *koinonia*, the life of Christians in their communities and parishes. Both cannot do without *koinonia* and both cannot remain together without *koinonia*! *Koinonia* is the communal social ground or sphere of orthodoxy and orthopraxy, of the service of God and the service of humankind, of *martyria* and *diakonia*, of kerygmatic-sacramental and diaconal mission for and with each other. The three dimensions, however, are not on the same level, as they are not of the same constitutive category. The church community has the character of being service for the sake of the relationship of God and humankind *and* for the sake of improving relationships within humankind. *Koinonia* can only do this when it *is determined* in its purpose-related structure by *martyria* and *diakonia*. This shows and makes possible all the more that its intrinsic value lies totally within this Christological identity, that is, proclaiming and presenting the Gospel of the redeeming God for all people and the liberating love of humankind through its own actions. Jesus sought the encounter and the company of people to give them his healing and liberating help and to proclaim the evidence of the merciful God and his kingdom within this real diaconia.

In effect then, there are "only" two *fundamental* dimensions to the existence of the Church, at least on the horizon of the concept of evangelisation: *martyria* and *diakonia*, which can never be realised outside the corresponding

---

8 As R. Zerfaß formulated them in 1974 based on S. Hiltner's classification, which had been raised by human science before it was associated with corresponding phenomena occurring in the New Testament. See R. Zerfaß, Praktische Theologie als Handlungswissenschaft. In: F. Klostermann/Id. (cd.), *Praktische Theologie heute* (München/Mainz 1974) pp. 164–177.

koinonia. However, *koinonia* must be more closely defined by the condition that it realises the *martyria* and *diakonia* authentically. Only then does the fundamental equality of all people and the reciprocity of all charismata materialise in *koinonia* so that nobody is entitled to produce dependencies from top to bottom in that the communication of words is conveyed as a ruling knowledge or the communication with people in need degrades the others to being mere objects of giving help.

Naturally, one cannot assume that every Christian and each Christian social form fulfil both the basic functions of word and deed thoroughly and equally. This would be an abstraction of the real possibilities and of a concrete, individual and collective theology of charismata.

By the term "collective charismata", I understand the fact that Christians join together, in a group or institution, with charismata directed in a similar way (for example, towards the "option" of a particular social work, again with different abilities and qualifications) to act more effectively and with more solidarity for others within this social form of the Church. In such *koinonia,* they attain a new quality which goes beyond the individual charismata, as a church that is on the spot. Thus, I maintain the legitimate partiality, the one-sidedness and the dominance of the presence of the Gospel in different social forms. The verbal and sacramental or the diaconal presence of Christ is made possible in the Church, precisely by the fact that both are manifested by means of different charismata and different communities all the more intensively for the necessary "one-sided" recalling of Christ *and,* at the same time, *that* both ensure that they remain in contact. If the "division of labour" in the Church does not collapse into sectoral separation and loss of relationship, then it is ecclesiologically legitimate and can justifiably be a socio-structural expression of the Christological "unmixed" combination of the service of God and the service of humankind in the Church.

2.2 Synopsis

The model suggested here of the areas of presence of evangelisation or basic functions of the Church can be depicted in the following diagram:

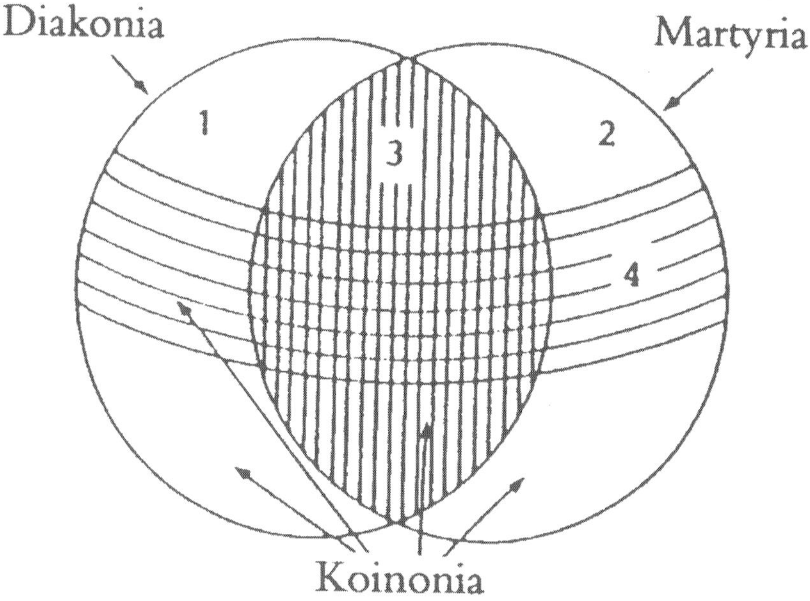

The overlapping circles represent the two basic dimensions of *diakonia* and *martyria* (in word and sacrament). In both, there are independent areas (1 and 2) such as the particular connection between diaconia and sociology (for the empirical analysis of social factors), as well as with the human sciences, which make qualified help possible. The relatively independent areas in *martyria* would be such areas as discussions of belief, the sermon and the liturgy, but also academic theology (with the appropriate partnerships of knowledge with philosophy, literature and linguistic science, for example). In these specific and characteristic areas of both dimensions, the other area is also necessary, but is only *implicitly* contained within it, in the condition of its being in another aggregation: Thus, a theology that reflects the dimension of *diakonia* in it will come to different results than if it develops only according to apologetic arguments. Conversely, a special diaconal spirituality is realised in a particular fashion on the basis of diaconal actions inasmuch as the relationship to Christ is experienced in the encounter with the suffering.

In many areas of life and deed, both dimensions will overlap each other as they are expressed in each other and *explicitly* "manifested" (3): when, for example, in a conventional parish (which normally concentrates on liturgical services, sermons and faith) social work groups are formed which realise the dimension of *diakonia*. Conversely, in a diaconal institution, its own theology will become explicit when its members (its social workers and their target groups) learn to speak to one another about their faith in real contact. *Diakonia* then incorporates *martyria* explicitly into itself when those involved in social care talk about their Christian motivation with each other and with the people they care for. In this area of the explicit realisation of the relationship between *diakonia* and *martyria*, both areas of presence of the Church learn how they live and exist within one another.

An entire congruence of both areas (= circles) every time and everywhere would be overtaxing and need not be postulated! The band that encircles both circles (4) shows the communication of exchange between both areas as they both learn to discover and value each other and also discover themselves in the other area. Here, the moments that otherwise belong to the independent areas of each dimension (1 and 2) come into contact with each other. In this band, too, much has to be communicated between the two dimensions, so that one may come to know the other from the dimension that is missing explicitly from the praxis in one's own area and life. This is important particularly because no one, and also no social form, is able to realise everything because of the limited charismata of an individual and the collective nature.

Let me now return from this point in my survey to *koinonia*. It realises itself here fourfold: as *koinonia* in both the areas of the basic functions of the Church, "concerned with themselves" (1 and 2), and in the area of encounter (3) where one explicitly expresses or realises the dimension of the other area in one's own and thereby provokes the possibility and necessity to establish contact with each other for the sake of mutual interest. That happens in the communication which encircles both areas (4, in which one hears from the other area, values its matter of concern, bears it with solidarity and discovers it within oneself at the same time as a matter of concern which, however, one cannot or will not *practically* follow oneself). The unity of *diakonia* and *martyria* is perceived, experienced and seen as important in the real *koinonia* amongst each other. Such determinations of the relationship of *diakonia* and *martyria* together and in each other refer to all scales and levels of their realisation: on the level of the diocese and charity organisation, the presbytery and social institution, the Bible group and social circle (in the parish, of different individual persons and within the same person concerning his or her different phases in life).

2.3 Diaconal Responsibility Of the Church's Ministers

From the perspective of *diakonia*, a characteristic social responsibility for the formation of the parish lies with the church officials and particularly the ordained ministers. It is a duty here which has a "hierarchical" quality inasmuch as it does not derive from the democratic majority but stands in "opposition" to this in a prophetic and critical way, for the civic majority of the parish can be so orientated that they do not allow the minority to have its say or they even suppress it. The minorities I speak of here are those that realise the diaconal relationship with those affected and support corresponding political options or are themselves affected. In such conflicts between the majority, which is distanced from *diakonia*, and a minority, which is close to it, between the "church from below" (democratically) and the "church which is totally down below" (socially), the church ministers have to flex their "hierarchical" muscles for the good of the latter and use their structural power for the sake of the powerless. On this horizon, the church's teaching is understandable because the first and last basis of the Church is not based on the democratic paradigm but on the paradigm of the "Kingdom of God" (which is given in the revelation) where the hungry are given food and the rich are sent away empty, where the lowly are raised up and the powerful are brought down (cf. Lk 1:51–53).

If one takes this option for the sake of minorities into the definition of democracy, that there should be no social contradictions within it and that, as long as this is not the case, the increasing importance of the poor is represented, then there should be no tension between fundamental democratising and the fundamental option. In this case, such an understanding of democracy contains itself the tendency towards social justice. In any case, the aforementioned tension must be thematised to avoid misunderstandings, whether the discussion is about the understanding of democracy itself or between the terms democracy and option.

If the church administration understands reality from the perspective of the poor and interprets from this standpoint of the "sign of the times", then it becomes open to criticism that it ignores the rich in all this. However, just the opposite is the case. A bishop in Brazil formulated it this way: "Of course I go to the rich, but I go to them after I've been to the poor. I visit the rich from the perspective of the poor!" The option for the poor prevents them from being grouped together with the rich as if the preaching of the Gospel could "pass over their heads" unaware of their specific situation. The option does not select out the rich, but makes clear their structural position in the real social life and thereby their social duty in evangelisation. Thus, it is not an option against the rich; rather, this option cares for them as the message reaches them according to the specific role they play in real circumstances. Whoever wishes to keep these circumstances out of the Christian faith also keeps evangelisation out of social contradictions and its history and reduces it to arbitrary words.

The definition of justice, mercifulness or humanity is best established from the standpoint of those who have to experience their lack personally and structurally. If one tries to define these terms separately from those affected, then they are deprived of their own interests. If the church administration learns to live and think from the viewpoint of the affected (like the USA bishops, for example, in their bishop's letter of 1986),[9] then the outlook on life and

---

9 Cf. N. Mette, Die kirchliche und politische Dimension der Caritas, in: H. Bogensberger/W. Zauner (cd.), *Perspektiven des Sozialstaates 2000* (St. Pölten, Wien 1990) pp. 53–66.

people gradually alters and becomes radical, and the path of leadership in the parishes also alters. The suffering not only have a right to be helped, but also have something important to say! The church ministry should make sure that in a Christian community the suffering always have the right to have their say and this particularly in the presence of those believers who are deaf in this respect. It should be understood that not only should church ministry speak as a lobby for the affected, but also that ministry works for social forms beyond such ambivalent caring for a situation where the affected may speak themselves. The so-called social "periphery" has great meaning for the "centre" and qualifies its real relationship to the Gospel. This will create more trust and willingness to cooperate on the part of the affected because they learn the importance of their lives and survival through social recognition and participating integration.

In Western European churches and parishes, one must warn against speaking of a "theology of liberation" and of "basic communities". As an example: even when democratic equality of all those baptised in our parishes is realised, this would not be a basic community as it is understood on the other side of the "Big Pond". For the basis there is not primarily characterised by these civic demands for freedom but by people in need and injustice (as well as by people who show solidarity with them), who take their own fate into their hands, define their situation according to the Gospel and organise their actions with the corresponding demands for liberation.

Who else should have the primary power of definition of justice than those who are the victims of injustice? There is no liberation that acts above their heads and hearts. Or to put it biblically: without listening to the message of the poor (here, disadvantaged people in general) there is no praxis of the Gospel, because otherwise the Kingdom of God does not set foot in the destructive conflicts of history.

Whoever wishes to preach the Gospel to the poor can only do so if she puts herself in a position where the poor themselves determine the liberating manifestation of the Gospel. For this reason, there is also, alongside the official church ministry of preaching, something like an equivalent unofficial "ministry of preaching" of those who live in need and injustice. If the preaching of the hierarchy "from above" does not seek this preaching of the hierarchy "from below", then the history of suffering and liberation in the Jewish-Christian tradition cannot be effectively linked with the suffering in the present for the sake of their liberation. Therefore, the spiritual and prophetic duty of the church official ministry lies in allowing and encouraging the prophetic and political preaching of the poor to take place: for their words are in fact connected with God, who wants them to be liberated.

For in the same way as the remembrance of the suffering and their liberation constitutes the horizon of the biblical belief in God, as tradition tells it, the stories of suffering and their liberation of the present are also not subject to a bourgeois democratic process, but have an implicit requirement for help and thus their need within themselves. A majority that is not at the same time representative of the perspective of the affected cannot decide on their existence and their obligatory claim. The stories of the victims are to be realised in a privileged way and taken seriously for the existence of the Christian and the Church: in liberating love and solidarity with them. One cannot decide upon the existence of past and present cases of victims and liberation by means of quantitative power (not even by the "power of the people"): moreover, not one jot of their stories or complaints should go astray. Only the word of the sufferers and people showing solidarity in the present gives the word of the people in the past who have suffered and shown solidarity its importance related to the present in a practical way. We have to discover that this direct connection to the poor belongs directly to the formation on the Church. In many cases this "other half" of the preaching is missing.

Therefore, the vital importance of suffering and disadvantaged people for the development of the church community must be brought to the fore against any superficial equality: not everyone has the claim to the same importance (in the ignorance of their different social status and personal situation). Moreover, the poor of the past and present have not only as much to say as the rich, but they have more to say than these others. Only this is the condition for the possibility that they are put on the same level as the others. One must listen to their descriptions and analyses of their situations as well as their stories and demands for change. Such a listening process has the holistic character of sharing life; in this way, the Church realises itself. Otherwise, it loses life and sinks back into the boredom of the insignificant because it has no direct contact with concrete need and is therefore not needed! Also, the needs of the Christians themselves sometimes have too little influence on the manner and way of community building. The competence for the diaconal way of life begins in the accepted plurality and perception of need in its own house.

Decisive for all this is the universality of the aforementioned competence of the poor: all poor people have this obligatory advantage due to their practical experience of need, not only the poor who belong to the Christian ranks. Such a right of the disadvantaged to receive attention cannot be split. Only the realisation of this fact frees the Church from the allures of indoctrination and authoritarianism and constitutes a liberating Catholicism, freeing itself from unnecessary limitations. Then, the Church risks a transition "beyond itself" that does the world good.

2.4 Social (and) Pastoral Care[10]

To prevent a serious misunderstanding which the above model could give rise to without further comment on my part, I would like to stress that *both* areas realise the redeeming or *saving* function of the Church in the world, with it and for it, and should not under any circumstances be divided from each other between "profane service" and "holy service". Thus, in the verbal and sacramental martyria, the healing (diaconal) service of Christ is also present in word. Thus, in the real *diakonia*, the resurrected Lord is also made present in the suffering and helping. *Diakonia* is in analogous "*perichoresis*" just as much a holy and divine service as the benevolent Jesus as a human being is the Redeemer and Son of God.[11] Valid for *both* forms of the realisation of evangelisation in several parts of the Church is the basic structure of the sacramental constitution of the Church as the one prime and original sacrament of salvation for the world, when it allows the offer of the belief in a loving God and the experience of God's love (of humankind) in the social behaviour of Christians to be "indicatively" experienced.

This view can base itself not least on an ecclesiology that is orientated on Paul's concept of *charismata* with its mutual dependence, which is to be realised in *koinonia*, of "carriers of *charismata*" or "*charismata* groups". One-sided charismata are then not only legitimate, but also necessary when they complement each other (also critically), interchange and thereby dispense salvation and liberation not only in teaching but also in praxis. The completeness of following Jesus is not easily possible in comparing each of us or our communities with the entire model of Jesus, but is guaranteed in a just as happily relieving as compelling way by the assembled serving of the different individual and collective *charismata* as supplements: in such a composition they realise the Church as the entire "body" of Christ (cf. 1 Cor:11–12).

Preaching and *diakonia* are related to each other in an analogous way as the "two natures" of Jesuanic, ecclesiastical and Christian existence and are undivided and unmixed in a relational (not identical) unity. Of course, preaching is always a *service* of word, but it is not the *same* as helping and liberating deeds. For this reason, preaching or catechesis cannot be interchanged with deed, and, of course, cannot replace it. Only when one keeps both areas apart are they able to criticise one another and break up ideologising identifications: when the minister preaches, then this is not all; above all, that is not *diakonia*

---

10 The conception of this term can be found in N. Mette, Sozialpastoral, in: P. Eicher/id. (ed.), *Auf der Seite der Unterdrückten?* Düsseldorf 1989) pp. 234–265.

11 The term "*communicatio idiomatum*" in Christology means that what you are able to attribute to the one nature (human) of Christ, you can also attribute to the other (divine); for example, if Jesus died on the cross, then the Son of God died on the cross, or, if Mary is the mother of Jesus, then she is the mother of God's son.

itself, not by a long chalk. Maintaining the word is not yet doing it. When the nurse carries out her duties, then this is not yet identical with her belief and with the preaching of the word. The actions of both have the same value but are not the same and need the respective supplementing of themselves (with regard to their own identity as well as the ecclesiastic identity through the charismata of the other).

If I consider *diakonia* and *caritas* here as a theologian, I carry out *theology* and do not think for one minute that this process is already identical with *diakonia* itself. My explicit diaconal action is located elsewhere. This does not exclude the fact that, within theology, there is also a diaconal component inasmuch as theology thematically concerns itself for *diakonia* or inasmuch as within the consensus of Christians the latter help each other in their *belief,* give fresh heart to one another and strengthen each other (Bible groups or discussions of faith, for example). However, such *diakonia in martyria* is again something different from *diakonia within diakonia*, as a disabled person is not only helped by encouragement in his or her belief, but also by the necessary physical help and social equality.

As the integral term of evangelisation also permeates the definition of pastoral action, the latter must also incorporate diaconal action. In such a context of evangelisation and of the Christian action defined by it, this means not only spiritual welfare, but also social, individual and physical welfare—also not only verbal preaching in the service and conversations of spiritual welfare, but also diaconal action in a healing community and in the liberation of the oppressed, in help for those in need and in solidarity with all who are disadvantaged. The lack of warmth and sincerity in the Church's pastoral care is based in many cases on its abstraction of how people are and also that faith is only understood, to a great extent, spiritually, in thought or institutionally, and occurs and grows rarely as an event that can be discovered particularly in an integral encounter. This happens, on the one hand, between people and God where God becomes human and where the human being may pray "Protect and heal us in body and soul" and, on the other hand, among people where there is not spiritual welfare without physical and social welfare. This starts with the access to all places in the Church for those in wheelchairs and leads to the sensitive perception of people's physical signs and reactions in their faces, gestures and demeanours as well as to the corresponding reaction to them.

III. Church for Others

1. *Introduction*

In a time when children demonstrate for their future and coming generations must fear that their death will coincide with the "apocalypse", with the collective death of humankind, where therefore the future Kingdom of God is plausible as a catastrophic break in history, Christian hope can no longer easily speak out in favour of a lineal continual transition of present history into the Kingdom of God (in the form of worldwide ecological and ethical progress) without not only supplying the hope for this "improvement of the world", but also preparing itself as quickly as possible for corresponding active changes. Thus, it is all the more important to learn about the socially unjust conditions from those presently affected as a highly necessary basis for solidarity and to act now with a view to the future potential victims and, as a responsibility to these people, to undertake everything possible that may prevent the collective death of humankind. Whoever says "what happens to my neighbour does not interest me" will also say "It doesn't matter what happens after I'm gone!" The condition for the creation of the necessary political majorities and national structures for action, so that such majorities come to being, is solidarity with the closest and most distant affected people of the present. Thus, the integral paradigmatic change mentioned above will be complete.

If the Church realises its own identity for the sake of social welfare and justice towards the outside as well as inside for the benefit of Christians and humankind as a whole, then it will discover its goal as it assists in making possible, struggling for and forming the more humane future of humankind. The Church can then refrain from its recruitment strategies towards the formation of a "club-like" identity.

Let me put my theses into the word of a German Protestant theologian whom I appreciate very much, Dietrich Bonhoeffer, who was killed by the Nazis because of his resistance against violence and oppression: "The Church is only the Church when it is there for other people". Bonhoeffer's assertion sounds resolute and provocative, especially if we think what its negation would be: The Church is not the Church if it is not there for other people, if—we might go on to say—it is there only for its own sake, merely as an in-group of believers with the appropriate ideological self-certainties and institutional structures, which then determine the character of the Church's social forms. "Existence for other people" is different. It definitely (also) means the people who really are "the others"—all the people who do not belong to the Church, as an institutional and doctrinal community of faith. It means especially the people who—

according to the faith and morals which the Church approves—count as unbelievers, sinners, outsiders, aliens. The Church is there to be there for these "others", to expand the opportunities of living open to them and their quality of life. And it has to do this through direct, helping and liberating encounters and groups, as well as by way of humane social structures and just economic conditions.

This is the Church's task, formulated in general terms. But it catches fire in the real and specific places where these "others" are suffering, the places where they are living in poverty and need, despised and oppressed, in unjust conditions, or where their very lives are threatened. These "ignition points" are not matters of choice. They are the places where the ministries of the Church are necessarily expended. The Church, that is to say, is only the Church when it helps those who need help, and helps the helpers to help, and when it liberates the oppressed and helps the liberators in their task of liberation: and all this irrespective of who these "others" are. This is the praxis in which the Church is authentically the Church, because its identity comes into being through service.

For the well-disposed, this perhaps sounds so obvious that its explosive quality, as criticism of the Church, may not at first appear or be grasped. Yet here nothing less than the Church's identity per se is in question. For here service for others is made the decisive criterion for distinguishing in the Church's praxis between its maintaining of itself as institution and its solidarity with others; between faith and ideology; between love and rule; between liberation and domination; between Baal and Yahweh—ultimately between godlessness and trust in God, or between anti-Christian conduct and discipleship. We sense especially that this touches the very nerve centre of the Church's self-development structures when we observe the history-long ambivalence of its defence of the faith and its defence of its own institutions, seeing these things critically against the background of unconditional service—which means service hindered by no inhibiting conditions.

2. *Neighbourly love in the Church and Its Limitations*

Let me go back briefly to the beginning of church history: As the Christian churches grew up, it was their inestimable achievement, on the basis of a new religious unity, to cross frontiers in their own social spheres. These frontiers had hitherto seldom been infringed upon; some of them—religious, ethical, political and socio-cultural—were heavily charged with restrictive sanctions. Yet, as the Church increasingly constituted itself as a group and formed its social identity, it inevitably created new dividing lines between what were now Christian congregations and their non-Christian environment. Here the development of the concepts "heathen" and "heresy" is significant.[1] There are certainly already movements running counter to this trend in the New Testament writings and among early Christian theologians—writers who stress love of one's enemies or unconditional service for all who suffer.[2] Yet we can detect an apparently ever-more dominant narrowing down of the universal character of neighbourly love to that of brotherly love within the Church.[3] Service for others finds its scope mainly within the limits of the new communities.

Of course, there is nothing to be said against mutual service in and among Christian congregations. However, it is then easy to lose sight of the fact that there are people outside the Church who are not only in need of redeeming faith, but who also require help in their distress and liberation from oppression. This aspect of the Jesus of Nazareth described by the Gospels recedes into the background, while doctrinaire apologetic and institutional demarcation lines between Christians and heathen, or between Christians and Jews, increasingly push themselves to the fore.

In the first three centuries the minority status of the Christian congregations, and the occasional oppression they suffered, may serve as an excuse for this development. But after the change of conditions under Constantine, this no longer applies. The Church was now on the way to becoming a majority with a share in state power, and it was precisely as its influence increased that the frontiers between Christians and heathen were drawn more strictly, against the background of the new conditions of power. As a result, non-Christians increasingly experienced their dissident status in the form of defamation, discrimination and maltreatment.[4] Christians and the Church ceased to be aware, spiritually, theologically and ecclesiologically, that this kind of conduct towards "unbelievers" was a slap in the face for the universal ministry, depriving the transmission of faith of its essential communicative basis, replacing it by an improper (because unchristian) more or less forced indoctrination and a press-gang type of integration. From here, not much stands in the way of developments in the Church's history leading to the "wars of religion", pogroms and "Christian" colonisations.

Here a contemptuous totalitarian ideology stands unspoken sponsor: unbelievers do not deserve humane treatment—or deserve it less than believers.

---

1 See N. Brox, Häresie. In: Reallexion für Antike und Christentum (Stuttgart 1950–) VIII, pp. 248–297; C. Colpe, Die Ausbildung des Heidenbegriffs von Israel zur Apologetik und das Zweideutigwerden des Christentum. In: R. Faber and R. Schlesier (ed.), Die Restauration der Götter (Würzburg 1986) pp. 61–87.

2 See P. Hoffmann, Tradition und Situation. In: K. Kertelge (ed.), Ethik im Neuen Testament (Freiburg 1984) pp. 50–118; M. Puzicha, Zur Aufnahme der Fremden in der alten Kirche. In: O. Fuchs (ed.), Die Fremden (Düsseldorf 1988) pp. 180–183.

3 See Brox 'Häresie' 255ff.; J. Becker, Feindesliebe – Nächstenliebe – Bruderliebe. In: Evangelische Ethik 25 (1981) pp. 1,5–18, esp. 10ff., 16ff.

4 See Colpe 'Heidenbegriff' pp. 72–82.

Consequently, it is easier to accept the sufferings of non-believers than the bitter experiences of Christians. Moreover, it is even legitimate to increase the sufferings of unbelievers, through pain and oppression, since they really deserve nothing else, or in order to bring them at last to true faith. To put it in simple terms: people may surely be forced for their own good "to get to heaven". The unbeliever can easily avoid suffering of this kind if she will only let herself be told what the truth is and enter the fold of the Church.

The ministering love of the Christian God is radical in its universality. It is wide open. This God loves human beings as sinners without any conditions and desires their salvations even before they change their ways (cf. Rom 5:8 and Jn 4:10). But this love is obscured if the ministering love of Christians is dependent on the condition that the sinner must first enter the institutional and ideological fold of the Church and adopt the good behaviour bound up with that. Christians and the Church would rather be preaching the Gospel to themselves if they spelled out the "limits" of their faith by tearing down the limits on loving service for all. The persecuted Jews and the Communist in the concentration camp, the AIDS-infected homosexual and the slandered man or woman seeking political asylum—all these people belong to the social domain of the Christian Church and its charitable service, and to the sphere of its political solidarity, simply because they claim help and need liberation. This prevents the mentality that is seriously prepared to help only if certain moral, ideological or institutional conditions are fulfilled.

3. *The Fruitful Tension Between Fellowship and Service*

If we see the problem in this light, then the concept of "brotherly love" is surely insufficient to cover "Church for others". It may also be too undifferentiated, since it does not distinguish clearly enough between *koinonia* (the fellowship of believers) and *diakonia* (service to the suffering, including strangers and opponents, which continually tears down the barriers of the "internal" fellowship). Moreover, brotherly and sisterly love all too easily suggests that service for others is exhausted in service for "the brethren".[5] But in fact fellowship to-

5 Cf. K. Lehmann, Nochmals: Caritas und Pastoral. In: Caritas 88 (1987) pp. 1,3–12, where it is not really clear where the main reference of the brotherly and ministering congregation lies. The general trend of the argument would suggest that it is *koinonia* rather than *diakonia*. This is shown, for example, by the use of the term "all" in the following quotation: "All are there for one another. All are members of the one body" (p. 9). On the mutual delimitation between *koinonia* and *diaconia*, and their critical complementation, cf., also R. Zerfaß, Der Beitrag des Caritasverbandes zur Diakonie der Gemeinde. In: Caritas 88 (1987) pp. 1,12–27,19ff., 22ff.

wards the inside and service towards the outside stand in considerable tension to one another in terms both of social psychology and institutional theory; for no interest group willingly puts someone at the centre who does not "belong" or hold the same opinions.

This tension will not emerge, however, if service is made over to a separate church organisation, as in the churches in Germany, which is the Caritasverband in the Catholic church and the "Diakonisches Werk" in the Protestant church).[6] The parishes then feel that they have been relieved of this task. If we look at the resulting practice, in the Church's *koinonia* (fellowship) and *diakonia* (service for others), we see that there really is unconditional ministry for all the suffering and oppressed; but this is confined largely to the initiatives and institutions of the Church's charitable associations. The Caritas, for example, has more than 28,000 institutions (hospitals, homes for the handicapped, social and counselling centres, etc.) and more than 300,000 full-time workers, thereby being the largest charitable organisation in West Germany.[7] But these initiatives and institutions are relatively cut off from the parishes. Consequently, the parishes could and can without embarrassment concentrate on "more essential" sectors of passing on the faith, through proclamation in word and sacrament. So, in over 50 per cent of West German parishes, service for others plays a highly reduced role, generally as a particular topic on special collection Sundays.[8] The other 50 per cent (especially the student congregations) are increasingly and unerringly sensitive to and aware of local needs. They concern themselves with the possible organisation of help and with supra-regional solidarity actions. Though here, certainly, local parishes should watch more carefully to see how far service is limited to believers. For example, does a Catholic kindergarten accept the children of immigrant Turkish workers?

This state of affairs cannot be considered satisfactory. The practice of the parishes is often considered legitimate, because the charitable organisations

---

6 C£ H.Steinkamp, Diakonia in the Church of the Rich and the Church of the Poor. In: *Gonoilium 24* (1988) pp. 65–75.

7 The institutions of the freely sponsored welfare organisations (the sponsor in this case being the Church) are 80 per cent financed by the state, the rest having to be supplied by the Church from its own income (which results from Church tax and voluntary contributions). Persons employed in the parishes and in special sectors of pastoral care amount to only about 10 per cent of the number employed in the Caritas organisation! But the corresponding awareness among those employed full time in pastoral care and in theology is certainly in inverse proportion to this representation of the Church's ministry in society, for among theologians and those concerned in pastoral care, the Church's expression of itself through service is seldom discussed. On the history and development of the Caritasverband, and on its relationship to the congregations, cf. R. Zerfaß, Organisierte Caritas als Herausforderung an eine nachkonziliare Theologie. In: E.Schulz, H.Brosseder and H.Wahl (ed.), Den Menschen nachgehen (St. Ottilien 1978) pp. 321–348.

8 See Lehman 'Caritas'. op. cit. 6ff.,11.

exist. But if the parishes make themselves primarily places for liturgical celebration and confessional ideology in the sphere of an ecclesiastically accepted religiosity and morality, they delegate the concerns of diaconal service (if they even know what these concerns are) to some other institution, away from the congregation, and this authority "represents" the congregation to all those in need. The parish certainly pays highly for this delegation in financial terms. But it is saved direct encounter with those affected.[9]

This "organising away" of people who are in need and on the fringes of society has catastrophic effects for the build-up of the congregation itself, as well as for the needy, the oppressed and underprivileged, in the area served by a given parish. For the problem of professional charity is that it easily estimates—and underestimates—as dilettante any non-professional, spontaneous, simple, every day, matter of course, effective ways of helping by "lay" people or their ability for service.[10] Yet without the "infrastructure" of minds orientated towards living with the affected, and the corresponding communicative reality of a wider social network, the highly cultivated professionalism of the charitable organisation is left in the air of specialist care and treatment, which is insufficiently carried over and continued in ordinary everyday life.

For example, the hospital treatment offered by the state and charitable organisations is highly necessary, especially for those suffering from AIDS in its acute stages; yet it proves relatively helpless when it comes down to the social contexts to which people with AIDS return, in their often relatively long symptom-free periods—whether they can live there in dignity (i.e., accepted and perceived as important for others) and whether they can discuss their situation, master it or endure it. The best counselling or care remains an unrelated experience unless there are also special, alternative social forms on an intermediary level (between family and the major social structures) in which those affected are not exposed to social discrimination but are given jobs, support and places to live. And the local churches would belong precisely to this "between" level.

Moreover, only the lived sensibility for service of Christians and congregations can probably perceive the need that lives beyond the zones of need defined by the charitable organisations and outside the receiver-range accepted by the financial bureaucracy.[11] The problems "the welfare state" has about accepting "the new poverty" in the highly industrialised countries belong here, though the real experience of the people concerned make this poverty undeniable.

---

9 See Zerfaß ‚Herausforderung' op. cit. 336ff' 341.

10 See O. Fuchs, ‚Kirchliche Gemeinde im Selbstvollzug der Diakonie' *Caritas* 88(1987) 6, pp. 280–293. See Steinkamp, Diakonia p. 70ff.

11 See Zerfaß, Herausforderung, *op.cit.* 334.

Because there is so little social contact with the handicapped, the distressed and those suffering from discrimination, we lose the particular "competences" which these people have to offer and can claim; they have a perception of what the Gospel means and the beginnings of a practical realisation of the Kingdom of God. Practised service always changes the witness itself, which is to say the proclamation of the Gospel, for learning how to think and live from people who are suffering means that the practice of faith is changed and radicalised in the context of options that are no longer optional but quite literally necessary—born of need. The suffering do not merely have a claim to help; they always have something important to say as well. That is surely why Jesus does not merely put a child in the midst as the object of helpful service (because "not yet being grown up" counts as a deficiency); he makes children the actual yardstick for "grown ups" in their dealings with the Kingdom of God (of Mt 19:13–14).

Here we can discover possible ways of learning, ways we can hope for, particularly in encounters with the suffering; for the helpers help those who need it and, anticipating that the suffering can help them, accept help in their turn. This help takes the form of disquieting, yet ultimately salutary questions put to their own forms of living, their attitudes, their suppression of weakness and powerlessness, their perhaps pathologising and alienating forms of behaviour, structures and ideologies. The person who suffers always has an essentially critical, transforming and intensifying quality for all concerned.

What is in question here, therefore, is not a new moralisation of service. It simply means being encouraged to expect and accept, even in such encounters—and there especially—a decisive message about more humane living. The "complementary community" comes about only in the mutual fellowship of helpers and those who need help, the healthy and the sick, the strong and the weak, where roles can be exchanged and where their possibilities and impossibilities do not have to be either left unused or suppressed, but can be "lumped together" to provide the great opportunity for a more humane church.[12]

4. *The Scope of Service in the Community of the Church*

Service for others provokes the breaking down of barriers in two directions, permanently stripping faith of its ideological character and dissolving institutional restrictions. Barriers *inwards* are broken down, because people who are in need belong from the outset to the centre of the Church and to its special sphere of responsibility, simply *because* they are in need (not, for example,

12 See U. Bach, Boden unter den Füßen hat keiner (Göttingen 1980) pp. 70–83.

because they "belong"). Barriers *outwards* are destroyed when Christians and Church work together with all non-Christian initiatives and groups, and with all men and women of good will, showing solidarity with those who—in their actions and in their siding with those who suffer, at home and abroad—aim to expose and combat social-political and economic causes of distress.

This dynamic, truly communicative exchange process between Church and society in the service which bridges the two is the mark showing that Christian and Church manifest their identity *through* service. The universality of service to people inside and outside, in and between Church and society is the historical and the specific situational expression of the Church's character as universal sacrament for the world. This universality of salvation in ministry as a whole means the criticism of all manifestations of the Church which, content with their own dynamic (and understandably enough, psychologically), try to fence themselves off, and, if necessary, to exclude "outsiders". This is so especially in the spheres where people only meet in liturgy and worship or where faith only seeks to assure of its doctrinal truth or moral standards.

Accordingly, while claiming unlimited scope outwards, wherever there is distress, ministry (*diakonia*) claims the same scope inwardly too, in a special sense: that is, within the community (*koinonia*) of the Church's own social forms. To deny divorced and remarried people admission to the sacraments is in this light behaviour hostile to ministry in the liturgical sphere (or in the conditions for admission to the sacraments laid down by canon law). Equally hostile to ministry is the longstanding contemptuous treatment of applications for laicisation made by priests (treatment in the interests of a law that is in any case theologically questionable). The result here is unnecessary conflict and oppressive inhumanity. And when the Congregation for the Doctrine of Faith, writing about the pastoral care of homosexuals,[13] denies them the title of "believes in Christ" (which is always otherwise applied in such texts to baptised and confirmed Christians), then a verdict prompted by sexual morality is standing in the way of humane dealings with people belonging to a fringe group. Strictly moral Catholics then do not offer these people the congregation's help, even for the sake of ministering to HIV-infected or AIDS sufferers.

In view of what I have merely touched on here, I am unable to accept the assertion that the unlimited scope of ministry "has, for example, no direct consequences for admission to the Eucharist".[14] Here a dubious distinction is made between ministry and liturgy which cannot be legitimated by Jesus's own behaviour, for his Last Supper was the ultimate expression and final seal of all the previous meals he shared with sinners and those on the fringes of society, and the seal too of the ministry of them he thereby lived. This cannot be separated from the sacrament of the Eucharist, any more than the Jesus we hear

[13] German text in: Verlautbarungen des Apostolischen Stuhls no. 72 (Bonn 1986).

[14] Lehmann, 'Caritas' p. 11.

about in the Gospels can be separated from the Christ of faith. It is for me too little and also considerably too wayward to talk merely about "an analogous relationship of interdependence between charitable service and Eucharist".[15] In the context of the Christological paradigm, we have rather to talk about a perichoresis—an unmingled intertwining of *Eucharist* and *diakonia,* the real presence of Christ in the sacrament and his real presence through the ministry of love in the community of Christians, and hence through the Church.[16] For the risen one Himself appears in strangers and the sick (cf. Mt 25:35–36), just as he is also really present, through his Spirit, in all those who help and liberate.

This interactive Christo-praxis between helpers and sufferers, the rejected and those who receive them, gives Christology in the sphere of faith and Christo doxology in the sphere of worship their all-embracing dimension, the dimension comprehending the whole of life. Faith and worship then no longer act as a blockade against unrestricted service. They are experienced as the enabling foundation and context of a service that devotes itself without if's and but's to the underprivileged, the sick and those in need. People who believe that their whole existence is founded in God until death and beyond, *can*—out of this inexhaustible fact of God's love—give themselves to suffering men and women. Since God's love is already theirs without reserve, they can give unreserved love themselves and spend themselves within the limits of their possibilities and the impotence they experience.

The saving universality of the Eucharist, and hence its "ministering" diaconal dimension, should therefore be maintained, at least for all baptised Christians,[17] so that in the Church people may discover that, in its own sphere, the Church deals with sinners (or those whom it seems sinners) in exactly the same way that God, in infinite readiness for reconciliation, encounters sinners: that is, in unconditional love—not merely after they have duly changed their ways, but beforehand, so that they *can* change, within the framework of their own possibilities. God's righteousness does not set up any meritocratic conditions. He justifies sinners and the godless. All Christians have a right to a praxis of

15 Ibid.

16 See O. Fuchs, The "Option für die Armen" als theologisches Prinzip für den christlichen Selbstvollzug von Individuum und Gesellschaft. In: A. Bucher et al. (ed.), *Die vorrangige Option* für *die Armen" der Katholischen Kirche in Lateinamerika,* Vol. 1 Eichstätt 1991, pp. 32–52.

17 I do not speak here of the invitation to *all* the suffering, or to all people of good will, to partake of the Eucharist, since this could also be interpreted as an appropriation of non-Christian helpers or people in need. The Eucharistic celebration is a special sphere for the *koinonia* of the Church, where *all Christians* can assure themselves of God's unconditional grace and love for human beings and where, in the power of this divine Spirit, they may be encouraged to practice similar unconditional ministry towards others. But, as in the case of baptism and faith, this (restricted) sphere of participation in the sacramental life of the church, with the resources conferred there, has as its purpose the passing on of what has been received—not through the strategy of "compelling them to come in" but in ongoing love.

ministry in everything that happens in the Church—a praxis in which grace goes before law and where love is freed from the constraints of morality. "It is therefore theologically and pastorally atrocious to give the impression that it is not love that is the fulfilment of the law and the first of the commandments, but rather complete identification with the Church's doctrine of faith and morals."[18]

The different conditions in which Christians live are always fragmentary. One person lives more in the sphere of explicit faith, another more in the sphere of charitable service, again others rather in the common life of the Christian community. It is only on the basis of mutual service, and in the acceptance of mutual *limitations*, that Christians can take one another seriously, and all the more so by exposing themselves to mutual criticism. The more the dimension of service is committed to being directly effective in all spheres of the Church's own life and social forms, the more the Church will itself internally become the social field *where Service is learnt,* and it can then offer this service "outwards", to everyone, all the more effectively, and with all the more experience. In this way *koinonia* (community) becomes the foundation for the universal *diakonia* (service) of Christians and the Church towards all human beings. It becomes the place where its own necessity and the necessity of others is discovered. But it is the place too for discussing helpful and liberating acts for those who need help, and for the helpers. So, unless the Church's pastoral ministry is service "inwards"—communicating the gracious God *there,* in the Church itself—it will hardly be able to provide the corresponding basic experience which is required for its ministry "outwards".

5. *The Situational Priority of Service as Principle*

In all cases service is the essential option which determines the ordering of all other priorities. This must be the fundamental policy or programme, as long as there are people who suffer in the area to which a congregation belongs, or in its sphere of experience, or in the remote sectors about which it hears. After all, there is not likely to be a time in the history of humankind that would not present some form of suffering and disadvantage. This is the permanent situation of this world (see Mt 26:11).

Nevertheless, there can be no primacy in principle from diaconia to martyria, from solidarity to liturgy and worship. Rather, it is about a dynamic and flexible relationship, in which the question of what is better and what is more important does not arise in principle, but only by means of kairological and

18 Zerfaß, Herausforderung p. 343.

situational answers.[19] So, in the Samaritan story (cf. Lk 10:30–37), in this emergency situation of a human being the help is more important than the worship service. But there can also be situations (above all situations of hopelessness and failure) in which it is more important to allow oneself to be gifted with God's grace in prayer and liturgy than to drive oneself even more into the overpressure of doing and overstraining oneself. Thus, Jesus again and again leaves people, even those whom he could heal, in order to root himself in the desert in the relationship with his Father, and then again to become capable of an even more radical self-giving in an emergency. Only when God's and neighbour's relationships are not in danger of instrumentalising each other can they, out of the their respective otherness, deepen and criticise each other.

But the Samaritan story remains just as true, and this story marks precisely this conflict: Christians and congregations are, in principle and from the outset, "the neighbour" of people in need, and they have to seek these people out and discover where they are (cf. Lk 10:36). It is not for the person in need to force her- or himself on the congregation's attention first of all, proving that she or he is their neighbour. They have to discover her or him, since they have made the fundamental existential decision that they will be the neighbours of the suffering. One cannot invest all one's energy in something or other—even if it is by no means bad in itself (liturgy and catechesis, for example). Service is not an optional subject in pastoral care. It is essential. This means that diaconia is not the option of the person who has to decide, but is dependent on the really existing need itself.

If people, in this context, speak only of "situational priority", this will easily impair the ability to perceive need and oppression, especially where the sufferers do not make themselves known, or are prevented by strategies of appeasement from crying their need aloud. Moreover, it is the fundamental priority of diaconia that will make people unerringly watchful to discern need, although here the background must be the also fundamental premise that suffering people themselves have the authority to define their situation and to plead their own cause. Recognition of this principle differentiates the explosive power of the concept of evangelisation and the praxis or theology of liberation from all other theological outlines.[20] People who from the outset accept the fundamental priority of suffering in their theology and spirituality will be able to perceive a specific situational priority, and they will avoid making the discernment of need and the discussion about active help depend (solely) on what

---

19 Cf. the discussion about the primacy of diaconia over the other self-realization of the church, Ottmar Fuchs, Solidarity and Faith, in: German Caritas Association (Ed.), Caritas 99 (Yearbook), Freiburg 1998, 19–34, 20ff.

20 R. Zerfaß makes a similar plea for a European "post conciliar theology" which views itself and realises itself contextually against the background of service *for* others. See Zerlaß, Herausforderung' pp. 324, 338ff.

they or others think best (unless they are the sufferers themselves, or have to do with them).

If we ask what ought to have a permanent "systematic" priority, before the merely situational priority of solidarity, then of course (in most cases) we arrive at the answer: the proclamation of the Gospel, liturgy and worship. Yet if we look at the Jesus Christ of whom the Gospels tell, we have surely to perceive that what he says about the Kingdom of God and about God is said pre-eminently in the context of encounters in which God has already acted as healer or where God has entered into dispute on behalf of the poor and despised. Therefore, recourse to this origin forces us to accept that in principle talk about God is not talk about God at all without the praxis of active ministry and that the praxis of ministry is always the point at which we can and may talk about God.

This is very important, because one does not have to be explicitly affected by the Gospel before one is able to discover the needs of other people.[21] If this were not so we should have to put down any solidarity and discernment of need that is not motivated by Christianity and the Church as "optional social work" and depreciate it as something that has nothing to do with God. Certainly, many Christians acquire greater sensibility towards the perception of suffering because they have been touched by the Gospel. But on the other hand, human need touches the love and compassion of many people directly, as we are told it touched Jesus. They practise the Gospel in the world, even though the Gospel is never mentioned.

For centuries, the Gospel was read by most interpreters of the Church without their being touched at all in the way we have described. Much suggests that it is only the perception of need which provides the material hermeneutics[22] for reading the Gospel in such a way that it has to do with the real hope: that there is a focal point in combatting necessity and oppression in the light of the Kingdom of God, because the Kingdom thereby acquires reality in the way men and women shape their lives. And it is this reality alone which has a future, down to the coming of that Kingdom and into the Kingdom itself. Accordingly, it is true to say that people who allow themselves to be touched by the need of others will never read the Gospel except with the eyes of compassion and will discover the corresponding faith. This will be so all the more if they encounter Christians and proclaimers of the Gospel who place a high value on all forms of diaconal service and link them with talk about God in the context of the Jewish-Christian tradition, though this link may be either explicit or forged through the recognition and gift of loving service.

21 Contrary to Lehmann "Caritas" p. 11, and also to P. Zulehner, *Das Gottesgerücht* (Düsseldorf 1987) p. 65.

22 On this "material hermeneutics" cf. O. Fuchs, The praktische Theologie im Paradigrna biblisch-kritischer Handlungswissenschaft zur Praxis der Befreiung. In: O. Fuchs (ed.), *Theologie und Handeln* Düsseldorf 1984) pp. 209–244.

6. The Use of Theology

But of what use are these reflections of a "practical theologian" in the context of the scholarly disciples, with the diversified organisation prevailing there today? Zerfaß does not take a very exalted view of their usefulness, because in his view scholarly theology is too bookish and not contextual enough. Moreover, he thinks that it is illusory for this theology to imagine that it can deepen the spiritual motivation of those concerned with it.[23] My own experience does not permit me any emphatic contradiction. And yet I am inclined not to set so little store by the reflections of university theology about service for others. After all, here a long overdue process is at last taking place within theology itself for it is trying in its discussions to arrive at a high, argumentative theological assessment of diaconia.[24]

Apart from this clarification of the significance of service in theology's own field, I should not like to discredit the—at least possible—effect of these endeavours (an effect which is also continually experienced in the relevant encounters). For one result is that the people engaged in pastoral care and proclamation are attaching increasing importance to this kind of ministry (or at least pay it lip service). And this means greater appreciation of all those in the congregation who perform the little and the greater services and are involved in social work. A change, step by step, in the awareness and spirituality of theologians (men and women) and of clergy would perhaps be a fruitful beginning—provided that one believes that awareness has to some degree genuine power.

I believe too that it is not pure illusion to hope that theologians may enter into an exchange of views, for example, with social workers, and that they may pass on their ideas as motivating help to the people concerned. But this exchange must be on equal terms and in the appropriate language. And it will be more fruitful if more theologians allow themselves to be affected by what they are told about the social field involved. Perhaps we are after all gradually rediscovering common social sectors, where theological concepts make their impact not as indoctrination and discipline, but as ideas, which put themselves at risk in confrontation with the narratives of those engaged in charitable service and let themselves be forged by these people's experiences and opportunities for faith.

Ultimately speaking, "contextuality" cannot be entirely denied to the theologians concerned with diaconia, because they themselves are often forced, with some anguish, to think about it, because of real experiences of personal suffering, and through the suffering of others. The reproach is of course still

23 See Zerfaß "Herausforderung" pp. 324,32~339.

24 Cf. O. Fuchs, Wie verändert sich das Verständnis von Theologie, wenn the Diakonik zurn Zuge kommt? In: *Pastoraitheologische Informationen 10* (1990) 25, pp. 175–202.

justified where this contextuality remains largely private and does not enter explicitly into the publications of these theologians. This is no doubt connected with the nature of European theology, which is largely argumentative and not sufficiently "narratively" sustained. This is probably the justifiable criticism of an insufficiently contextual theology: that individual contexts are insufficiently brought into the discussion of principles and are insufficiently accepted. That is to say, they are not sufficiently used as starting points and tend to be forgotten in subsequent reflection. Yet these individual contexts have a dignity as "arguments" of a special kind, for which rational argument is no substitute. One would often like to know even from theologians the places and starting points of their specific concern.

This would in itself be the beginning of a change in theology from professionally academic thinking to personal and positional reflections in the context of individual experiences, not merely with books but also with human life and suffering. It would mean entering the context of certain suffering people, and of corresponding projects nearby, as well as entering into active and political solidarity with people far away. But certainly to achieve this, and with this in mind, theologians would courageously have to try out and discover a new language. Particularly theologians belonging to the "First World" will need much conversion before they can press forward a theology which is there for other people and which finds expression in ministry for others. But in entering on this path theology may perhaps become a driving force that—though its efficacy must not be overestimated—cannot be ignored in a Church that is constituted through service for other people.

7. *The Messiah's Sensibility and Solidarity*

Theology reflects especially the biblical foundations of Christian faith and deed. What do the actions of Jesus of Nazareth, the praxis that the Messiah himself combines with the term and will of God, look like on closer examination? How does he treat the poor, how does he behave concerning diaconia and how does he treat the suffering? How do the disadvantaged become not only receivers of his help and liberation, but also people who have important things to say and who, in turn, represent help and rewarding experiences for the lives of the helpers. I would like to present several examples that appear to me as decisive for our topic as a whole.

7.1 Jesus Deals with People in a "Physical" and Gentle Way

Despite some of the formal reductions in the existent texts by corresponding literary schemes, many of the stories of encounters with Jesus in the Gospels have still retained their original character of unavoided corporeality. Jesus allows the leper to approach him and touches him (cf. Mt 8:3) and allows the woman who had suffered a haemorrhage to touch him (cf. Mt 9:20). Jesus does not hesitate also to mix his spittle with the earth to rub into the eyes of the blind man (cf. Jn 9:6). It is also a part of this manifestation of human contact that Jesus allows time for conversation (cf. Mt 15:21–28) and that he often reacts and acts in the most sensitive and appropriate way towards the people and situations. In this feature, I think for example of the encounter with the adulterous woman (cf. Jn 8:3–11). Jesus does not accuse her; rather he downgrades the self-appointed judges and their moral laws, which are, literally, written in stone and can easily be used as stones. Silently he writes in the sand in the earth and thus rescues the situation and the "sinner". No person deserves physical punishment because of actual or alleged infringement of moral principles! The fact that Jesus reacts in this way to the situation is one aspect in his way of treating people in person.

When one considers that here literary reworking of real encounters of Jesus are concerned, then one can hardly imagine the warmth of feeling and trust, the communicative and therapeutic power and the physical dimension in his encounters intensively enough! The overcoming of the fear of contact with ill people, outsiders and lepers is the helping and merciful power of the Holy Spirit in the saints of past and present days, who confirm the security of their lives in God and as a result of such belief (like Francis of Assisi) kiss and embrace the lepers.

7.2 Jesus Heals and Forgives

Jesus realised the existence of physical and mental need around him and, in liberating encounters, healed the sick, drove out demons and forgave sins. The fact that Jesus appeared as a worker of miracles is amazing but not unusual for his contemporary socio-cultural environment. Jesus thus practices a "conventional" form of healing for that time. He confronts the experiences of pain and reacts to them in the most effective way possible. According to A. Suhl, the miracles are "a definite protest against real human suffering, against the suffering of the ill, the maimed and the isolated".[25] The stories of miracles are

25 A. Suhl (ed.), Der Wunderbegriff im Neuen Testament (Darmstadt 1980) pp. 1–38 (Introduction), p. 38.

therefore not (only) there to support the belief in the authority of God in Jesus (such belief should be based after all in the message of the resurrection); they rather also refer to his praxis of realising the existence of need, of wanting to communicate with the suffering and to help them as much as possible and to show solidarity with them.

The sobering and principally diaconal basic structure of the stories of healing may not be disregarded in favour of the mounting stylisation of the term "miracle", which is already present in the New Testament, or in favour of the ever popular and even new modern tendency to debate about this term! The miracles are not the "be all and end all" of Christian belief! They are not really important. Because if you believe only in Christ's miracles, then you easily forget the purpose they have, the purpose of diaconia. The miracles have no meaning for their own sake, quite against the anthropology of general religions concerning the miracles as religious belief's dearest child.

The healing of Jesus is not only closely linked in meaning with the message of redemption, but his message of redemption is also closely linked in its material effect with healing! If one cannot refrain from referring to the miracles, then one must see the miracles in their strict functional context of diaconia; God confirms in the miracle of healing the fact that Jesus may go beyond the existing natural or legal norms for the sake of suffering people. The miracles are thus a "judgement of God" for the radical diaconia of Jesus at any time and in any place against anything that could prevent and obstruct this diaconal action.[26]

The motivation for this helping and liberating behaviour of Jesus is his compassion and often affectively described mercifulness (the need of humankind moves and shocks him; cf. Mt 9:36; Mk 1:41; 6:34). "Primarily the poor and the sick learn what it means that they are more important for Jesus—and for God, as Jesus tells us—than even the Sabbath, the law. Mercifulness thinks and acts according to the suffering people."[27] The miracles make clear the prevalence of diaconal behaviour. "Only the realization that God places himself through the miracles on the side of action which breaks through the norms, removes the uncertainty and leads to the praise of God" (Mk 2:12).[28]

Jesus brings the suffering person into the innermost centre for this reason and makes him into the inter-relative centre of his words and deeds. In this way Jesus takes the man with the withered hand (cf. Mk 2:27–3:6) from the periphery and places him in the centre, in this case in the centre of the synagogue. This is enormous, because the centre is the place where the *Torah*, the word of God and God's self, has its place. We are not concerned here with a mere centre of locality, but a theologically determined centre. Also worthy of

26 Cf. M. Dibelius, Die Formgeschichte des Evangeliums (Tübingen 6/1971) p. 144.
27 H. Seibert, Diakonie – Hilfehandeln Jesu (Gütersloh 1983) p. 35.
28 G. Theissen, Urchristliche Wundergeschichten (Gütersloh 1974) p. 118.

mention here, alongside the aforementioned stories, are his encounters with lepers, tax collectors, prostitutes and sinners. Many parables also belong here. The groups of poor people of that time receive their place in the centre because of their need for help (not because of any other precondition than that of hopeful expectation) and because of the fact that Jesus comes into such encounters with them. All this shows that the encounter with those needing help and with the weak belongs in the centre of every Christian communication and also in the Christian social form. In the moment of encounter with a person in need of help, nothing else is more important than this person, who needs recognition, an enhancement of status and support without regard to his or her culture, race, religion or denomination. His or her life is eternally valuable in the eyes of Jesus and his God. Christians, as the followers of Jesus of Nazareth, must learn this eternal value of the suffering in their own way of life.

Exactly such moments of encounter with the disadvantaged are the special place where Jesus teaches and where he speaks of the loving God and the message of the Kingdom of God. The Kingdom of God is here not a utopian ideal without a place in which one must believe and in which one can only believe, but is already, at least in part, a real manifestation which one can see! The credibility of Jesus lies only in part in his words about the Kingdom of God and about God. His main credibility lies in his diaconal experiences with God and in his diaconal acts for the people. To put it the other way round, Jesus interprets with his message, in effect, "only" that which he does![29] The diaconal experience has thereby a central character of conveying the message, inasmuch as it partly makes possible the real experience of the Kingdom of God which has become credible exactly because of it. The great importance of such an action in the message and the life of Jesus is shown in his call to follow him in a realistic way. This is possible to see in the story of the two brothers (cf. Mt 21:28–32), where the one son says no to his father's request to go to the vineyard, but in the end acts positively, whereas the other son who says yes does nothing. The first son is shown to be right by means of his deeds.

7.3 Jesus Expects Decisive Messages from Those in Need of Help and Justice

When Jesus encounters suffering or "stigmatised" people, as well as those characterised in any way by loss and disadvantage,[30] as well as by guilt, he places them in the centre of the current communication (cf. Mk 2:27–3:6). Jesus

[29] Cf. R. Zerfaß, Predigt im Prozeß der Gemeinde. In: id. (ed.), Mit der Gemeinde predigen (Gütersloh 1982) pp. 30–49, p. 36.

[30] According to E. Goffman's definition, cf. id., Stigma (Frankfurt a. M.) 1976, pp. 9–30.

places the child in the centre who, then as now, is not an "equal" person because a child is not capable of taking a full part in official worship (or today does not belong to the achievement-orientated society) and is thus not yet an adult. He does this also against the attempts of his disciples to turn the children away because they did not consider them important enough to meet him. At the same time more happens; the children and the fact of their childhood are displayed as an orientation of meaning for the adults and for the disciples who do not take the children seriously. They are made a measure against which a person has to learn how to deal with the Kingdom of God. The child is thus not placed in the centre to be an object of helping actions but becomes itself a personal criterion for how the so-called adults should behave towards life, humankind and God (cf. Mt 19:13–14; Mk 9:36). Jesus thus says: "Truly, I say to you, whoever does not receive the Kingdom of God like a child shall not enter it" (Mk 10:15). The healing of the blind man (Mk 10:50) also shows that those affected have something to say. For Jesus does not heal him without being asked, but expressly asks "What do you want me to do for you?"

Jesus turns the tables: You can learn particularly from the young and from the weak how to deal with God and humankind. The weak but not the strong are the meaning-giving principle for following Jesus. This applies in two aspects. The strong (in this case the adults) open their perspective and put the young and weak in the centre. And they allow the formation of their community with one another and with God to be determined by these weak people. It is then clear that justice in a real context can only be determined and defined by those who have been deprived of justice. They have the competence for it.

This moment of Jesus's communication with the suffering (in which they are credited with a particular meaningful competence) is revealed in an amazing way that has been almost ignored to date, in his healing encounters with the so-called possessed. The latter know who Jesus is, that he is the Son of God (cf. Luke 4:41). The "possessed" have something true to say.[31] The suffering are therefore not only the target group of Jesus's liberating action, as he treats their problems, but they are accepted as important individuals exactly because of their suffering and they have something decisive to say. Therefore, in *diakonia*, *martyria* (preaching) of a particular type takes place. As when one meets the son of humankind in suffering, one can be certain that they are not only the target group of *diakonia* but are and become also a creative group of the *martyria* in the Church.

31 Cf. O. Fuchs, Theologische Aspekte zur Interaktion mit psychiatrischen Patienten. In: Wege zum Menschen 40 (1988) 2, pp. 87–95.

7.4 Jesus Supports the Suffering in Public

It is well known that Jesus not only came into small groups but, on many occasions, was not afraid to make use of "mass communication" and openly and pointedly made his position clear. The argumentative discussions with the religious leaders of that time also belong to the public and political side of his actions. There are also very few parables in which, along with the individual encounters, a structural political perspective is not apparent in the choice of those involved. A classic example of this behaviour is contained in the parable of the Good Samaritan. In the answer to the question of the Pharisee "Who is my neighbour?", the definition of this term follows not in an abstract way, but pragmatically, that is, within the course of the action, but in two directions: on the one hand, in the direction of the narrower, interpersonal social area (i.e., the helping deed) and, on the other, in the direction of a sharp social criticism of the existing prejudices, since it is the Samaritan who helps after all (cf. Lk 17:11–19).

In this as in many other stories, the structural aspect of sin is also involved and thematised. The prototype of those who belong to the negative group in the actual context is connected in the story with positive actions. The religious outsider is the one who helps the other, who is for him a stranger and an outsider. The story is thus also directed against the collective downgrading of the people concerned. The Samaritan is not on the level of the recounted story, but is on the level of the story between the narrating Jesus and his listeners, most certainly the victim; Jesus opposes his "status as a victim" by making him a model in the story and thereby attacking the ethno-centric stereotypes which debase those who do not belong to one's own people.

The biblical stories are not divisible between the collective and the individual. They unfold their meaningful energy for the relationships between people as well as for those between social systems, groups, societies and peoples. One must remember the stories of the prophets, whose socio-critical involvement in the context of their belief in *Yahweh* (as the helper of widows and the poor) is constitutive of their message. The aspect concerning structural sin between peoples becomes clear in Isaiah 7:1–9 where King Ahaz has to decide between a military alliance or renouncing it by means of trusting in God.

In the authentic following of the Old Testament socio-critical prophecy, Jesus lists the decisive social contradictions by name in his public speeches (cf. in particular the Sermon on the Mount in Luke 6:20–49) and exposes them: "Blessed are you poor ... but woe to you that are rich!" An individualisation or therapisation of diaconia cannot be justified. Political diaconia forms moreover an integral part of Jesus's redeeming treatment of the sick and the oppressed. The analysis of social, political and institutional reality must be seen as an essential moment of his preaching itself. Belonging to diaconia are not only the immediate giving of help and the reduction or removal of suffering, but at the same time the search for the political conditions and structural origins which create suffering and the resulting socio-political and economic position. This has to be seen as an integral part of the term "diaconia".

7.5 In Diaconia, Jesus Risks Becoming an Outsider and Oppression

Jesus's relationship with the sick, the poor and the guilty along with his public support for these groups provokes the accusation of being possessed himself. His contemporaries judge his actions to be pure folly (cf. Luke 11:14ff.). His non-conformism and dissidence for the sake of diaconia appear to be signs of dangerous madness for those in power and eventually lead to his crucifixion. Whoever treats the suffering and oppressed with radical help and redemption attracts the anger of those who possess power at the expense of the disadvantaged. Jesus does not give up his struggle for humankind, however, right up to the end. Precisely the "rich" are for him the real "fools" because they cling to deceptive and inhumane security and strategies that have no future in the Kingdom of God (cf. Luke 12:20).

7.6 Jesus's Relationship to the Diaconia of God

One wonders where Jesus obtained the power to consistently lead such a life right to the end. The answer to this question leads us to his relationship with God, which means here that he believes in the God of Israel and finds himself in the tradition of the communication of the people with YHWH. Thus, he prays with the words of the psalms and prophetic texts; he knows the old stories of God's helping and redeeming treatment of his people. Jesus experiences the relation to God in a way that is incomparable in its intensity. He finds his own word for this, namely "Abba", the child's word for a good and loving father. This is why he seeks refuge for weeks on end in the desert. This is why he tells of the love and justice of God in parables. This is why he believes in the coming Kingdom of God. That is why he laments at the end, in a situation of extreme physical and spiritual need, with the words of Psalm 22 (cf. Mc 15:34).[32]

These are only indications of how much his relationship with God formed the centre of his existence, how much time he invested in this relationship and how vital his encounters in prayers in the form of an I/you dialogue were. God

[32] Cf. O. Fuchs, Die Klage als Gebet. Eine theologische Besinnung am Beispiel des Psalms 22, München 1982.

is not a mere word for humanity but is a real helping and liberating partner in this life and beyond, who cannot be preached and represented in the history of humankind in any other way than as the advocate of human beings who need help and liberation. For Jesus, God and his Kingdom not only become concrete praxis in interhuman deed, but also in the relationship with God which can be experienced as reality through belief and which underlies the human relationship with other people in a facilitating way.

B. Contexts and Challenges

I. Christian Identity as Non-identitarian Gift and Task

Everybody gets his or her life without doing anything for it. Birth, as the fundamental basis of identity, is free, it is given unconditionally. In the Christian context we say: birth is pure grace. What does this mean, this fact that life and identity are first *given*, for the personal and political responsibility of and for human beings? Many people find themselves in families or socio-political conditions in which they cannot experience life as gift and in which they are hindered by merciless structures from developing their personal and cultural identities in justice and freedom. Nevertheless, how can this original experience, that life is *given*, *give* strength and hope, to retain and to develop one's own identity in difficult situations and to fight for better conditions?

1. *Introduction*

I would like to outline in my following text how Christian identity can be a gift for life *and* for solidarity to the inside *and* to the outside. What are the criteria of such a religious identity, in whatever time and space it may happen? How can religious identity be experienced as a resource that gives strength and power to live, to endure what you cannot change, or to fight against the power and violence of oppression and iniquity? We will see that this is not only a religious question, but a political one, too. Because religious attitudes can sharpen political and social situations; sometimes they are the most effective elicitors and flow heaters for violence and terrorism, because they are able to legitimise everything. This refers to non-religious belief systems as well.

There is no need to decide the argument about whether socio-political or religious motivations are the leading ones for oppressing or revolting violence and in both cases for killing others. But as I said, sometimes the religious influence is the deepest and most effective, especially if the people concerned are not poor but have money enough, like normally the Jewish settlers and occupants in Palestine. We have examples enough showing the religious effect even when there are no social problems. Many people who are willing to use violence, whatever purpose it may be for, for example terrorists from different areas, come from rich families. Then, the naked religious ideology leads the motives.

However, in most cases religious fundamentalism comes out of the roots of social problems, and gets sharpened by religious attitude, or vice versa, or simultaneously. Here the danger of fundamentalist reactions touches the Palestinians, too. Most of the Palestinians are socially deprived of rights, and many of them are therefore disadvantaged and unemployed. Mostly it depends on the situation and on what kind of religious identity has been shaped in the respective religious communities. Exactly this is my question, too: What role does what religious identity play in shaping the identities of individuals and their collectives in different times and spaces?

If there are political differences, then there is mostly a possibility to discuss it. But if there are religious questions involved, especially fundamentalist attitudes, then normally there will be no possibility to discuss anything. Therefore, it is important to concentrate on the issue, what kind of religious identity we have and have to foster.

Therefore, for the sake of the future of all countries in the world, we have to ask the question: How do you deal with your religious tradition and heritage? How do you transform your religious identity, individually and collectively, into dimensions and motivations that do not exclude and degrade others, who are in certain respects different from us, to a faith which includes everybody unto the universal salvation and solidarity? This question of our own and others' religious identity is so crucial and important: Can people everywhere experience that they are desired, accepted and loved by other people so that they are able to accept others themselves and campaign for their welfare, too? This is a great religious hope: that if people realise the unending, never exhaustible love of God, then they are gifted with the strength we need so badly, with the power of solidarity with everyone.

I guess that many of you will be surprised, maybe astonished by what I have to say. I do not want to diminish religious faith. Instead my aim is to deepen the Christian or Islamic faith (in which religion takes place) to the heart of each belief, not to venerate God but to give God the greatness and magnanimity God *is* himself and she is to be praised for: inexhaustible mercifulness. I am sure that this deepening of our faith will bring especially the Christian faith to its own core and heart of identity. Tolerance will overtake difficulties only if it is rooted in a certain realisation of the Christian faith itself. I believe every religion has its own possibilities and resources for similar transformations and to take up the responsibility to avoid fundamentalism in one's own complex identity.

2. *Love as a Given?*

The sociologist Hartmut Rosa distinguishes between two different maps or profiles of human beings in the world[1]: a map of judgements and a map of desires. Desiring and being desired are more profound and are to do with the area of emotional affection (or aversion), while judgements relate to moral and ethical attitudes and lead to fixed principles.

Love could be that which connects the two: it extends into the depths of desiring and being desired and grounds corresponding attitudes and judgements. The most profound human experience is to be wanted and welcomed in love—either by other *people* or, in the area of religion, by a *God*. The Bible contains powerful texts in which God encounters humans on the level of passionate desire, for example, in Hosea 11.

People who have been loved and are able to love, who have thus received the gift of love in both ways, share a profound experience: the experience of their existence being desired and welcomed unconditionally. The person who loves wants their loved one to *be*, to be there, to live, to exist. To be wanted from birth, even from conception, is a gift; a person's existence becomes a gift because it is wanted. Rich findings surely await those who search in poems and stories, in poetry and prose, for the traces of this connection between infinity and love, between love and an existence that is desired and wanted, between love and the pain of death. "It is what it is, says love," writes the German poet Erich Fried in one of his poems. Here is a brilliant insight: love desires being and protects that which is.

To love a person means to say: You must not die. This thought of Gabriel Marcel highlights an experience which the Christian faith extends to include the love of *God*. To be loved by God means that God says to us: once born nobody must die. Are humans permitted to hold these ideas and hopes even in relation to the existence of all humanity, of the world, and of the whole universe? Raising the question: What is the motive for why all of this is and exists, for why there is not nothing? "Is it love?" In the musical "Fiddler on the Roof", Tevye the milkman puts this question repeatedly to his wife, Golde, and the quality of their life together allows him to answer yes to it; we may put the same question to the creator. In asking "why?" and "what for?", we are not simply asking whether there is a God who made all of this; we are also asking *why* God made all of this. What is his and her motive? Is it God's amusement to witness the blossoming and destruction of life—similar to how, in ancient Empire, gladiators were fed well and kept healthy to enable them to butcher each other? This sort of God would not add anything to atheist evolutionism: for in

1 See Hartmut Rosa, Weltbeziehungen im Zeitalter der Beschleunigung, Berlin 2012, 382.

the end there is no difference between believing in a cold God (even if cold "merely" towards others) and believing in a cold universe.

3. *Love Enhances and Encompasses Everything*

It is the quality of such experiences that touches the membrane of the world beyond and of infinity. Most religions hold to the faith that God is merciful. It is because God created humans out of love that we may hold the hope that God will not let humans perish, the hope that the divine love will not allow a human existence to fall into empty space at the point of death but will hold it. When my father died in 1987, my mother insisted that the inscription on the gravestone should include his name as well as the sentence: "God is *love* and *life*."

If an unending God is love, then his or her love is unending. That which is loved is saved, and if love really is God—that is, if love is limitless and infinite—everything is loved and everything is saved. As the First Letter to the Corinthians says in chapter 15, the key question is ultimately: is the wholly impossible possible for us—is life saved beyond death and calamity?

But: Just like that, as though all evil and suffering had not happened, had not been experienced? With what conditions? Or is it unconditional? And what impact does this unconditionality have on people with their respective memories and experiences of life? Because if every loveless action was not negated, ignored and considered undone even in eternity, that would be a contradiction to universal love. In the last judgement nothing that happened must and will be lost. Everything re-appears and is elevated into the state of being infinitely loved in the horror that was experienced or the joy about what happened.[2]

From the vantage point of this inexhaustible love which can be fully experienced in the last judgement, all lovelessness is condemned even more sharply; all pain about pain and suffering inflicted on others are extended into divine infinity. Because God never withdraws love as a punishment, we will be able to experience deep remorse—not as a condition of reconciling grace but as its consequence. The pain of any punishment inflicted outside the scope of this love would never reach the human heart, would always fall short and would be itself excluding.

This judgement of grace applies to all humans, and the same criterion applies to believers. Different options of religious commitment are judged by the "fruits" (see also Matthew 7:16) they produce following Matthew 25: "For I was hungry and you gave me food." (Matthew 25:34): That is, by the motives on

2 Vgl. Ottmar Fuchs, Wer's glaubt wird selig ... Wer's nicht glaubt, kommt auch in den Himmel, Würzburg 2012, 98–106.

the basis of which people in need were welcomed. Nothing is said about faith in the last judgement.

4. *Political Implications*

This leads to the political implications of my reflections. There is a spiritual provocation here which poses an enormous challenge to social policy and global politics. We urgently need both: ways in which we can imagine our identities as being loved—as a source of a solidarity that transcends personal benefit. The global financial crisis highlighted how unscrupulous investors find themselves in a system which allows them to gamble away hundreds of billions of dollars or euros: money which over decades would have been sorely needed to effectively stem the exponentially growing poverty and oppression of human beings. A similar point applies with regard to the ecological survival of humanity and planet earth.

We need models and discourses of solidarity that make an impossible possibility into both a practical desire and an element of our discourse regarding accountability and responsibility[3]: that of extending to the children of the world as much solidarity as to one's own children, beyond one's immediate social ties and beyond personal benefit. Those who refuse to share now are already engaged in killing and will have to kill a million-fold later in the wars about distribution. Horst-Eberhard Richter's title "Those who refuse to suffer will have to hate!" has achieved acute global significance[4]. Those who refuse to share will have to hurt, disadvantage and, ultimately, exterminate others.

Those who do not experience love are unable to love. As an inexhaustible grace, "impossible" religious faith might be able to enhance "being loved" as a resource for humans to draw on. Individuals receive this message against the background of their varying psychological constitutions. Although allowing oneself to be loved unconditionally is encouraging news, for many it also amounts to a difficult challenge. Because of deficiencies in their experiences with other people, many people are, in fact, unable to open themselves up to this. This leads to a search for safety and redemption through meeting conditions rather than through letting go within an honest, unconditionally loving relationship. In this world, unconditionality works in a strangely paradoxical way: to make itself experienceable at all, it must grasp and transform these circumstances. A key teaching of the theology of grace is borne out here: nei-

3 See Ottmar Fuchs, Wohin mit der "Angst im Abendland"?, in: Adrian Loretan, Franco Luzatto (Hg.), Gesellschaftliche Ängste als theologische Herausforderung, Münster 2004, 119–135.

4 See Horst-Eberhard Richter, Wer nicht leiden will, muss hassen, Hamburg 1993.

ther physical and mental "health" nor sinlessness is necessary for experiencing the loyalty of God's love. In this regard, the Bible itself presents a flexible God.[5]

This world always requires adjustments and compromises that involve if-then arrangements dependent on the given social circumstances. The more conditional and thus the more uncertain these circumstances are, the more individuals feel compelled to prioritise their own safety, even in magical ways, to find some sort of firm ground to stand on. What individuals achieve here, they project onto the divine and experience as acceptance by God. This is the basic issue of any fundamentalism. Nor can the problem be resolved by postulating that one has to be able to allow oneself to be loved in this way. This apparent solution would only exacerbate the problem. The only way forward consists of an acceptance that can actually be experienced.

5. *From the Very Beginning: Theological Equality*

For Hannah Arendt, birth is the event "through which every human being once appears in the world as something uniquely new".[6] All life is preceded by the gift of being created, that is, being born. Thus, birth is already the grace of being wanted and loved unconditionally by God and having been brought into existence for this reason. Birth is free just like a lifetime is free. This grace does not represent arbitrariness but total unconditionality. Birth makes grace experienceable within creation. Josef Wohlmuth uses the metaphor of a "non-determinable beginning" to characterise the nature of birth.[7] This refers not only to individuals, but analogically also to different groups of individuals, cultures, peoples and societies.

Being chosen to be loved is thus not identical with the biblical notion of being chosen to believe. Being loved coincides with creation or, on the individual level, with birth. God's love is shown not only at the point of being chosen for faith, but also already at the point of creation and through everything that is created. To restrict God's love to those who have been chosen is one of the most fatal mistakes religions make, both because this diminishes God and because of the consequences for those people who do not belong to the chosen ones. Birth is the primordial justification in the sense of St. Paul's explicit theology of justification, according to which all are loved by God as they are, without any conditions so that they are able to change out of this love. All of us are desired by God whoever we are and whatever we are going to become. Therapists say that for humans the most important thing is to be and feel desired.

---

5 See Jan-Dirk Döhling, Der bewegliche Gott, Freiburg i. B. 2009.

6 See Hannah Arendt, Vita activa oder vom tätigen Leben, München, Zürich 2002, 167.

7 Josef Wohlmuth, Die Tora spricht die Sprache der Menschen, Paderborn 2002, 88.

To be sure, Christians continue to be chosen in a special way: through faith they *know* of this infinite love of God, may trust in it and live life out of this faith. God alone gives the gift of faith, far from the fateful exclusivism of fatalist ideas about predestination according to which God predetermines who does receive the gift of faith and who does not and is therefore condemned. This is not the remit of choosiness: its remit is vicarious reception on behalf of all.[8]

What is the difference then between the faithful and the others? Simply put, whether I do or do not know that someone loves me makes a huge difference. And this is the great gift we have received in terms of the love of God. Therefore, faith is itself the gift of being chosen and nothing else. For faith involves believing that God loves even without this faith, unconditionally and regardless of what people do with it. Where God's unlimited grace, in the form of infinite love for all people, is part of the experience of faith, it mobilises the human heart as a powerful source of good and engenders universal solidarity with others (even those who are completely different), especially with oppressed people, faith communities, cultures and ethnicities.

Thus, the notion has to be abandoned that those who do not believe in the Christian way lack something: they already have "everything"—life and, in it, they realise the love of God. To impute some sort of deficiency to those who believe differently or not at all undermines their status as children and (following the pastoral constitution of Vatican II) a people of God, which everyone is given through birth, and it also undermines the radical love given through the radical gift of birth. Simone Weil offers a fascinating insight here: "One of the most precious delights of earthly love, that of serving the loved one unknown to him or her, is possible in the case of God only by being an atheist."[9]

Every human being has been called into life. But not everyone is able, within the context of their lives and socialisations, to experience the givenness of birth for what it is, as a blessing.[10] The conditions of this world may run counter to the unconditionality of birth, or they may support its realisation. Faith as well as the churches, in their message, hopefully support and facilitate experiences of blessing and celebrate the explicitness of the universal grace of birth which, however, occurs and exists without them, too. Thus, the German theologian Karl Rahner reminds us that, through sacraments and preaching, the language of the Church presents and makes conscious that which is the case in all places and can take place in all places: "Did I not bring Israel up from Egypt, the Philistines from Caphtor and the Aramits from Kir?" (Amos 9:7), and, hopefully, the Palestinians from Israel's oppression!

---

8 See Ruth Fehling, "Jesus ist für unsere Sünden gestorben.", Stuttgart 2010.

9 See Tomas Halik, Geduld mit Gott, Freiburg i. B. [2]2011, 5.

10 See Fuchs, Wer's glaubt, 64–72.

6. *Mission from the Christian Perspective: a Liberating Release*

To burden each other with if-then demands is the first sign of friendship or love receding. Those who cling to others do not understand the balance between love and freedom. The same applies, and even more so, to our relationship to transcendence, to God. Faith is not the condition of this love, but the space where it is experienced explicitly.

Everyone can love and be loved. Believers may add—in a low-key way—that this love is to do with God and that their faith includes the experience of God's inexhaustible love which gives strength to do good, and they will be all the more believable to the extent to which they exemplify this acceptance of others in their lives. This faith makes it possible to understand that which is other but can also surpass it in so far as that which is other must be protected simply because of its birth, that is, unconditionally. All people are loved by God, unconditionally. There is no need to believe to be loved. This happens in any case

This is where Christianity's truth lies: in telling all those who are born that they are wanted by God and helping them to realise this experience, without conditions, following the theology of justification: precisely as people who are sinful and far from faith, even before you have changed, you are loved infinitely by God. And this will remain the case even if you never change. Not because God is indifferent to how we live, but God's response is different, not in terms of the intensity of his love, but in terms of the difference between joy and pain within love, based on God's substantial empathy in Christ: in terms of solidarity with the victims and in terms of accusation of and reconciliation for the perpetrators. To suggest an anthropological analogy (familiar to parents who do not withdraw their love from sons and daughters who may have made questionable choices, may have gone wrong ways in their eyes): the intensity of God's love always remains the same; the difference is that love given to sinful people becomes painful—a "cross to bear", as it were—whereas love given to good people is a joy.

Whether individuals turn to the churches, saying "here is where we wish to be and stay", or whether they remain in their own life spaces, religions and cultures, is out of anyone's control. From this perspective, "mission" is already successful when individuals discover the depth of this unconditional love in their own religions: the mercy of God features in every surah of the Qur'an. When, for example, inspired by the way Christians believe in and live the unconditionality of God's love, Muslims deepen their own corresponding traditions and trust in their own faith's ability to remove any limits to God's love, all has been achieved.

Years ago, I was told about two families, one Muslim, the other Christian, who were neighbours and got along together very well; they were helpful and friendly towards each other. And one day the Muslim lady tells her Christian neighbour: "I cannot go on believing that you don't go to heaven." Where people, through their own faith, allow themselves to be redeemed of a fearsome and excluding God in this way, Christian mission has been successful. In Christianity we have traditions in which believers do not wish to come to heaven, if there was even one human being who would not be saved, whoever he or she may have been as sinner or as unbeliever. I mention for example only Theresa of Avila and Charles Peguy.

7. *A Profligate Approach: Unchained and Unchaining*

So I plead for a "light" or "weak" faith, in parallel thought to the notion of a "weak reason" of the philosopher Gianni Vattimo.[11] By this he means a deliberating which does not try to be superior, which refuses to play the Platonistic emperor over life counting abstract victories against realities. It is a light faith, not because it contains light things (the cross is not such a thing) but in the way we live it as an undeserved present, which we do not "possess". According to St. Paul in 1 Cor 7:29–31: to have it as if not having it. Faith and God are not possessions. It is a faith loosening and throwing away the chains of enforcing people inside and outside the communities, by unchaining the faith and unchaining the believers from fear and oppression. This is the future of religions. Otherwise, they would make everything worse and should disappear.

Belief in God is a free extra; it is not necessary for living a good life, nor for living a good life that benefits others. For this, only one thing is necessary: the human experience of tenderness and acceptance. No one has to explore God through religious language games. Christians demonstrate that being chosen to believe in such a God is good and beneficial, that it makes available resources and strength to show solidarity beyond personal boundaries. But there are no necessary and compelling reasons for having to believe to achieve salvation.

In this sense, faith is as overflowing and superfluous as the miracle of profligacy at the wedding at Cana (see John 2:1–12). It is interesting and surprising to note that in John, Jesus' first miracle is not a healing miracle, and there is no shortage or deficiency to address. The people there have already had enough food and drink. And now they are being given even more, even better wine. No one here is in need, at least not in this particular situation. What is more, no less than six water jugs holding a hundred litres each are filled to overflowing. Everything is turned into wine. Isn't this wasting a miracle on lavishness? Of

11 Cf. Gianni Vattimo, Ideologie oder Ethik. Von Marx zum schwachen denken, Lörrach 1988 (Information Philosophie, 16, 1988, Nr. 4); Peter Hardt, Klaus von Stosch (Hg.), Für eine schwache Vernunft?: Beiträge zu einer Theologie nach der Postmoderne, Ostfildern 2007; Michel de Certeau, Mystische Fabel. 16. bis 17. Jahrhundert, Berlin 2010.

course, it is wonderful to see and celebrate life delighting in wine, that is, faith. And it is in this sense, because in many situations faith is experienced as a powerful sustaining force in life that it is experienced as indispensable.

Faith is free, is "gratis", it is not necessary, but it is precious, inexhaustibly precious, just because it is not necessary. And the perspective of faith makes many things in life appear even more precious than they already are, but also even more painful than they already are. But both already exist anyway.

Similar to art, music and poetry, faith is an overflowing luxury: no one has to visit the opera to be able to live. And yet, a beautiful concert casts a glow, as it were, onto all of life. And this is what people "waste" their money on. Hence, following the French philosopher George Bataille, faith is correlated more with the anti-economy of profligacy than the economy of purpose.[12] With our sensitivity enhanced on the basis of this love relationship, life resonates in empathy with the sorrow of those who are sad and the joy of those who are happy. And this is done not in return for what has been received, not out of obedience; it is done out of a carrying empowerment.

How special it is to be allowed to fall in love. How lucky one is to have good friends. What is special about all of this is that none of it can be simply produced or even enforced. They are examples of those extraordinary experiences of love that do not diminish everyday experiences of loyalty and mutual solidarity, but yet they are more than these. They are not necessary for living a valuable human life, but they have the power to deepen the experience of life enormously.

Praise and worship of God demarcate the spiritual space where a "useless" God is experienced—"useless" in the sense that God is never fully identical with any experience, purpose or intention[13], and this dynamic of continual growth extends into eternity and is forever open-ended. The realm of faith is a heterotopia in the sense of the French philosopher Michel Foucault, a place of otherness within the world "governed by wholly different laws and visions, where things follow an altogether different order".[14] Whoever believes in God in such a way will never be tempted to deify him- or herself.

---

12 See Robert Ochs, Verschwendung. Die Theologie im Gespräch mit Georges Bataille, Frankfurt a. M. 1995.

13 See Ulrike Bechmann, Das Lied der Weisheit, in: dies., Klaus Bieberstein, Weisheit im Leiden, Stuttgart 2007, 39–77, 60.

14 Hans-Joachim Sander, Einführung in die Gotteslehre, Darmstadt 2006, 34.

8. *For the Sake of Other Identities*

The more people and cultures there are that are actually allowed to develop their own identities, the more they are able in this self-respect to also open themselves to self-limitation and self-relativisation regarding other areas of life and people. What is valid for people is also valid for cultures: where an individual is able to experience the importance of her own existence in a situation of social recognition and acceptance, which is maintained despite its inconsistency, then she can dispense with having to borrow her identity from the collective identity of a larger "community" for the sake of her feeling of self-esteem. Where ego strength is allowed to develop, one does not need to instrumentalise others to compensate for one's own ego weakness. The more one enters the depths of life, the less one needs expansion in the breadth. The more one is allowed to learn to love and accept oneself, the more one is able to grant this to others.

This is an eminently important connection that is also applicable to cultural units: where they are allowed to find their strength in themselves, they do not need any hegemony over others. Then, one can dispense with being only interested in the maintenance of conventions; instead, one can be interested in living one's life intensively. Singular wholeness leads to the removal of power over the whole. Then, it is possible to look at oneself from the outside, because there is an outside at all (and not claimed as an area which should not be outside but should be integrated into one's own identity): for example if somebody judges his/her own context from the foreign perspective of another culture or if he/she lets themself be criticised by members of another religion. It is an integrated part of their every living identity, not to remain always in one's own context but to look at the own identity with the eyes of other identities: to take over the perspectives of others, especially of those whose viewpoint discovers ourselves as rather limited or as people who are not solidary enough with them or even cause injustice and poverty among them.

Those who can accept, value and criticise themselves in their limitations do not need any colonial limitlessness to experience themselves as important. Exactly this equal openness towards all beings is the test of authenticity for the difference between genuine and fascistic entirety. Fascistic entirety is namely in a position to activate, in a highly cunning manner, emotional levels in a mass of ego-weak people to an extent that they believe that chauvinistic and extensive claims to power over others are actually their own deepest desires. But this is a manipulated effect in which the pathos for the power over others prevents genuine self-realisation in realistic self-moderation.

9. The Universalisation of Christian and Churchian Solidarity

Christianity can refer to its own long history of misinterpreting God's universality, which has cost millions of people the possibilities of living, freedom and finally life itself. Religion inhibits solidarity whenever it restricts God's love to the own area and considers all those who don't belong to their own faith not worthy of solidarity. This would be a *heavy* faith, like having a possession to defend, including God. But God needs no defence. In the Bible God allows accusations like in the Psalms and the book of Job. On the other hand, religion always accelerates solidarity if it grants God's love to all people and experiences the own limited area as a learning field where the inwardly directed solidarity turns towards the outside.

Every religious chauvinism applies God's mercy only *to itself* and thus renders itself universal in relation to others, thus completely losing sight of God's mercy for all God's creatures. Universalistic and thus integralistic strategies form the sharpest contradiction to removing one's own borders against the background of the only existing universality, namely God. The problem "inward-outward" has never stopped being a problem. Especially from the Israel-Palestinian conflict we know: The letter of the Bible alone does not save from a religiously entitled withdrawal of solidarity; this is only done by the the spirit and the intention respectively with which the Bible is read, namely that dynamism expressed in the Bible itself towards a more merciful God and a more universal inter-human solidarity. The Christian creed thus coincides with human rights.

II. Rooted in the Life and Passion of the Cultures

1. *What Does "Contextual" Mean? Preliminary Clarifications*

The term "contextual theology" is experiencing a boom at present and, as a result of its increasing popularity, is in danger of becoming an umbrella term and so of losing its clarifying profile. When I, as a Christian, a Catholic, a European and a German, seek a more precise understanding of this term, then I should not overlook the fact that my understanding of contextuality is itself influenced by my own factual contextuality and limited; that is, it also belongs to what is open to discussion. Other forms of theology and other churches in other contexts also lay claim to other nuances of experience and understanding. But, exactly here lies the first insight: theological thinking is also worthwhile when it is not universally valid in general abstraction, but sees itself as an offer for the "others" to test it.

A context can be defined as the spatial and temporal reference point of human existence, whereby the latter (be it as an individual or a group) itself has an effect on this context and influences its stability or change. Thus, for the term of cultural contextuality one can justifiably employ the term "cultural ecology" inasmuch as the fluid dependency relationships between differing factors are named in a context. As in natural ecology where whole areas of life cannot be neglected or even destroyed because other living organisms would not live or survive otherwise, so it is with cultural ecology. With reference to our subject: in situations where faith and the Church do not relate to the vital expressions of life in a culture, then they destroy themselves partially or totally.

The adjective "contextual" is thus first a formal aspect, at least in contrast to other qualifications in theology (for example, Evangelical, Catholic, dialectic, kerygmatic theology, etc.). Primarily, the principal statement here (which generally applies in its formal scope) is that every form of theology, every statement of believing and every church formation exists in a certain social environment which can be separated from others. Without this connection to life, there would be no relevance of the Gospel to life; it would just be a meaningless collection of words. If this premise is true, then, for the sake of consistency, it must also be considered that human life and belief manifest themselves individually as well as culturally in different and contrasting forms. In calling for contextuality one must also have a positive understanding of plurality. Plurality, however, would still be too imprecise if one did not include in its definition of the equality of the differing fulfilments of life in the Gospel. The words of the North American theologian Robert J. Schreiter relating to the relationship between Christianity and non-Christian religions and cultures are even more applicable to the Christian ecumenical movement, to the relationship of Christian churches existing in different cultures. Schreiter said that the respective manifestations of cultures should be able to communicate their views and claims to others in a way that does not dominate the latter. According to Schreiter, we may never again revert to all-embracing or graded universalism where one cultural manifestation of the Gospel, although it always arises in a limited, partial area, nevertheless becomes universal in a form in which churches in other cultures have to submit to this cultural version of Christianity.[1]

The theory of incultural rootedness presented here is not only valid for the more Catholic viewpoint concerning the theology of creation, namely that all cultures are already filled with the creative power of God before each acceptance of the revelation in itself (despite the contamination by sin). It is also valid for the more Protestant assumption that only through the process of belief does God's spirit allow humankind and culture to accept the justification of this sinful and contaminated existence and to experience it as an area of grace. If God's unconditional acceptance of sinful existence is a part of this justification, with a wholeness that includes even those parts that go against God, then God gives us the right to live and survive as such. The Christian faith is a condition where we experience God's justification in a very authentic way, but it is not the condition for the justification itself, which may be experienced in other religions as well. Otherwise, faith itself would be an achievement that must be fulfilled to obtain God's justification, which would then no longer be unconditional. Precisely speaking, we are not justified by faith but by God.[2] In essence, both trains of thought arrive at the same option, namely that human, cultural and religious existence is or may be seized down to its very roots by the grace of God and the faith of humankind.

Thus, I would like to distinguish between a wider or a formal and a narrower and aim-orientated understanding of the term "contextuality": 1. All is contextual, even the theologians who do not want to be contextual but absolute and universal (like God is): their complex of God[3] is through and through contextu-

1 Cf. R. J. Schreiter, Abschied vom Gott der Europäer. Zur Entwicklung regionaler Theologien, Salzburg 1992.

2 Cf. O. Fuchs, In der Sünde auf dem Weg der Gnade, in: Jahrbuch für Biblische Theologie, Bd. 9, Stuttgart 1984, 235–259.

3 Cf. H. E. Richter, Der Gotteskomplex. Die Geburt und die Krise des Glaubens an die Allmacht des Menschen, Reinbek 1979.

ally conditioned. And: sin and evil are contextual, too. Contextuality is not a legitimating term on its own.

2. My aim-orientated understanding of contextuality is strictly bound to the criterion of the Kingdom of God, that is, of the *basileia,* as Jesus Christ gave us through his life and cross. Therefore, I am looking for the contextualisation of the *basileia* in its respective context, in a twofold way: first to see, to realise, where the *basileia* already lives (L. Boff: Before the Missionary was God)[4]. Second: to increase this reality with the help of God and by means of our whole existence. The realised and necessary manifestations of the *basileia* localise the sources of the criteria: in the context itself and in challenging encounters with other (maybe alien) realisations of the *basileia* in the past and in the present; in the Bible, church history, history of cultures (concerning the victims and the experience of social and spiritual liberation) and the many cultures and religions of the present.

This is a vivid life process about which nobody has an Archimedic point of view, not even the Bible, the pope or other clergy. Even the incarnated Christ did not claim a point above the life and history of humankind. Thus, the criterion comes out of the life, written or lived: in every love, deed of justice and protection and in every act of belief in a human-friendly transcendence. Such experiences are evidently experienced as good, healing and liberating. All these experiences are manifestations of the Kingdom of God, wherever they start and develop. In Christological terms: our criterion must be the living Christ in the world without whom we can never recognise the Christ in the Bible.

In finding oneself in one's own culture, also its hidden depths are always involved and, from the perspective of the sufferers, breaking these open is concerned with a ploughing up of the past, leaving deep furrows behind. This is the most important way to create a specific *life force* from one's own history, namely to prevent the sufferers from suffering for a second time if one forgets because one does not want to see particular sufferers at the time either externally or internally and therefore one suppresses all sight of them. Only those who endure their own truth in this respect do not need to produce any scapegoats to mask their own depths. When we are blocked in many respects from treating the sufferers outside of our own country seriously and from organising our actions accordingly, then this blockage is connected with our homegrown suppression. The silenced sufferers of the past also make the living sufferers of the present silent. It is also possible, however, that a fixation in the present on the sufferers of the past only allows them (even if their situation

4 Cf. L. Boff, Gott kommt früher als der Missionar. Neuevangelisierung für eine Kultur des Lebens und der Freiheit, Düsseldorf 1991.

has changed) to be seen *as such* in the present and the others are overseen.[5] What is suppressed or fixated on in history leads inevitably and repeatedly to such reductions!

2. *Contextualisation from the Very Beginning*

Even the briefest of glances at the history of our religious tradition sufficiently demonstrates that it always has been a history of contextualities, changing in time and differing in their local nature. And this has been the case from the very beginning. It belongs to the principle of the incarnation of God that Jesus did not become culturally independent and only a biological human being, but that this incarnation happened within the context of a specific historical, cultural, religious and political situation of the people of Israel. From this context Jesus takes his words and the resources of meaning with which he interprets his own message and in this way "makes himself understood" by his opponents and also by those who are open to his words and deeds. He creates in this larger context a situation of community with the men and women who begin a new life with him.

After his death, it is through the remembrance of him, which was made possible by his resurrection, that Jesus lives on as the risen Christ with or in the community, whereby the respective contexts of the new communities mould the different points of emphasis in belief or in the formation of the Church. In such a way, the Hellenistic communities which resulted from Paul's mission differ to such a degree from the Jewish Christian communities that massive differences of opinion arise (in the conflict between Antioch and Jerusalem) which can no longer be solved by a consensus of opinion.[6] On closer examination, considerable contrasts, even conflicts, can be seen between the different theological communities of the authors of the Gospels and the authors of the letters in the New Testament (as, for example, between the theology of community of the First Letter to the Corinthians and the community structure of the Pastoral Letters).

In the New Testament it already becomes apparent that where the remembrance of Jesus and the belief in the resurrection have actual relevance for the life of humankind there is a simultaneous fusion of faith and life, of transferred contents and current interests of life. Only then does the Church find itself on the way to the "fullness of life" which the Gospel of John holds so dear. The ecumenical movement of the Christian church thus begins already in the New

5 Cf. O. Fuchs, Die Stimme der Leidenden ist heilig!, in: Bibel und Liturgie 67 (1994) 2/127–142, 130ff.

6 Cf. O. Fuchs, Zwischen Wahrhaftigkeit und Macht. Pluralismus in der Kirche?, Frankfurt a. M. 1990, 62–87.

Testament. And it is one of the most inspired features in the process of canonisation that the latter is not subject to the primary criterion of agreement (consensus), but that it retains the contrastivity of the different traditions. This intra-textual gathering of different contextually mediated forms of beliefs and churches possesses a generative quality for the further progress of the ecumenical movement.

We now have the basis of the Old and New Testament that possesses a constitutive quality for the future, not only in its content, but also in the structure of its origin, that is, in its contextually conditioned contrasts. Simply the fact that these different realisations of the *one* remembrance are treated as a normative content is a convincing sign that in the future not only the remembrance, but also the contextual realisations possess normative energy for the present and also for the future. This train of thought is only applicable if one is prepared not to fix this intratextual relationship between memory and context exclusively, but to interpret it generatively, that is, as being productive and reproductive and to apply it in the respective relationship between the written word and each new present and situation. The following graph may illustrate the process from its beginning with Jesus:

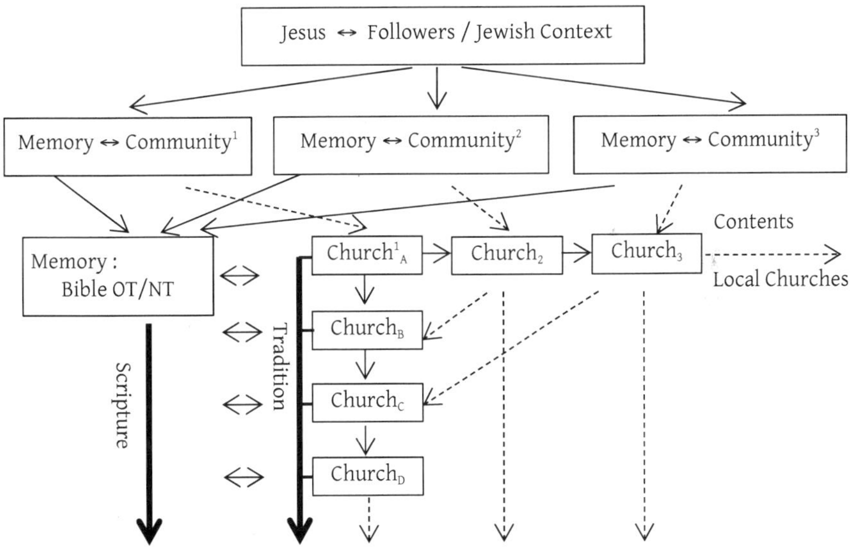

Thus, throughout history there is a permanent reference back to the written word which in an unchanged form accompanied the course of history, whereby this reference becomes more relevant for life the more contextual it is allowed to become, in other words, the more it has to do with the life of human beings and the more it comes into contact with their joys and sorrows. In this way, different manifestations of faith and church also occur in the history of the Church, both synchronically and diachronically—synchronically in the simultaneous existence of locally different, cultural basis positions and diachronically in the progression of time and in the related cultural and situational changes in and between the churches in different periods of time.

3. *Context and Tradition*

Without an apologetic gesture, I will at least refer in passing to the fact that the reverence, taught in the Catholic church, not only for the written word of the Bible but also for tradition can be viewed as an expression for the fact that contextually conditioned, limited and enabled existential realisations of belief are themselves an actuality of Christ's spirit in history. This insight then casts a particular dignity on the contextualities of the respective present: they too have the character of "a self-expression of God in the event of Christ through the Holy Spirit".[7] This statement is not valid in a positivistic sense, of course. Moreover, contextuality confirms the fact that failure and sin belong to life and to the historical condition.

Every contextuality, be it past or present, is always subject to two "suspicions": on the one hand, the suspicion of shaping God's spirit within it and, on the other, of blocking or betraying it. This mutual "suspecting" must take place interculturally on the same level. There is no place here for a Eurocentric surplus of better self-suspicion towards the churches of other countries. The standard for mutual criticism as well as self-criticism remains the respective connection to the biblical message, which has to be developed from one's own contextuality. We may empower ourselves to place different emphases onto the realisations of the message, just as in reverse no compromises for ourselves and others are allowed when suppression, destructive treatment of God's name and the scaling down of life of ourselves or others are involved. The more one can accept that the biblical texts were written by people who often did not practically meet their own theological claims, who were limited and also sinful, the more a mutually critical relationship can develop in reference to the Bible. Self-discovery in the Bible can not only be achieved in structural analogy, but also requires the criteria of the previous hermeneutic of Christ, who lives in the cultures, in which the structural analogies are strictly linked to the experiences of the suffering, the feeling of undivided, compassionate pity and the theological perspective of the universal benevolence of God.[8]

The tradition of the Church in its own traditions is thus itself a fundamental expression of its inculturations concerning the life of the Church as well as theology. In this way, in a review of the past we can discover which contextual

7 Cf. W. Beinert, Art. Tradition, in: id. (ed.), Lexikon der katholischen Dogmatik, Freiburg i. Br. 2/1988, 513–515, 515.

8 Cf. O. Keel, Bertold Brecht und das Erste Testament, in: Bibel und Kirche 50 (1995) 1/2, 13–19,18.

references both of them allowed themselves in the course of history and which catastrophic consequences there were when this was hindered with violence. The fact that Catholic theology sees the reference to tradition, along with the reference to the Bible, as the constitutive source of the Church's identity is an impressive piece of evidence for the just as decisive power of the respective contexts which form the basis of these traditions. Tradition and context are the historical or systematic descriptions of the same process, namely to guarantee faith's relevance for life in the self-fulfilment of the Church and to give prominence to its theological relevance.

Vatican II sees this connection very clearly when it reconstructs the principle of tradition of the Catholic church as its pastoral principle that has to be realised. It must be made clear, however, at this point that pastoral, in the way Vatican II understands it, means nothing other than the side of the Church that deals with experience and action. Pastoral is thus not a reduced term for the work of the officials in the Church,

but is a term for the fulfilment of the contact of the Gospel (the subject of which is all believers) with life, in faith as well as in actions.

Unfortunately, precisely this Christian church which has highlighted the relevance of tradition in its dogma has itself often enough not held a high opinion of the plurality of different contextual references, either diachronically or synchronically. Where the reference to tradition is treated in a monopolistic way, however, and where it is robbed of its contrastivity and is forced onto the same level as the interests of dominance, it functions as a relationship of oppression in the service of a collectivist rule by the Church. The past and the present will then lose their creativity and liveliness. The churches of the Reformation are considerably more advanced in their mutual practice of recognising differences and reciprocal relationships: in their "ecumenical movement" *they* realise de facto the importance of that contextuality which the Catholic church asserts in its systematic reference to tradition.

Seen from this perspective, the traditions are the result of a formerly vivid exchange between word and life, message and situation, content and history and, in the end, Christ and existence. In this existence, Christ appears in many different forms of the Church, in different biographies and cultures. This process began in particular with the so-called missionary work among the heathen, that is, with the step the Christian faith took from the Jewish culture into other cultures, without leaving the Jewish culture entirely. It is thus present simultaneously in culturally different forms of the Church. If one wanted to stop or abandon this continuing process at one point in time, then one should have done so right at the beginning, namely with the prohibition of missionary work among the heathen taking place without circumcision, and, in doing so, one would have reduced the culture of Christian belief exclusively to the area of Israel. However, this would be a crass violation of the canon of the New Testament.

The transitions and replacements did not always take place so successfully, however, in the sense that the culturally different manifestations of Christian existence in each case were accepted and the "handshake of community" was exchanged, which contains within it the joint last supper and mutual diaconia, that is, mutual support, appreciation and protection. Whilst accepting all the problems of historical analogies, it may be asserted here that the Roman church in the Chinese debate relating to rituals[9] reacted in the same way to authentic Christianity in Chinese culture as if Jerusalem alone had asserted itself in the early church and had prevented the progression of the Christian faith into Hellenistic culture. In seventeenth century, Rome wanted to force the Chinese Christians to use Latin in the same way as the agitators in Jerusalem who were accused by Paul of forcing the Greek Christians to adopt circumcision and to live as Jews (cf. Gal 2:14).

4. *The Presence of the Resurrected Not Only with His People of Israel*[10]

A basic process of fundamental religious strategy consists of making the history of its own beginnings absolute. This ideologically fixed identity of origin, which is projected into the past and is exclusive, corresponds to the equally exclusive feeling of superiority in the present. In contrast, those advocating the equal treatment of religions and cultures must also include in the discussion the contra-effective historical ideology that is responsible for such self-deification.[11] The way of plural cultures is not viable without the reconstruction of a plural historical conscience. In our context, the following question in particular arises: is Jewish, Hellenistic, European or any other history the lasting cultural norm for Christianity on its way into all other cultures?

As the question of whether the Eurocentric Christian culture should be the norm for Christian identity in other peoples arises in the discussion of inculturation, so also arises the question of whether the Jewish history of its roots can be the permanent and sole norm of understanding for a Christianity that is

9 Cf. K. Schatz, Inkulturation und Kontextualität in der Missionsgeschichte am Beispiel des Ritenstreites, in: M. Pankoke-Schenk/G. Evers (ed.), Inkulturation und Kontextualität. Theologien im weltweiten Austausch, Frankfurt a. M. 1994, 17–36.

10 The generative quality of the inculturative incarnation, not quite according to F. W. Marquardt, Die Gegenwart des Auferstandenen bei seinem Volk Israel, München 1993.

11 Cf. M. Raheb, Ich bin Christ und Palästinenser. Israel, seine Nachbarn und die Bibel, Gütersloh 1994, 96–108. Concerning the difference between the existential and universal claim of absolutivity cf. O. Fuchs, „Sein-Lassen“ und „Nicht-im-Stich-Lassen“!, in: K. Hilpert/J. Werbick (ed.), Mit den Anderen leben. Wege zur Toleranz, Düsseldorf 1995, 132–160, 151ff.

pluricultural. Similar questions can also be directed towards Hellenistic hermeneutics, of course.

Jesus Christ, who is rooted in Judaism, can only be understood from his Jewish context. This fact can be interpreted in two ways: for all the further receptions, Christ in all the other cultures can only be "understood" from Jesus' Jewishness. The other interpretation would be: the fact that Christ in Jesus was a Jew permanently confirms the radical contextuality of this event. Exactly for the reason that Christ's presence in Jesus is only understandable from his Jewish background is Christ's form of existence in other cultures only to be understood based on *their* cultural identities. In the first case, a universalisation of a singular fact takes place through its superiority and, in the second case, the uniqueness of the other is experienced at the same time in the uniqueness of this event and thus the equal meaningfulness of its contextual hermeneutics for the pluricultural experience of Christ. Accordingly, we would have the same responsibility as we have towards the Jews towards the Palestinians. The relationship to the Jews would then be a kind of torch that enlightens all our relationships. It is a pity that this is not often the case in the Jewish-Christian Societies in Germany. They do not open their eyes to look at all the suffering people, but blindfold themselves by an exclusive positive discrimination.

If we express this in Christological terms: God's son has not become human on a supracultural level but became human as a Jew. Here, the incarnation shows itself as inculturation. More recent Christologies of the present, in particular in the context of local theologies of liberation, have as their basis the *self-evident experience of the origin* that Christ lives especially in the suffering (Mt 25:35–40) and in the person showing solidarity (to a certain extent incarnated in them). In recent years this "option for the poor" has joined with the "option for the others", the disrespect of whom initially makes the option for the poor necessary. As a result, the belief is increasing that something resembling an *original* way of existence of the historical Christ in all cultures and religions also exists.[12] God's presence in history is only universal when it has a multicultural character which justifies the dignity of all cultures—not only morally claimed, but also christologically and thus theologically (in terms of pneumatology).

The incarnation of God's son in the Jewish context is a context of lasting importance in order to understand and to encounter (not to be) *this* incarnation of Christ. At the same time, every interpretation of this fact that gives cultural and religious predominance to it is forbidden. This would be the inadmissible universalisation of a contextual event, a human disrespect for the incarnation through de-contextualisation, that is, generalisation by destroying the particular realities of them. This allows us to raise the thought: what the

[12] Cf. O. Fuchs, Ökologische Pastoral im Geiste Teilhard de Chardins, in: Orientierung 59 (1995) 10, 115–119.

people of Israel are for the understanding of Jesus is for the understanding of Christ in other people's *culture and religion*. In all cases these contextual prerequisites to understanding are naturally always ambivalent and therefore they require all the more an urgent movement towards the historical becoming of reality of the respective presence of Christ in them. After all, chauvinism and totalitarianism were and are present in no small quantities worldwide.[13]

In principle, we may say that God could have been incarnated in every religious and cultural context. This view does not reduce the importance of Israel for the "first incarnation" and its religious hermeneutic[14] in the category of a parity, intercultural duty for encounter and advice, but it does not tie this importance to a claim, free of ambivalence, to absolute right as if God had only been able to be incarnated in this religious area alone. It must not be forgotten how critically Jesus struggled with his own environment. In this obviously hypothetical consideration, the mentality is nevertheless concerned with whether other cultures and religions would have principally come into question as possible locations where God, who became concrete in the Jewish or Christian religious sphere, could have become a concrete reality of life in the same way. Only then do we believe in a universal God who, in a similar way as we believe God to be with us, is able to be effective with mercy in a different way with other peoples.

Therefore, I speak out against the exclusive (that means non-generative) dogmatisation of the incarnation of Christ or of the Kingdom of God in Jesus the Jew. By asking hypothetically: could Christ not also have lived, fought and failed in other cultures and times? The incarnation through Jesus the Jew is a historical fact that cannot be generalised in the way that every historical and cultural context must repeat this historical version of the incarnated Christ by copying it in a fundamentalistic way. The incarnation would quickly become a fossil, a petrification, its own mask. What we will say about the Bible as a reading book (see below chapter 8) must also hermeneutically refer to the content

---

13 Cf. H. Arendt, The Origins of Totalitarianism, San Diego/New York/London 1979, XII ff; I. Shahak, Jewish History, Jewish Religion. The Weight of Three Thousand Years, London/Colorado 1994; Keel, Bertolt Brecht und das Erste Testament 17ff. C. Thoma gives the following clarification: "Anti-Semitism is an ideologically rigid attack against the distorted understanding of the selection, segregation, history and uniqueness of the Jewish people including their alleged concomitants: obstinacy, their fixed ideas, feelings of superiority, plans for dominance, xenophobia against others" (Das Messiasprojekt, Augsburg 1994, 181). If, however, on the Jewish side, feelings of superiority and xenophobia were established, then, we can conclude, the criticism of them is neither ideologically rigid nor the expression of anti-Semitism, but the claim for humane options for all without exception. Cf. G. Aran, Jewish Zionist Fundamentalism: The Bloc of the Faithful in Israel, in: M.E. Marty/R.S. Appleby (Ed.), Fundamentalisms Observed, Chicago 1991/94, 265–344; F. Langer, Wo Haß keine Grenzen kennt. Eine Anklageschrift, Göttingen 1995.

14 Cf. V. Küster, Models of Contextual Hermeneutics. Liberation and Feminist Theological Approaches compared, in: Exchange Vol. 23:2 (1994) 9, 149–162.

of the Bible, to the story of Jesus, to the revelation of it. From this incarnation we learn how the incarnation of Christ was lived and realised in a unsurpassed perfect way in the Jewish culture in order to learn (by taking our own context into account) how such an incarnation of the Kingdom of God can be believed and realised in one's own life, sorrow and joy.

This Christology is combined with the theology of creation, since we take into account that the creation has been carried out by the preexistent Christ (before Jesus) himself and will continue by the postexistent Christ (after Jesus) in the following different cultures as well. Paulo Suess writes, "To make the history of one people into the normative history of origin of other people means to destroy both histories. In Christianity, neither an identity of soil, nor an ontologically (ahistorically) or historistically fixed identity of origin is concerned, but a plurihistorical identity of way."[15] Accordingly, we can assume a plurihistorical and pluricultural presence of God in the peoples—not romantically, but analogous to Jesus among sinners, but not powerless because of it, but with the "power in the relationship" (C. Heyward)[16] of love, friendship, pity and justice. In the following, I intend to embark on the search for possible "principles" of such contextuality.

5. *Contextualisation as Inculturation at the Grassroots*

From the above it is clear that the term "contextualisation" is closely linked with the term "inculturation" and the intercultural qualification of the Church's relationships. To explain the history and background of the term "inculturation" lies beyond the scope of this paper; nevertheless, two quotations can serve to show that it can be reasonably employed here. First, we have the term "enculturation", which comes from the field of ethnology and describes how the members of a particular culture are included in this culture from birth onwards and are socialised.[17] The transformation of this term to that of inculturation is a theologically motivated word creation (neologism) that has its roots in the Christian principle of incarnation.

This corresponds with the opinion in the Catholic missionary paper of Vatican II where, in section 10, it says that the Church should encounter other cultures with the same incarnatory dynamic "as Christ himself took up in his

---

15 P. Suess, Welche Identität für das Christentum?, in: Orientierung 58 (1994) 21, 233–236, 236; Cf. O. Keel, Die Diffamierung des Ursprungs, in: Neue Wege 88 (1994) 3, 71–78.

16 Cf. C. Heyward, Und sie rührte sein Kleid an. Eine feministische Theologie der Beziehung, Stuttgart 1986; E.A. Johnson, She Who Is. The Mystery of God in Feminist Theological Disourse, New York 1992, 270 ff.

17 Cf. T. Sundermeier, Inkulturation und Synkretismus, in: Evangelische Theologie 52 (1992) 192–209, 194.

incarnation from the social and cultural circumstances of the people with whom he lived".[18] The study "Religions, Religiousness and Christian Faith" undertaken by the Protestant churches in Germany and the churches of the Arnoldshainer Conference (Gütersloh 1991) also states: "But the history of making Christianity indigenous is ... the history of God's condescension. God enters with his words into the worlds of thought and feeling, which the witness seeks. He does not remain outside or on the surface."[19] In these statements, in the fundamental features we have reached a respectable consensus of opinion between the churches.

A. Roest Crollius quite correctly noted already at the beginning of this debate that the term "incarnation" is an insufficient formulation that does not manage to illuminate the complete happening of Christ.[20] A decisive, but not the only manner to elementarise the criteria for the inculturation of the Gospel is the analysis of how the Jesus of the Gospels acted in his religious and cultural environment. We find Jesus there as someone who values life above all, who acts for those whose quality of life has been diminished, as someone who exerts himself for the victims, but who is close to those who cause suffering and the sinners and who offers reconciliation. We experience him as someone who employs the term of God in a healing, redeeming and sharing way and who very carefully acts with what we now, in theological terms, call transcendence for the benefit of humankind and its respect. We find him as someone who brings the Word of God into contact with humankind, not with suppression and as a burden, but as something strengthening and redeeming.

Such a definition of inculturation is open to the ambivalence that each culture has within it. Despite the appreciation one has for the achievements in human culture (also in so-called Christian cultures), one must refrain from idealisation or even romanticising. "The inculturation of the Christian message does not take place where it does not question the cultures whether they serve life and the liberation of mankind or confine it in bondage and in the power of death."[21] Nevertheless, when the inculturation of Christian existence is concerned, there is always the need to first accept a cultural context in its own identity and from its deepest roots as a necessary condition of life and its shaping. In this context, one must trust in and support an all pervasive formation of

---

18 Cf. E. Nunnenmacher, Art. Kultur, in: Lexikon missionstheologischer Grundbegriffe (ed. K. Müller and T. Sundermeier), Berlin 1987, 134–139, 138.

19 Studien Nr. 115, cf. H. Rzepkowski, „Religionen, Religiosität und christlicher Glaube" und „Redemptoris missio", in: Evangelische Theologie 52 (1992) 262–276, 269f.

20 Cf. A. Roest Crollius, Inkulturation und Inkarnation, in: Bulletin Secretarius pro non Christianis 13 (1978) 136–140.

21 Cf. F. Weber, Gewagte Inkulturation, Basisgemeinden in Brasilien: Eine pastoralgeschichtliche Zwischenbilanz, Mainz 1996, 302.

life by means of one's own Christian existence in the same deep-rootedness as the power of Christ requires it. If the contextual formation of the Church does not reach that place where the cultural centre of a people is, then it divorces itself from the decisive central life force for the benefit of the Gospel. Such a church formation not only goes against ecological, but also economic and eventually ecumenical interests because a cultural self-realisation and thus the cultural realisation of others are not allowed.

Another insight is also linked with the above: namely, the more people and cultures there are who are actually allowed to develop their own identities, the more they are able in this self-respect to also open themselves to self-limitation and self-relativisation regarding other areas of life. What is valid for people is also valid for cultures: where an individual is able to experience the importance of his own existence in a situation of social recognition, which is maintained despite its inconsistency, then he can dispense with having to borrow his identity from the collective identity of a larger "community" for the sake of his feeling of self-esteem. Where ego strength is allowed to develop, then one does not need to instrumentalise others to compensate for one's own ego weakness. The more one enters the depths of life, the less one needs expansion in the breadth. The more one is allowed to learn to love and accept oneself, the more one is able to grant this to others.

This is an eminently important connection, which is also applicable to cultural units: where they are allowed to find their strength in themselves, they do not need any hegemony over others. Then, one can dispense with being only interested in the maintenance of conventions; instead, one can be interested in living one's life intensively (as Else Laske-Schüler once formulated it). Selective wholeness leads to the removal of power over the whole. Then, it is possible to look at oneself from the outside, because there is an outside at all (and not claimed as an area that should not be outside but should be integrated into one's own identity): for example, if somebody judges her own context from the foreign perspective of another culture or if she lets herself be criticised by members of another religion. It is an integrated part of every contextuality not to remain always in one's own context but to look at the own identity with the eyes of other identities: to take over the perspectives of others, especially of those whose viewpoint sees us as rather limited or as people who are not in enough solidarity with them or even cause injustice and poverty among them.

Those who can accept, value and criticise themselves in their limitations do not need any colonial limitlessness to experience themselves as important. Exactly this equal openness towards all beings is the test of authenticity for the difference between genuine and fascistic entirety. Fascistic entirety is namely in a position to activate, in a highly cunning manner, emotional levels in a mass of ego-weak people to an extent that they believe that chauvinistic and extensive claims to power over others are actually their own deepest desires.

But this is a manipulated effect in which the pathos for the power over others prevents genuine self-realisation in realistic self-moderation.[22]

In examining the term "inculturation" more closely to allow a more precise definition of the term "context", we have at the same time resisted the danger of misunderstanding the respective contexts in a too superficial or extensive manner. In dealing with inculturation, the vertical, deeply rooted levels in the respective identity and culture structures of individual and collective existences are particularly concerned. In simple terms, at issue here is the realisation of faith in the concrete life of people in all their cultural areas and social relationships. The Gospel then reaches the experiences of life and suffering of humankind and no longer acts with empty words and terms but discovers symbols and acts that are able to give good or better messages. The groundwater of human existence then flows to the Gospel; that is, the often submerged hunger for God and the vital desires of people, particularly of those who are suppressed and poor.

6. *Syncretism as a Necessary and Ambivalent Dynamic*

In such a frame of context, the process takes on a new meaning that has to date been mostly disparagingly termed as syncretism. If it is true that culture is almost universally linked with religious components and is thus a mixture of social and religious elements, the question arises: What is the relevance of this for the inculturation of the churches or of Christians?

For example: if the Islamic religion is an integral part of Arabic culture (like nearly everywhere, a culture is connected with religious sediments, that is, it is a mixture of social and religious elements), then the question arises: what does this mean for the inculturation of the Arabic Christians and churches? Does this not mean that the churches at least partly have to take Islamic presuppositions to express themselves in this culture? This question raises the problem of syncretism, as a term that is mostly dealt with critically and defensively in the theological discussion. However, on closer examination one may realise that there has been no offspring of a lively religion without syncretism: Even the YHWH religion of Israel could not have arisen without an encounter with the foreign God *Yahweh* of the Midianites.[23] A similar process took place when the Christian faith shifted from the Jewish to the Hellenistic environment, with the result that the Jewish hermeneutic presuppositions of the

---

22 Cf. O. Fuchs, Gott hat einen Zug ins Detail. „Inkulturation" des Evangeliums hierzulande, in: id., a. o., Das Neue wächst. Radikale Veränderungen in der Kirche, München 1995, 55–95.

23 Cf. E. A. Knauf, Untersuchungen zur Geschichte Palästinas und Nordarabiens am Ende des 2. Jahrtausends v. Chr., Wiesbaden 1988, 145f. und 171.

Christian faith and the Jewish preconditions for the up-building of church communities faded into the background. What the Jewish context has been for the Jewish Christians should have been, for example, the native religion of the Amazonian Indians for the indigenous Christians. This refers in structural analogy to the Palestinians in a Muslim-dominated culture as well. Concerning this freedom, our church history was and is mostly failing. Therefore, Boniface felled the tree of the indigenous religion and imposed Latinisation and centralisation in early Germany, thus depriving those tribes of their own original cultural identities. Here, as in many other historical examples, the inability to establish a responsible syncretism shows itself as the inability to inculturate the Gospel.

Thus, syncretism can be regarded as a positive process if we trust in the Christ through whom creation has taken place, including the creation of religion (not beyond sin but contaminated by it), and if we trust in the Christ who did not abandon this creation when it fell into sin and suffering, but stayed with it and endured it. The scriptures and the Christian tradition give the explicit manifestation of this general fact, because nobody can say that the Bible and church history are beyond sin or not contaminated by it, and because nobody can say that Christ would not be within this process.

Maybe the hypothesis is right: whenever religions cut off their constructive relationships with their cultural-religious context, then they became ghettoised, lifeless and fundamentalist. There may be periods of particular self-finding and segregation in religious history, but never forever and never totally. The Second Vatican Council made such a change from a church that rotates around itself to a church for the sake of and with the others.[24]

Thus, the duty to consult the Jewish-Christian origin does not destroy one's own cultural identity, but fosters—like every free and reciprocal relationship—the development of an own language for the religious dimensioning of reality. Thus, S. Schmidt asks if it is not urgent "to develop a new catechetical dictionary which will be of necessity more distant from the biblical frame of reference?"[25] Schmidt argues from a linguistic-analytical standpoint regarding the problem of changeability of metaphorical language in favour of the ease of communication of religious truth in new contexts. In doing so, he advocates the freeing from biblical metaphors to a form of expression that facilitates a certain communicability in a specific context. In the rejection of any form of positivist ideal language that maintains its own truth through asserting that it issues its own metaphors "unmetaphorically" as descriptive terminology, he directs his attention to the changeability of metaphorical language. When does

24 Cf. O. Fuchs, God's People: Instruments of Healing. The Diaconical Dimension of the Church, Bern/New York 1993.

25 S. Schmidt, On the problem of Metaphorical Language and the Communicability of Religious Truth, in: ET-Bulletin 6 (1995) 2, 130–136, 135.

the relationship between metaphor and life contain truth? In any case, not in the sheer repetition of the same metaphor (as compulsive coherence to tradition), but in a particular connection between metaphor and life. Jesus himself was the one who broke through the existing coherence of religious metaphors as the power-forming legitimisation of a practice that controls the people. It was the prophets and Christ acting in this way "who confronted the traditional cohesion of their religious group with a different approach to the truth, an ethical one". And he asks further: "Can the cohesive power of our traditional religious language be confronted with divergent approaches to the truth, e. g. philosophy, sociology, psychology, the sciences?"[26]

Every culture has its own approach to its reality and to the creativity to seek new metaphors to express the depths of religious experience and respect between people in the best way.[27] Schmidt writes: "In my opinion, we can no longer maintain that the revelation is to be found on the level of supplementary supernatural information. Jewish hermeneutics has always been conscious of this datum. Christians and non-Christians have the right to hear that a number of traditional data have no other truth than that of metaphorical statements; they have the right to distinguish the metaphorical from the non-metaphorical."[28] Accordingly, for Christians, the link to tradition occurs in the sense that they never lose the self-critical contact to the biblical tradition in order to examine for themselves in this necessity for encounter if their own new metaphors evoke that transcendental and human relationship that was "previously" evoked by biblical metaphors. Above all, there is the examination of whether the metaphors can be related to the ethics that are told by Jesus: in his dealing with tradition, humankind and sinners, in his freedom from violence and in his willingness to testify to this connection between religion and life, up to the deepest form of testimony, to the "martyrium".

7. *Cultural-normative Origin of Identity?*

Paolo Suess, in his studies on the "Historical Project of the Poor Others"[29], drew attention to the problematics of a hegemonial and exclusive culture of origin in Christianity for the radical recognition of other cultures. However, Suess does not give more intensive thought to the Christological quality of this position: in

---

[26] Ib. 135.

[27] Cf. O. Fuchs, Literarische Prosa und biblische Geschichten. Was heißt erzählen?, in: Theologica Practica 18 (1983) 3/4, 28–40.

[28] Schmidt, ib. 133–134. Cf. G. Bodendorfer-Langer, „Sie ist nicht im Himmel!" Rabbinische Hermeneutik und die Auslegung der Tora, in: Biblische Notizen 1994, 75, 35–47.

[29] Cf. P. Suess, Ein gewisser Exodus. Zum historischen Projekt der armen Anderen, Sao Paulo 1995 (manuscript).

the related radicalisation of the dogma of incarnation together with the dogma of the pre- and post-existence of Christ, not only in God, but also in creation. This existence of Christ is universal in the sense that it forms the lasting origin for the evolutive power of God's Kingdom in its relation to creation and history. It is also universal in the sense that it can selectively attain a historical appearance in the manifestations of solidarity, justice and transcendence that increases hope.

If the fact that, from a Christian perspective, the historical Christ is also present in non-Christian religions is under discussion at this point, then this does not occur in the voicing of demands for exclusivity, but with the intention of being able to think about the equal importance of other theologies in the heart of our own theology. This not only happens as the application of a Christian ethical imperative "to tolerate" people and their cultures, but also as a *locus theologicus* that is central in the self-realisation of our own conceptional theology. If the equal and so justice-seeking recognition of others is not rooted in the core of one's own theological identity, then it is tainted with the risk of a lesser normativity and thus with an arbitrariness which is likely to increase in certain situations. Only that which is constitutive for one's own identity is constitutive for the ability to enter into relationships and for their quality.

I am in agreement with Suess in his criticism of J.B. Metz and J. Ratzinger. Every "cultural-normative identity of origin of the Christianity hinders the cultural subjectivity of the poor others".[30] Of course, there is no pure Christianity without culture. It has been there from the beginning in cultural state of matter. However, this does not justify the view of Metz that "the culture from which Christianity cannot simply rid itself ... is the European-Occidental culture, which has been assimilated from the Jewish and Greek-Hellenistic tradition."[31] Rather, this fact of the cultural connection of Christianity is to be interpreted much more radically, namely not as exclusively normative and so expropriating, but generative and appropriating. The specific form of culture of a historical epoch—even if it is the so-called identity of origin—should not be allowed to patronise other cultural identities in a type of transcultural generalisation and to act as guardian. "Under the conditions of a normative Christian culture, there is no inculturation. The others, too, have an identity to defend which is rooted in culture and history."[32]

If Ratzinger, on the other hand, wants to exchange the, for him, disagreeable term "inculturation" with the term "inter-culturality", then he is led by the, at first sight, tempting thought: "We cannot repeat the process of incarnation as we want in the sense that we, so to speak, repeatedly remove Christ's

---

30 Suess, ib. 5–6.

31 J. B. Metz, Wider die zweite Unmündigkeit. Zum Verhältnis von Aufklärung und Christentum, in: J. Rüsen a. o. (ed.), Die Zukunft der Aufklärung, Frankfurt a. M. 1988, 86.

32 Suess, ib. 7.

flesh and offer another in its place."[33] Are the conditions of this sentence dogmatically sound? This may be doubted since Ratzinger ignores the Christology of creation here. It is not "another flesh" which Christ is offered, but his own in other shapes. We cannot talk about arbitrariness in this context either, if we strictly differentiate between the constructive presence of Christ (which is hopefully the case in the bounds of the Church) and the destruction of this presence. Then, the essential drawing of boundaries does not take place primarily between the Church and its environment, but between Christ and non-Christ in the environment *and* the Church. "Ratzinger stands in conflict to the views of church teaching which determines 'inculturation' by incarnation and imitation (of Christ, O.F.) and relates the 'breach of conversion' not to prehistory and culture, but to the 'powers of death' and the 'structures of sin.'"[34] Thus, it is his flesh which Christ took on in other cultures "a long time" before and after his incarnation in Jesus and which he takes to himself in the specific "Body of Christ" in a contextual local church.

One cannot think of a subordination here when the Christ in Jesus or in the Church encounters the Christ in cultures and in other religions. It is an equal "self-relation" of Christ in his own rich dynamic of identity in the history of the world and in the history of the Church. The Christ incarnated in Jesus encounters himself, so to speak, in the excitingly different forms of his existence in other cultures. It is then true to say, "what happened in the history of the Jewish people is, despite its uniqueness, a multidimensional example, not for repeated copying (normatively), but for contextualising imitation (paradigmatically)."[35] The model function of this event towards other cultures thereby takes on not only a clear aspect of their freedom, but also the necessary aspect of their otherness.

In addition, one should not act as if the biblical, Jewish, Hellenistic or Occidental expression of Christianity in history were free from ambivalence. Already in the Gospels, Jesus is encountered not as "*cultura pura*", that is, as "pure Jesus", but the Gospels themselves are the result of a (regarding content) more or less successful, in any case lively encounter with him. Not Jesus is writing here, rather those who met him personally or encountered him in the preaching of the Church, and this writing takes place already in connection with contextual one-sidedness, restrictions, additions and contaminations which also result from the weaknesses and susceptibility to guilt of these believers (for example, in the restriction of universal love for others to those of the same faith, in anti-Judaism as a result of a situation of oppression and minority, etc.).

---

33 J. Ratzinger, Der christliche Glaube vor der Herausforderung der Kulturen, in: P. Gordan (ed.), Evangelium und Inkulturation (1492–1992), Graz 1993, 9–26, 19.

34 Suess, ib. 8.

35 Suess, ib. 9: Normative for Christians is, in addition to this, the duty to encounter the presence of Christ in the Jewish context.

The Church has never said that the authors of the Scriptures were without sin. Although this encounter is obligatory for Christians, it is still so free that the Christ who is also living in those who are alive now (which is reconstructed in the Catholic church from the perspective of the theology of the sacraments in baptism and confirmation as the giving of the spirit) possibly has not only more, but also better and more necessary things to say.

However, the question still remains as to the condition for the possibility of other cultures to hear about the incarnation of Christ in Jesus of Nazareth, which is paradigmatic for the Christians, and to develop a Christianity which is explicitly formed by their own culture and so to develop local original churches. One may postulate a special relationship to the historical origin of the Christian faith and the Christian churches, in particular in the biblical tradition. Only which relationship? In any case, not that of subordination, but that of the necessity of an equal encounter, to a certain extent in the sense of a diachronic, inter-religious and inter-cultural relationship, whereby the result of this consultation remains open. The character of a duty to take part in this encounter and to regard this "partner of origin" as equal to oneself, and to accept him as the necessary, continuous, critical "prophecy from outside" regarding one's own cultural form of Christianity results from the self-obligation of Christians and churches, in so far as they wish to call themselves "Christian". For non-Christians there can be no such talk of a duty to let themselves be advised by these Jewish-Christian traditions. The meaning of revelation becomes clear for us only in the living Christ in history who, for us Christians, is recognisable and identifiable from the perspective of the inter-cultural encounter with Christ in the Jew Jesus and from the transfer of perspective which results from this.

8. *The Passing on of Faith in Relation to the Bible, Church and Context*

Dealing in a reductionist way with humankind's reality does not allow one to see how that eternal bountifulness of life, promised by God, actually explodes into the manifold vitality of people and cultures and blossoms within them. The strength of the religious basis communities in Brazil, for example, does not come from the "Theology of Liberation" (this is merely its discursive expression), but from the centuries-old cultural depths of the indigenous peoples' history of piety and resistance. Without this first book of cultures, the second book, the Bible, has no meaning if one believes that its message has any connection to people's lives. Faith achieves its redeeming power only from being rooted in culture and history. The written word without the book is like a puppet without its puppeteer.

The Bible is a source of discussions for mutual dialogue, even arguments, for exchange of meanings and lives, but—and this is to be stressed—on the same level. Thus, the Bible is a book for learning to know the experiences of life and of God in the past including the resulting different concepts and self-confidence of the people. Learning is a mutual process that does not subjugate the learners but enables and empowers them to their self-realisation in the face of the past. The education of liberation is the frame of reference for the term "learning".[36] Since all who want to learn from the Bible are themselves in their own lives "learning books", which the Bible texts have to learn from, too. As St. Augustine said once: There are two books that are crucial, the book of life and the book of the Bible. Without the first the second would be lifeless and dead to the extent that it makes things lifeless and leads to killing in the real sense of the word, as the biggest genocide known so far in history of circa 80 million Indians in so-called Latin America proves. In this respect, we have to rethink the term "revelation" anew. If we understand the relationship to the revelation merely by terms of servility, of subjugation, then there is always a hierarchy implied which tells the people what they have to believe. Further on, there is always a superiority implied which is to be maintained as the more true and the better against other churches and religions.[37]

What is the relationship between the Old and the New Testament on the one hand and between the Church and different cultural contexts on the other? I would like to draw the parallel in the following way; the connection between the explicit Christ or of the Kingdom of God which he represents in the NT and the implicit Christ or of the Kingdom of God as it is represented in the OT is a pattern for the connection between church and context: on the same level of value without superiority of the NT over the OT and of the Church over context. Such a Christology is again linked with the theory of creation inasmuch as we accept that creation was brought about by Christ himself and that creation continues to exist through the pre-existent Christ (before Jesus) and through the post-existent Christ (after Jesus) in itself and so in the different cultures as well. As the OT can be understood as the written context of Jesus and of the NT (at least partly), so the several cultures are the context containing the Kingdom of God and its oppositions, which therefore need Christ to be realised in them as well. I dare to utter the sentence: what the Jewish culture was and is for the understanding of Jesus, every other culture is for realising and enhancing the living Christ within contextual churches. Not only the Jewish understanding of

---

36 Cf. B. Uphoff, Kirchliche Erwachsenenbildung. Befreiung und Mündigkeit im Spannungsfeld von Kirche und Welt, Stuttgart 1991.

37 Cf. J. Hartung, Love Thy Neighbor. The Evolution of In-Group Morality, in: Sceptic 3 (1995) 4, 86–88.

God can be a basis for the Kingdom of God, but also other cultures and religions, both in their ambivalence.

I would like to stress the point that there is no qualitative superiority of the NT over the OT. The quality of the Kingdom of God happens in both, more or less "quantitatively" or gradually. Therefore, the hermeneutic key or the criterion is not the Jesus of the NT exclusively, but the wider reality he stood for, the Kingdom of God. This kingdom of mercy and justice, of a loving and liberating God, is not confined to Jesus, but belongs to the OT as well and all cultures and contexts. We can also put it into the language game of the children of the universal God if we interpret these terms consistently. Brothers and sisters are of equal value as such and they have to deal with each other accordingly. In this way we have traced fundamentalism to its deepest roots: where any superiority vanishes. Accordingly, the OT is crucial for the NT, but in a free way of vivid encounter as Jesus encountered his Jewish context: in critical reciprocity and parity in the horizon of the *basileia*. Consequently, in the same free way the context is crucial for every other—always partly—realisation of the Kingdom of God ("partly" in an eschatological way: the fulfilment at the end will be brought about by God himself).

And now to the relationship between the whole Bible (OT and NT) and the holistic contextual existence of the Christians and churches in their local environments. I would like to make the proposal: this relationship should also be seen in the paradigm of a necessary (not only helpful), provocative and challenging, free and equal encounter, as a crucial reading and rereading in which much can be learned (in the way I explained above). It can be imagined in a kind of reciprocal intercultural relationship in the common horizon of the Kingdom of God.

This hermeneutic horizon of mercy and justice and of a liberating transcendence (even if it is expressed in different, even foreign manifestations) is necessary in order to discover God's will in the Bible. Without it we would always use the Bible for destructive means as has happened often enough. Such a congenial contextuality is no longer formal but aims at the growth of the Kingdom of God in one's own environment: raising necessary conflicts and martyrdoms, as we can read them in the Bible. Thus, the Bible gives us a specific story book in which we can rediscover in another form, from a foreign perspective, what we do in our life and struggles, thereby finding hope and encouragement. Sometimes the encounter with biblical texts really can become a diachronic encounter with the entire otherness of God's presence, which we need to detect, to judge and to deepen our own reality. Such a constructive relationship shows itself as a fine example and learning field of intercultural relationship in the horizon of the Kingdom of God or the spirit of God which lives where he/she wants to live. In such a relationship, this connection to the Bible develops into a ray of light which illuminates and enlightens all our relationships.

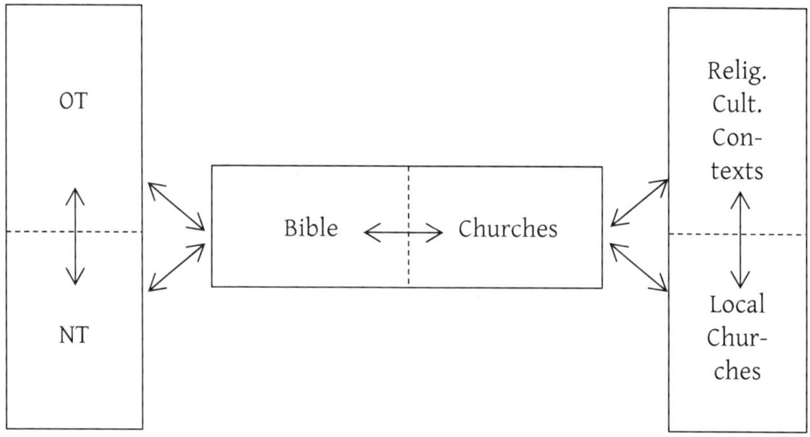

Maybe this sketch will illustrate what is meant. Each of the three rectangles is divided into two halves that are connected by an arrow indicating similar relationships and exchanges: necessary but free in their implementation, obligatory as such but of equal reciprocity between themselves. (They have diachronic and synchronic aspects; diachronically as the history which stands behind the text of the OT and synchronically as the "present" encounter with the scriptures and their religious and cultural context.) This encounter was realised intratextually between Jesus and the early first Jewish-Christian and then Hellenistic churches and their Jewish context or the Jewish origin. This encounter has to be realised extratextually between the living churches or Christians and the Bible as a whole: the same relationship that took place in the Bible takes place between the Bible (as the permanently unaltered synchronic result of the history of faith communities until the canonisation) and the churches in different times and countries. In the same way as the Bible consists of a major relationship between two realities (see the small arrows leading to the OT and NT), the churches are the unmixed but undivided integrated connections of the two realities, that is to say of the religious-cultural contexts and the local communities of faith. Thus, the horizontal rectangle connects the Bible with the churches in the same way as the two vertical rectangles connect the OT and the NT or the cultures and the local church communities.

One must not forget that all relationships are of the same basic communicating structure as developed above. This proposal raises the problem that such an elementary equality of both sides would affect and question the self-confidence of being in the position of more truth and uniqueness than the other side. But there is no other way against any kind of fundamentalism than to encounter each other on the same level of mutual acknowledgement and appreciation between human beings, synchronically among living people and diachronically between people, who lived in former times but encounter us through their texts. For all communications between human beings must be reconstructed on the same level, even and especially to those whom we do not understand or who are alien and strange to us. Otherwise, there will always be a source of chauvinism and racism. This is not only a question of the universal validity of human rights but theologically speaking of the insight that all human beings are beloved sons and daughters of God and sisters and brothers of Christ. This paradigm refers not only but also especially to the sinners and other-believers, whom God loves and justifies unconditionally. Of course, there is a decisive difference concerning the manifestations of the kingdom or spirit of God within the life and history of humankind. But this border—as we know from our own experience and church history—goes through the middle of all realisations of churches, religions and cultures. The more we as Christians look outside in this way, the more we will discover the insight that practically we are sinners ourselves although we claim to know somewhat better in our revelated faith.

In the Bible we find the repenting sinner as the obligatory hermeneutic to understand Jesus's message of *metanoia* (cf. the preaching of John the Baptist, cf. Lk 3:3) and the tax collector praying in the back of the temple: "God, be merciful to me a sinner!" (cf. Lk 18:13). The more we realise (seeing and doing it) the Kingdom of God, the more we can claim uniqueness in front of others. But this statement can only be understood with its dialectical counterpart: We cannot realise the Kingdom of God without the deep confidence that the grace of God enables us. Exactly this leads us away from "*kauchesis*", to a misconception of oneself and a boasting attitude toward others.

III. The Challenge of Plurality

The complicated plurality of the so-called postmodern society in its different realities and modes of life requires not only professionalism in "soul care" but also intensive changes of the structures in which pastoral practice takes place: especially concerning the categorial, the parish and the living space ("Lebensraum") orientated pastoral manifestations. At the same time, there may be the danger that such an enhancement of different pastoral places loses the connection with the Christian tradition, especially if the structural responsibilities of the pastoral care are structurally separated between church and state.

Christian belief has no other "transcendence" than the remembered one. How can the different personal and societal beliefs of transcendence be opened for this semantic of God? Or is this endeavour not necessary at all? For example: Is it appropriate to support people to convert guilt into sin?

How can both necessities be combined with each other: The necessity of the structural pluralisation including its network and the necessity to be rooted in the identity of the Christian, especially biblical past? For example: How can the theology of grace be connected with the achievement of professionalism? How can the meaning of a profiled godlike practice (narrated in the Bible) be saved from being forgotten, the worst sin in Israel? How can the fact that many pastoral areas and communications—for the sake of possible spiritual and diaconal results—are not able to speak explicitly of Christian roots and motives be connected with the solidarity of the other pastoral areas?

1. *Pastoral Care Projects in the Context of an Overall United Pastoral Conception*

1.1 Plural Places and Spaces for Pastoral Activity

In many places the Church has increasingly come to find itself within a variety of communities, institutional and service settings. Even though the parish is the first thing to spring to mind, a many-faceted ecclesial landscape has emerged within congregations and parishes as well as between and beyond them because of individual (and thus plural) demands, increased mobility and the differentiation of life spaces (which are not identical with places of residence; the variety of spaces for choice, communication and relevance available to individuals)[1]. The range extends from different groups within a congregation right through to life space-oriented pastoral care involving a presence of the Church in relevant locations, both rural and urban, where people encounter each other in a culturally and socially diverse society. Pastoral care in the city (city pastoral) is such a form of church life space orientation in so far as here people from various places of residence come together, sometimes for specific events, at other times simply for a chat. The more the societal presence of the Church moves beyond the residence-based parish towards manifestations based on life spaces, the more individuals can have a choice within the Church or even between churches depending on their milieus, circumstances and issues.

However, to be aware of those differing circumstances under which the churches exist, the various loci must pay attention to each other so that passage between them remains possible[2]. If that is the case, both believers and officials within a parish will know exactly, for example, where a young person can find a more relevant pastoral location within another city. There may be a continuing role for residence-oriented parishes[3], in particular when it comes to the experience of being rooted in a community: the resulting social and spatial continuity offers young people the opportunity to become familiar with the sacramental life of the Church where older people, if they have made that choice, have ceased to be subject to the pressure for mobility. But it may be anticipated that the majority of people, firmly at home as they are in their distinct life spaces, will approach the Church via context-specific pastoral care and undergo a corresponding catechesis of faith.

Similarly, given these changes, parishes will not be able to avoid undergoing processes of transformation towards greater inner pluralisation with a strong emphasis on communication, for example, by initiating, supporting and contributing to various social forms alongside each other. This may take the

1 Cf. Michael N. Ebertz, „Lebensraumorientierte Seelsorge" im Bistum Mainz, in: K. Vellguth (Hg.), Missionarisch Kirche sein, Freiburg i. Br. 2002, 142–154; cf. ders., Aufbruch in der Kirche, Freiburg i. Br. 2003.

2 Cf. zum Konzept der Gesamtpastoral Rainer Bucher, Jenseits der Idylle. Wie weiter mit den Gemeinden?, in: ders. (Hg.), Die Provokation der Krise, Würzburg 2004, 106–130; ders., Die Neuerfindung der Gemeinde und des Pfarrgemeinderats, in: Lebendige Seelsorge 55 (2004) 18–22; ders., Neue Zeiten und welche Kirche? Die Konstellationen des Religiösen und die Reaktionen der Pastoral, in: Walter Krieger/Balthasar Sieberer (Hg.), Wie religiös ist diese Welt?, Limburg 2002, 25–51.

3 This statement is only possible the background of still relatively lively congregations in the parishes in Germany, but probably also in Austria, Switzerland and England. It is certainly also connected with my own biography and my pastoral activity as pastor that I do not like to kill a living reality, with all its ambivalence, even before it is dead. But it is just as clear to me that the parish has not only a chance, but a theological raison d'être only if it de-monopolises itself with regard to other forms of presence of the church and at the same time makes itself available for these and spends itself on them.

form of small Christian Bible sharing communities, although in Africa it was these co-existing social forms that have saved the African churches from disintegration into ever-larger missionary areas of pastoral care.[4] This example also illustrates the necessity of trans-regional communication between the local churches in the various parts of the world. Indeed, lessons could have been learned from this pastoral strategy by the German-speaking areas, namely the establishment within each major pastoral area of pastoral sub-areas with enhanced communication structures. Examples include strategies to avoid the marginalisation of existing smaller parishes as well as schemes to explore and develop new forms of encounter between Christians, increasing content orientation (for instance, as is the case there, by a constitutive reference to the Bible) as well as external responsibility. Let us not forget that the number of Catholics who sympathise with the Free Churches and their more intensive communication structures is increasing. Pastorally, too, the world of the churches is moving closer together, with both analogous problems and possible solutions.

With a view to the sociological and thus theologically significant objections Michael Ebertz has made in highlighting the ambivalence of the local parishes[5], there is only one case in which I accept a role for the parishes in the transformation of pastoral care just outlined: namely if a parish carries out its own transformation and "dissolves", as it were, in its ambivalent aspects; if it becomes a residence-oriented personal community and thus the driving force for change away from the old parochial principle and if it is able to recognise and evaluate itself in its partiality vis-à-vis other forms of pastoral care[6]. But the parish must not supervise and control new pastoral opportunities but recognise them and support them outside its own field; it must not overlook places of social interaction but recognise and support smaller-scale forms of encounter; it must appreciate the variety of personalities and be capable of "passing them on" to other pastoral social institutions; it must display greater permea-

---

4 Cf. Klaus Vellguth, Eine neue Art, Kirche zu sein. Entstehung und Verbreitung der Kleinen Christlichen Gemeinschaften und des Bibel-Teilens in Afrika und Asien, Freiburg i.B. 2005.

5 Cf. Ebertz, Aufbruch 80–121. With regard to its territorialist monopoly, the community then undertakes something like a constructive self-deconstruction because of the necessity not to hinder but to promote the overall pastoral care. It would then have a considerable reference function for the fact that existing institutions can also transform themselves into new responsibilities.

6 This is then a new appropriation of the local space. In this context locality itself is then a performance of habitat-oriented pastoral work: 'Localism as a reaction to globalization processes is something else, that is a reflected, a made, a created, a constructed localism. It is something different from localism in pre-modern times, which was lived unreflected, so to speak. The old localities are then something new in terms of life-space, they get a new meaning" (Michael Ebertz in a discussion protocol accompanying the LOS project).

bility between inside and outside, neither locking some people in nor excluding others; it must prevent questions of taste turning into social boundaries or, put differently, when making a choice of taste, it must not lose sight of the fact that this is always only a part of what the Church is; it must focus its attention on the addressees and their experiences, life events, experiential individuality and communicative capabilities so that acceptance of other external pastoral loci as on par with its own theological and ecclesial quality goes hand in hand with changes in the inner structures of the parish community.

Such would be the shape of a future overarching or aggregated pastoral conception: flexible and responsive to change as well as stable and firm in everyday life; agile in detail as well as well cross-linked in the wider network; with a minimum of centralism and protected by an overarching canopy or roof; accessible as well as demanding: for people with loose ties (who focus on processes and projects rather than the longer term) as well as for those with densely woven and enduring commitments. As a precondition, the different modes of pastoral care must respect each other: in the community, in the hospital, among young people and in the city; they must know each other in relevant ways; finally, they must allow people to move into other areas again and keep those transitions free of sanctions[7]. These transitions also encourage a mixing or mutual permeation of the old and new pastoral units, allowing the intensity of this permeation to differ depending on the respective institutions and initiatives.

---

[7] This would also include an electoral tolerance towards the simultaneity of non-simultaneous forms of church presence, including the option for believers who believe themselves at home in conservative, above all certain liturgical forms. This aspect is, of course, also a provocation for the existing parishes, insofar as they themselves are capable of assuming this responsibility to point to other forms of implementation of the church and thus to hand over their 'own' people. No social form of church may declare itself under the hand as fatally necessary, but has to spell out the freedom of the Gospel also on the level of the freedom of choice of church social forms. This is the sign of the times when 'postmodern' challenge and church self-constitution are mutually opening up. One can certainly argue about the equilibrium of the different forms of the church, especially with regard to the social challenge. Here a new capacity for conflict is required not only between persons, but between the church forms of presence, which can be vehement but in the end is able to leave the final judgement about the better truth to the future judgement of God. This spirituality can then also make it possible that mutual solidarity is not denounced for the sake of solidarity with the many different people, subcultures and milieus.

1.2 "Community" within the Joint Pastoral Conception[8]

I wish to apply a particular distinction to the diversity of the present pastoral situation of the Church among people, using the Christian notion of community to add greater precision. If indeed the Church is present in all those present societal manifestations of the Church, we are again faced with the question of at which point we can speak of a community. Church exists "wherever two or three are gathered together in the name of Christ" (cf. Mt 18:20). In his name people are gathered wherever they meet Christ in those who suffer, believer or non-believer, without any exception (for example in pastoral care in the hospital) and in those who are harried and disadvantaged (cf. certain areas of its social work) (cf. Mt 25: 35–40). Again, believers are gathered in his name when they hear his word or reflect on their lives and actions from the perspective of the Christian message in Bible meetings or in adult education. It is obvious: not every one of the aspects that are part of the Church's integral identity, i.e., its realisation in preaching, welfare *and* social work, liturgy *and* community, is always explicitly in every single ecclesial locality; rather, there are different emphases depending on the situation and the needs of those involved.

As far as pastoral transformations of the Church within the parish, categorial pastoral care and life space-oriented pastoral care are concerned, I advocate a specific understanding of "community" over against other social forms of the Church. This is a normative concept, even vis-à-vis the parish, which is thus not simply identical with this explicit constitutive Christian concept of community. For the sake of those concerned and involved, it is necessary that many pastoral loci represent "merely" specific or individual aspects of the Church's whole identity; by the same token it is essential that there are forms of Christian community that approximate its integral identity, in particular regarding the relation of sacrament and belief, of Eucharist and community. This theological concept of community is open to all social and organisational forms but does not have to be fully realised in each of them. It is in those social forms of Church that a focus on current addressees is brought together purposefully and programmatically with a diachronous focus, i.e., the focus on believers known from the Bible and tradition who are already dead and on their diverse social contexts. Thus, congregations make available for the present not only what can be appropriated easily and quickly but also what is experienced as difficult and problematical. Other social forms of church, too, are involved in this: But it is the characteristic task of the communities to engage with this set of pastoral issues along with a social conditioning that carries this givenness of the past over into the present as grace and judgement.

---

8 Integrated congregation within the aggregated pastoral conception.

At the core of these issues is the sacramentality of the whole Church manifested in remembering symbols and in necessary actions, where the givenness of God's history with humanity is celebrated as a present and real experience. Elements of a future theology of the Christian parishes in the context of life space-oriented multidimensional pastoral projects include their pro-existence for all other social forms of the Church, spiritually and practically as well as hermeneutically in so far as they make explicit symbolically the implicit sacramentality of that which, externally, is not immediately recognised as such; they further include their willingness to embody their continuity with the past not exclusivistically but on behalf and for the sake of others, prepared to surrender it at any time. Such a community can no longer impose itself only upon the traditional territorial structure by claiming exclusive validity and making other forms of existence less important or even impossible for the Church. If it did, it would lose its dignity as a congregation in accord with the overall pastoral approach of the Church. Furthermore, its self-positivism would prevent it from perceiving, within its own liturgical centre, those dimensions where the negativity of human life is acknowledged and expressed or the negativity of God experienced, more often than not through a dialectic of experience and sacramental symbolic events[9].

Therefore, both are needed in the aggregated pastoral conception of the Church so that it is a body both gathered and sent: social forms rooted in the Church's diachronous and explicitly sacramental identity as well as social forms of nuanced communication between believers, and between church and society. Equally importantly, conversations with the past and present must appreciate, protect and permeate each other in their theological ideas and with practical solidarity. From this perspective, there are two basic forms of being the Church in the world that pay justice to its identity and incorporate an emphasis on communication in postmodern times: that of *rootedness* and that of *cross-links or networking*, both enriching each other for the benefit of an enhanced *communication* and inculturation of the Gospel and for the sake of more and radical humanity.

From the very beginning, since the first communities as we encounter them in the New Testament, baptism and the Lord's Supper have been central to the self-realisation of the Church in small-scale communities. Hence, I suggest limiting the concept of integral community to those social forms of the Church that explicitly link community and Gospel in a sacramental way. But it would be a misunderstanding if this concept of community were to be restricted to existing parishes (among which, in any case, there are some that are not able to celebrate the Eucharist for prolonged periods); rather, this concept of

---

9 Cf. Ottmar Fuchs, Eucharistie als Zentrum katholischen Glaubens- und Kirchenverständnisses, in: Thomas Söding (Hg.), Eucharistie. Positionen katholischer Theologie, Regensburg 2002, 229–279, 235–241.

community cuts right across all pastoral forms and may be present in all of them, sometimes temporarily, sometimes permanently. Thus, parishes can constitute a community, and so can monastic communities, and so can pastoral care in the hospital in as far as the sacrament of the anointing of the sick and the Eucharist take place in the hospital chapel.

Hence, neither the necessary pluralisation of pastoral care into society nor the call for inner and outer cross-links should be allowed to lead to a "total categorialisation" of processes of ecclesial self-realisation and thus to a relative dissolution of their identity as being gathered and sent as they become explicit in community pastoral care. For the latter gains its life from communication, not only with the present, but also with the past, and especially the biblical past. If the parishes fail in this respect—either because they resist rather than take on board the transformations towards an integral pastoral conception as outlined or because they stop functioning as sacramentally integrating (because of a lack of priests)—new integrative loci for the identity of the Church need to be found to experience the collective corporate identity of the Church described above.

We must not see these various forms of community and other forms of existence of the Church, between the integral pastoral areas and the areas of general soul care, in terms of an opposition between essential and non-essential. Rather, the sacramental form offers an experience that is present in other manifestations too: that "whenever two or three are gathered together in his name" Christ is present or, put differently, that he is present in the encounter with those afflicted by suffering and injustice. The same applies to the relation between liturgy and new liturgical forms in the sense of a service of rites[10] offered to those who are distant and to non-believers. The Eucharist and the other sacraments continue to be the sources of those liturgies, not in the sense of the Eucharist downgrading their value but by means of their givenness through grace, which is celebrated in the Eucharist and is present also in the other liturgical forms. It is the same "water", so to speak, that waters all other pastoral areas from this source and makes them an experience of grace. Those loci, in turn, channel crucial life back into the celebration of the Eucharist, into the universal relevance for people's lives and the transcending of boundaries inherent in it.

Hence, the ecclesial sacraments and other rituals allow a certain amount of movement between each other, which is a gift that may enter the consciousness of the faithful. For theologically specified though it can be, the "added value" of the Eucharist in the context of the explicit remembrance of Christ's life, cross and resurrection (that dialectic between the source of the water and the water itself, as it were) is not a value of which humans can be proud as if

---

[10] Cf. Michael N. Ebertz, Diakonische Riten – Riten bei Gelegenheit, in: Karl Schlemmer (Hg.), Auf der Suche nach den Menschen von heute, St. Ottilien 1999, 120–137.

they had created it themselves. It is itself a gift seeking to bestow itself and be bestowed.

Yet the importance of the explicit congregations within the general pastoral landscape continues to lie in their ability to point those who are open and want to know about them towards forms of ecclesial community that offer an experience of the explicit sacramentality of what they do and experience in their own space. Thus, if carried to extremes, the differentiation of pastoral care might endanger the integration of the Church. Pastoral differentiation needs guidance to safeguard the Church's overall identity: *horizontal* cross-links through movement between them on the one hand and *vertical* roots (in tradition and in remembrance through symbolic drama) through the community on the other.

A certain degree of differentiation will always be necessary to increase inner and outer communication in a way that is attractive and enriching for both insiders and outsiders. Then, the heritage can be passed on through communication with a view to the future. By the same token, our appreciation of tradition will gain in nuance because it is seen to generate different profiles of relevance geared towards specific clienteles and situations on the basis of particular experiences and pastoral circumstances. The secret of integration with both the past and the future is more differentiation; the perennial secret of differentiation is an integration that, on the basis of cross-links in content and communications, lends the differences their differential value in the first place, in the whole identity of the Church.

In the future, the temporary forms of community where, at specific times or for longer periods, sacrament and life are experienced concurrently (for example, in the sacramental celebration of baptism or the Eucharist on specific occasions in a life space-oriented sector of pastoral care) will probably continue to exist. Alongside these, however, forms of community will remain necessary where sacrament and life are bound up with each other *permanently*, in a sense "vicariously", for areas where this is not the case[11]. *For the time being,* this is done chiefly in the parish communities. But this may change in the future and we will have to look very carefully to see whether a congregation is temporary or permanent.

---

[11] About this representative proexistential meaning of the Eucharist for the other liturgies, liturgical theology and pastoral theology would have to be thought out even more carefully. Here only so much: It is part of the sacramental mission of the Church to be Sacramentum mundi, that is, to act for the world, be it in direct encounters and opportunities for change, be it in the representation of those places where the sacrament cannot (yet) be celebrated for disparate reasons and where other symbolic forms are discovered. If sacramentality is in principle bound to pro-existence, then this also applies to the relationship between sacramental and non-sacramental liturgy. For this concept of representation in the Church see Ottmar Fuchs, „Stellvertretung" – eine christliche Möglichkeit!, in: Theologische Quartalschrift 185 (2005) 2, 95–126.

2. *Consequences of the Practice of Pastoral Care*

The distinction and correlation between the discovering of opportunities and the developing of rationales may illuminate the issues under discussion: Integral practical projects are chiefly a discovering of opportunities, seeking as they do to make a sociologically identified possibility accessible to pastoral intentions. Academic theology, in contrast, is concerned with serving a project by elaborating the underlying rationale. In literary terms, this is the distinction between narrativity and conceptional theology—effectively that between pastoral care and dogma, which need each other and cannot exist in separation. Of course, arguments are provided in the course of practical activities and opportunities and deciphered in the area of theology, but the point is to make a distinction between them to describe their nature while acknowledging overlaps. In this, note must be taken of two criticisms that theology makes of practical projects: first, if and when it is human performance or achievement that draws all attention and if the fact that neither humans nor God is simply at our disposal is not acknowledged; second, wherever and whenever the parable of the talents (cf. Mt 25:15ff) is not taken seriously, which brings the future judgement into view. Ernst Käsemann's insight remains true: Grace that does not become active is an illusion. At the same time, all activity without an awareness of grace amounts to human hubris (*kauchesis*, see Rom 3:27). Both grace and activity are related above all to the notions of freedom, grace, judgement, human relevance and the transcendence.

2.1 In the Context of Freedom

The various individual areas of pastoral care must always claim considerable freedom for themselves. Theologically speaking, the theology of creation for pastoral care is explicated by a creative freedom, resisting demands of continuous self-legitimation vis-à-vis professional theologies or the promulgations of the ecclesial authorities. In this freedom there is an increased risk of failure, ephemerality, shortness and intra-ecclesial denial of acceptance. Theologically it is probably fair to say that God has exposed creation to the risk of freedom and takes this risk again and again in the biblical stories between God and humans; God's pastoral policy towards us is, so to speak, not a history of surrender but one that releases beings into freedom along with all creation.[12] The

[12] This does not yet mean that this freedom is at the same time a complete argument for why there is suffering and sin and evil in the world. For the existence of evil is not yet sufficiently clarified with this freedom. Even the future heaven will be a place of freedom, outside this alternative, and the question remains why heaven was not created in the beginning.

freedom risked in pastoral care the more it moves into processes of solidarity with those concerned is creative and hopeful, but it also experiences new responses and might have to face jealousy, stigmatisation or exclusion. The risk of injury (in the passive and the active sense) is always very high.

Therefore, all practice of pastoral care is always in need of structural support by the state and the Church in order to have an opportunity to build up its strength in substantive terms and develop the ability to be able to expose itself, after a trial period, to appropriate evaluation. Hence, experiences of pastoral instability—containing as they do the hope that they will provide opportunities for the future—need more support including theological appreciation. At this point the suspicion arises that ultimately, because of the self-propelling dynamics of taken-for-granted structures and institutions, the fact that God cannot be pressed into schedules is lost to view along with God's freedom and mystery. The experiences of being on a journey and of fellowship on the journey, along with the corresponding insecurity—in positive terms, an openness for new perspectives—were imposed already upon Israel by God through Hosea when it had become too contented with the status quo.

Thus—to use the Biblical picture—a kind of wilderness or desert approach to pastoral care exists: moving away from the meat pots of Egypt, from certainties that turn out to be deceptive, and into the open field of grace and judgement as Hosea demanded Israel to do. The point of comparison here is not so much the wilderness as the going out, and being driven out, into an area that is as yet unexplored but where every step leads towards the presence or indeed the—this time acknowledged and thematised—absence of God. Ecclesiology and "ecclesiopraxy" should take issue with this existence in the desert not only with regard to individual believers but also with regard to pastoral social forms.

2.2 In the Horizon of Grace

Both in the memory of Christian tradition and in theology, there is another way in which this type of pastoral care triggers a deeper experience: in so far as we will have to anticipate the Spirit of God's ability for surprises as we encounter it in people as well as in our own new ideas, because there are new spaces where grace is encountered, for example when new ideas and experiences for one's own Christian identity are triggered by people we meet in specific spaces, and when areas of ecclesial pastoral care are not sealed off and kept separate but allowed to gain new significance. Then such spaces become loci for the experience of the grace of God among humans. Whenever pastoral care focuses in a characteristic way on its addressees, we will in special ways experience and look out for what is literally *there* among humans of God's reality, of the reality of the Holy Spirit: how they actually live their lives, how they succeed and thrive, how they suffer, what they lament, what their longings are and where problems press on them.

If these are places of encounter with people affected by sin and suffering, we must appreciate the theological extension and motivation that, from the perspective of the Christian Gospel, it is in "problematic cases" that God is especially close to us. Here, the focus on the addressees links in to the Gospel's focus on the message. At the same time, this theological perspective raises a critical dimension through the question of how those areas or even islands of pastoral care may be valued theologically, and in this context especially in terms of service for others, for even pastoral care cannot cover all eventualities and do everything for everybody. A pastoral policy that is humane and "merciful" and takes place in the hustle and bustle of the world has to make choices about where to concentrate its efforts given the limits of resources of time and energy. More often than not, excessive demands on the self are just the flipside of self-idolatry.

From a systems theory perspective[13], a distinction can be made within organisations between a programmatic focus on conditions and a programmatic focus on ends. The former refers to all those structural processes and relations in an organisation that are given and repeatable. Those actions follow a pre-given, sometimes prescribed, format, for example, applying for a passport at the local council office. By contrast, a programmatic focus on ends exists wherever new aims are formulated and new ways of achieving them must be developed and established. In the area of liturgy, existing formats such as the celebration of the Eucharist belong to the first "programme", while the development of new liturgical formats aimed at inviting outsiders in for a joint experience of a symbolically mediated depth of life requires a lot of effort and preparation.

Taking place largely in the context of re-modelling the presence of the Church for specific purposes, many projects and experiences in pastoral care share in the intensity of effort required for formulating new aims and remoulding formats. From the perspective of the theology of grace the concern may be raised about how far those involved not only perceive, and co-create with, the communicative grace inherent in a given project, but are themselves sustained by a structural grace that relieves them of having to build up something from scratch and raising support for it, for grace is not only an interpersonal dimension but also a structural one, in so far as there are institutional and liturgical conditions that make possible and sustain human life and Christian existence. Locating grace only in interpersonal relations, in proper chari-

[13] Cf. Niklas Luhmann, Soziale Systeme. Grundriss einer allgemeinen Theorie, Frankfurt a. M. ^{6}1996, 432f. (im Kapitel 8, Struktur und Zeit); id., Organisation und Entscheidung, Opladen/Wiesbaden 2000, 263ff.

ty, but not in the area of the structural justice of existing laws and systems is to withdraw from individuals any support capable of creating merciful and just structures. Hence, a distinction must be made between a constructive and a destructive legality or structural conditioning[14].

Thus, while a programmatic focus on conditions might hamper the future of an institution if it obstructs new developments, with a programmatic focus on ends care must be taken to put in place, within projects, structures capable of supporting new formats. The perennial question is how quickly new ecclesial or pastoral forms or formats can or should be institutionalised without leaving their original power. For theological and sociological reasons, it is important avoid apprehensiveness towards new conditionings. More importantly, we should look at them carefully and ask whether or not they can be justified from the perspective of the theology of grace, especially where the development of new symbolic frameworks and rituals or of new routines is concerned.

Hence, what sociologists term a programmatic focus on conditions is theologically highly ambivalent—an ambivalence that in fact keeps open the possibility of exploring the potential theological depths rooted in the givenness of sacramental actions: Here, in symbolic actions something is given to us which we do not have to create but which nonetheless unlocks a new reality for us. At this point, with a view to certain projects especially in the area of individual pastoral care and social work where those in charge face permanent demands and the relief provided by institutionalisation is just about sufficient to keep them going, it may be suggested that a renewed orientation towards the integral community forms of ecclesial realisation could be helpful: it might deliver the kind of grace-mediating structures that provide the necessary motivation and strength in other areas, encouraging solidarity towards the unstable situation of new pastoral forms in existing, institutionally solid pastoral formats.

This is not new: any theology of community adopting the motto that only those who participate in the official activities offered by the parish form part of the community remain ignorant of the kind of strength a large (though decreasing) number of people draw from parish worship for a humane and Christian everyday pastoral care in their life spaces. From this vantage point, the slogan "only those who get involved experience community" is revealed as a monopolisation and ideologisation of the parish community vis-à-vis all those pastoral manifestations that have always existed unprofessionally in different formats but hardly featured in the official self-image of the parishes, especially concerning the area of social work.

---

14 Cf. Christoph Lienkamp, Theologie des Gesetzes aus dem Kontext des jüdisch-christlichen Gesprächs, in: Rainer Bucher/Rainer Krockauer (Hg.), Macht und Gnade. Untersuchungen zu einem konstitutiven Spannungsfeld der Pastoral, erscheint Münster 2005; auch Rainer Bucher, Neue Machttechniken in der alten Gnadenanstalt?, in: ibid.

2.3 A Strict Focus on the Addressees

A frequently invoked motto of pastoral care is a phrase coined by Klaus Hemmerle: "Let me learn about you, about your thinking and talking and questioning, how you live your life, so that I may learn anew the message I am to deliver."[15] Bridging two millennia, this sentence could also serve as a heading for how Jesus approached people. His adversaries had a point when they called him a wine drinker and a glutton. They realised what his strengths and greatest abilities were, namely sitting down with people and sharing meals with them, being invited, and seeing eating and drinking together as the time to speak out and deliver important, liberating messages. The meal stands as a sign for his breaking up of conventional forms of community, inclusion and exclusion, for he is invited by people whom others no longer invite and whose invitations they no longer accept. But Jesus is also open towards the opposite side: he accepts invitations from the rich and those holding religious power. In this case, an encounter becomes a place for delivering critical messages, but that too is possible only because Jesus gets involved with those he meets, opens himself up towards his addressees and responds to them.

Even in the Sermon on the Mount, an instance of mass communication, he differentiates between addressees and specifies the particular relevance of his message: "Blessed be the poor, woe to the rich!" Therefore, a focus on the addressees is a corollary of a focus on the message. The latter cannot exist without the former because the situation of the addressees is an integral component of the message itself: it is the situation that makes specific aspects of the message relevant in special ways.

What use is there in claiming the extraordinary significance of one's message if there is no communication to relate to those who are meant to receive and rejoice in the message? The pathos of truth is no substitute for communication, all the more so because the truth of Christianity is a truth that is realised only when it is accepted in its relevance. Indeed, the real religious question is not whether or not there is a God, but whether or not there is a God to whom we matter and who makes this known to us as the experience of salvation.

Now pastoral care often faces the criticism of focussing more on the addressees than on the message, with it being argued that the addressees[16] must

---

15 Klaus Hemmerle, Was fängt die Jugend mit der Kirche an? Was fängt die Kirche mit der Jugend an?, in: ders.: Spielräume Gottes und der Menschen. Beiträge zu Ansatz und Feldern kirchlichen Handelns. Freiburg i. Br. 1996, 329.

16 There was already a similar argument in the Vatican reaction to the working priests with the insinuation that they would no longer be evangelically oriented because they are entering the target group orientation with their professional life: cf. Annette Schleinzer, Die Liebe ist unsere einzige Aufgabe. The testimony of Madeleine Delbrêl, Ostfildern 1994. The Second Vatican Council, on the other hand, rehabilitated the employment of priests

not be allowed to eclipse the message. This criticism does not do justice to the projects themselves, but it may be taken seriously as representing a particular concern (apart from the justified criticism that the critics, in their classic pastoral fields, probably do not allow the differentiation of addressees to differentiate the message sufficiently, with the result that the fixed claims and situational abstraction of the message fail to address people's concerns and thus lose their relevance for life). This leads me to my last point.

2.4 Openness to "Transcendence"

In speaking of transcendence[17] I am concerned with something that can be said in focussing on the addressees and that transcends this relation—be it in the experience of a grace beyond our own powers and achievements or in the hope for a reality beyond our own. Such are the "*transcendalia*" related to the grace of God.

At the same time, there are *transcendalia* that are related to interpersonal responsibility. First, there is a presupposition of a communicative focus on the addressees as well as an opening up towards greater inner and outer solidarity. For example, those who work closely with unemployed people in pastoral care in the workplace are sometimes faced with the problem of decreasing solidarity between different groups of unemployed people (especially between German and foreign employees). The reference to the New Testament as well as Hemmerle's phrase makes it quite clear that something can be said on the part of Christians that presupposes current experiences but goes beyond them in innovative ways by motivating them toward an overbridging solidarity. Here we may also ask what the external relations of the respective projects are, how they allow themselves to be modified by them, and where they offer and seek solidarity.

Second, an openness to transcendence includes the explicitness of a specific relationship with God. The possibilities and formats for encouraging, supporting and accommodating such an openness to transcendence are manifold. In fact, it might be interesting to ask those managing or otherwise participating in the projects of pastoral care about such experiences. We would probably discover new ways in which people open themselves up to this mystery of their lives in their specific biographical situations and life spaces, where there are blockages and where unexpected opening is experienced. The fact that this

and assigned in its pastoral conception a constitutive weight in evangelization to this addressee orientation of pastoral work.

17 Cf. to this term and the reality meant with it Karl Rahner, Grundkurs des Glaubens. Einführung in den Begriff des Christentums, Freiburg i. Br. 1976, 42–46, 61–79, 145–147, 157–165.

kind of sensitivity and receptivity to what theology calls the transcendence of life, coupled with the dynamics of an accompanying open-endedness, exists would do no harm to the focus on the addressees; it would actually deepen it so that people feel acknowledged and taken seriously in the depth of the transcendence bestowed on them in their situation.

Incidentally, this not only applies to the domains of communication and social work but also explicitly to religious areas as well. To illustrate with a somewhat simplistic example: take a group of people who regulate their lives on the basis of horoscopes as the chosen life space. In this case, a focus on the addresses would involve not only empathy with the underlying sorrows, fears and needs, but also the concern that a belief in horoscopes does not put a premature stop to the longing for transcendence as though there were no further transcendence beyond simplistic promises of fulfilment of day-to-day desires and religious yearnings. The critical contribution of a pastoral care focussed on the addressees would be to point out that further-going mystery that is not part of self-produced and self-controlled magic. For all ecclesial pastoral care happens in the horizon of a God who bestows the index of being unfinished upon all human belief and action so that there is nothing that we can bring to a conclusion ourselves; rather, everything that is human is also penultimate and brought to its ultimate conclusion only by God.

This applies also to the pastoral care itself. According to Karl Gabriel, "only in the tension to the transcendence-locked reality of the everyday life the potential power of spiritual Christian resources for a new pastoral culture reveals itself."[18] What is in view here is not precipitate promises of fulfilment of human longings for transcendence but also pastoral care itself, learning as it does through a continually unstable focus on the addressees to change existing relations from the viewpoint of that which is always new and other.[19]

For notwithstanding the necessity, in the horizon of the future judgement, of our mutual responsibility to engage in rigorous self-criticism already in the present (cf. Mt 25), the final judgement is for God to make. This does not downplay our effort and engagement, but it does eliminate their ambivalent aspects: patronising know-it-all attitudes, arrogance and hubris; in short, it eliminates all that which St. Paul calls self-indulgence or i.

In summary, I plead for a sole care that is connected with increasing solidarity and must not be separated from solidarity, and where solidarity is not separated from the Christian revelation of God him/herself. Both belong together

---

18 Karl Gabriel, Zukunftsfähigkeit der Theologie, in: id., Johannes Horstmann, Norbert Mette (Ed.), Zukunftsfähigkeit der Theologie, Paderborn 1999, 7–15, 10.

19 Cf. dazu und vor allem auch hinsichtlich der theologischen Unabgeschlossenheit der pastoralen Tätigkeit selbst Ottmar Fuchs, Theologie aus der Erfahrung des „Mysterium Dei", in: Pastoraltheologische Informationen 24 (2004) 2, 68–104.

mutually carrying and enriching each other towards the dynamic transcendence of a *semper maior* (always more!) in human relationships and in relationships with God. To achieve this aim, we need the local structural tensions between different realisations of the Church: to the inner side concerning the unblocked solidarity, to the so-called outside and concerning the openness to the explicit Christian message, routing in the inside of the churches' memory. We need the personal-communicative tension especially in soul care, helping individuals concerning their problems and within this help leading them cautiously to overbridging solidarity with others and helping individuals widen their relationships with transcendence as it is experienced in the Christian faith. For example, to convert their guilt into sin in front of a God who loves the sinner unconditionally so that he or she *can* change their life for the sake of others.

The local structural tension is mirrored in the personal communicative dynamic and vice versa. Both need each other. Pastoral care needs the structural background as a basis which corresponds to its own tensions. The term congregation or community has the double meaning that not only people come together but also that the explicit whole identity of the Church happens (in preaching the Gospel and celebrating the sacramental symbols). Here Christians come together for the sake of both areas in pastoral care, the areas of *martyria* and *diakonia*.

1. Church and state/society have to be interested in "soul care": as immediate help and indirectly against the local and global decreasing of solidarity and for the sake of solidarity which can be shared beyond one's own advantage.
2. Within the whole pluralistic pastoral responsibility of the Church, each manifestation has its own profile (especially between the inside and outside of the Church as institution) *and* should have its supporting context. At the same time an aggregated pastoral concept combines the gospel-orientated identity of the Church with the areas of pastoral care without damaging their freedom but deepening their intensity.
3. Pastoral care happens in the context of freedom and the horizon of grace, strictly focused on the addressees and open to the transcendence towards the dialectic experience of a meaningful relevant and at the same time hidden and mysterious God.

IV. Suffering in the Practice of the Christian Faith in God

Introduction

If death bursts violently into an active life, if a deadly disease destroys the existing form of self-empowerment in respect of life, in this extreme whether faith in God can also keep up with these experiences is shown. In a very specific, unsurpassable explosive way the relationship between power and religion breaks open here in the question of what "might" still remain on the horizon of the religion if a person is at the mercy of his or her last powerlessness. When the question arises about the "might", this is what, in terms of religion, still comes into a relationship in view of the powerlessness of violence, disease and death and beyond, which can be viably supporting and allows for hope.

Here the Christian message here is able to provide information: Christ's suffering and death are an expression of the love of God who is capable of empathy. Suffering is not outsourced from a suffering-free God. The Christian drama of the relationship between love and death, which pervades world literature as a question motif and signals the question horizon of human life in this literary "tip of the iceberg", is an occurrence of its own and one that is highly generative for the life of the believer.

Because God lets suffering get close to Him in Jesus, because "since then" the resurrected Christ has kept the wounds of humankind in God, because the Spirit of Christ continues to "groan" in those suffering (cf. Rom 8:26) and moans because he encounters every suffering person in a lasting historical presence (cf. Mt 25:42–43), because he does not leave the sin of people to be the boundaries between humankind and God but goes beyond these boundaries (cf. 1. John 4:10): because He shows solidarity substantially and existentially with those suffering, Christ provides suffering with a "transcendence" into God and, therefore, never releases the transcendence of God again from an imminence in the suffering person.

The Christian dealing with experiences of suffering, in particular in the field of disease and dying, of physical and spiritual pain, in this connection depends on the situation and person in contradiction: I focus, also with biblical replies and narrative shares, directly on the God-related speech acts of faith, on the supplication, accusation and praise, with different degrees of tension between resistance and surrender.

1) The *prayer of supplication (or bidding prayer)* presents one's own concerns and

needs before God, looking for ways to escape or overcome the hardship. Here is lamenting and weeping, not as an accusation but as an expression of pain and powerlessness hoping to be heard. The success of the supplication is, however, unfairness vis-à-vis those whose supplication does not lead to success. In the recognition of the sovereignty of God, the supplication can lead to surrender to God's will, to God's unfathomable mystery.

2) The *lamentation* before and against God, by contrast, confronts the suffering and love of God and expresses the difference between promised salvation and experienced affliction. Theology's answers to the theodicy question to justify God cannot reassure us. Forty per cent of the Psalms are such conflict and accusation texts. After such prayers had been criminalised as quarrelling in the practice of the Church for centuries, they gained immense significance with the emancipation of believers from ecclesiastical obedience structures, a constantly growing, almost exploding significance, supported by a suffering-sensitive theology, which in turn carries this fundamental conflict into the relationship with God itself.[1]

3) At the end of the lamentation, too, there is, in biblical terms, praise of God, a *surrender* but one that has gone through resistance and reached a special "maturity". It is the recognition of the mysterious God who is released from any instrumentalisation. God is praised as the one who brings everything to a good end in an intangible future. This praise of God often occurs counter-factually to the current experiences, i.e., it must not be confused with thanks for something, but formulates thanks as a promise for a future which does not yet exist.

1. *Invocation: Dialectics of the Own Wish and God's Will*

1.1 Trust in the Prayer of Petition

One way to deal with suffering in Christianity and other religions is the prayer of supplication. In the petitionary prayer, a person asks God for something close to their hearts. This uttering of one's own wishes and needs to God is a very significant "addressing" of God. On an interpersonal level it is actually the worst communication breakup to say: "I will never ask God for anything again!" This also applies to the relationship with God, if relying on the assumption that what is important to a person is also important to God. In particular, if people really wish for something, a genuineness is manifested that should

1 Cp. Ottmar Fuchs, Der zerrissene Gott. Das trinitarische Gottesbild in den Brüchen der Welt, Ostfildern 3/2016.

not disappear from the relationship with God, if one wants to come into contact with God with their heart and soul, with their feelings and wishes and wants God to take them seriously. Consequently, the prayer of supplication also plays a central role in Jesus' prayers (e. g., Mt 7:7–8).

If people stand before God in a prayer of supplication and formulate their *own will*, this is a vehement description of their own affliction. This is an act of wilfulness. The verbalisation can, however, permit some distance from the self. The rush of one's own aspirations to God must not render "Thy will be done!" impossible. First, it needs to be noted that God also takes people seriously in their obtrusiveness and wilfulness (e. g., Lk 11:5f). The own "position" must not be withheld or given up. The surrender is not a blind self-submission. It goes through the tension between one's own wishes and "Thy will be done".

In relying on the granting of a hearing, the *freedom of God* is already designed so that people are addressed differently, maybe "completely differently", without giving up the hope that "at the end of the day" God wants the best for them even if their own wish is not fulfilled, even if the hearing occurs in a completely different manner from what was fantasised about. God will be bigger once more and also more unfathomable than one's own supplications: this, too, is part of the Christian prayer of supplication!

The therapeutic effects of such praying should not be underestimated: whoever elevates wishes and concerns to a verbal expression in a dialogue creates a linguistically and psychologically effective delimitation, a setting, a framing a concern. Formulated through the linguistic awareness, it cannot grow like the unspoken "abyss" at the bottom of the emotions of a person into mostly unjustified ulcers that make the days and nights exceedingly depressing. This applies to both big and small everyday concerns and to concerns of conscience that people have because of their guilt. Such praying reveals that one can again see life and people also outside one's own concerns, so that a bad partial experience does not overshadow one's whole life and paralyse constructive acting.

The prayer of supplication does not, by the way, slide into magic but is actually a strong relationship, since the relationship is carried forward even if the prayers are not fulfilled. Popular piety has not resulted in a breakup of relationships despite all disappointments and sufferings. This relationship is too strong, stronger even than all "if/then" temptations. This does not exclude that people lose their faith in the presence of the worst experiences of loss because God has not helped them. They then look for other ways outside of religion, or they persevere in accusing God whom they cannot forgive for all of this.

1.2 Unfair Answering

Whether something is experienced as an intervention of God, an intervention of answering (if a surgical operation is successful and one recovers), or not is a matter of spirituality. Without doubt there are experiences of evidence which occur between a prayer of supplication and an answered prayer and which belong as such to the inner circle of biblical spirituality. In faith, the answering of a prayer is possible. One cannot deny God's interference or intervening because this would likewise be an inadmissible access to God's freedom. The experience of intervention would, however, become a magical access if one made it a condition for the relationship with God, because there are also opposite biblical prayer experiences, namely that God does not answer and remains hidden (e. g., Ps 88). One can thus not "count" on God's intervention; there is no "if/then" relationship.

One has, however, to make the experience that it appears coincidental when God intervenes or not; one has to expect that one cannot count with God, that at the end of the day one is dependent on oneself and a possible "intervention" by God in turn is experienced as both motivated and unmotivated. If one considers that God in certain biblical texts God does not intervene and that God's "being the Lord" in this life has a different meaning than a forceful self-assertion, one may claim as a biblical spirituality a relationship with God in which no intervention in this form is expected anymore, in particular since any salvation or non-salvation of one or the other reinforces the inner-worldly strong dynamics of unfairness.

This is not directed against the experiences of answering, but is a plea in favour of a spirituality which gratefully accepts the answering and not only fails to reject it in respect to others but co-represents their wishes in one's own praying for a spirituality which can release the requested intervention of God for oneself to God. This spirituality opens itself up to solidarity with all those people who do not experience any salvation. Jesus is in solidarity with them, too. He rejects God's intervention on the cross.

This does not mean that God's spirit and hence God's might did not have any effect in history and that there are no criteria for the identification of this might. In this eon, however, this is not in a self-praising arrogant attitude but in the speech act of praying, lamentation and accusation, hope and supplication, the gratitude and praise of God. At any rate, it would be good for Christianity, after centuries of an often unbridled and disastrous identification of the "others" of historical and biographical events with the intervening acting of God (which always excludes those for whom God does not intervene), to have in this respect a long moratorium of renunciation. In faith, too, it is possible to consider salvation or non-salvation as a coincidence; nothing must be identified with God's intervention or non-intervention. Gratitude and lamentation are possible in both cases because God remains responsible for everything that happens in Creation, be it in the linguistic game of intervening or of coincidence.[2]

2. Resistance

2.1 Lamentation: Resistance and Hope

Lamentation has already been addressed. In the terminology it becomes clear: if I ask somebody for *something*, the accusation is directed at the person who is considered *responsible* for their own condition. In this case there is a claim for something, too, i.e., salvation, but in the highly conflicted relationship of the lamentation. This dimension of a relationship crisis and a crisis talk is not (yet) part of the supplicating prayer or is no longer part of it. To formulate it more strikingly: the supplication wants *something* of God; the lamentation wants to hold God responsible. The lamentation is a prayed conflictual talk with God.[3] It deals with the obvious breach of confidence in God as an issue of confidence.

The most well-known prayer of lamentation in Christian faith is Psalm 22 with the vehement initial question "My God, my God, why has thou forsaken me?" In addressing the question, the emergency condition is attributed to God, claiming from God what had been promised in terms of salvific experience and has not yet been fulfilled but that is now incomprehensibly and shockingly no longer the case. God denies Himself.

Jesus prays this psalm in the human and God-forsaken distress on the cross (Mk 15:34). In this deep distress, Jesus relies on a prayer of his people that is now at this moment available to him as an expression of prayer because it is an offensive prayer that springs from a situation of distress and of being unanswered (in the double meaning of this word: referring to the situation and to God). Nonetheless, it is already an intensive taking up of a relationship with God.

Psalm 22 (abbreviated)
2. My God, my God why have you forsaken me?
Why are you so far from saving me, from the words of my roaring?

---

[2] Cp. Thomas Markus Meier, Dürrenmatt und der Zufall, Ostfildern 2012.

[3] Cp. Ottmar Fuchs, Die Klage als Gebet, München 1982; ibid., Lamentation, in: Hansjakob Becker u. a. (Hg.), Im Angesicht des Todes, St. Ottilien 1987, 938–1024; Thomas Hieke, Schweigen wäre gotteslästerlich, in: Bibel und Liturgie 71 (1998) 287–304; Jahrbuch für Biblische Theologie, Band 16, Themaband: „Klage", Neukirchen-Vluyn 2001; Bernd Janowski; Konfliktgespräche mit Gott, Neukirchen-Vluyn 2003.

5. In you our fathers trusted.
They trusted and you delivered them.

7. But I am a worm and not a man,
Scorned by mankind and despised by the people.

12. Be not far from me, for trouble is near,
And there is none to help.

15. I am poured out like water,
And all my bones are out of joint.
My heart is like wax, it is melted within my breast.

16. My strength is dried up like a potsherd,
And my tongue sticks to my jaws,
You have brought me into the dust of death.

20. But you, O Lord, do not be far off!
O you my help, come quickly to my aid!

22. Save me from the mouth of the lion,
From the horns of the unicorns: You have heard me!

23. I will tell of your name to my brothers,
In the midst of the congregation I will praise you.

In a fervent way the praying person presents their distress to God. In the middle of this distress, where a person does not see any way out, an energy of hope is breaking up in the encounter with God, which is even bigger than the energy of an atom. It is something unbelievable among humans that at this point of suffering disaster they hope against all hope! Biblical praying shows that it is exactly here that God "breaks through" in human life. In going through the lamentation, in not having to hide their own situation before God, in the deepest valley, the miracle occurs. The lamentation turns into an immediate certainty to be answered: "You answer me, you are with me, you deliver me!" (Psalm 22:22b).

Nothing has happened yet externally, but internally the relationship with God has radically changed; it is not only believed that God is near if one is fine, but also that God is near or even nearer in affliction and suffering. This breaks up every "talisman dear Lord", every if/then in the relationship with God, e. g.: "If I am fine, You are near!" or: "If I am close to You in my faith, I should be fine!" God is no longer instrumentalised for wellbeing. Why should one believe if one has nothing, no benefit from it?

In the conflictual talk of the lamentation the believer learns to let God be God and is given the hope that this sovereign God is always close by, in particular in the deepest distress. In a counter-factual manner, people stick to the "good" God. With the accusation not only traditional perspectives of the submission of God to one's own wishes but also the submission to God are broken up. In this way the self-conscious person regains confidence in God in a different form.

Erich Fromm refers to these psalms as dynamic, because their objective is for the praying person to change. They are texts in which you come out differently from when you went in. "It is the seeming paradox that the despair can only be overcome if you have experienced it in its full depth."[4]

For Jesus, too, nothing changes on the cross. God does not intervene, not in this case and as God often does not for humankind. And we do not know why! There is no miracle that conjures the distress away. Nonetheless, there is a miracle, namely that the prayer encounter with God in distress gives rise to a new and now unconditional trust, namely that God is near in distress. It is is wrong to think that wellbeing is a sign of God's proximity and distress is a sign of God's distance, although this calculation might be a temptation.

2.2 No Winner Discourse

God reveals no answers within the meaning of an explanatory knowledge except God's co-being with humankind. Faith does not need any winner discourse. It is not about apology within the meaning of wishing to be right in a dogmatist society.[5] Nor does God have to be justified, as Job's friends believe (Job 3–5).

It is characteristic that in Psalm 22 the initial question "why" is not answered anywhere. Nor does Jesus provide any explanations for why there is sin and suffering. He rather accompanies those suffering and stands in a reconciliatory way side by side with the sinners. And finally, on the cross, at a place of extreme remoteness from God, Jesus claims the proximity of God. Nonetheless, he is rescued. This is embodied by the Christian faith in his resurrection, in his rescue beyond death. For this reason, this psalm has become the mourning prayer of men and women left behind, who followed Jesus between his death and resurrection. In this way this mourning prayer with its hope for rescue becomes a spiritual possibility for the eyes actually to be able to open to per-

---

4 Erich Fromm, Ihr werdet sein wie Gott, Reinbek 1980, 168.

5 Cp. Ottmar Fuchs, Von der siegreichen Apologie zum verletzbaren Denken und Handeln, in: Bernd Elmar Koziel (Hg.), Apologie und Glaubensrechenschaft zwischen Konfrontation und Korrelation. Überlegungen zur Struktur gegenwärtiger Fundamentaltheologie, Würzburg 2017, 383–403.

ceive the epiphany of the crucified Christ and believe in his resurrection (e. g., Lk 24:13–35).

In the confrontation with the immutable, it is easy to identify phases of mourning going through the lamentation process and in respect to which God is claimed in the prayer as "a companion in mourning and dying". There is the shock, then the protest, then the danger of despair and then the breakthrough of a new calm and strength in dedication.[6] This is, however, only possible because rebellion was accepted, because devotion does not prevent resistance but only materialises in or after it. Against the backdrop of the unaffirmable disasters that people experience in themselves or others, there is a fight for an affirmative being which does not know anything and hopes for everything.[7]

In the presence of distress, the believer realises that God listens and answers. This "answer" means: the salvation is already firmly decided in God. It is a reality in God. It is "only" a question of time until the praying person will learn about it. The lamentation process as reproduced paradigmatically in Psalm 22 constitutes the concentration of a process that can take minutes, or days, weeks and years, even decades and a whole lifetime. At the end it proves true in the salvation through the resurrection. The self-interruption of the praying person in the middle of part of the verse of Psalm 22:22: "From the horns of the unicorns (i.e., in particular in suffering)—(and then unexpectedly) you answer me, you deliver me (also against all appearances)!" is best characterised with a dash. The time between these two fragments can be a long time of speechlessness and silence, also of loss of faith during which one stops speaking and does not know how to go on, until speech comes back because one knows how to proceed. Here speechlessness and shortage of speech interrupt speech. This is the critical time during which we no longer know how we can still pray.

According to Paul, the spirit of the risen Christ takes over further praying by proxy, by bridging the silence and appearing with a groaning which we cannot express in words because it is itself totally part of the distress which makes us speechless (e. g., Rom 8:26–27). He prays our prayer when we can no longer do it and he even does it on the level of suffering with the suffering person (not with a nonchalant remote control). He can do it because he is the risen *crucified* Christ. He has taken for himself a horror that makes people speechless: but in it he can find a word to the father in our place, for he is the crucified *risen* one. In this way, the Spirit of God not only occurs in the praying person as long as they speak, but also stands in for them when they have become speechless: against the backdrop of affliction and the remoteness of God experienced therein. In the latter the spirit of the resurrected Christ is likewise

---

6 Cp. Yorick Spiegel, Der Prozess des Trauerns, München 1973, 57–89.

7 Cp. Jürgen Werbick, Was das Beten der Theologie zu denken gibt, in: Johann Baptist Metz/Johann Reigersdorfer/ders., Gottesrede, Münster 1996, 59–94, 69ff.

still in solidarity with his groaning and contributes it to and against God like at the time on the cross where Jesus experienced the forsakenness of God and prayed the beginning of Psalm 22. The incarnate God represents in God the lamentation against God. From this perspective, too, the prayer of lament is the interactive execution of negative theology.[8] With Christ the believers have a might in God to whom they can say everything and lament about everything without having to fear being sent away as insubordinate or being punished as quarrelsome.

2.3 Eschatological Event

Most lamentations are not heard in this world. Consequently, in what it claims and in what it hopes, the lamentation bridges the boundaries of death. If there is a hope for the victims of history, then it must be assumed that their lamentation does not fall silent upon death but that it continues beyond death as a request to God, but above all as an accusation of the perpetrators. This is the only way for hope for the victims not only to survive but also for justice when they can lament before God. Under this aspect the resurrection of the dead proves to be a condition for the last (death) cry of the old world being at the same time the first (birth) cry into the new world. And the coming judge will stand on the side of their lamentation and accusation; it will allow and support them in the tribunal of the Last Judgement. The lamentation is, therefore, also an eschatological event because it is hoped that God not only answers with salvation but will also answer at last the numerous "why" questions arising from the suffering of humankind. This answer will not be poor; it must not be given below the level of the suffering.[9]

A part of this answer will be that God reveals to us by way of an experience what has already shown in God's incarnate and suffering son, namely that God was never remote from us and experienced in Christ the suffering and lamentations of humankind. We also believe in the almightiness that has been necessary to bear all those sufferings throughout history. Whoever has done this in their life, for example by staying with seriously ill people and not running away, knows that this is not a small matter but requires a lot of strength. It is, therefore, possible to imagine that only an almighty God can be so close to all people without exception in their suffering, that God can bear and jointly bear it.

---

8 Cp. Bernhard Casper, Das Ereignis des Betens. Grundlinien einer Hermeneutik des religiösen Geschehens, Freiburg/München 1998, 124 und 93f.

9 Cp. Ottmar Fuchs, Das Jüngste Gericht. Hoffnung über den Tod hinaus, Regensburg 2018, 67–82.

In the experience of the worst negativity, the cry for and in accusation against God is not given up. This is not yet enough. The mentioned tension is pushed to the limits through a very concrete prayer and at the same time stretched and relaxed to the infinite: it is the prayer of the praise of God, the doxology. How is it to be understood, provided that one can actually understand it at all?

3. *Dedication to God's Secret*

3.1 The Doxology of the Praise of God

At first sight, lamentation and praise seem to be related to another in the same way as fire and water. But if one takes a closer look, the prayer of praise does not have the same relationship as the prayer of thanksgiving to the lamentation: because the prayer of thanksgiving cannot be said in distress. The prayer of praise can, however, do this, because in this third part of Psalm 22 God is praised and the whole world is called upon to praise God. However, the deplorable situation of the praying person has not changed.[10] It is not in the situation but in the relationship with God that everything changes.

In going through the lamentation, the relationship with God has, however, changed, from accusation to praise. How is this possible?! It is probably the craziest thing we encounter in biblical praying, because the existing ascriptions are literally displaced: if one wants to attribute the prayer of praise to a wellbeing situation, this order of spiritual speech acts is thoroughly broken up. The doxology is not only married to the prayer of thanksgiving, but it also has a relationship with the lamentation!

In Job 2:2 the mentioned connection is described with hymnal precision: "Naked I came from my mother's womb, and naked I will depart. The Lord gave and the Lord has taken away; may the name of the Lord be praised!" Out of affliction he succeeds (or rather he is given the blessing) in turning his sight away from himself to the great Creator God, the God who is almighty, who stands above everything and who is greater than everything, also the affliction of Job.

Job's word is not an indistinct qualification and trivialisation of life meaning in which it actually doesn't matter what is given and what is taken. Here, too, it is not about highlighting God as an arbitrary God who doesn't care how

---

10 Concerning the change from lamentation to praise in Psalm 22, verse 22b, although distress has not yet changed, cf. Augustinus R. Müller, Stimmungsumschwung im Klagepsalm, in: Archiv für Liturgiewissenschaft 28, 1986, 416–426; Antoon Schoors, Warum hast du mich verlassen?, in: Geist und Leben 57, 1984, 193–199.

he deals with people. God is not to be made smaller and uglier, but greater, greater than our own misery so that a space for a possible salvation opens up in God. Doxology allows faith in God against all appearances.

The human powerlessness experienced by Job is not the last thing that remains to people; it remains and is always the second but last compared with the actually last, compared with God. Job does not consider himself more important and does not think his own misery is more important than God's. Even if it sounds paradoxical: the humility of worshipping uplifts us by still thinking that God is not taken up in the affliction of humankind but is with His infinite mystery infinitely more than a person can perceive and experience. Although God is not acting in a wholesome manner, God's nonetheless assumed power to act is praised in the Creation and history.[11]

Job does not turn his experience of misery into a totalitarian yardstick for the judgement of God. He lets God be greater than everything he experiences once more. It is a God-empowering praise of God and redeems the person from self-deification, be it in her power or powerlessness, by "deifying" the powerlessness in such a way as if it and hence death were not able to live up to the mightiness and almightiness of God.

3.2 God Is Greater than "Everything"

In doxology faith is based on the fact that God is not taken up in the prayed for or in those owed something or in the suffering. Because if God were not, in addition to everything else, almighty in an intangible and infinitely mysterious way, we would not have any hope beyond our limited joy beyond the affliction and beyond death.

But where people accept this presentiment, where they have it given to them, everything is always possible on a large and small scale, as Elie Wiesel narrates in his "Trial of God".[12] In Shamgorod, the Jewish community meets for the service. Based on their misery of persecution they place God on trial and accuse him up to a conviction because he has forsaken his People in this way. As soon as the judgement has been pronounced, the rabbi stands up and invites the community to the most important praise of Israel, the main prayer during the Shabbat celebration, comparable to Job's hymnal praise of God.

The most fascinating thing in the praise is that people, regardless of their situations, ignore and refrain from their situations and focus on the recogni-

11 Concerning the polarity of might and mercy as the core to the spirituality of praise of the Psalms, cf. Dorothee Steiof, Das Gotteslob der Psalmen im Spannungsfeld von Macht und Gnade, in: Rainer Bucher/Rainer Krockauer (Hg.), Macht und Gnade, Münster 2005, 88–102.

12 Cp. Elie Wiesel, Der Prozess von Schamgorod, Freiburg i. Br. 1987.

tion of the unintelligible, intangible and almighty God. In this mystery, which is not easy to instrumentalise for our current life, which goes beyond all accesses to God, there is actually the hope in this life and beyond, a hope that is rooted in His mystery, not in our knowledge and acting.[13] It is the spirituality of letting go.

In the doxology no if/then game with God is possible anymore, and it is also absolutely unnecessary. If the biblical spirituality does not come to nothing, but if it actually reveals the direction of content of this mystery, namely that God is in the deepest abyss of His secret and at the same time the deepest love and salvation, there is no need for any accesses. Accesses and deals exist only in a context with limited resources. In the case of God there are, however, no conditions. This dissolution of boundaries is exactly what doxology draws attention to.[14]

For Job and Wiesel a reference was made to swinging into liturgical forms of prayer. The cult has a proxy task,[15] by bringing to mind in the securing of the ritual the reality that also applies "independently from experience" and is the reality. It continues to "pray" although a woman or man can possibly no longer pray from their situation.[16] In the ritual, mercy is still present before the experience, also independently from it, in order to be experienced as such as far as its pre-givenness is concerned.

The doxological liturgy becomes an area of idiosyncratic "sacramental" steadiness, namely the blessing to be told in every case and to experience that God and hence the hope is always greater than the happiness and affliction of humankind. The ritual is hence not only a compressed expression of human experience but is also opposed to the latter and represents a reality which can also be counter-factual in respect to experience. What the ritual brings to mind is a promise which is at present not yet at home in many respects in the experiences of people but may be experienced with a view to hope, and often enough against all hope (cf. Rom 8:24), as something which is nonetheless already in a certain way present reality.

The ritual represents the non-experienced, the outstanding. In the ritual the answer of God is occurring as it goes along now and will rescue in future, which is decided in God and is hence genuine but cannot yet be experienced. This applies obviously in particular to the ritual of anointing of critically ill or

---

13 Cp. Karl Rahner, Die unverbrauchbare Transzendenz Gottes und unsere Sorge um die Zukunft, in: Schriften zur Theologie, Bd. 14, Einsiedeln 1980, 405–421.

14 Cp. In this respect Mary Jo Leddy, Radical Gratitude, Orbis Book 2002.

15 Cp. In this respect J. Christine Janowski, Bernd Janowski, Hans P. Lichtenberger (Hg.), Stellvertretung. Theologische, philosophische und kulturelle Aspekte, Neukirchen-Vluyn 2006, 227–264; Ruth Fehling, „Jesus ist für unsere Sünden gestorben". Eine praktisch-theologische Hermeneutik, Stuttgart 2010.

16 Cp. Ansgar Franz, Klage als Ernstfall des Betens, in. Ulrich Willers (Hg.), Beten: Sprache des Glaubens. Seele des Gottesdienstes, Tübingen 2000, 435–475.

dying people: given the inevitability of death, the salvation from death is crazily enough believed in here.

Facit: Christian coping with suffering, especially in the area of illness and dying, of physical and mental pain, is quite contradictory: I concentrated on the tension between resistance and submittal, both relating to the relationship with God. Submittal seeks ways to come to terms with God: by giving oneself up to the will of God or to the profound mystery of God, maybe accepting one's own suffering as an atonement for one's own guilt, or to sacrifice it for others, either as an atonement for others or as an endowment so that other loved ones must not suffer. Here, too, there is lamenting and crying (especially in the piety of the people) not as an accusation, but as an expression of pain and helplessness, with the hope of being heard.

The resistance to God, on the other hand, confronts suffering with the love of God and expresses this difference between promised salvation and experienced disaster. God gets deprived of the justification for such a contradiction. Even the theological answers of "theodicy" to justify God are not accepted. Forty percent of the Psalms are such texts of conflict and accusation. After centuries of religious practice such prayers have been criminalized as rebelling; nowadays they gain an ever-growing, almost explosive meaning, accompanied by the emancipation of believing people from ecclesiastical obedience structures, supported by a theology that itself brings this conflict directly to God.

C. Hermeneutical Keys of Memory

I. Memory as Encounter[1]

1. *Encounter with the Past ...*

In our relationships we try to get known to each other, to experience encounters between living people, learning from each other, reacting upon each other as persons with all our capabilities of thinking and feeling, of accepting and refusing, of understanding and being unable to understand, of being understood and not understood, of more spontaneous sympathy or more feeling of distance, which takes time to bridge!

However, Christians not only encounter living people, but also dead persons as we know them from our own experience (our departed friends and relatives), from the Tradition of the Church and above all from the Bible. This is true especially for narrative texts, in which "real" men and women encounter each other or God and thus invite us to meet the narrated people by identification or counter-identification. Thus, these stories become narratives of our identity. The communion of the saints not only embraces the living saints (according to St. Paul), but all the saints who believed in Christ before us. Besides: Paul calls us saints not because we will lead a holy life, but because the Holy God gives us unconditional love and justification as sinners before we have achieved anything. This insight into the twofold Community of Saints has important consequences for the relationship with the text of the past, especially with biblical texts. It is my aim to unfold some of them!

This understanding of biblical texts as representations of persons (concerning the authors and the people talked about within the stories) gains a special meaning for us Christian believers when we read biblical texts: For we believe that the main author who is behind every text and story is God, first in Israel and then in Jesus Christ. Therefore, reading the biblical text is always—at least in an indirect way—an encounter with the self-revealing God, revealed by

1 With the Interlude "Joshua fit the battle of Jericho ..." by Ulrike Bechmann, concerning paragraph 2.

means of biblical stories. In the text we meet God's grace and will; especially in the Gospels we meet Jesus, as he meets us. In him we actually meet the living Son of God, and it is Christ we will meet again. Thus, the encounter with the past is a present encounter with Christ himself and reaches the future of our lives and of the whole earth as well. The texts of the past are not merely past texts, but are an utmost importance for our life and future, even beyond death.

"Hermeneutics" mean translation in a special way: not only to translate a text into another language, not only to understand a foreign text mentally, coming to us from another land in another time, but to meet a text like a person, which sometimes I do not understand, sometimes I even oppose. A text (containing human experiences with people and with God) is not only a piece of paper with written lines, but it is a kind of representative of a person who lived in the past. Therefore, I plead for an understanding of biblical hermeneutics as an encounter, which almost implies all that an encounter between living people qualifies.

Therefore, my concern is with both these things: (a) exactly grasping the content and structures of meaning within the text and (b) grasping no less exactly one's own situation. More precisely: what meaning do the readers extract from the situation they are in—for themselves and also for how they understand the text? The meanings they extract from their own context are linked, of course, to their desires and aspirations, and so are not free from the general ambivalence to which human desire is prone. The history of the uses to which the Bible has been put does, to be sure, bear witness to the twin dynamic of meaning waged between semantics and pragmatics, the good and the bad contending. When humans link what they read in the Bible to their own lust for power, their thirst to exclude those who do not belong, they will draw legitimation, from Scripture too, for the acts of destruction they then embark on. We are left appalled to find that up to 1986, the South African United Reformed Church justified the violent regime of apartheid wrought by the white descendants of the Boers as an integral element of their Christian faith on the basis of biblical theology (using the biblical texts that portray Israel's chauvinism). We are left shocked at the violent and unfair settlement policies of fundamentalists Jewish – in doing so they will please the God of their Bible.

2. Let Joshua 6:1–7.16–21 Be an Example![2]

We will experience an encounter with a biblical text of violence by means of the story of the fall of Jericho (Joshua 6:1–7.16–21). We all know the story of Joshua and Jericho. But as a reminder hear are the main parts of the story.

Text:
1 Now Jericho was shut up inside and out because of the Israelites; no one came out and no one went in.
2 The LORD said to Joshua, "See, I have handed Jericho over to you, along with its king and soldiers.
3 You shall march around the city, all the warriors circling the city once. Thus you shall do for six days,
4 with seven priests bearing seven trumpets of rams' horns before the ark. On the seventh day you shall march around the city seven times, the priests blowing the trumpets.
5 When they make a long blast with the ram's horn, as soon as you hear the sound of the trumpet, then all the people shall shout with a great shout; and the wall of the city will fall down flat, and all the people shall charge straight ahead."
6 So Joshua son of Nun summoned the priests and said to them, "Take up the ark of the covenant, and have seven priests carry seven trumpets of rams' horns in front of the ark of the LORD."
7 To the people he said, "Go forward and march around the city; have the armed men pass on before the ark of the LORD."
(As the story goes, Joshua did all according to the commandment of the Lord.)
15 On the seventh day they rose early, at dawn, and marched around the city in the same manner seven times. It was only on that day that they marched around the city seven times.
16 And at the seventh time, when the priests had blown the trumpets, Joshua said to the people, "Shout! For the LORD has given you the city.
17 The city and all that is in it shall be devoted to the LORD for destruction. Only Rahab the prostitute and all who are with her in her house shall live because she hid the messengers we sent.
18 As for you, keep away from the things devoted to destruction, so as not to covet and take any of the devoted things and make the camp of Israel an object for destruction, bringing trouble upon it.
19 But all silver and gold, and vessels of bronze and iron, are sacred to the LORD; they shall go into the treasury of the LORD."

[2] Cf. Ulrike Bechmann, The Woman of Jericho: Dramatization as Feminist Hermeneutics, in: Lipsett, B. Diane/Trible, Phyllis (Hg.), Faith and Feminism. Ecumenical Essays, Louisville 2014, 183–186; also id, Sarah and Hagar: A Feminist European Perspective on Actual Controversies, in: Lipsett, B. Diane/Trible, Phyllis (Hg.), Faith + Feminism. Ecumenical Essays, Louisville 2014, 161–181.

20 So the people shouted, and the trumpets were blown. As soon as the people heard the sound of the trumpets, they raised a great shout, and the wall fell down flat; so the people charged straight ahead into the city and captured it.
21 Then they devoted to destruction by the edge of the sword all in the city, both men and women, young and old, oxen, sheep, and donkeys.

Many of us have stood there, looking at the old walls of one of the oldest cities in the world. When we as Christians meet the persons in the story we normally side with Joshua and the people of Israel. Joshua, who follows Moses to lead the chosen people to the Promised Land, is someone who cannot fail. We follow him; we stand on his side; we admire how the walls of Jericho come down—and all of this only by marching around with the ark, blowing the trumpet and shouting aloud at the same time. With Joshua and the people of Israel we trust God's word, even if it is as wondrous as it is at the sight of the falling walls of Jericho. We even have a song for that story.

Song: "Joshua fit the battle of Jericho ..."

The Jericho Woman
(to be performed)

"Hello. You don't know me, but we met already in the story. I'm a woman fom Jericho. You don't know me by name—by the way, my name is Nachla. I'm one of the forgotten ones. But I'm there in the text, in the last verse you just heard..."men and women, oxen, sheep and donkeys." You see, I'm one of those women.

I want to meet you. You are going with Joshua? Well, the wall of Jericho is still there and the gate is open. I'll show you around a bit if you like. You know, we live in a nice city. We have a fountain that never dries up, not even in the summer. This is important, because Jericho can be a hot city, especially in summer. Because of the water we have all this greenery here! You can see a lot of fruit trees all around the city. And palms! Many of them.

Look at the wall and the big gate. It is necessary to have it and to protect it well. Many travellers and merchants come to our city. We are a rich city! Come with me down our main street, I'll show you our temple. Isn't it a fabulous building? Perhaps you can get a glimpse through the open door of all the silver and gold vessels that are in there! We are really very thankful to our gods to live in such a good place.

But come to my house. You must be thirsty. I can offer some milk and fruit. Here is my house. Look, these are my children. I have three. Here, my daughter is 12. Isn't she a beauty? And I can tell she is bright, too! I really have to find a good man for her who likes her. Oh, here comes my youngest child. He is three years old. He likes to play around with our donkey. And you know, we sometimes think that the donkey likes him best, too.

But, look at the sun, time is running out. You have to hurry to join Joshua again. You must leave before the gate is closed. If the gate is closed, nobody can go out or in. So, hurry up to go back. Tomorrow, when the sun rises, the wall will fall down. The city will be burnt. Joshua will take all the silver and gold for his God. You know, the God of Joshua has no mercy at all, not even for the old ones or the children.

So go now, and tomorrow we will meet again—and you will kill me."

3. *... But with What Intention?*

We see: Biblical texts can be dangerous for us if we misuse them as legitimations for forgetting the victims and for degrading those who do not belong to our group; then they become very dangerous for those who are forgotten and excluded. Violence begins with wrong identifications.

This brings us to the insight that the encounter with the Bible has to take place with an intention which leads this encounter in the "right" direction. Concerning the Joshua text, this would mean that only victims of oppression—like African-Americans in the United States—are entitled to sing the song "Joshua fit the battle of Jericho", expressing their hope that God will destroy the walls of exclusion and oppression. Others should be in solidarity with the victims to judge the situation from their perspectives. They should sing another text: "Listen to the people of Jericho ..."

These leading motives and motivations are the condition for understanding the texts according to the spirit, who should guide every reception of the Bible. For example, this spirit differentiates between biblical texts that should be imitated and those that we should use as mirrors of our destructive longings and thus reject. All texts of biblical revelation are important, of course, but in different ways: For example, if we believe that we meet Jesus in suffering and oppressed people, then all biblical stories in which people bring others into pain and oppression are written for us so that we can detect the permanent danger of our temptation to do evil.

Let us look at a biblical story that demonstrates the necessity of having a "prophetic" spirit that points to the decisive perspective, that communicates God's will to the listener or reader! Let us listen to 2 Sam 11:27–12:9!

When the wife of Uriah heard that her husband was dead, she made lamentation for him.

When the mourning was over, David sent and brought her to his house, and she became his wife, and bore him a son.

But the thing that David had done displeased the LORD, and the LORD sent Nathan to David. He came to him, and said to him, "There were two men in a certain city, the one rich and the other poor.
The rich man had very many flocks and herds;
but the poor man had nothing but one little ewe lamb, which he had bought. He brought it up, and it grew up with him and with his children; it used to eat of his meager fare, and drink from his cup, and lie in his bosom, and it was like a daughter to him.
Now there came a traveller to the rich man, and he was loath to take one of his own flock or herd to prepare for the wayfarer who had come to him, but he took the poor man's lamb, and prepared that for the guest who had come to him."
Then David's anger was greatly kindled against the man. He said to Nathan, "As the LORD lives, the man who has done this deserves to die;
he shall restore the lamb fourfold, because he did this thing, and because he had no pity."
Nathan said to David, "You are the man! Thus says the LORD, the God of Israel: I anointed you king over Israel, and I rescued you from the hand of Saul;
I gave you your master's house, and your master's wives into your bosom, and gave you the house of Israel and of Judah; and if that had been too little, I would have added as much more.
Why have you despised the word of the LORD, to do what is evil in his sight? You have struck down Uriah the Hittite with the sword, and have taken his wife to be your wife, and have killed him with the sword of the Ammonites.

David reacts as one who was not intended: He identifies himself wrongly with the false man. But Nathan makes clear: He has to identify with the wrongdoer, the perpetrator. The prophet provokes the real and true hermeneutics between David and the story: The parable itself does not achieve this result. Nathan personifies the perspective, the option, which leads the encounter with the text. Thus, Nathan is the hermeneutical key in this story: to repent before God and thus to accept God's unconditional acceptance of the sinner and, concerning human beings, the willingness to deal mercifully and justly. All of this happens for the sake of the victims of oppression and destruction. God is on their side. This is the most important criterion of the hermeneutics of biblical and actual stories.

I propose to designate the guiding relationship between situation and meaning by the term *steering factor*, which I understand as the basic normative intention. It tells us in which direction a possible, or probable, authentic understanding of the text might lie—in critical cases *must* lie. Or, to put the question negatively: What are the preconditions whose absence leads to misunderstanding and misuse of the biblical texts?

Yet to argue thus is to catch myself in the act of presupposing criteria that play a determining role in—and I mean *in—the* biblical texts themselves. The insight that this is so, however, requires closer inspection and justification:

a) The steering factors themselves derive from the leading intentions of the biblical texts (cf. Nathan);
b) I deem above all two things to be critical steering factors within the Bible:
   - *a willingness to repent and*
   - *a readiness to be compassionate and to deal justly.*

I go on to maintain that without these steering factors coinciding on the pragmatic level, no adequate reception on the semantic level is possible. Both kinds of readiness, coming as they do from the texts themselves, steer the relationship between situation and meaning. When, in my following remarks, I look at each of these two criteria more closely, I will be in no sense be claiming to have spoken the last word. Though I hold them indeed to be crucial, I am well aware of how much they bear the marks of my own situative background.

4. *The Readiness to Repent*

The *first criterion* for a *readiness to repent* comes directly from the Bible; indeed it can be seen as something of a personal constant shining through many of the stories it tells. Opposing it is the motif of hardness of heart. For believers, the fact that others do not hear God's message, and do not shape their life accordingly, is so paradoxical that they are even willing to ascribe the striking of these unfortunates blind to God. Jesus also can do nothing when people are obdurate in this way (cf. Mark 6:1–6a). Only those with a readiness to repent can glimpse what God has in store for them. This readiness boils down to us perceiving that we are as sinners, whereupon we can awaken to God's message. This act of insight into our nature shatters our hardness of heart. Not for nothing does the preacher of repentance, John the Baptist, come before Jesus the Messiah does. He is the one who personifies the hermeneutic I have in mind. Those unwilling to recognise their sinful ways for what they are, to turn full circle, in act and thought and move towards the love of God and one's fellows, as Jesus proclaimed and set forth, will *always* read the Gospels wrongly, will misuse them in defence of their personal or collective circumstances.

Speaking of John the Baptist, Helmut Merklein opined that the crucial opposition is not to be sought between salvation and judgement, but in whether one submits to judgement or not. "The alternative, therefore, is not salvation or judgment (or flight from judgment vs. judgment), it is acceptance or non-acceptance of God's impending wrath. In the first instance, passage of judgment leads to personal renewal, in the second, to final annihilation...Who submits to God's judgment shall be renewed, who seeks to evade it shall die." To relate to God's judgement and so tread the path of practical repentance is, and this is grounded in the texts themselves, the condition for any possibility of accepting the message of Jesus. Text-externally extrapolated, we have to do, therefore, also with the pragmatic conditions for the possibility of understanding the biblical texts. Therefore, it is that the concrete readiness to repent becomes the material-hermeneutic requirement for reading the Gospel texts authentically.

The readiness to repent to which I have been alluding constitutes, in light of this basic proclivity to sin that is our fallen condition, a principal aspect, one might say a universal-pragmatic precondition, for grasping the Gospel message, more, at any rate, than does any possible aspect of urgent import in whose situate sinfulness we are directly involved. Not least, the readiness to repent is an indispensable way station if the Gospel message is ever to percolate through to, and concretely influence, the real world of persons and situations. Without the readiness to repent, our faith would never seek an outlet in action, as a result of which it would lose its power to transform our lives. Therefore, what is called for is not so much rethinking faith itself, but rather changing the way we act, which is sorely needed if we are, in turn, to tap the depths of faith. Who stands directly before God, knowing that she or he is now at the end of all striving, needs to ponder that story of the tax collector standing at the back of the temple, who has no illusions, face to face with his Maker and God, that he still has a very long way to go in terms of his faith and practice (cf. Luke: 18:13).

Self-knowledge of this kind does not diminish us (nbefore God or before our fellow humans); rather it delivers a bleak and unvarnished insight into ourselves and our biographical, historical and social situation or, to take the negative, it reveals our lurking potential for bad and worse than bad. We have no mandate to make ourselves better before God than we are, on pain of forfeiting His affection. Rather, particularly on the plane of justification theology, God's compassionate solicitude is given in advance and unconditionally. In God's presence, we even do not have to justify ourselves, which might in itself entail grievous consequences for others (given our propensity for scapegoating others while claiming the moral high ground for ourselves).

Thus, this further plane of a principled readiness to repent develops *sui generis*, until it is sensitised to the point of seeing, with particular clarity, those who are, or who will soon be, victims

a) of the refusal to repent and
b) of human sinfulness,

both of which are directed at God (on a scale ranging from self-aggrandizement to self-adulation) and at humanity (in the withholding of help or by actively inflicting harm). This brings me to my second criterion, a *readiness to be compassionate and to deal justly*.

5. *The Readiness to be Compassionate and to Deal Justly*

If the readiness to repent involves turning inwards and working with the raw material of our nature, then the second of our two criteria refers to our relationship with other people and groups. Content-wise they belong together, and each constitutes a different side of the self-same reality, which is this: the perspective of God's own compassion and justification, as accepted into and activated within our own person, so much so that we do not begrudge others, nor do we withhold from them the compassion and justice that is their due.

Thus, that the poor and the afflicted have a particular status can certainly be seen as a biblical leitmotiv. Relentlessly hammered home, and demonstrated again and again, is that they are better placed than their more fortunate fellows to fathom God's justice and enter God's Kingdom. Not that this diminishes the universality of the biblical message; rather the contrary: only thus does it gain the ability to link up with the differing and contradictory situations humans find themselves in, the better to gain real "traction" with them (as opposed to merely sliding over the surface). Even the rich and powerful are addressed in the Gospels: yet what they are told is pitched differently than it is for the poor. What *is* universal is that the message also reaches them that they are sinners. But the manner in which they sin and the manner in which they are tempted differ greatly. The message for the poor in the Gospels, and from the Gospels, is not, therefore, that penury is their lot; rather the message enfolds the rich in a quite specific way, namely it enfolds them in terms of how they relate to the poor. This is a literal necessity, because otherwise God's justice is but a pretence because it does not reach the victims of injustice. And so social status may be said to overlap with a certain hermeneutic status.

This steering I have been referring to in the reception of the biblical texts renders incumbent a *comparative situative analysis*, where the situation of the biblical actors, those whose stories are told in the Bible, is compared with the situation of persons extraneous to the Bible who are trying to grasp its meaning. The substantive delimiting of meaning production is grounded, therefore, in a quite specific relational determination as between textual (and contextual) situative perception and evaluation. Our reading of the Bible must be contextual in the sense that the related and real situations correspond in their social structure, or, in the negative case, when their non-correspondence is discerned. As when in Matthew 25:35–40 Jesus Christ is moved by pity to identify with the stranger and the needy; as when in the Sermon on the Mount, again moved by pity, Christ beatifies the downcast, then we can say only those can identify with the categories of persons addressed who have had, and can draw on, comparable experiences of their own. Thus, if we are to identify with those who are part of God's Kingdom, we must include the sick, the stranger and the needy in how we define our own faith and actions. Had Francis of Assisi not identified with the rich young man whose story is told to us in Mark 10:17–35, his conversion would likely not have happened. Had, instead, Francis identified with "poor Lazarus," he would have never fathomed his own truth, nor that of the biblical texts, meaning, in end effect, he would have evaded both repentance and calling. In every case, therefore, of drawing on biblical texts, the parallel social and personal situations of narrated text and current situation must "fit". Social status has a hermeneutic quality, in that thinking and being, interpretation and context, all duly feed into each other.

At the bottom, what is at stake here is always the issue of power, as between domination and impotence, as between the way of violence and that of the cross. If the Gospels are to be binding for all of us (and not just on the plane of generalisations, but in all concreteness of application), the different situations covered in its pages must be factored into the reading process, so that with such luminosity, such a lack of ambiguity, they actually come across to us as they really are. Rich and poor may, indeed must, be able to identify their "opposite numbers", as it were, through the biblical texts, seeing past the differences in circumstances. This holds too for the mighty and the ground down, for those who belong and those who have been excluded, and so on. What the poor man can do therefore finds its counterpart in what the rich man can, namely that the latter accepts the Gospels most condignly when in following Jesus he repents in ways that benefit the poor man, thereby freeing himself from the need to fear for his possessions and power. Those to whom the Sermon on the Mount is addressed (the needy, the persecuted, the doers of deeds of peace) are not, at least not in the Bible, spoken to in their *general* humanity; rather they are analytically identified in their situated contexts as real-world addressees of what Jesus is preaching and are thus brought into a specific relationship with the Good News. This text-internal pragmatics possesses constitutive meaning too with reference to the text-internal pragmatics of interaction with the texts. Each biblical reading, if it is of the right kind, then becomes a motor for how we ourselves analyse our situation from the perspective of justice and the need for compassion. Accurate perception of situation, then, is the key to greater accuracy in the specification of self-directed (or even other-directed) perception within the biblical texts.

Therefore, out of deference to human dignity and the especial dignity of those who suffer, as attested by many biblical texts, particularly those telling of the prophets (of both sexes) and of Jesus himself, it is necessary to reject or pass over passages in the Bible when they themselves neglect this basic option I have explained. Failure to heed this hermeneutic steering factor cannot be legitimised by the expedient of citing certain quite specific biblical passages; attempting to do so always constitutes an abuse of the Bible. Thus, if we wish to resort to violence, we cannot do so by adducing cases in the Bible where the protagonists did as much. In particular, biblical texts which, for a variety of historical reasons, regulate the inside-outside relationship with the intent of degrading and subordinating, can and may not be produced in support of strategies in the present day, whose aim, express or covert, is to humiliate and ostracise. Any identifying with such biblical texts to promote and justify the expulsion and suppression of other persons or groups cannot be condoned for the sake of the better, more humane texts in the Bible, and one might add the whole Judeo-Christian tradition (which at its core preaches love of our fellows, including those who are strangers to us, and it does not balk at extending this same love to our enemies). To see why, we need only consider a fundamental dynamic, one that starts with self-love, passes through love for others, and then transcends itself by refusing to exclude strangers and even those who would do us harm, a dynamic that cannot be stopped, just like that, by some biblical text or other that has somehow remained frozen at the level of self-love. Rather what we must do is invoke the lead texts, those in whose inspired words this dynamic culminates and then judge all the others by *their* light.

6. *Responsibility of the Churches*

At last we have to go back to the encounter of the living believers, of ourselves. Though we might find evidence for this dynamic to a more and more merciful God, to more and more solidarity and justice, there is one question that remains unanswered: What is the basis on which believers' take the decision for such prioritising in dealing with biblical revelation? How can we talk of the will of God in a criteriologically sound way, given the variety and diversity of texts? There is only one answer to this, and it is an ecclesiological and pneumatological one: as and when believers read the Bible in the spirit of the God whom they believe to be love and freedom, in the spirit of the risen one and his judgement on human violence. For this transformation to be firmly and plausibly established (against many of the plausibilities of Church and society), a social context is needed that *sustains* this perspective, this "hierarchisation" of the biblical texts, through internal and external interaction. Now, how do we arrive at a compass for balancing, or better, constituting the reception of biblical texts in this very specific way? For actively violent texts are important too, albeit in a different way than other texts, namely as an explicatory or analytical hermeneutics, as a negative foil of our existence in the face of the renunciation of violence for the sake of fellow human beings and God.

The more God's people tell each other the relevant stories (or hear them told about "saints" and exemplary figures past and present), the more that *willingness to delegate all violence, both current and eschatological, to God and to God only—conscious of the permanent danger and temptation of taking violence into their own hands*—will develop. The biblical message exposes our profound sinfulness, that is, our violence, and at the same time proclaims a God who accepts sinners back into his love and justice and, at least according to St. Paul's theology of justification, refrains from violent punishment. Those who in their proclamation and belief are able to join God in this unconditional love will from the very heart of their being no longer be driven to violence. Grace alone can conquer violence.

Thus, I come to the encounters between the Christians and the churches on the one hand and all human beings on the other. In particular, the Church has to explain, but also, positively like Nathan, to *provoke* the existential and social nexus that is a condition for the Bible not being misunderstood. Here too, biblical reception is a function of the shape the Church is in, and vice versa. The more diaconical the Church is, the more it will understand the Gospels. Biblical hermeneutics and diaconia feed off and disclose each other; they mutually reinforce each other. Without having clarified the issue of power from the diaconal perspective, or without having attempted to at least clarify it there can be no biblical hermeneutics worth the name, nor can the Church realise its own true self. What we need is a Church where the faithful do *not* cite biblical texts in justification of some status quo in their own lives and the compromises they see fit to make—we need a Church where the faithful submit to God's judgement and let God justify them (in the sense spelled out by the Apostle Paul), so that as sinners unveiled, and yet at the same time accepted and reconciled, they may tread, or dare to tread, the path of ever greater charity of spirit and righteousness.

Once more, the social forms of the Church emerge as the external condition for the possibility (or impossibility) of this perspective on the Bible's internal variety. There is no hermeneutics of the text without such prior hermeneutics of the context. Social hermeneutics leads to biblical hermeneutics and vice versa. If Christian and ecclesial existence accepts discrimination for the benefit of the less fortunate in the name of God, rather than chasing their personal advantage, certain biblical texts (and their context) will disclose their meaning quite differently. *People treat the Bible the same way they treat each other and outsiders.* And certain biblical texts engage our lives because we have a longing for them, a faint experience of them.

7. *Responsibility for Sensitive Liturgical Remembrance*

The history of reception concerning the story of Herod, who does not want to share his power and therefore has to kill the children of Bethlehem (Mt 2,16–18), is an impressive example of how the Churches should take up their hermeneutic responsibility:

7.1 Christmas Idyll and Child Murder in Bethlehem

What characterises humanity again and again in a terrible way are mass murders and genocides. In the memory of the victors they are instrumentalized as strategies necessary for the maintenance of empire or for the spread of one's own people. The suffering associated with this on the part of the defeated and annihilated people is thus made invisible.

There is also talk of mass murder in the context of the Christmas story in the liturgies of the churches and before that already in the New Testament. The story of the murder of children in Bethlehem is found in the Bible in the New Testament in Chapter 2 of the Gospel of Matthew and belongs to the Christmas story, i.e. the story of the birth of Jesus of Nazareth.

My question here is not whether the infanticide actually took place or not. Certainly not, because King Herod was already dead at that time, but probably he could have done it, in the same way as he eliminated rivals out of his own family by murder.[3]

As far as the number of murdered children is concerned, the tradition largely had an idea of mass murder: 14,000 in the Greek area, 144,000 in medieval assumptions, and finally in recent times realistically measured by the size of Bethlehem one to two dozen, if it happened at all. The text itself is intended to increase, it emphasizes that all the boys and in addition all the boys in the surrounding area were killed. Therefore, the number is already potentially open upwards in Matthew's case.

For me, the most important historical fact is that this story exists in a text which in turn has a historically provable history of reception. For the latter, it is irrelevant whether the story can be historically proven, unless this evidence is thematized in the reception itself.[4]

That is why it is nonsense when Protestant Bible criticism (Switzerland) writes with a derogatory undertone: "The murder of children in Bethlehem is unanimously regarded as not historical. Nevertheless, every year on 28 December the Catholic Church commemorates the 'little first martyrs' with the 'Feast of Innocent Children'". If one wanted to apply the criterion of historicity to all liturgical commemoration days in Christian ecumenism, not many would remain. But the texts in which people believed in the narrative are historical and have their effect up to the present day. And it's this impacting story that mat-

---

3 Cf. Helmut Bouzek, Der Kindermord in Betlehem – Faktum oder Fiktion?, aus dem Ökumenischen Heiligenlexikon – https://www.heiligenlexikon.de/Literatur/Kindermord_in_Bethlehem.html, abgerufen am 27.2.2019.

4 Cf. Felix Albrecht, Herodes der Große und der Kindermord zu Bethlehem (Mt 2,16–18) aus historischer und narrativer Perspektive, in: S. Luther u. a. (Hg.): Wie Geschichten Geschichte schreiben. Frühchristliche Literatur zwischen Faktualität und Fiktionalität, Tübingen 2015, 139–154.

ters. Thus, in the title of the 'Feast of Innocent Children', the murdered children are at least remembered, even if the liturgical texts then again almost continuously subordinate this memory to the messianic dignity of Jesus.

7.2 Liturgical Instrumentalization

The liturgical memory of the murdered innocent children takes place one week after the actual birth feast. If one looks at the liturgical calendars of the Catholic and Protestant Church, one is not concerned in them with the suffering of children, not with the horror of mass murder, but rather with this event being subordinated to the Christmas event as an additional confirmation and thus deprived of its own force.

In the evangelical agenda, the Gospel meets on the first Sunday after the feast of Christ, in the Catholic missal the 'innocent children' appear at least in the title of the day, but then the innocent children are used for the glorification of the born Christ. This is the prayer of the day: 'Father in heaven, the innocent children have not praised you with words, they have glorified you by dying'. The introduction to this feast day reads: "Fathers of the Church have praised the child martyrs who were granted the privilege of dying not only as witnesses to Jesus, but on his behalf". This assumption in the history of salvation deprives the children of their subject character and the event of its object character. No less problematic is the giving prayer: "Lord our God, you have given the crown of martyrs to the innocent children, although they were not yet able to confess your son with their mouths." Here a double thing becomes clear: on the one hand the unquestioned claim of the children as martyrs and witnesses for the Messiah, on the other hand the cryptic idea that otherwise the crown of heaven does not belong to all those who do not confess the Son with their mouths.

7.3 Subordinate to the Messiah?

The fact that this instrumentalization of the murder of children for the confirmation of Jesus the Messianic King already takes place in the text of Matthew does not make the whole thing any better. At least Jeremiah is still quoted in it, whereby the event then acquires a certain intrinsic value, "a cry was heard in Rama, loud weeping and lamenting: Rachel cried for her children and did not want to be comforted, because they were gone" (Mt 2,18). In this respect the word of the prophet Jeremiah in favour of the prophet Jesus is fulfilled. At least there is still talk here of screaming, crying, lamenting and not being comforted. Even if this then serves the fulfillment strategy as a whole.

Herod always had to secure his dominion. The empire strikes back; it is built on violence and oppression and cannot allow another power to become strong or stronger. Especially when this other one comes with another power, with the power of love and peace and justice. What actually happens later on the cross could have already happened to the child Jesus and was prevented at the last minute. But at what price?

For the price of sacrificing other children. And here strangely something like a claim, like an instrumentalization of child murder for the new 'King' the Messiah, for the truth of his mission and for his authority, happens. Like other similar birth stories of important leaders and powerful kings and emperors in the ancient times, from Moses to Augustus. Thus already in the Gospel the murder of children and their memory has only a *relative* meaning. Investigations show that this instrumentalization is continued for centuries up to the liturgical models of the churches.

Only Christian art, with its massive images of the child murder of Bethlehem, reproduces the self-esteem of this suffering in drastic images that try to correspond to the force of this event. The suffering of children and mothers is made visible. Here one defends oneself against the deficit of empathy in the relevant church texts:

'Pieter Brueghel the Elder painted the infanticide as a village scene in the Flemish winter landscape, reflecting the atrocities of the Spanish occupiers. Also Giotto, Fra Angelico, the older Cranach and Rubens created versions. The bloodbath of the children became the epitome of the fifth commandment: YOU SHOULD NOT KILL! It symbolizes the vulnerability of humans, our powerlessness, our unbillable intrinsic value. A human, disarmed as a child. Children are blameless. They are not responsible for ideologies or their battles. The child murder exposes and marks the ultimate evil, the total war.'[5]

7.4 The Empire Strikes Back

In the biblical text, Herod stands for those who impose and maintain their rule without regard to the suffering of human beings, always striving not to make this suffering visible. The Herod story is a generative story for the analysis of such relationships throughout history. It's the inability to share power for the sake of the powerless.

This inherent weight of the Herod story for the perception of history in general, and also of the history of modern Bethlehem, does not or only seldom

5 Christoph Dieckmann, Murder of children: All babies dead! Whether Bethlehem or Aleppo: The murder of children always marks evil par excellence, in: DIE ZEIT Nr. 53/2016, 24 December 2016.

occurs in the liturgical and sermon texts of the church, because in the church reception the idyll of Christmas outshines everything else apparently.

In the Gospels, however, this dignity of the Messiah is shown quite differently in terms of content, namely in the fact that Jesus attacks all asymmetries and does not beatify the rich, but the poor. Not the violent, but the peaceful. Not the victors, but the subjects. From this perspective, the feast of innocent children is not to be subordinated to the birth of Jesus, but to be put on an equal footing. The juxtaposition of these festivals in the Christmas season is then a programmatic juxtaposition for each other, insofar as from the perspective of the Messiah born in Bethlehem the view is directed towards the most helpless and powerless people, namely to perceive such victims everywhere in history and in the present and to stand up for them. Thus, the Birth Feast of the Messiah intensifies this messianic view of human history and the present. And with a view to the importance of the crib in Luke it is also remembered that, as the cross of Jesus already appears in the crib, such a commitment costs much, sometimes everything.

With this view to Jesus himself who has not overlooked or neglected the poor and oppressed people, the Christmas story must be constitutively linked to the child murder story, not the latter as evidence of the former, but as the terrible context in which the Christmas story itself takes place. The Christmas story of the birth of the Messiah does not exist without its confrontation with the opposite empires in which it takes place.

Rachel, the second wife of Jacob, is remembered at Bethlehem, "Rachel's Tomb", traditionally a common "Holy Place"; for Jewish, Christian and Muslim worship. The political conditions of the occupation and new security barriers make the grave accessible only for Jewish worship.[6] Meanwhile, Rachel's Tomb is listed under the Arab name as a UNESCO World Heritage Site, which led to fierce protests by Israel.

In the present Bethlehem one experiences and feels this confrontation: the Church of the Nativity and the Wall, the weeping Rachel and the exclusion of the Bethlehemitic population from entering her place of memory. They are not allowed to identify with the suffering and pain of Rachel on the spot. Christmas should not only be celebrated in the Christmas church, but also at the closed doors to the tomb of Rachel. The struggle against the instrumentalization of one's own oppression and suffering for imperial power is a Christmas struggle par excellence in which the Messianic, helpless as it seems, gains strength.

6 Cf. Elise Aghazarian, Andrea Merli, Lucia Maria Russo, Ingeborg Tiemann, Rachel's Tomb. An Alien in Her Hometown? Perceptions from the Other Side of the Wall, Berlin 2010; Fred Strickert, Rachel Weeping. Jews, Christians, and Muslims at the Fortress Tomb, Collegeville 2007.

8. *Holocaust Remembrance as an Ongoing Breach*

I begin with the remembrance itself and continue with the necessary conditions of the possibility of such a memory.

At first: The remembrance of the deadly breaking of human lives cannot leave theological discourses unbroken. This remembrance puts the past theological discourses under the judgement that they should not have been as they had been. Auschwitz de-bridges, deconstructs all thoughts and concepts which are not able to give up their untouched continuity, which overbridge the contradiction between death and life, victims and torturers too fast and are not able to let themselves be interrupted by the sight of deeply suffering people on the one hand and unbelievably cruel people on the other hand, of the ones who suffered and the ones who did evil. There must be a remembrance for the sake of the Holocaust itself: to accuse the one, who did evil, and to honour the victims, to feel deeply horrified what we could have been in this past situations. But who wishes to fulfil this demand?

Second, I concentrate my question upon the challenge on the necessary present context of facilitating this Holocaust remembrance in and by means of the churches, so that they will become a kind of leading example, a kind of lighthouse, in this important duty. What kind of challenge and change does the Christian self-realisation have to face so that Christians and churches will be *able* to remember the Shoah forever?

May I put it this way: we do not violate this Holocaust remembering concerning its own value, we rather let it become not only the centre of our sorrow, but also the centre of our present responsibility, if we search for the meaning, the consequences which come out of this remembrance for ourselves. The same works the other way around: if we do not realise the suffering people and the ones who cause their suffering presently (even, especially, if we should be it ourselves), then there is no chance to build up an appropriate remembrance. If youngsters are not educated to respect each other and other people, to feel compassion when solidarity is needed, then the Holocaust remembrance will not only lose its meaning but also its context. Especially the churches who have bad and good experiences in combining memory and life, traditions and actual responsibilities, have to take up this task, if they really want to realise the challenges of their own remembered origin in the cross of the victim Jesus Christ, who sacrificed himself for the victims and for the reconciliation of the perpetrators as well.

The connection between the Holocaust remembrance and the Christian theology and churches is a complex one: First of all it is not merely a question of postulation, which can provoke defensive reactions, but above all a question of building up the social requirements which evoke an inward demand, an earnest desire, for this remembrance in order to feel compassion with the past victims as well as with the present ones. Only appropriate stories of the present time can open this perspective to history. Whoever refuses to feel sympathy for the suffering, will forget the victims. Whoever does not want to risk the battle against the perpetrators must forget their evil deeds. There are two sources to facilitate such a vulnerable theology: respective sensitive encounters with remembrance and appropriate encounters in the present social reality. Both sources need, enable, deepen and radicalise each other.

All empirical researches on the question of how the Holocaust remembrance can bridge the gap between the eyewitnesses and their future absence come to the result that the present younger and the future generations will forget this memory if they do not find important interest in it, if they cannot combine their problems and desires of living with this remembrance. If their problems are not the problems of universal solidarity and their desires are not longing for justice, then there will be no hope of not forgetting the past victims and of being horrified by the past penetrators. If the Christians and churches miss this responsibility concerning the past and the present time, then they miss their identity.

We need everywhere a religious faith which opens the mental ideological prison of religion, which enhances solidarity to all people as well as confidence in a God whom we have not to excuse nor defend, whom we must not use as a legitimation for our own wicked purposes against others, who gives liberty and love to everybody—will be and will become a reality everywhere.

II. Suffering as a Hermeneutical Key

1. *Biographical Context*

We need a spirituality that opens our eyes to the disadvantaged and gives us strength to get involved in responsibilities and actions, which sometimes cost us disadvantages and pain for the sake of suffering people. Or you can take my theme this way: That I try to give reflecting and meditating words to the impressive liturgy we had once in Palestine: when we knelt down in front of pictures of the suffering land and people, with deep respect, compassion and solidarity. It is a kind of verbalisation of what we already realised in this Liturgy. It was a divine service because in suffering people we encounter, according to Matthew 25, God's son himself and we will be judged by him in front of them! We felt how true this is.

We all come out of our own personal contexts. Sometimes those personal experiences mirror special trends, which you can analyse in major parts of a whole country. Therefore, I think that in this case my own biography has at least some significant elements of how people in Germany "invented" history concerning the Israel-Palestine conflict, especially in the fields of Christian attitudes. Those trends have mostly descriptive and normative implications, which show already the significant mixture of inventing history between seeing and judging, preparing new or old actions, including their legitimation by this kind of inventing the past, which always heads the future as well.

I myself do not belong to an oppressed people. And what I want to say comes out of the perspective of someone who has to think about Spirituality which is necessary for those who has to build up solidarity with people who are in pain: in personal pain and in pain which is caused by oppression and humiliation!

The following reflections have their roots, not least, in a problematic I myself find deeply moving. With hindsight, I can recognise it as a significant plank in the autobiographical contextuality that has also marked my pastoral-theological research and teaching. I think of my first intensive reading on the Holocaust, which reaches far back into my early youth. I was traumatised by the same helpless feeling that often overcomes descendants of wrongdoers, because one can no longer intervene in the past or change anything. The victims remain unalterably dead, beyond recall. To reach back and save them is just not possible. They, the victims and the perpetrators, are outside the reach of our deeds. This feeling of impotence with respect to the past in my case sought and found a special outlet, a "reparations" of sorts, in the form of a solidarity extended, come what may, to the upstart state of Israel. In 1969 I spent time on a kibbutz, Mishmar David by name, situated about halfway between Tel Aviv and Jerusalem.

I rejoiced with the Israelis at the successful Six Day War, and I was glad to have the burnt-out Jordanian tanks pointed out to me. At the time, I wouldn't have minded if Israel had pressed on recklessly and captured territory even beyond the Jordan. The Arabs for me, deeply impressed as I was by the book and film of Leon Uris's "Exodus," were enemies of Israel and so they were my enemies too in what I can only describe as a bizarre projective case of transference. I saw them as seeking to annihilate the Jews just as the Germans before them had done so gruesomely. And that the Jewish liberation groups in the course of gaining their state had resorted to terrorist means, as I well knew, seemed to me only logical given the circumstances. After what the Germans had done to the Jews, the Jews in what is now Israel, first the Zionists and then later the Israelis, had an indisputable right to settle wherever they chose in this Biblically sanctioned land of theirs, to conquer it, defend it or even enlarge it by force. That I was projecting wildly from one historical actor to another is now clear, but I failed to notice it at the time. The Palestinian Arabs, who had had nothing to do with the Holocaust, nonetheless had, in my imaginary world, to suffer as scapegoats for what the Germans had done. That they too were on the receiving end of violence hardly trickled through the mind-set I had then. That coming out lopsidedly, in a totalitarian leap of faith, for the Jews in Palestine meant discriminating against the Arab populace and so practicing a kind of reverse racism, which likewise evaded my young understanding.

Only in the 1980s, after I made a number of trips to Israel and Palestine, did my experiential world develop a few cracks, minor at first then growing ever deeper. Especially in direct encounters with Palestinian Christians I came to see the other side, compounded by several truly horrifying individual experiences in this connection.[1] Since then my radius of reality has changed, so that now I often feel the pinch in this "dual loyalty" of mine for both the Jewish and Palestinian people. I know this much only: I will no longer let myself to be browbeaten into thinking that the Palestinians are not genuinely beleaguered, that they are not victims of structural injustice. No invoking of the Jewish state's need to defend itself, no matter how understandable in its own terms, can justify such a politics of occupation. But black-and-white stereotypes of the other kind are no answer either, as if the Palestinians were blameless and the Israelis the sole guilty parties. There is simply too much terror, whether structural or of the acute kind, on both sides for this to possess even a shred of plausibility. Nobody is free from blame in this conflict. Not that it is true that the

1 Cf. Ottmar Fuchs, Ortsbegehung palästinensischer Erfahrungen und Theologie, in: Pastoraltheologische Informationen 17 (1997) 1–2, 79–98.

afflicted need be blameless to have a claim on our solidarity. Alone the extent of their suffering is what counts.

Now I know that the Palestinians are the victims of structural injustice and oppression! But black-and-white stereotypes of the other kind are also not answers as if only the Palestinians were victims and the Israelis had no victims to lament. To realise the suffering people honestly always bridges existing borders between the collective bodies of groups, societies or nations, also between Palestinians and Israelis, as the Parent's Circle shows in an impressive way. But because of this it is important to realise the difference that the whole body of the Palestinian people is disadvantaged and oppressed and the collective victim of the State of Israel, its Military Forces and the Superpower behind it!

2. *Careful Awareness and Analysis*

Going back to my own biography, I want to point to the danger of obscuring matters when one is fixated on one's status as victim, even though one's situation in real history has *changed* in the meantime. What at first inspection seems simple enough, namely to see the pain of others, turns out to be full of difficulty. At first, I myself didn't see the pain of the Palestine people!

To ideologise one's historical status as victim or perpetrator operates for the present purposes. If the Christian reception of the events of Christ's Passion and death on the Cross was such that the Jews not only were (as it seemed to some) perpetrators but also would be and *remain* perpetrators, meaning, of course, that they were fair game for persecution whenever it pleased someone—then we would have a case where perception of a unique historical situation, whether real or alleged, was bolted down for all future situations.

But such ideologising of historical situations can also occur over the status of victim. When the Palestinians cry out against the organs of the Israeli state and strive against these for justice and self-determination, they are being neither anti-Semitic nor anti-Jewish. For in this they are not expressing an ahistorical ideology, running through all situations, such as that "the Jews" are always and everywhere to be despised and fought. Their resistance is rather the outgrowth of a *current* situation, in which they sense, in the here and now, that they are being unjustly treated by Jews and Jewish institutions. If Israel wasn't Israel, but some other state, the Palestinians would, would *have* to, react just the same. For the state of Israel, too, it follows that there may be no ahistorical fixation on any possible status as permanent victim.

We cannot be expected to ask the Palestinians to sacrifice their self-experience as victims of injustice on the mnemonic altar of any past status Jews have had as victims of injustice in another country. To think contextually is not to ideologically freeze historical situations; rather it is to strive incessantly for a reality-sensitive, socially critical analysis of the contradictions, such as they are between power and powerlessness, between justice and injustice. This is always the problem of violent revolutions—that violence now remains, only turned against others! And it is a strange historical experience, that former victims, having reached power, refuse to become victims again in such a way that they fail in suffering with the victims; they create themselves again.

The above arguments cast doubt on each and every category of election. The ambivalence of the election paradigm runs through religious history like a thick trail of blood, nowhere more than in the history of the Christian churches in their changing political contexts in which the purely religious belief in one's own elected status has allied itself all too easily with political, chauvinist and racist systems of rule. In the Bible as also in the Church itself and in religious history generally, there are probably two versions of what we may call the "election, to be chosen by God" theorem, the practical consequences of which are, in each of these cases, radically opposed: a) the exclusive claim to be chosen against the others and b) the claim to be chosen for the sake of the others.

In the case of a), those who do not belong are consigned to the godless (this in two senses: that of subjective unbelief and that of God's objective indifference to them, or even active spurning). In the case of b), the pointedness of God's historical presence in His chosen people is not reduced to themselves, but is construed as a pledge in favour of the universal salvation of all nations and all humankind: God blesses Abraham to be a blessing. There is still a portion of exclusiveness, but it is understood as a special, in this respect exclusive, vocation for radical inclusive behaviour in solidarity with all suffering people, without any exception! This kind of election needs an inclusive realisation of itself.

3. *Sensitive Comparison or the Way to Find Options*

What we need badly is the praxis and the theory of suffering-sensitive comparison. This applies especially to the readiness for comparison between one's self-perception as disadvantaged and a willingness to scrutinise the still greater, or perhaps incomparably greater, distress that others are in. To be ready to make comparisons of this kind requires seeing, recognising, evidence in both oneself and others experiencing suffering.

But the thing about claiming victimhood is not always so straightforward. This was indeed the key to the refined propaganda of the Nazis, as when they defined the Jewish people as a "bacillus" threatening to infiltrate and destroy an otherwise healthy collective German body. Said Alan Bullock, noted Hitler expert and World War II historian: "Hitler trained his gaze on those sizeable number of Germans who shared his paranoid sensitivities and who saw themselves as preyed on by plotting capitalists, those on the left, Bolshevists and Jews." Against such a strategy of inverting, of "turning on its head", the true nature of things, there is only the counterstrategy of downplaying—as an exercise in self-relativisation—one's own alleged victimhood, as from looking at real disadvantaged and suffering people. That is why, under the Nazis strenuous efforts were made to stop the German people, in their majority, from seeing the suffering of the *truly* suffering for what it was. For this to happen, the Allies had first to arrive and force local populations to actually see what had been going on under their noses in the nearby concentration camps. For if people had grasped the horrors of the camps in their full dimensions, many would probably have reacted with the one feeling the regime could on no account permit: compassion.

Therefore, across all borders and boundaries, we need a spirituality of radical incorruptibility that refuses to pick and choose and divide off against one another, an ethic that opens our eyes to people afflicted by poverty, injustice and oppression. The voice of this ethic will not just need to be heard in one's own little corner, but everywhere where victims are met with or where they cry out in protest.

Empirical studies have shown that most persons in German society feel they have been badly done by in some way or other. Eighty per cent are not satisfied with their life. Evidently a top-down scale applies in assessing disadvantage. Our focus is not on the many who are worse off than we are; it is on the small handful, the lucky few who can afford ourselves more than we can. Therefore, our gaze, and with it the scale by which we make comparisons, wanders upwards, rarely downwards. And so it is that most of us go through life thinking of ourselves as permanently on the losing end. This can make our people incapable for solidarity. One way of snapping out of such self-fixation, and perceiving the truth of our situation for what it is, is not to look only at ourselves but also at others, for example, comparing ourselves to the boat people on the Mediterranean Sea who die in the water and too few care.

There is another inevitable problem in that we have to accuse God himself: We are likely to come out for *those* persons in distress to whom we have, in one form or another, cognitive ties (either we know them or we know *of* them) or affective ties born of empathy or of shared resistance. In doing sensitive comparisons we are not able to go beyond our own radius of resources, time, knowledge and emotionality, even thought there are suffering people somewhere else no less deserving of help. We often cannot prevent our solidarity from disadvantaging others than those it was aimed at helping. We can only recognise that they are in principle no less deserving, prevent becoming wholly indifferent to them. Now I am here and cannot be with my friends in SA. Positive and negative discrimination are two sides of one coin. Even God, in helping one group of people cannot avoid damaging others (e. g., the Egyptians in the story of the Exodus).

4. *Power of Compassion*

Grace in the Bible implies that God has mercy on us. And God shows mercy even, indeed especially, when we are guilty of wrongdoing. Jesus Christ is the incarnation of this mercy. In the Gospels we encounter Jesus as someone who mirrors God's compassion in his own actions. Jesus interacts with men and women in distress—the sick, the outcasts, the victims of injustice, in that he bridges borders and does it with a deep-seated compassion that has the power to steer action. The Greek expression mostly translated as "to take pity" loses much of the dramatic force of the original, which means to be so shattered by how another is struck down by suffering and fate that one feels it deep within one's bowels, that one's stomach literally turns, not from disgust but from pity (Lk 15:20; Mt 9:36ff.). Nowhere and never is God's pity impeded, nor is it anywhere or at any time qualified by an "if-then" such as: "you wouldn't have needed pity now if only you'd done the right thing"—as if someone only deserves pity if she bears no responsibility for the mess she is now in. Pity also pierces through to the level where calculating any sort or the pursuit of private interest is no longer possible. It pierces through all barriers, through all ideologies and prejudices. It is proof against that hardening of heart, that averting of our gaze, which would seek and find reasons why we should not be so moved. The word for pity in my native German is *Mitleid*, meaning "shared suffering" or "suffering along"—and the English "compassion", of course, has the same core meaning.

Now compassion in the sort of society we have today is not exactly a highly prised good. The society we live in is profoundly suspicious of compassion, despite the need for it being greater than ever. We might even call compassion an endangered species. Let me endorse the German psychotherapist Horst Eberhard Richter's judgement: "Sadly, compassion has become something of a laughingstock. In truth, it is *the* life-preserving faculty period." Compassion is especially at risk from the mass display of suffering in the visual media; our capacity to react becomes deadened as a result; we succumb to "compassion fatigue". Yet it need not always be so: sometimes the images go straight to the heart (and to more than a few hearts too, as the volume of donations that pour in shows). Yet it is not too cynical to suppose that those who respond are the ones, the not too numerous few, who have kept the "soft tissue" of compassion from hardening over in their daily lives. We often tend to associate compassion with something frail and fragile, smacking of helplessness and a lack of resources. It is said it is not a good idea to be overcome by such feelings; otherwise, we will take our eye off the ball and end up trampled by life. Therefore, we should keep our compassionate urges on a tight leash, or at least make prudent use of them. It is also true that many a sufferer will say he does not want your pity—and he is probably right in saying so, for pity can be of the condescending sort, and no one can judge that better than the intended recipient. Indeed, a fine eye is needed to tell both kinds of "pity" apart.

The great pre-war Austrian writer Stefan Zweig, in a novel called "The Impatient Heart", described this "twofold pity": "There are two kinds of pity. The kind that is fainthearted and sentimental, that signals but an impatient heart, impatient to get away from being embarrassingly stirred by somebody else's misfortune. Such pity has nothing to do with the other pity, as when we suffer along with another. It is but the instinctive fending off of alien suffering from one's own soul. As for the other kind, the only kind that counts—it is a pity that is as unsentimental as it is creative, the kind that knows what it wants, the kind that is determined to go through thick and thin, patiently and with a humble heart, until it has exhausted all its energy, only then to tap into even more."

What does matter is that we should remain vulnerable in the depths of our being, that our soft tissue should not be allowed to become hard tissue, so that it no longer responds to human suffering in a vital way. What matters is that a path can be found to our affective depths, that we do not barricade these off from being "moved".

There can be no progressive justice adequate to human dignity, without compassion being part of it, such that it can detect those laws that "lack" access to justice. And vice versa: There can be no progressive compassion without the corrective of justice—a justice that implies those for whom we feel no particular or immediate compassion but who are still in need of justice. Only by making the latter link can we save suffering people from exposure to the arbitrariness of empathy felt or empathy not felt. So there can be no justice without a compassion that delimits justice, and there can be no compassion without a justice that delimits compassion.

5. *Christian Martyrdom*

Christianity can refer to its own long history of misinterpreting God's universality, which has cost millions of people possibilities of living, freedom and finally life itself. Religion inhibits solidarity whenever it restricts God's love to the own area and considers all those who don't belong to one's own faith hardly or not at all worthy of solidarity. On the other hand, religion always accelerates solidarity if it grants God's love to all people and experiences the own limited area as a learning field where the inwardly directed solidarity turns towards the outside. We have to make these resources of the religions fruitful, first in our own Christianity. There may be a possibility of a kind of secular spirituality of solidarity, but as Herbert Marcuse (in his book The One-dimensional Man) and Jürgen Habermas newly stated: the secularisation did and does not give the necessary alternatives, the strength and motivations which carry the necessary deeds. Demands alone give no strength to fulfil them.

This imposes a specific dynamism on the Christian existence namely not to render oneself universal but to detect God's universal grace in the world and to help shape it. The problem "inward-outward" has never stopped being a problem. The letter of the Bible alone does not save us from a religiously entitled withdrawal of solidarity; only the spirit and the intention respectively with which the Bible is read, namely that dynamism expressed in the Bible itself towards a more merciful God and a more universal inter-human solidarity.

Faced with a threatening lack of the success, faith preaches that it is never in vain to act toward justice and mercy, even if it does not seem to be fruitful. The Gospel contains the eschatological message that only mercy and justice are the realities which fulfil God's Kingdom on earth and which will find eternal realisation in God's Kingdom. The option for the poor is not a programme of success but provokes additional experiences of powerlessness and failure in particular for those who take it seriously. To be able to believe that God (in the meaning of Roman 8:26) helps carry this powerlessness and sighs with us, that God in the co-suffering Christ does not exclude himself, is the consolation of the Christian message which strengthens action and perseverance.

From this perspective, and if Christians don't want to give up God's mercy in a merciless world but preach and realise it, the coming decades will mean following the cross: Jesus has not paid back the violent attack in its own coin but turned the intensified evil and gave it back as doubled love. Thus, God allows herself to be drawn into the history of humankind and willingly becomes a sacrifice for the sake of the victims. A Church that forgets its martyrs forgets itself because it forgets its roots in *the* martyr, Jesus Christ. This highlights a certain attitude which can be found within the Bible itself: Wherever someone accepts suffering violence in someone else's stead and does not respond with violence, we see in him or her a realisation of the example of the suffering servant in Second Isaiah and of the suffering Son of God praying for his violent tormentors even from the cross (cf. Luke 23:34), returning the violence he suffered as love.

In their commitment to the life of others, Christians in many countries go so far that this "overstepping of borders" costs them their lives. Faith without remembering them is like preaching resurrection without the cross. Whoever stands for God's de-limiting justice for the sake of those who are excluded must be prepared to be restricted and excluded in her or his own life chances. This is the message to the rich countries in the Western hemisphere; this is the message to Israel as well: Israel has to share and to risk disadvantages in order to gain free Palestinians as neighbours.

III. How to Deal with Violence in Biblical Texts

1. *Introduction*[1]

Quite unsurprisingly, since September 11, 2001, Christian believers have been facing a deluge of knowledgeable reproaches regarding specific biblical texts, namely those that not only legitimise violent destruction and murder of people who think differently but actually call for it. This provides our fellow contemporaries with further arguments for giving short shrift to Christianity along with institutionalised religion in general. Here we have, as it were, recent acquisitions *ex negativo* to society's collective and cultural consciousness. Those at the receiving end are having a hard time in the face of violent incidences from the history of the churches which are now pressed even more forcefully in the face of the current devastating suicide attacks by Muslim fundamentalists (who in their turn harness their own holy book, the Qur'an, for their purposes). The frightful ambivalence of all revealed book religion has become a talking point.

We need to both counteract this particular sentiment and take it seriously by giving account of how we intend to handle those texts from the Bible, for the existence of such passages cannot be denied. But people allege that we apply a hermeneutics of imitation to them: Whatever the Bible says Christians are allowed to, and indeed have to, imitate—in doing so they will please the God of their Bible. The fact that—unlike in the past—they do not do so (and in fact shamefully avoid such texts in their liturgy and everywhere else) is due to modernity, the Enlightenment and the universalisation of human rights, but not to the Bible. Such critics among our fellow contemporaries in society adapt a particular hermeneutics and at the same time reject it: they assume that all biblical texts are of an equal standing as guidelines for a Christian lifestyle and may be appropriated accordingly.

This problem cuts right to the heart of practical biblical hermeneutics, and its resolution, though delicate, must not be delayed. Reassuringly, the varied character of the biblical texts allows for some freedom as far as their reception is concerned, but it offers less reassurance regarding the critical flanking of this freedom on the background of texts that claim it not only for oneself but

---

1 Cf. concerning the following considerations in more detail (especially concerning the problem of God's violence as an ambivalent token of his inapprehensible mystery) Ottmar Fuchs, Praktische Hermeneutik der Heiligen Schrift, Stuttgart 2004, 438–461 (444–448).

also for others—to the point where the life and survival of the other as the subject of this freedom are paid for by a reduction in one's own freedom and life. The biblical texts are quite diverse on this point. They arguably represent both ends of the scale: the destruction of the freedom of others as well as a veritable devotion to safeguarding it.

Such a fundamental criticism of biblical hermeneutics retrieves exactly those problematical texts from our own unconscious denial and places them squarely in the public domain. We are left wondering at our own helplessness and inability to properly account for them and indeed at our failure to even start to identify conceptional hermeneutic solutions to these issues.

Yet there aren't any easy answers; at the most there are pointers to a constructive hermeneutics of violent biblical texts. For we can neither eliminate the passages concerned from the revelatory canon by branding them unbiblical, nor reconstruct their reception in the horizon of a positivist, unilinear understanding of revelation. Inner-ecclesial attempts to defuse the issue by downplaying it will no longer do either. There is nothing left to hide—the texts have become public property in a qualitatively new way through negative appropriations. Just as abstaining from communication is a way of sending a message, so is not facing up to the violent texts.

Face up we must, furthermore, to the defensive smoke screens which, though in various ways they do have some efficacy, ultimately fail to satisfy and need clearing up. Among them are: first, extenuation and mitigation through translation; second, anesthetisation of what is understood as poetic licence; third, contextual interpretation, i.e., the historisation of texts in terms of the problem of violence obtained at the time of origin only; fourth, metaphorisation, implying that the stark images are no more than stand-ins for something else—but that does not cut much ice, because the imagery is a significant part of reality as it helps to construe the content! Fifth, liturgical deflection (for example, by avoiding texts in readings); sixth, educational instrumentalisation and relativisation, based on the notion that we need the texts to learn where violence will lead us and that studying the way the "enemy" is constructed will help us see through and thwart the process in our own reality; seventh—perhaps the worst mitigation strategy of all—denigrating the Old Testament as an inhumane "preliminary" stage or imperfect phase of faith history proper. Ultimately, all these cop-outs lack an appreciation of the profound ambivalence of God and humans themselves.

Those texts are not archaic, inhumane stories that we might smugly distance ourselves from, deeming ourselves more "advanced". Up to the present day, the lesson of history is a different one. The Bible confronts us remorselessly with the hidden depths of humans as well as with those of God. What will remain true is St Paul's statement from Romans 15:4: "Whatever was written, was written for our instruction." But how is it meant? Definitely not as a training in wickedness!

Which are the texts concerned here? Some brief examples will give a flavour of their forcefulness. A survey of the material reveals the following scenario among others: The Lord himself wages a war against the enemies and destines them to total destruction (Isaiah 34:1–17; 63:1–6). God calls for revenge upon other peoples and for their annihilation (Numbers 31:1–20; 1 Samuel 15; Deuteronomy 20:10–20; 25:17–19); God chastises his own people and shows his wrath by delivering them to their enemies (Lamentations 2; Deuteronomy 28: 15–68); God uses violence against individuals (Job 16:6–17; Psalm 88); a curse calling on God to destroy the enemies (Psalm 109; Psalm 137:7–9; Psalm 139 19–22); God restores his servant who accepts violent humiliation to atone for the sins of others (Isaiah 52:13–53:12); God judges and scolds "before the eyes of the lamb" those who "worship the beast" (a reference that arguably includes the imperial cult) (Revelation 14:9–11, also 19:11–21).

2. *Hermeneutical Explorations*

2.1 The Signature of God's Eschatological Power over History

The biblical texts about God's violent intervention hold a lesson for us: Tendencies to reduce belief in God's power over history to stories about a God that helps individuals must be reversed, thrown open and universalised into collective (concerning the people and all peoples, just like collective lamentation) and cosmic (concerning the whole world, as did the flood in Noah's time) dimensions. At the core of such lamentation lies not doubt about God's ability to intervene because God does not exist or is too weak, but distress at his failure to intervene even though he could. Why does he not step in mightily? Why does Jesus not call on the heavenly hosts (cf. John 18:36)? The belief that he will never intercede because he cannot intercede is tempting for the victims to resign to and the perpetrators to be reassured by. But that is a delusion. Here the biblical texts about God's violent interventions remind us never to forget that God can intercede and surely will do so ultimately, with unimaginable might (described in Revelation), wiping out violently and uncompromisingly all destructive violence, destroying the freedom of evil and the "violence of injustice".

This eschatologisation of God's power to intervene at the end of history is, at the very least, what must not be suppressed. Otherwise there would be no hope of justice, and the victims would be lost forever. This would be so if there were no resurrection of the dead. Yet as death is the last and ultimate violence against life, only a more powerful force can lead to the resurrection of the dead and put an end to death.

What is at stake is not only human ambivalence, but the negative dialectic in God's action and in our relationship to God, indeed, the ambivalence of our images for, encounters with, and experiences of God. Oddness will always remain here and we will have to bear with God in his strangeness, his ineffability and hiddenness, in both suffering and violence, for what continues to be fatal and incomprehensible about the pertinent biblical texts is the fact that God's intervention is experienced not only as the power of authority but indeed as naked violence. God's intervention for the benefit of the Israelites is experienced as brutal destruction by the Egyptians (i.e., outside this authoritative relationship with God). God continues to owe them their salvation. With great care, then, we might suggest that somehow both love and violence are rooted in God, that within the mess of history, God commits himself lovingly to someone or to his people while at the same time inflicting injustice or violence on others. Ultimately, it is hoped that God's love will bring about the kind of violence that will universally create a new world without suffering and death, where neither God nor humans desire to cause injustice and no longer have to. Before that, however, all evil and suffering must be crushed. Such would be the eschatological origin of biblical texts of violence.

2.2 Not Imitation but Delegation

There are a number of texts, among them the cursing Psalms, that delegate the violence to God because those concerned are themselves victims lacking any capability for it: "O God, break the teeth in their mouths!" (Psalm 57:7; cf. Psalm 3:8). But do such delegation strategies apply also in cases where those concerned do have such power? Is God's power called on only to compensate for one's own weakness? Is this a matter of principle applying to all situations? Clarification will come only from a hermeneutics that generalises the semantics of those texts on a meta-contextual level. As a matter of principle, even in situations of acute hatred, the cursing Psalms' demand to renounce becoming a source of violence and to delegate violence to God applies to those capable of violence as well. This is certainly not the highest form of spirituality, but still a necessary one that can prevent the worst in a potentially violent situation and, above all, block knee-jerk reactions. Those not yet ready to turn the other cheek will at least hold back their own violence in appealing to God for it. But does this not mean instrumentalising the relationship with God to satisfy instinctual drives? Perhaps God wishes to help with this particular historical problem? The questions remain open.

Again, relevant texts are not only from the Old Testament but also from the New Testament. St. Paul radicalises the issue in Romans 12:17–21: The prospect of divine revenge not only prevents violence, but also makes love of the enemy possible or, more precisely, loving action towards the enemy, which, eschatologically speaking, actually amounts to hatred of the enemy. Again, this is hardly the pinnacle of anti-violent motivation. But it does offer a biblical strategy for dealing with the violence of texts and of human desires in a constructive way, preventing at least violence of human origin from affecting others. Ultimately, delivering someone to God's wrath means delivering them to God's mercy, which leaves the question unsettled for the moment. In the end, everything is left to God's autonomy and thus to the justificatory activity St. Paul described so intensely.

These reflections on a delegatory hermeneutics of violent biblical texts leave us with the renewed realisation that those who rely on a revelation must never take violence into their own hands. Taking God's violence seriously means taking it seriously with him as the starting and the end point—a covert swap of roles allowing humans to exert it is precluded. A practical hermeneutics of discipleship, of the kind conceptualised in discipleship of Jesus, is definitely out of bounds here. There can never be a unilinear hermeneutics in relation to the violent texts, neither one of discipleship nor of comprehension, nor of approval.

2.3 Being Alarmed at Ourselves

There is thus no uniform hermeneutics that could be applied to all biblical texts. Woe to the people if we get our categories mixed up and, for example, read violent texts in the category of a hermeneutics of imitation. Rather, given the variety of texts in the Bible, we should expect hermeneutic approaches to vary correspondingly, ranging from imitation hermeneutics to hermeneutics of confrontation and challenge where the biblical texts disclose to us our real or potential nature, leaving us alarmed at it and revolting against it. Being mutually dependent, the hermeneutics of self-explication and the hermeneutics of confrontation constitute the sinner's repentance! Both may be termed forms of confronting hermeneutics provided that two aspects are kept in mind: explicative confrontation with the self and self-activating confrontation with violence.

Then, our reading of the violent texts will have an even more forceful impact as, in the light of repentance, through self-critical "identification", they will reveal our own part in being actual or potential perpetrators. Thus, our horror at the texts merges with horror at ourselves and at our temptation, on reading the texts, to wish for such a violent God and such violent solutions to our problems!

Thus, the texts facilitate self-knowledge and also disclose to us our own susceptibility to violence in order to warn us in time and protect us against outbreaks of violence. There is no use—especially not to others—suppressing them if we do not want to face them, and this includes violence that others inflict upon others. Is it fair to say that our refusal to face violent texts reveals our refusal to face our own hidden depths or actual (especially structural and global) realities of violence? The resulting marginalisation and scorning of the Old Testament (because of the allegedly low level of ethicality of its violent texts) has always been tied up with an actual proclivity towards violence against the Jewish people! Hence these texts have indeed been written for our education so that from the catastrophic rifts of revelation we may come to see our own flaws and may open ourselves up to those violent texts which present the severest of all criticisms of violence at the same time.

Therefore, eliminating specific violent texts from the Bible on account of their incompatibility with a particular image of God revealed in other passages is no solution. This would be to repeat Marcion's mistake of making the Bible "holier" than it is. If, then, we stay true to the Church's tradition of seeing all those texts as integral to the biblical canon of revelation, we need different hermeneutical approaches in order to take the various texts seriously in exactly the way they are to be taken seriously. In this way, we reaffirm that all biblical texts have revelatory status while their content is plural and sometimes contradictory and must be accessed through a corresponding plurality of approaches.

Hence the notion of biblical revelation as something entirely good, holy and salvific is discredited. Holy Scripture makes no pretence about the unholy. Its character as revelation derives from the fact that it presents encounters with God in a variety of situations and against the backdrop of the ambivalence of human longing and thinking. The Bible is God's revelation as reflected in humans, their evil and their bad traits, their hatred and their love, their oppression and their justice. As soon as God enters this ambivalence through his actions they become part of it and their divine "purity" is tainted.

The Bible has not been purged of the profound ambivalence of creation and human existence; rather, they are integral elements of the multi-faceted encounter of God and men and women. It abounds with instances where humans misunderstand God (and vice versa) and in this is no different qualitatively from the later history of the churches, the history of the ambivalence of the religions and of the encounter of humankind with God and vice versa. The Bible reveals the misunderstandings, the dark sides, the often explosive ambivalence of encountering the divine, to later generations so that they may become aware of the ambivalence of their own faith: alarmed at themselves and fearful of God. The dark mysteries of humanity, creation and God are not banned from the Bible. Rather, in the stories of the Bible, we encounter the mystery of our violence and of the power which God has over history and which in the present eon cannot be explained without ambivalence.

2.4 A Martyrial Criteriology

Finally, I want to highlight a certain attitude which can be found within the Bible itself, even though it calls for an active decision on our part. Wherever someone accepts suffering violence in someone else's stead and does not respond with violence, we see a different kind of "violent text": for example, the suffering servant in Second Isaiah, the suffering Son of God praying for his violent tormentors even from the cross (cf. Luke 23:34), returning the violence he suffered as love. Both scenes presuppose a context of violence in reality and could, especially for Christians, suggest a specific hermeneutics of violent Biblical texts which Horst Eberhard Richter put in these words: "Those who don't want to suffer must hate!" So do the violent texts seek to educate us about self-discrimination for the sake of others, even the perpetrators, in other words, to endorse martyrdom?

This is not the martyrdom of suicide bombers who, rather than breaking free from the vicious circle of violence, augment it ad infinitum. One of the "signs of the time" may be found in the increased necessity for Christianity to take a stance in a wider argument about the correct understanding of Christian martyrdom[2] vis-à-vis an emerging societal interest in the concept and to bring out the specific nature of Christian martyrdom: "It is better to suffer defeat than to prevail by violence."[3] Those in view here are those who, for the sake of justice, share when there is time to share to avoid having to kill later (cf. Matthew 2: 13–18), those who, for the sake of keeping violence in check, suffer and withstand more (direct and structural) violence than they inflict, starting right from the first small discriminations; those who ultimately prefer being killed to being a killer.[4]

Are these the violent texts that provide an authentic inner-biblical key to Christians and indicate the "centre" of meaning and interpretation for all other violent texts? This perspective establishes an interrelation between the different texts, maintaining their multiple perspectives, and at the same time it drives on a particular dynamic which cares about their equal validity while challenging hermeneutic carelessness. Here, we have a hermeneutics acknowledging all forms of human and religious violence. It is also critical because it undermines violence by surrender, euphemising neither active nor passive violence, neither the violence inflicted nor that actively suffered.

They are counter-texts of intransitive against transitive violence: Servant and Son of God inflicting violence upon themselves, allowing it to be inflicted upon them, juxtaposing the non-violent force of their own bodies. The body is

2 Cf. O. Fuchs, Mission (Missionsorden) – auch im 21. Jahrhundert gefragt?, in: Zeitschrift für Missionswissenschaft und Religionswissenschaft 86 (2002) 3, 163ff.

3 Kamphaus, Gewaltanschauung 126.

4 Cf. J. Sobrino, Die Erlösung der Gewalt, in: Concilium 33 (1997) 4, 486–494, 491ff.

their resistance. The "heroes" and protagonists here are not the subjects of violence, but those subjects who non-violently rise against the violence wrought by others and who expose themselves to it (vicariously) for the sake of others. They are not objects in this process because they are and will be in charge of their decision. They could decide otherwise: run away rather than hold out; call for or apply violence rather than resist with their own life and body (which the opponents need to clear away before carrying on or, indeed, deciding to refrain from doing so); destroy the perpetrators rather than protect them. After all, Cain has a mark put on him so no one would kill him without attracting the sevenfold revenge of God (cf. Gen 4:15).

Still the question remains: The approach outlined remains an externally applied set of options, because as they stand the texts are presented with no valorisation or prioritisation. What is the basis for prioritising our critique of violent texts away from transitive and onto intransitive violence? From inflicting onto accepting suffering? For the texts of martyrdom too portray violence, albeit substantively and perspectively different: with a view to the victim rather than the perpetrator. The texts that criticise violence are part of the Bible, but what prevents readers from prioritising those legitimising violence over the martyrial ones? The Bible itself, for one, does not. The ambivalence it contains is that of life itself, that of our lives.

Nevertheless, it is important to establish an intra-biblical authenticity for this perspective and identify relevant texts. Once this perspective is adopted, we discover significant texts taking it up and grounding it within the Bible. I will try to sketch the line from the Flood to the Gospels—the crucial rainbow, as it were, considering that in Genesis 9:17 YHWH promises never again to intervene with such violence and that in the Gospels Jesus gives the command to love one's enemy rather than calling on the heavenly hosts. The relevant intra-biblical dynamic appears to be notably robust, all the more so since there are no positive texts capable of establishing a reverse counter-dynamic of equal validity.

3. *Outlook*

3.1 The Path of the Church

Though we might find evidence for this dynamic, there is one question that remains as yet unanswered: What is the basis on which believers' take the decision for such prioritising in dealing with biblical revelation? How can we talk of the will of God in a criteriologically sound way given the variety and diversity of texts? There is only one answer to this, and it is an ecclesiological and pneumatological one: as and when believers read the Bible in the spirit of the God whom they believe to be love and freedom, in the spirit of the risen one and his judgement on human violence. For this transformation to be firmly and plausibly established (against many of the plausibilities of Church and society), a social context is needed that sustains this perspective, this "hierarchisation" of the biblical texts, through internal and external interaction. Now, how do we arrive at a compass for balancing or better constituting the reception of biblical texts in this very specific way? For actively violent texts are important too, albeit in a different way than other texts, namely as an explicatory or analytical hermeneutics, as a negative foil of our existence in the face of the renunciation of violence for the sake of fellow human beings and of God.

The Christian Creed could provide such a compass through its substantive dynamic of God's descent and self-emptying in Jesus Christ and his resurrection and the resurrection of humankind. The more God's people tell each other the relevant stories (or hear them told about "saints" and exemplary figures past and present), the more that willingness to delegate all violence, both current and eschatological, to God and to God only will develop—conscious of the permanent danger and temptation of taking violence into our own hands. The biblical message exposes our profound sinfulness, that is, our violence, and at the same time proclaims a God who accepts sinners back into his love and justice and, at least according to St. Paul's theology of justification, refrains from violent punishment. Those who in their proclamation and belief are able to join God in this unconditional love will from the very heart of their being no longer be driven to violence. Grace alone can conquer violence.

Once more, the social forms of the Church emerge as the external condition for the possibility (or impossibility) of this perspective on the Bible's internal variety. There is no hermeneutics of the text without such prior hermeneutics of the context. Social hermeneutics leads to biblical hermeneutics and vice versa. If Christian and ecclesial existence accepts discrimination for the benefit of the less fortunate in the name of God rather than chasing their personal advantage, certain biblical texts (and their context) will disclose their meaning quite differently. People treat the Bible the same way they treat each other and outsiders. And certain biblical texts engage our lives because we have a longing for them, a faint experience of them. This kind of appropriation of biblical texts remains a constant challenge throughout our lives, until the final surrender in death. Thus, in conclusion, we return to the passage in Romans that expands on St. Paul's statement that everything has been written for our education: "...so that by steadfastness and by the encouragement of the scriptures we might have hope...Welcome one another, therefore, just as Christ has welcomed you, for the glory of God" (Romans 15:4, 7).

Can we find a "plausibility" for this in our faith and proclamation? It would be high time, so that a millennium of mainly violent Christianity can be succeeded by a millennium where Christian existence embraces surrender and "vicarious" existence rather than the subjugation of others, empowerment rather than the exerting of power.

3.2 ... Towards the Bible's Fourfold Conception of Violence

We derive the strength for this not only from the hope that God's ultimate power over history and the secular forces will one day be manifest, but also the fact that even now God accompanies us on our ongoing path of blocking and reducing violence, just as on the cross he walked this path right to the end, so he will walk and endure it with us. That is the root of his credibility: he will eventually exert his power for the benefit of justice and mercy because even now he gets involved in the necessity of justice and mercy and its consequences. If God does not intervene now, if he did not interfere on the cross, this does not mean she is not able to interfere. The reason why in the present he intervenes in the form of the one who bears violence and sends back love remains hidden from us. But one thing is made plain by this: God does not sit on the fence and does not abandon humans in their violent actions, but gets involved and, in doing so, indicates how to deal with them.

Thus, in the Bible we find a fourfold conception of violence: First, one that makes perfectly plain to us our profoundly violent nature; second, one that embraces the compromise of forcibly expressing human hatred and desire for violence but delegating its implementation to God; third, one where the Servant of God on the cross endures our violence in all its fierceness, returning it as reconciliation; and finally, one that makes unambiguously clear that the omnipotent God has both the power and the intention to eventually use violence to put a stop to the violent and destructive forces of the world and establish an eternity of surrender and non-violence.

Corresponding to these conceptions of violence, there is a hermeneutics of confrontation (in exposing our violent nature and triggering resistance against it), a kind of hermeneutics of delegation (as the compromise between expressed aggression and abdication of violence), a properly theological hermeneutics of martyrdom (a willingness to pay with one's life for one's renunciation of violence) and an eschatological hermeneutics (in hope for and awe of God's powerful intervention to destroy violence at the end of time). These hermeneutic perspectives contain partially interlocking and overlapping triggers that are paramount if anyone is to open themselves up to the biblical message and form their lifestyle correspondingly.

This would be an adequate Christian reaction to modern plurality by means of the responsibility for a justly based plurality in and between societies, and for intra- and interreligious tolerance and criticism. This is where biblical hermeneutics and present Christian lifestyle meet and enhance each other.

IV. Biblical Laments Wherever People Suffer[1]

1. *Context: World Day of Prayer 1994 and 2024*

In 1994 the World Prayer Congress for Women took stock of the situation of Palestinian Christians and made their Order of Prayer the basis of a worldwide of divine service on the first Friday in March. The women attending the Congress had, as it happens, needed a lesson or two from the downtrodden; some of them had, in various trips to the occupied territories, grasped the situation and, in particular, spoken with Palestinian women about their plight. They were left in no doubt as to how greatly the Palestinian people as a whole feel that their present situation is one of oppression, of intolerable hardship, of crass illegality. In the Order of Divine Service, the Palestinian women offered up in prayer verses from Psalm 142, a song of lamentation. Perhaps that was why this practice of theirs touched off an at times vitriolic debate, especially in the Protestant churches.[2] Here I shall concentrate on the following chief charge that was laid: for Palestinian women to pray with a Jewish psalm of lamentation is to disinherit the the Jewish people, because these prayers, taken from an original text referring to the land of the Jewish people and its history, are now being used against Jews in their own land, and by non-Jews, too, who are outsiders. *Publik-Forum*, a German periodical, fielded a provocative headline: "Prayers Against Israel?"[3]

It is to this controversy (which will probably recur in 2024, when again the Palestinian Christian women will be the centre of the divine service) that I will devote my presentation. My topic is: Who is entitled to pray the Jewish psalms of lamentation?[4] This is a challenge for practical biblical hermeneutics, too. Taking us well beyond the immediate context of origin, it is clear that thorny questions involving a pragmatic set of criteria for a biblical hermeneutics await us, questions concerning the extent to which not only textual semantics can be

---

1 Significantly expanded version of my paper: „Wer darf die jüdischen Klagepsalmen beten?" in: Biblisch-Theologische Studien 44 (Biblischer Text und theologische Theoriebildung), Neukirchen-Vluyn 2001, 135–161.

2 The whole controversy is documented and analyzed in S. Klein: Dokumentation zum Weltgebetstag 1994 aus Palästina, Düsseldorf 1995 (Klens Verlag).

3 Cf. Klein, Weltgebetstag 1994, Document 27; cf. on this controversy also O. Fuchs, Die Stimme der Leidenden ist heilig!, in: Bible und Liturgie 67 (1994) 2/3, 127–142.

4 On the debate on the Hermeneutic relationship between Bible and the situation in Palestine itself cf. U. Gräwe, Kontextuelle palästinensiche Theologie, Erlangen 1999, 119ff., 230–275.

made the touchstone for arguments of intellectual hermeneutics, but also the specific relationship, practical and theological alike, prevailing between

a) situation and person and
b) the texts themselves,

i.e., between pragmatics and semantics in their reciprocal intentionality, a matter that is, in itself, fraught with ambivalence, inasmuch as pragmatics can shed light on semantics, but also has the power to obscure and destroy it. In a way, what I would like to do here is pick up on a debate that has by now been largely forgotten, namely over "materialist" readings of the Bible, which is a debate over the extent to which such readings need modification if they are to contribute to a more broad-based discourse, one that transcends and subsumes previous debate concerning this nexus but only within quite specific theologies (which are readily affirmed or downgraded by noting their indebtedness to leftist thought). From these we also derive an understanding of the following chief rubric for a topopractical criteriology of biblical hermeneutics, this being construed as a criteriology specifying the link between biblical semantics and a location-sensitive pragmatics (where location refers to *situation and person*).

2. *A Topopractical Criteriology of Biblical Hermeneutics*

2.1 The Hermeneutic Force of Personal and Situative Circumstances

Any text, and a biblical text is no exception, has a life of its own, which no one can entirely control. Even the author can only formulate it in terms of, and via, his or her own situation and intention, but then has to let go of it, to confide it to a future with multiple times and persons. Future recipients of the text, each coming from his or her own discrete angle, will forge a personal relationship with the text. But if the text is not to be mere grist for the reader's mill, to have a life of its own, transcending this reception or that, it cannot be assigned any old meaning, as if it could be pressed into service, expropriated, for any purpose at all. After all, it may conceal within itself idiosyncratic semantic structures, suggesting that though its reception is not completely fixed, it is—to an extent—circumscribed and hedged in. The text opens a generative space of meaning, but also contrives to limit and steer it through the semantic field it represents. But just how is this done?

To answer this, I propose to designate the relationship between situation and meaning by the term *steering factor*, which I take to mean the basic normative intentions discernible in the overall semantics of a text or texts (for present purposes, the Bible as a whole)—failure to attend to which on the pragmatic level (i.e., in how we relate to the text) constitutes the syndrome we know as misunderstanding or abusing a text or texts. Such steering factors are not positivist in the sense that we need but attend to them to understand the text correctly. Yet they do tell us in what direction a possible, or probable, authentic understanding of the text might lie—in pivotal cases *must* lie. The question can be put in another way. What do we have to bring to bear from within us, in terms of text-external preconditions congruent with the basic thrust of the text content, if we are to succeed in truly experiencing the text-internal meaning as a text-external meaning? Or, to put the question negatively: What are the preconditions whose absence leads, with some automaticity, to misunderstanding and abuse of the biblical texts?

In attempting to answer these questions, my concern is always with both these things:

a) exactly grasping the semantic structures within the text; and
b) grasping no less exactly one's own situation.

More precisely: what meaning do the downtrodden extract from their situation—for themselves and also for how they understand the text? What meanings they extract from their own context is linked, of course, to their desires and aspirations, and so it is not free from the general ambivalence to which human desire is prone. The history of the uses to which the Bible has been put does, to be sure, bear witness to the twin dynamic of meaning waged between semantics and pragmatics, the good and the bad contending. When humans link what they read in the Bible to their own lust for power, their thirst to exclude those who do not belong, they will draw legitimation, from Scripture too, for the acts of destruction they then embark on. They deem unquestionable certain texts that seem exactly to corroborate the motivations and ideologies they most need if they are ostracising or, in the most extreme case, exterminating the others who have drawn their ire. The theology of the United Reformed Church in South Africa had no difficulty coming up with chapter and verse justifying, in terms of revelation theology, the racist stance it had adopted towards the blacks.

But this does not mean that only good, tolerant, blameless persons can read the Bible correctly. For anyone who deems themselves such, free from ambiguity, is, from the perspective of *kauchesis* (in the Pauline sense of self-aggrandisement and pridefulness, see Romans 3:27), not especially likely to take seriously, in their own personal pragmatics, the meaning of the biblical texts. Thus, the whole thing cannot be relegated to the moral plane, as if we only had to be morally good and to have acted accordingly, to then understand the Bible.

In opposing the arbitrary use of biblical chapter and verse, our primary concern must be this to bar perpetrators, i.e., the rich that exploit and the powerful who oppress, whether in person or structurally, from citing whatever they can come up with, after a trawl through the Bible, in justification of their deeds of inhumanity. To do otherwise would be a perverse way of relating to the God of the Bible, who in the best texts and the ones that matter most surely takes the part of those who cry out and suffer and who calls upon powerful oppressor and rich man alike to repent. It is therefore only right that this text-internal fact should define the text-external hermeneutics. Those who fall victim to injustice may pray the psalms of lamentation. But the perpetrators of injustice may *on no account* do so, perhaps out of some keenly felt sense of regret that their efforts to close with their victims have borne so little fruit. Obvious though this point might seem, it is still necessary to make it.

The poor, the threatened, the disadvantaged, the "battlers", all have a direct and immediate right to identify with parallel persons, or groups of persons, in the texts and to relate the words they spoke to their own lot. They have, at all times and in all places, this right; nor is there anyone who can strip them of it (just as none of them can take it from anyone else) when it comes to rediscovering themselves and their situation in the biblical texts and in the Christian tradition, which is as much as to say they can define where they stand now, on the plane of God's message, placing themselves the more sharply in the context of injustice. This universal pragmatic—namely that the needy, when they read the Bible, may identify with the needy in its pages, while those who join with the needy in solidarity may, when *they* read the Bible, identify themselves as those who, in the guise of the needy, have clothed and visited Jesus Christ Himself in prison (cf. Matthew 25:34–40)—this universal pragmatic, I say, constitutes the "head start in experience" given to those laid low by suffering and injustice, but also to those too who come to their rescue, and that in terms of the same Kingdom of God that has been promised them within the Bible itself.

The gradient of hermeneutic competence would then feed back into one's faith and proclaiming of the Word, inasmuch as those so afflicted, as well as those who show solidarity with them, have a special place in the churches when it comes to linking our belief in a God of compassion and justice, such as the Bible teaches, to the situation we find ourselves in today. To be sure, this implies a special aptitude for preaching the Word not only in the clergy, but also in the needy, in those who suffer, in those who show solidarity with those who suffer. When congregations neglect this diaconical dimension of the Church, they cut themselves off from the social experience they will need if they are to understand.

In particular, the Church has to explain, but also to positively *provoke*, the existential nexus that is a condition for the Bible not being misunderstood. Here too, biblical reception is a function of the shape the Church is in, and vice versa. The more diaconal the Church is, the more it will understand of the Gospels. Biblical hermeneutics and diaconia feed off each other, mutually reinforce each other. Without having clarified the issue of power from the diaconal perspective, or without having attempted at least to clarify it, there can neither be a biblical hermeneutics worth the name, nor can the Church realise its own true self. What we need is a Church where the faithful do *not* cite biblical texts in justification of some status quo in their own lives and the compromises they see fit to make—we need a Church where the faithful submit to God's judgement and let God justify them (in the sense spelled out by the Apostle Paul), so that as sinners unveiled, and yet at the same time accepted, they may tread, or dare to tread, the path of ever greater charity of spirit and righteousness.

2.2 Diaconal Awareness Instead of Ahistorical Ideologies

If the contradiction between compassion and ruthlessness, between dealing justly and dealing unjustly, between the victims and those that victimise, if this contradiction merits such a prime hermeneutic rating, we must ponder next what lets us see for what it is, or alternatively renders us blind to, this contradiction when it crosses out path in the real world. Here I want to point to the danger of obscuring matters, as Paul says, of "seeing through a glass darkly" when one is *fixated* on one's status as victim or perpetrator, even though one's situation in life may have *changed* in the meantime. What at first inspection seems simple enough, namely to recognise affliction when it is stares you in the face, turns out to be full of difficulty.

To ideologise one's historical status as victim or perpetrator is, for the present purposes, to operate thus: one allows oneself to become fixated on a unique historical situation and in a way that is "trans-historical": by which I mean that it spills beyond its historical context of origin. For example: if the Christian reception of the events of Christ's Passion and death on the Cross was such that the Jews not only *were* (as it seemed to some) perpetrators (waiving the point that this interpretation, historically seen, does not hold water) but also (in the sequel and for all time—in some travesty of "original sin") would be and *remain* perpetrators, meaning, of course, that they were fair game for persecution—*then* we would have a case where perception of a unique historical situation, whether real or alleged, was bolted down for all future situations as a basis for perception, no matter how different the context.

The same holds for the anti-Jewish texts in the New Testament, which can be put down largely to historical and theological squabbling in a movement sprung from Judaism and in the process of growing a new identity, with a concomitant need to set boundaries and to stake out distance. The situative character of these texts consists in them naming the felt problems of the day, the danger being that we identify them so much with the revealed Word of God that we think that Christian faith, from now on in, no matter what, has to be anti-Semitic. A grievous error. Apart from the fact that, in so proceeding, we would no longer be taking the revealed character of the Gospel texts seriously, precisely where this very attitude was being broken through, namely in the person of Paul, as we read him in Romans 9–11, where Jews who do not find their way to the new faith will also, at the end of days, partake of God's boundless justification.

But such ideologising of historical situations can also occur over the status of victim. When the Palestinians cry out against the organs of the Israeli state and strive against these for justice and self-determination, they are being neither anti-Semitic nor anti-Jewish. In this they are not expressing an ahistorical ideology, running through all situations, such as that "the Jews" are always and everywhere to be despised and fought. Their resistance is rather the outgrowth of a *current* situation, in which they sense, in the here and now, they are being unjustly treated by Jews and Jewish institutions. If Israel wasn't Israel, but some other state, the Palestinians would, would *have* to, react just the same. For the state of Israel too, it follows that there may be no ahistorical (i.e., freed from all scrutiny) fixation on any possible status as permanent victim. One may, at best, especially from the German perspective, positively suspect the ascription may well be merited; indeed in the past it was, with very few exceptions, but verification has to come from the facts, not from *a priori* conviction in advance of the facts.

The accusations made by Palestinian women at the 1994 World Prayer Congress are therefore not theologically anti-Semitic, but they are situatively critical of Israel. We cannot be expected to ask of them that they sacrifice their self-experience as victims of injustice on the mnemonic altar of any past status Jews have had as victims of injustice in another country. To think contextually is not to ideologically freeze historical situations; rather it is to strive incessantly for a reality-sensitive, socially critical perception of the contradictions, such as they are, between power and powerlessness, between justice and injustice.

The whole thing becomes vastly more complicated when *we in Germany* hear the voice of the afflicted Palestinian people. It goes without saying that Germans are, and should be, careful before exposing Jewish organs to criticism. Not one's own fantasies and projections, but alone the voices of the afflicted themselves, can be the yardstick for such critique, which, for the sake of the afflicted, may not then be silenced or censored. If listening means anything, it means letting others have their say. The controversy we witnessed at the 1994 World Prayer Congress of Women was sparked by this very issue: May we, in our own country, let Palestinian women have their full say, a say that was full of bitterness? May we then, coming from where we are and have been, show solidarity with them? Could not their situative criticisms of Israel be taken here, *mis*taken here, as ideological anti-Semitism? Shouldn't we, therefore, tone down or palliate the laments of these Palestinian women, to prevent them from being peddled as anti-Jewish sentiment and boycotted?

Posing these questions is no less important than answering them in a context-sensitive way. What can be heard *here* (in Germany) as anti-Judaism is *there* (in Palestine) no more (but also no less) than saving preservation of self-maintenance of identity. Probably we will not escape seeing that our discrete German context cannot be so generalised as to drown out the cry of the Palestinian people. But from the perspective of Palestinians, this same German context is just a chink in the big picture, one that might bear historically, etiologically, on their own situation, but which cannot be said to be part of, or have derived from, their own experience. And so we arrive at this general conclusion: Palestinian Christians may, given their situation, pray the biblical psalms of lamentation, as indeed may all Christians everywhere, when they find themselves in sickness, distress or extremity.

2.3 Election by God: Exclusive or Generative?

The above arguments cast doubt on each and every category of election, if election means that some, many or most, are excluded from the fold. This religious trope envisages not only a top-down division of the world, but also a permanent (whether openly waged, repressed or spiritualised) war for the right to be elected in the stead of others. In the Bible as also in the Church itself, and in religious history generally, there are probably two versions of what we may call the "election theorem", the practical consequences of which are, in each of these cases, radically opposed:

a) the exclusive claim to election and
b) the proexistent (being there for the people) responsibility for election.

In the case of

a) those who do not belong are relegated to the godless (this in two senses: that of subjective unbelief and that of God's objective indifference to them, or even active spurning). In the case of
b) the pointedness of God's historical presence in his own domain is not reduced to this point, but is construed as a pledge in favour of the universal salvation of all nations and all humankind. One's own election seals not only the fact that one is elected, but also that, because this is so, all other people, albeit differently, now fall within God's radius of salvation. Here one's own election is so conceived as to let it be overtaken or else withdrawn, if (and to the extent) others come to experience, discover and taste true election themselves.

The ambivalence of the election trope runs through religious history like a thick trail of blood, nowhere more than in the history of the Christian churches in their changing political contexts, in which the purely religious belief in one's own elected status has allied itself all too easily with political, chauvinist and racist systems of rule, whether actual or simply striven for. Much, no doubt, is gained when Jews and Christians recognise each other in their respective claims to election, yet such a joint claim to being thus singled out would itself run afoul of the ambivalence in election ideology by means of an exclusive claim, if this were to imply a claim to election derogatory to the rest of the world. Not less than with one's own election, such a joint, albeit contrasting, claim to election would have to possess a certain generative character, which I will describe in the words of F-W Marquardt concerning Israel's status as the first elected of God (here he is following on from Karl Barth), namely that Israel's history, being the "indispensable linchpin between God and man's whole history on earth", should therefore be seen as a "microscopic, exemplary, representative distillation of all of history".[5] This means, in all likelihood, that the structures of hope and liberation, which in Israel's history were (and are) lived out or rendered necessary, are ready and available for manifestation in the different contexts of other peoples and religions. Thus, the (temporal) primacy of Israel's election is stripped of its exclusive flavour. Therefore, Marquardt praises the importance "that Jewish humanity possesses for all humanity" on the plane of a biblical *pars pro toto* dictum, that "the universal inserts itself always and only at the apex of utter particularity".

So Jews and Christians do belong together, to make the point again, in ways different from others. I see therein, operating with undiminished intensity, the "new hermeneutic situation" bequeathed by Auschwitz, if (and precisely for that reason) they do not want to know themselves blocked in their universal dynamic by fixation on the Jewish-Christian nexus. This is particularly true in view of the pressing political imperative, at once geopolitical and local, to ubiquitously oppose racism and fundamentalism, not to systematically exclude millions of people. If here the Jewish-Christian relationship turns in on itself and its own problems, and, for example, puts down the theology of liberation, without trying, at least, to grasp the latter "from the inside out", then it is itself contributing to provincialising the memory of Auschwitz and draining it of its force. Not that there is any lack of Jewish and Christian theologians to point out that despite Auschwitz being so singular in its horrors that it cannot be hitched to—instrumentalised by—just any moral bandwagon, we may never (just because it is so singular) forget, with Auschwitz in mind, "what humans, so called humans, are capable of". Nor can we ponder the memory of Auschwitz without having a tension befall us, a fear we can never quite shake off, that the same horrors will resurface again, somewhere else and at some other time, to show what humans are capable of doing to humans. In this sense we

5 *F.-W. Marquardt*, Die Gegenwart des Auferstandenen bei seinem Volk Israel, München 1993, 18.

must read Metz's lament and admonition: "Few indeed associate the crisis of humanity around us with Auschwitz..."[6] For were this not so, a destructive problem complex that has so far chiefly pitted Christians against Jews would only be displaced to another level, that of non-Christians versus non-Jews.

2.4 Victims Caught Between Self-experience and Comparative Evidential Critique

If the Bible can only be authentically read in terms of a readiness to repent, a readiness to obey the promptings of mercy and justice, then we can say that gravitating to, and seeking out, situations of exigency, situations where this readiness can be channelled to those whose claim to it is greatest, now takes shape as an integral part of this *material* hermeneutic which is rooted in the real odds. What, however, at first sight seems non-negotiable, transparent to a point where it cannot be rationalised away, namely when someone is a victim and not a perpetrator, does it turn out, on closer inspection, to have its share of problems, especially concerning the balance between one's self-perception as a victim and a willingness to scrutinise, with an eye honed for comparisons, the still greater, or perhaps incomparably greater, distress that others are in. To be ready to make comparisons of this kind is to consent to see, to recognise, evidence in both oneself and others of experienced suffering, evidence that, through time, becomes ever more unquestionable. Any averting of one's eyes, in the name of some false comparative hierarchy, would be tantamount to falsifying the hermeneutic situation.

As a first point: The victim's right to protest and cry out is indivisible, as is her right to be recognised and taken seriously. There is no exclusive right to victim status, as in the maxim: if it is *us* who were—are—victims, then others can't be. Or, if *we* are victims of historical circumstance, then there is no way that others can have felt history's sharp teeth; rather these others are rivals or enemies and should be seen as such. Reality, as ever, is more complex. Only when others are glimpsed as victims in their own right is it possible to seek jointly for ways and means to reduce the weight of *both* burdens of suffering, fear and non-freedom. What matters in each case is that the respective experiential worlds of those who experience their situation as unjust, as boding ill for them, should be taken seriously, with nothing taken away or denied, and that, as a result of this, the closer and the remoter contexts open up and the analytic nexi as well, which is to say no more than this: no work of analysis may be compiled over the heads of those in distress. Becoming attuned to how the

6 *J.-B. Metz*, Theodizee-empfindliche Gottesrede, in: id. (ed.), „Landschaft aus Schreien", Mainz 1995, 81–102, 102; also 84:

downtrodden experience themselves is no guarantee that the imperatives of the hour will be objectively perceived (given that being attuned easily turns into being inured); it is however the *sine qua non*, if there is ever to be any gravitating to relative objectivity.

But the thing about claiming victimhood is that it is not always so straightforward. When Christians identify with Christ as victim, as sacrificial offering—and in German both are subsumed in one word, *Opfer*—and then go on to "counter identify", as it were, with Jews as the seeming wrongdoers, the better to foment pogroms against them or to lend legitimacy to such, then we begin to perceive the nature of the beast. The rub is that even here the perpetrator can "somehow" manage to stake out a claim to victimhood. This was indeed the key to the refined propaganda of the Nazis, as when they defined the Jewish people as a "bacillus" threatening to infiltrate and destroy an otherwise healthy German body politic. Said Alan Bullock, noted Hitler expert and World War II historian: "Hitler trained his gaze on those sizeable number of Germans who shared his paranoid sensitivities and who saw themselves as preyed on by plotting capitalists, those on the left, Bolshevists, Jews, the dictates of the victorious Allied powers."[7] Against such a strategy of inverting, of "turning on its head", the true nature of things, there is only the counterstrategy of downplaying—as an exercise in self-relativisation—one's own alleged victimhood as from the perspective of the actual victims—to be effected by resolving to perceive all victims, inside and outside, for what they are—with particular reference to those who, as a result of one's constricted fantasies of ongoing victimisation on one's own turf, are being ostracised and imperilled (and growing in numbers) by the hour. That is why, under National Socialism of the Nazis, strenuous efforts were made to stop the German people, in their majority, from turning their inverted view of things "the right way up"—by seeing the suffering of the *truly* suffering for what it was. For this to happen, the Allies had first to arrive and force local populations to actually see what had been going on under their noses in the nearby concentration camps. For if people had grasped, beyond dissembling, in their full dimensions the horrors of the camps, many would probably have reacted with the one feeling the regime could on no account permit: compassion.

Therefore, across all borders and boundaries, we need an ethic of radical incorruptibility and integrity, an ethic that refuses to pick and choose and divide off against one another, an ethic that opens our eyes to people afflicted by poverty, injustice and oppression. The voice of this ethic will not just need to be heard in one's own little corner, but everywhere where victims are met or where they cry out in protest—and this in deepest principle. If taking victims seriously does not possess ubiquitous and universal evidential force, so that in derivation from such evidence (and there is nothing higher) all else has

---

7 A. *Bullock*, Die Genies des Bösen, in: Der Spiegel 45 (1991) 25, 108–129, 119.

to be ranked and a broad empirical perception of the interconnectivities put in place, then we will only find that the number of victims keeps growing. Then, the only option at least some of the downtrodden have, or think they have, is to withdraw into exclusive self-solidarity, which others equally downtrodden will take as a snub to their own cause, as a withholding of solidarity. Nor may this principled and unconditional attitude be checked and balanced, or in any way restricted, by operating some gradient, or scale, for the rational or ethical quality of the afflicted (for who would here be able to sit in judgement?). Supposedly "backward" victims, or those thought in some way to be morally vulnerable, may not have their right to recognition as victims downplayed or disputed.

Nor is this all just a problem of the past; it rears its head in the present. Empirical studies have shown that most persons in our society feel they have been badly done by in some way or other. But statistics tell another story: the truly disadvantaged are far outnumbered by those who are keen to define themselves as such. Evidently a top-down scale applies in the assessing of victimhood. Our focus is not on the many who are worse off than we are; it is on the small handful, the lucky few—ourselves, for the most part—who can afford most of the good things of this earth. Therefore, our gaze, and with it the scale by which we make comparisons, wanders upwards, rarely downwards. And so it is that most of us go through life thinking of ourselves as permanently on the losing end, as perpetual losers. This, however, is not the situation we are truly in, at least not objectively. One way of snapping out of such self-fixation, and perceiving the truth of our situation for what it is, is to look down rather than up, when making our comparisons. We should take in the plight of the many who don't even have the bare essentials at home, but even more away from home, out there in the wider world, where all too often we find people who lack the essentials of bare existence, who all too often face not only that but also an attendant risk of torture or death. This—to first inspection—simple example shows how hard it is to achieve a portion of honesty and openness. But without these qualities, it is unlikely we will expose ourselves to the "evidence" of those that actually suffer, or if we do, that we will have any precise yardstick by which to measure victimhood or rank degrees of suffering.

This principled stance towards the victims of repression and cruelty, of injustice and destitution, signals in the first instance a critical attitude towards the extending of solidarity in small dollops in the here and now—for this invariably bears the mark of personal relationships in our own lives, of constraints placed on our freedom of action. We are likely to come out for *those* persons in distress to whom we have, in one form or another, cognitive ties (either we know them or we know *of* them) or affective ties born of empathy or of shared resistance. In the teeth of this inevitable *factual* constraint, there is time and again a need, on the level of *principle*, to go further and recognise that, even beyond our own radius of knowledge and emotionality, there are victims no less deserving of help, even if their deserts be such that we cannot, or cannot fully, feel them on grounds of prior identifications in our lives. Then, we will not get a situation where victim is ranged against victim, in competition for our sympathy; none will then be beyond the pale of commitment born of solidarity. Although we often cannot prevent our solidarity from disadvantaging other victims than those it was aimed at helping, we can indeed, by recognising that they are in principle no less deserving, prevent them from becoming wholly indifferent or from experiencing that solidarity extended to the one is just code for suffering aggravated in all the others. When solidarity for the one is a zero-sum game where the others necessarily have to lose, positive and negative discrimination are two sides of the one coin. With its limited resources, church development aid for poor countries constantly runs up against this problematic of flipping the coin, of deciding which victim to assign priority to over the other; dissonance is a permanent feature of such work, as aid workers well know.

Between the extremes of the victim perceiving him/herself as victim and the victim as perceived by others who are not themselves victims, we can postulate a complex dynamic of responsibility feeding into an ever more ubiquitously extended solidarity with victims.

This dynamic unfolds in a number of phases:

First, there is the stage where the afflicted actively perceive themselves in their extremity and need, i.e., the victim in his (internalised) status as victim. And we can say that the greater the extremity, the less the afflicted will pick up on the sufferings of others—whether persons or whole peoples—and be *able* (i.e., have the psychological reserves) to show solidarity with them; least of all, of this we can be sure, will they have any time for any victims there *may* be among the perpetrators, especially when what is involved are structural contradictions that need sorting out in structural disputation. Realising that this is so extenuates a failure to discern that there are victims elsewhere, inhabiting other places—not that this means, from a Christian perspective, that license is now granted to engage in acts of violence, which will only add to the sum of victims elsewhere, including among the perpetrators. With Jesus it is abundantly clear that, even in direst extremity, He would not make victims of his enemies. He prays on the cross for them *too* to be forgiven (cf. Luke 23:34).

A *second* stage is when we reach the point of accepting, when the threat to us and ours is not so life-threatening, that other victims in similar circumstances do not have to be banished from our awareness: as when jobless workers with different backgrounds or ethnicities do not let their solidarity wither—i.e., do not resort, as sadly some unemployed German workers have done, to making convenient scapegoats of those foreign workers in their midst who are still working—but rather stick together, across the various divides, and experience ourselves as equally victimised by the same (or similar) circumstances, against which we can now make common cause. The specific ill of unemployment would then not isolate, but bring people together, empowering them as fellow sufferers.

And there is a *third* stage: The less our status is that of the ground down and the outcast, the more we are well situated in life and "sitting pretty"—the greater our responsibility is to achieve a growing perception of victims everywhere, in both our own country and abroad, not the least of whom are victims in countries that have been declared, perhaps by our political principals, to be "the enemy". For in this stage we do not have the excuse that, because all our resources are focused, and necessarily have to be, on our own situation, we have none left over to give to other victims; we do not have the excuse not to see their plight or to lift a finger on their behalf. Given that this is so, most of us in the developed world have no right to rein in, or ideologically blinker, our sensitivity to victimisation wherever it occurs. But human limits do operate. It comes down to, with all the good will in the world, us having enough energy in reserve. The more we focus on victims coming from a certain direction, the more our responsibilities are likely to grow towards them, meaning there is just that much less of us there to simultaneously commit to other victims. But then how much greater our responsibility is to at least ensure that this focused commitment of ours does no harm to other victims, on pain of us becoming accomplices. We must therefore keep an eye on the network effects.

In a real world where so many sharp edges rub up against each other, it would be naïve to expect that between our resources and the principles enunciated here perfect harmony will prevail. No one gets out of here with their hands completely clean! And knowing what it is like to get nowhere, despite all efforts, is par for the course, is a virtual certainty. It is important, however, that we should not try to hide our frequent impotence, our inability to make a difference; we should not ideologically "airbrush" out of the picture—or worse, legitimise—the risk we run, when trying to help, of acquiring guilt or, worse, the fact of having acquired it. This experience of having failed instils in us at least a readiness to accept justification by God's mercy, even as it prompts us, renewed, to again tread the path of repentance. Thus, that at stake here is not "just" diaconia, but also the pragmatic precondition for an authentic biblical hermeneutic, becomes clear once more.

I will conclude by sharing some thoughts on how the criteriology proposed here can be applied to biblical hermeneutics. Pivotal remains for me the perspective of our God-given ability to repent and to walk in the ways of compassion and justice. When such a practice is in place (or at least the desire for it is there) we then have the existential hermeneutic plank we need to read the biblical texts and hope to understand them. As prolegomenon, and to ground what I will later have to say, I will first discuss how compassion has the power to open our eyes to let us take into our hearts the victims around us and so can foster in us an ability to deal justly.

3. *Preconditions and Detailed Explication*

3.1 Compassion's Power to Touch Our Hearts

Grace in the Bible implies that God has mercy on us. The various stories it tells can probably be described in their totality as "dramas of God's mercy". On this theme there is impressive textual witness (see, for example, Hosea 11). And God shows mercy even, indeed especially, when we are guilty of wrongful doing or guilty of having become having hardened our hearts. God's mercy is bestowed on the suffering person as such: though God is not indifferent to whether we are innocent or the architects of our own misery, his mercy is not conditional on our innocence.

In the Gospels we encounter Jesus as someone who reflects God's compassion in his own actions and who renders it palpable. Jesus interacts with men and women in distress—the sick, the outcasts, the victims of injustice—and he does it with a deep-seated compassion that has the power to steer action. The Greek expression mostly translated as "to take pity" loses much of the dramatic force of the original, i.e., to be so shattered by how another is struck down by suffering and fate that one feels it deep within one's bowels, that one's stomach literally turns, not from disgust but from pity (cf. Luke 15:20; Matthew 9:36ff.). Jesus can do nothing but take in the scene before Him; he lays aside what He was doing, stands just where He is and then does what has to be done. Nowhere and never is his faculty for pity impeded, nor is it anywhere or at any time qualified by any "if-then" quibbling and caveats, such as: "you wouldn't have needed pity now if only you'd done the right thing"—as if someone only deserved pity if she bore no responsible for the mess she is now in. Pity also pierces through to the layer in us where calculating of any sort or the pursuit of private interest is no longer possible. It pierces through all barriers such as the urge to punish or exact vengeance, through all ideologies, prejudices and the so-called laws of nature, as vented in tensions, conflicts and enmities. Pity of this kind is non-negotiable, is irreducible and cannot be revoked, precisely because it wells up—to switch metaphors—in our hearts, our stomachs, our kidneys. It is proof against that hardening of heart, that averting of our gaze, which would seek and find reasons why we should not be so moved. The very immediacy of pity as a response—its evidential character—reflects the immediacy of the prior suffering. The word for pity in my native German is *Mitleid*, meaning "shared suffering" or "suffering with another"—and the English "compassion," of course, has the same core meaning, albeit at a Latin remove.

Now compassion in the sort of society we have today is not exactly a highly prized good. Rather the contrary: the society we live in is profoundly suspicious of compassion, despite the need for it being greater than ever. We might even call compassion an endangered species. Let me endorse Horst Eberhard Richter's judgement: "Sadly, compassion has become something of a laughingstock. In truth, it is *the* life-preserving faculty period."[8] So it is that compassion is especially at risk from the mass display of suffering in the visual media; our capacity to react becomes deadened as a result; we succumb to "compassion fatigue". Yet it need not always be so: there are times the images go straight to the heart (and to more than a few hearts too, as the volume of donations that pour in shows). Yet it is not too cynical to suppose that those who respond are the ones, the few, who have kept the "soft tissue" of compassion from hardening over in their daily lives. We often tend to associate compassion with something frail and fragile, smacking of helplessness and a lack of resources. It is said it is not a good idea to be overcome by feelings for others; otherwise we will take our eye off the ball and end up trampled by life. Therefore, we should keep our compassionate urges on a tight leash, or at least make prudent use of them. It is also true that many a sufferer will say he does not want your pity—and he is probably right in saying so, for pity can be of the condescending sort, and no one can judge that better than the intended recipient. Indeed, a fine eye is needed to tell both kinds of "pity" apart. It is interesting to note that, unlike pity, talk of compassion carries no such duality of meaning and needs no qualification. We need to tell false and true pity apart, but compassion is undivided and is synonymous with true pity.

Thus, there is a need to differentiate within the concept itself. Many an instance of pity turns out to be of the self-pitying kind, as for example is the case with pity born of fear, a fear that we ourselves will be overtaken by the same suffering that has laid low the person we pity. Behind this pity is a need to defend ourselves, for deep down we feel guilty at being so much better off than the other—at least so far. In such pitying of others, our true aim is to strike a bargain so we will never ourselves end up in this situation, nor is this bargain we strike entirely displeasing to us in a narcissistic way. Displays of this kind, therefore, proceed from self-pity. Such pity can ultimately become a deadly weapon, achieving the precise opposite of what saving pity, the other kind of pity, would achieve: to bolster the will to live, to instil a sense of worth in the other. We have all heard of physicians or care workers handling patients with extreme disabilities who find—more often than the patients themselves do, it must be said—that they can no longer stand the strain of their work, who then are dangerously tempted to do away with their charges before their time

8 In a television interview with Bettina Böttinger on Westdeutscher Rundfunk in 1999.

is up (whether by administering lethal dosages or by terminating a pregnancy in an act of "prenatal selection") or resort to euthanasia, so-called "mercy killing". "Deadly pity" was what Klaus Dörner called this kind of pity.[9]

The great Austrian writer Stefan Zweig, in his novel "The Impatient Heart", expressed this "twofold pity" with a force of his very own: "There are two kinds of pity. The kind that is fainthearted and sentimental, that signals but an impatient heart, impatient to get away from being embarrassingly stirred by somebody else's misfortune. Such pity has nothing to do with the other pity, as when we suffer along with another. It is but the instinctive fending off of alien suffering from one's own soul. As for the other kind, the only kind that counts—it is a pity that is as unsentimental as it is creative, the kind that knows what it wants, the kind that is determined to go through thick and thin, patiently and with a humble heart, until it has exhausted all its energy, only then to tap into even more."[10]

To pick up on this culture I am proposing that creative and life-sustaining suffering along with life's victims is not to insist that we can, always and everywhere, bring a radical depth of feeling to bear. What does matter though is that we should remain vulnerable in the depths of our being, that our soft tissue should not be allowed to become hard tissue, so that it no longer responds to human suffering in a visceral way. What matters is that a path can be found to our affective depths, that we do not barricade these off from being "moved". For it is upwelling from the depths that break through the incrustations and coagulations in us, that enable us, for the sake of suffering humanity, to let mercy go before justice; that dispel the coldness that would otherwise penetrate everywhere, affecting faith too. After all, true pity is the emotional ground of forgiveness and so of faith in a God of forgiveness.

In the long history of humanity's encounter with this God of forgiveness, as described in the Bible, we find a mutually reinforcing link between compassion and justice, with a tendency, through time, to ever closer integration. The interpersonal dimension too evinces this same tendency. There can be no progressive justice, nothing adequate to human dignity, without the theme of compassion being part of it, such that it can track down those who "lack" access to a justice that should be becoming ever more universal. And vice versa: There can be no progressive compassion without the corrective of justice—a justice that tracks down those for whom we feel (perhaps because we lack intuition) no particular or immediate compassion but who are still in need of justice. Only by making the latter link can we save victims from exposure to the arbitrariness of empathy felt or empathy not felt. Therefore, there can be no

[9] Cp. *K. Dörner*, Tödliches Mitleid. Zur Frage der Unerträglichkeit des Leidens, Gütersloh ^{2}1989.

[10] *S. Zweig*, Ungeduld des Herzens. Roman, Stockholm 1943, 228.

justice without a compassion that delimits justice, and there can be no compassion without a justice that delimits compassion.

3.2 A Concrete Case: Solidarity in Prayer

I begin this last section by drawing a modest balance. Our initial question was: Who may pray the Jewish psalms of lamentation? The answer is now clear: without reservation, all those that are victims of penury, injustice and violence may do so, all who from the depths of their distress reach out to the God of salvation or who cry out in bitterness for justification from a God who has averted His face, as they think—no matter from what nation or country they come. To set bounds to this universality would be a form of racism, tantamount to bluntly curtailing God's universality in history, which I take to mean God's universal willingness to take the part of the afflicted. The stories in the Bible testify to God's loving kindness, to use the older English term. But the fact that *only the victims* of sickness and suffering may pray the psalms of lamentation does *not* mean they can do so *arbitrarily*; rather they are subject to critique in the form of a semantic-pragmatic *ratio* feeding into a biblical hermeneutic—and it is *this* that I have tried to elucidate.

So where are *we* now? What follows for us if we attempt to take our bearings from this topopractical criteriology, if I may call it that. The psalms do not cloak the oppositions between poverty and richness, between sickness and health, between oppression and freedom; instead they make a virtue of juxtaposing them and show God as siding with the battlers, the losers, the downtrodden. Faced with these oppositions, where are we then to position ourselves? If it happens that we are ourselves the rich, the oppressors, or those who close their eyes to what is going on, then, at least for now, these prayers from the deep past are not our prayers and not our texts. If, nonetheless, we lay claim to them, and offer them up in prayer, we rob those on the losing end, along perhaps with much else besides, of the language of suffering that alone is theirs.

And if we insist on doing so, the oppositions between rich and poor will be crudely papered over, and those in the psalms will be tamed and have their teeth drawn. Among us too there are the poor (call them the *neo* poor) and the rich, the sick and the healthy; there are those that have been cheated of their right to work or equal treatment, and there are those who have profited at their expense. The first mentioned in these oppositions will be able, among us too, to pray the psalms of lamentation. Yet in global comparison with the millions of hungry and oppressed people (and peoples) around the world in zones on this earth of direst poverty and lawlessness, we still come off as significantly better off, which is not to say we do not need to differentiate among ourselves.

What does it mean for many of "us" —I leave out, for argument's sake, all those who in one way or another are disadvantaged or sick, in body or in mind: it goes without saying that all these too "are" the sorely pressed whose plight the psalms voice—what then does it mean for us when we, in our country, pray the psalms? Is it right for us to do? And if so, *how* should we do it?

We may do it in the following way:

- *By listening when we pray:*

Without grieving, we cannot and may not pray the psalms of lamentation. We grieve with the destitute and the oppressed who here voice their situation of utter loss, who cry out in prayer, and who—in that we attempt to pray in their words—all over the world, wherever they may be, similarly weep, cry out and raise their voices in accusation. And we will the more truly *pray with them* these psalms, the more we listen to these texts, *hear the cries of suffering* on the page. Then we pray these psalms of lamentation not directly, not "for their sake"; rather, we pray them as "*hearers of the Word*" in that in praying we hear the cries of the needy. In doing so, we let the world of suffering into our lives. It is the same world as the one we live in, but so often we do not wish to see it in this light, not least because we dread its claws, dread that we too will be made to suffer. To listen thus as we pray is to enclose the suffering of the world in our prayers. It is the condition for a spirituality that sees us, our human environment, our village, suburb or city, our country and the wider world *through the eyes of the needy.*

- *By praying with a penitent and contrite heart*

Once we have picked up on the voice of suffering, once it truly reverberates within, we are not far from a condition of repentance and contrition that will let us see with open eyes, hear with listening ears, those who are suffering, whether they be nearby or far off; now we are ready to take up the struggle for compassion and justice. Praying this way impels us to see where we are ourselves situated in the contradictory human scheme of things, and not to repress what we discover—or rather *un*cover, for it is not likely to be congenial—but to accept that it is so. Not least, we confess our sins and pray for forgiveness, for a new beginning in which we may be set free, such as is articulated often enough in the psalms—and when we do this we find that what we have done has urgent and immediate explosive force or subversive potential. We acquire a sense of how utterly dependent we are on justification by God's grace, of the necessity for repenting our sinful ways. Here the material hermeneutics has come full circle: for when we have demonstrated our readiness here, we can now see more deeply into the psalms and the other biblical texts.

- *By praying in memory of the victims*

Praying the psalms of lamentation with a listening spirit has, however, not just a synchronous but a *diachronous* dimension, in that such listening also involves remembering the victims of history, those who have prayed, or lamented, in the same or similar words; not least, and precisely here on this plane, it involves remembering Christ's self-sacrifice on the cross, the point in history where victimhood and sacrifice were revealed as *one*—for did He not, in His dying agony, pray in the words of Psalm 22? Prayer of this kind, with one ear trained on the past, by virtue of the solidarity it extends to the victims of history, becomes in itself a prayerful readiness to repent, concentrating the other ear to the present suffering—the point being to inject into the present a greater cutting edge of concern, a greater willingness to act now to remedy injustice, so that in future far fewer of us will have to pray like this, so that in future many more will be free from poverty and oppression. Sensitised by the prayers of the needy, Christians will rightly strive to make contact with them not in the abstract but in the real world, at home, in the congregation and in wider society. They will not turn away when the needy are there before their eyes. Such praying in the Psalter's words of lamentation can drive especially those who, right now, have nothing to lament, or not very much, into concrete diaconia with those who lament from the depth of their being.

- *By praying jointly with sufferers*

If, to date, I have been considering a form of prayer that, face to face with those whose suffering is great, is willing to listen, reluctant to put words in their mouth to appropriate language that is theirs by right, then there is too another form of prayer, one that takes the part of sufferers and stands in solidarity alongside them, one that makes the case against God and humankind. When in the Israel of old a man visited a sick friend, he would, after visibly commiserating with him and listening in silence to his friend's laments, join in with him in lamenting. The visitor would not come out against his friend, nor would he, this least of all, take God's part against him; on the contrary, he would take the invalid's part against God, demanding *why* He had let this infirmity strike down his friend and clamouring for an answer—all in a process of prayer that proceeds from rebellion to acceptance, from resistance to resignation. The visitor placed himself on the side of the sufferer, while demonstrating by his readiness to take his part and share his pain the fact of his compassion and solidarity. All of this was done without a hint of symbiotic-colonial condescension: even in the act of taking upon himself the other's sufferings, he kept some distance so as not to expropriate the latter's voice or dignity. Who prays in this way with those who suffer does not abandon them.

So in this manner too we may pray the psalms of lamentation with the afflicted: in communion with them, though not in the sense that we obscure the situational and role differences between them and us, but rather, in that we range ourselves *alongside* them in a feeling of togetherness, making their struggles our own. This will chiefly block often embarrassing attempts, born of some cramped urge, to acquaint sufferers with the causes of their suffering, either by quoting some framework of reference or, worse, trying to see their plight through God's eyes, daring to take God's part against them.

- *By praying on behalf of others*

Here it is only right to mention, on a cautious note, that when we pray the psalms of lamentation we may only do so as *proxies* for the real addressees, those whose crying out in prayer has now grown still, who can no longer, so great is their pain and desolation, think any thoughts at all or utter them with their lips, who may even be beyond having a God to whom they can address their prayers. Thus, the psalms are a prayer for intercession of a special kind. We pray them on behalf of the afflicted so that the plight that has befallen them may be restored to memory, and we argue their case for compassion before God and humankind. We pray these in their stead, as intermediaries, and this is what we pray: that they may, if it is still possible, find new trust and new hope towards God and humankind. Perhaps a solidarity in companionship with the spirit of the Resurrected One, Christ Himself, may be discerned here, with Christ who, in our hour of weakness when prayer dies on our lips, intercedes for us, even then, with a sigh that we cannot express in words and that passes all understanding (cf. Romans 8:26).

- *By praying in anticipation of what is in store for us*

Not least, we may pray the psalms *because of what is in store for us*. We should so "learn" from our solidarity with the needy, who received it from us in the here and now, in intimate familiarity with the processes by which they lamented (and perhaps managed to win back a measure of trust), that when our turn comes, and we find ourselves on the losing end of life, hedged in by pain and misery, that we then may dare to pray and also know how to. Also, it is possible that prayer offered up now will have anticipatory value, as if we were proxies *for our future selves*, if it should ever happen, at some bleak hour, that we can no longer pray and lament.

It turns out that we may, after all, pray the psalms of lamentation, despite not being ourselves afflicted or oppressed, not being in pain or on our deathbed; yet, for the sake of God and suffering humanity, we must never do so in such a way that the sufferers disappear or are forgotten. On the contrary: we must do it in such a way that they, precisely for that reason, find a place in how we internalise our spirituality and practice our Christianity in front of God him/herself. By being thus included, they will provoke us to change our bearings and modify our vantage point—leading, not least, to an improved material-hermeneutic situation and a deepened grasp of the biblical texts.

4. *Advocacy for the World Day of Prayer 1994 and 2024*[11]

To say it upfront: During the 1950s as a student the documentations about the mass extermination of Jews in the Third Reich shook me up so much that I am still ashamed to be a German whenever I meet Jewish citizens here or when I am in Israel. My co-responsibility for what our fathers and others did, or respectively did not prevent, drove me frequently to Israel during my college years to make contact and on some occasions by picking cotton and apples in a kibbutz for months. Also in my theological work the issue of a Christian theology after Auschwitz is always present and has never let me go. And the fact that God in Christ did not only become a human being but a Jew is for me the decisive contextual axiom of Christology itself.

These points are made not only as a preventative reference for my not wanting to be called anti-Semitic for my following thoughts, but that I am foremost concerned with that *undivided* orientation toward the victims, which in my own life story first and continuously was burnt into me with the memory of the Jewish Holocaust.

Two concerns are important: the *liberation theological* and the *contextual.* I want to question seriously the way in which they were brought together in the concrete conflict regarding the Women's World Day of Prayer 1994, and will probably be brought together in 2024, with the theses: The women were right to let the Palestinian women speak without censoring them.

The Protestant theologian Friedrich-Wilhelm Marquard sees the special character of biblical-Jewish thought in the fact that it "perceives the general always only as the tip of the most particular"[12]. I find this a very good description of biblically oriented contextuality. The "only" expresses clearly that the general as general does not exist. Universality in and of itself is only a fiction which then all too easily turns into an ideological evaluation of the particular when it is pulled over the different situations. Some did not sufficiently avoid that temptation because they defined the terminology of context (at the expense of the Palestinian women involved) to require including Jewish women in the preparation of the World Day of Prayer 1994, too, and thus they suggested without discussion that the Jewish women were in the same situation. That, however, is by no means the case. There are clearly different contexts of life

---

11 Cf. *Stephanie Klein*, Dokumentaton zum Weltgebetstag 1994 aus Palästina, edited by the German World Prayer Day Committee, Düsseldorf 1995, document 36, first published in: Publik-Forum 22 (1993) 22, 18–20.

12 *Friedrich-Wilhelm Marquardt*, Die Gegenwart des Auferstandenen bei seinem Volk Israel, München 1993, 18.

and faith. If one does not want to differentiate here, one could relinquish the terminology of context because it no longer includes the particular.

For example, it is problematic to judge the contextual theology in South Africa (with the example of the KAIROS document[13]) and the contextual situation of the Palestinian women by two different standards. If one was dealing with the KAIROS paper in the same way as with the statements of the Palestinian women, one would have to accuse the Blacks that did not deal constructively enough with those who live in the cities and regions of the Whites, where wealth, economic means and capital are hoarded (perhaps with the request: Why don't the Black women from Soweto cooperate with the White women from the wealthy neighbourhoods? Everyone who knows how much those two contexts are separated from each other can have a hunch about how nonsensical such a request is aside from the fact that through such requests for communication the structural contradictions are personalised and minimised). Or regarding the indigenous people in the Amazon: Should the indigenous women begin a dialogue with the wives of the white settlers or gold diggers so that their voice is legitimate?

Furthermore, by demanding the dialogue as someone who is standing on the outside (kind of from a bird's eye perspective) and by binding the evaluation and legitimacy of what the Palestinian women express to the fulfilment of that request, Europeans show themselves often as people who have gone through the "enlightenment" of universalist reason, who are better informed about and can better judge the situation and the connections than the ones who are involved themselves.

But herein lies the exceptional dignity of the World Day of Prayer women—that they let the voices of those involved be heard authentically and uncensored: that they did not dare to intervene in the text, according to the motto: the Palestinian women would really have to say such and such so as not to offend anybody.

By the way, I ask myself why one did not accuse the World Day of Prayer services of earlier years of "false contextuality". For the texts have always been produced in that same way, been translated and taken seriously: for example, when the women from Guatemala described their situation and in this case information was given to the women of the World Day of Prayer; solidarities were built months before the country moved into the headlines when Rigoberta Menchú was awarded the Nobel Peace Prize.

Moreover, in the intensive preparation for the World Day of Prayer excellent contextual work was done at the base und publically, including documentation of discussions and with complementary questions from the audience, but always with respect for those who speak from the particular country. This

---

[13] Cf. Albert Nolan, "Kairos Theology". In De Gruchy, et al. (Ed.), Doing theology in context. South African perspectives, Maryknoll 1994, 212–218.

also includes the respect for the composition of the World Day of Prayer committees in the respective countries and thus also for their context.

Regarding the Jewish women in Israel, some speak about "immediate neighbours". Having strange ideas about the local situation: "Jewish women live next to Palestinian ones." This is neither true for the Gaza strip nor for most parts of the West Bank (and if it occurs, then there is often an unbridgeable separation between Arab women and Jewish settlers, aside from language problems). Contextuality is not only an ideal term but also a situational one in regard to content in as much as it elaborates, on a basis that ranges from different to contradictory, the life situations and the structures in a local area ignoring, especially in local proximity, how poverty and oppression collide. Hardly anyone will claim that, to pick a drastic example, the torturers and tortured have the same context even though they are damn close to each other within the same prison. And when one recalls the fact that the text of the Palestinian women does not name the alleged immediate neighbours' (Jewish women in Israel) repression, then one can only speak of the projection of someone who stands far on the outside: for the supposedly repressed world is so present that it is presupposed as self-evident. One would rather have to talk about the careful reserve of the women.

The Jewish women of Israel who would have been named as "close" are those who are in solidarity with the Palestinians and therefore demonstrate "in black" (the small but important group of the "women in black") on the streets of Tel Aviv and Jerusalem against the politics of occupation. They show clearly enough who is in solidarity with whom here.

What I find especially angering is the way in which that one deals with oppressed people in general and women in particular. It punches every theology of liberation right in the face to accuse those who are oppressed that they would perceive reality only through their own tears and thus undifferentiated and distorted—as if one could not expect anything else from women but one-sided emotional expressions.

It is part of the essence of Latin American base communities that they are not about liberalist indifference to various ways of life and perceptions but that the perspective of the victims, the poor and oppressed can claim a preferential option for competence of truth. Reality is to perceive from their perspective. The relationship to the biblical message is also shaped from their perspective. This is true for the "Catechism of the Peasants of Peru"[14] as well as for many other experiences in Latin American and African countries.

It is also part of the right of the base communities to identify with the poor and oppressed mentioned in the Bible and to define their own situation theologically from there. No one so far has told the peasants of Peru that they must

14 Cf. *Equipo Pastoral de Bambamarca*, Vamos Caminando. Machen wir uns auf den Weg!, Freiburg (Schweiz)/Münster 1983.

not identify themselves with the poor and disadvantaged and the oppressors and the rich with the other respective characters, with all the self-critical potential that the texts always also bring toward the poor regarding repentance to fellow-creatureliness in their situation. If the Gospel shall indeed touch really existing historical situations in a way that is important for life, then this can never happen without such identification.

It remains even more veiled why just for the Christian Palestinian women such an identification is interpreted as naïve and unhistorical, since the entire interpretive horizon of liberation theology is saved: namely by the fact that here *suffering* humans identify with suffering humans as they are mentioned in the Bible, see their situation through this meeting and gain hope. As a consequence of a real contextual theology between history and the biblical text, the disregard of the tears of the Palestinian women retroactively therefore also shows itself as a degradation of the weeping women in the Gospel.

The fear of arbitrariness in dealing with biblical texts can only be contained by refusing to allow perpetrators, i.e., exploiting rich people and oppressing powerful ones, to use biblical texts to legitimate their inhumanness. This would be a perverse dealing with the biblical God who in the best and decisive texts of the Bible strictly stands on the side of the lamenting and suffering ones and who calls the oppressors and the rich to repentance. Without having clarified the issues of power, there is no appropriate biblical hermeneutics, biblical interpretation. Within the contradictory contextuality between power and powerlessness, one also has to search for the decisive distinction between a national "theology" in a chauvinist context of expansive superiority on the one hand and the theology of the people in the context of liberation from oppression and misery on the other.

To prohibit the identification of the Palestinian women with corresponding biblical texts because in the texts in the New Testament chosen by the Palestinian women the women are Jewish is literalistic fundamentalist reading of the Bible. This interpretation would have to lead to the situation that on principle no non-Jews were allowed to identify with the persons in the Gospel. The Christian proclamation as a whole could hand in its resignation. And in a new breaking of images one would have to rip out the Way of the Cross in a church in Soweto, for example, because there Jesus' Way of the Cross is painted into the daily way of the cross of the Blacks.

Two further remarks: Some facts are only half reported and as quickly as lightening subordinated under the desired argumentation: If, for example, many Christian Palestinians are leaving the country, then the reason for that lies not in a majority Muslim society which is heated up in fundamentalist ways—anti-Christian and anti-Jewish—but primarily in the many obstacles for Arabs in the Occupied Territories (through all that makes up a military administration, from the refusal of passports to the restrictions of movement and the confiscation of land. One has to imagine the relative lawlessness that is shown by the fact that the military administration holds all the powers, legislative, executive and judicial). Add to this that a greater percentage of the Christian Arabs has achieved higher educational levels and thus has better chances to build a new life somewhere abroad. How much, by the way, some like to blow the anti-Muslim trumpet here certainly reveals a greater inability to differentiate within the Muslim world than their own accusation of the Christian Palestinian women in regard to theirs. Are we really forced to foster solidarity with the Jewish people on the back of racist discrimination of Islam?

Conclusion: For the sake of authentic liberation theologically oriented contextuality it might be wished for many of us to let the ideologically veiled view be illuminated and clarified by listening to and looking at the unveiled view through the tears of the victims. Regarding our German past and situation let it be noted: next to the negative discrimination of the Jewish community or world, which is not without problems, and especially for us Germans, it veils the view toward the non-Jewish victims in Palestine. The great Protestant theologian Helmut Gollwitzer said it thus: "Not-an-anti-Semite is not the one who thinks that he is not one, but the one who does not demand anything more from a Jewish state than form other states." At stake is the radicalisation of the memory of the Holocaust, especially for us Germans in the sense of a vehement struggle so that no victims are ignored or diminished. The former Chair of the Central Council of the Jews in Germany, Ignatz Bubis, fought not only against the discrimination of Jews in our country, but he also advocated for the rights of other groups who are threatened by growing right wing fascism, for example, the Sinti and Roma. Furthermore, one probably cannot project the Jewish victims (especially) of (German) history on the present Jewish population in Israel so that these are considered the same victims. Exactly that would be a diminishment of the Jewish victims in Germany.

Thus, at stake is a contextual theology that is done *with* those involved, not by lecturing them. When those who suffer open their mouths, one must not forbid them to speak. Rather, we have to learn to modify our views and systems from the perspective of their words. It is not our task to normalise the voice of the victims but to enter into a relationship with them and to ponder what it means if we as Germans in the context of our own history take seriously the suffering of the Palestinian women. But that is *our* task and not the responsibility of the Palestinian women. Therefore, it also is not the task of World Day of Prayer to smooth the voice of the victims to prevent exactly this controversy.

D. Towards a New Mission

I. Christian Mission in a Pluralistic World

According to the Pastoral Constitution of the Second Vatican Council "mission" can be understood as a certain dynamic within the pastoral self-realisation of the church. This dynamic shows itself towards the outside by a universalisation of the Christian and ecclesiastical pro-existence in the diaconal as well as the preaching area (and in their mutual connection). In view of the actual rather ambivalent processes of globalisation the mission of the churches has the growing responsibility to realise the belief in the universal grace of God by means of the global preaching of God's mercy and justice and of the corresponding diaconal deeds. By this mission will become the mainspring of the appropriate interrelations and intentions in the global Church. This mission towards the outside requires the radicalisation of the Christian and ecclesiastical existence inside the Church and its social manifestations, which means to enter, rooting in the grace of God, a dynamic which risks disadvantages and characterises the mission towards inside (for the sake of the universal mission towards outside) in the horizon of the theological term "martyrium". By this, mission becomes the basis of the dynamic of the "*semper maior*" in the pastoral identity of the Church in which something of the unending universality and unconditioned love of God is mirrored in the history and stories of humankind.

1. *The Example of a Missionary*

To state beforehand: It is my opinion that, in view of the present situation in society(ies) and the global challenges, the mission of the Church has become more necessary than ever. I start with a very concrete reflection on our topic and from there shall arrive step by step at the basic structures of Christian mission. The following example demonstrates at the same time how in future, e. g., in the new century and millennium, Christian mission should take place. During the last millennium, mission was so much seeking violent victory and blanket conquest of the world that, despite the incalculable good which it without doubt created, and which must not be denied, Christian mission was always tempted and often succumbed to forcing other people to total submission. The latter ranged from withdrawing their right to shape their own life to even taking their right to life away. Instead of imposing devotion to others on themselves, they acknowledged persons and people of different thought and religion as equals only if they integrated into their sphere and more or less gave up their own identity. The *prior* recognition of *all* people as "God's children" within the horizon of God's universal grace was a rarity displayed by certain persons and communities.

This example will also show clearly how one person manages the qualitative leap from the one strategy of spreading the Christian faith to another mode of imparting it, how she breaks through to it and becomes moved by it. This biography demonstrates what a qualitative leap awaits Christianity between the old epoch of the last millennium and the hopefully new epoch of this millennium. If Christianity will not break through to the new quality and thus to a radicalisation of its identity, then it has finally not understood the signs of time and history and will degenerate into one of those religious sects and organisations whose main aim is to recruit members, and to do this with all possible means to sustain its own organisation. Only a qualitative leap into that identity which, in the face of the cross, has been engraved by the one whose name it carries can save Christianity from degeneration to such a level of atrophy.

I tell the story of Father Rudolf Lunkenbein. We find this Silesian Father in 1970 in Merúri with the Bororo Indians in the Amazon area of Mato Grosso. He has been given the order to evangelise this tribe. Soon he realises: The whole tribe faces extinction. And this is not nature's doing but has been caused by people. In the background is the clash with the white landowners and settlers who penetrate deeper and deeper into the territory of the indigenous people and are close to distributing everything among themselves. Because the former have increasingly lost the basis of their life, the rainforest, they have given up. Since the mid-1960s they have stopped erecting new huts and have also stopped caring about their own language. The women drink the juice of a forest plant which inhibits conception. For six years no children have been born. The whole tribe has resigned itself to die. This is thesituation into which Father Lunkenbein enters as a missionary with the order to preach the gospel to these people.

But how can you bring the message of a living God to people whose right to life is begrudged from outside, who cannot be revived inwardly, who wish for and seek death? In this situation the Father quickly realises: One cannot talk about the message of life if chances for living are not created simultaneously. One cannot speak of God's redemption without talking about liberation from injustice and the borders of death. He thus writes: "First it is necessary to help these people to find the way back to life...to show them what they have in themselves, what inner strengths they neglect, what magnificent traditions they let go waste. I have supported them, I have defended their rights."[1]

Against this background one understands how happy Father Lunkenbein was about the first baptism, not only because children were re-born into God's grace but because they were born at all. Through Father Lunkenbein the Bororo Indians regained self-confidence, courage to face life and hope. Within this experience the gospel too could gain ground: the confidence in a God of life and God's son who comes with compassion and justice. This was what the father demonstrated. The confidence in life, which Father Lunkenbein conveyed to the indigenous people, became the basis of confidence in God.

On 15 July 1976, Father Lunkenbein and the local chief were shot dead by white settlers in the courtyard of the mission station. The settlers were angry about the revival of the tribe they believed finished and wanted revenge for the fact that, with the help of Rudolf Lunkenbein, a land survey in favour of the Bororo Indians had taken place. As a result, the settlers were forced to return the land which rightfully belonged to the Bororo Indians. Deeply mourning, they decorated the dead priest with their chief's ornaments. He had become one of them, and thus they grieved as if for one of their own. In the spirit of the Apostle Paul, Lunkenbein had become an Indian for the Indians (see 1 Cor 9:19–22). Thus, he became a martyr of the practice and theology of liberation which aims to connect God's justice with justice among people. He has not been the last martyr and he was not the first. But he is presented here to represent all of them. In particular, he also stands for the many catechists, men and particularly women in the Amazon region who are similarly courageous in encouraging people and who stand up for them.

Initially Father Lunkenbein wanted to become a missionary in the old sense of the word, namely to bring the faith to the "unbelievers". But then he entered into a situation which first demanded a totally different missionary testimony, namely to give up one's life in the fight for life and survival of these people. This connection developed its own dynamism. At some time he must have recognised the alternative: Do I get more involved or do I get out? He could have gotten out, the more so as there were confreres in his own congregation who preferred a certain neutrality and non-interference, who understood mission in the old restrained sense of spreading religious faith which does not very much enter into the conflicts of the world.

At some time Lunkenbein decided to stay on and to stand firm, not because he wanted to interfere but because, as a Christian and priest, he felt himself pulled into this clash about life and death. He did not seek martyrdom but got entangled in it in the manner described through the situation and the people. Finally, he did not decide against this claim. He stayed on; he went along with

1 H.-G. Röhrig, Lasst uns leben. Ermordet für die Rechte der Indianer, Bamberg 1978, 14.

the affected; he endured the situation with them and thus risked becoming a victim himself for the sake of the victims. In contrast to quite some of his predecessors in previous centuries, Lunkenbein did not threaten the life of the tribal people to make them convert, but he protected it and valued their lives so that, through such an encounter, they would be able to believe in a God who wants them to live and to survive. He stated: "In the commitment for life God's love and the Bororo Indians quest for life become visible."[2] Lunkenbein clearly recognised that mission is not marketing to gain members but active participation.

In Father Lunkenbein I see a model for that process in which spreading the Gospel and practising solidarity universalise and radicalise each other: universalisation in as far as the Gospel message which proclaims salvation in the form of human solidarity is granted, awarded and given to all people; radicalisation as this motif can pull one into a dynamism which "finally" risks also the own abandonment in history for this God's gift, something which can never be ordered but enabled in the context of a relationship with God which carries this abandonment whereby this relationship reaches in itself the quality of adoring devotion and devoted adoration. This devotion to God (as confidence in his power on life, justice and reconciliation in history, beyond history and beyond death) deepens the devotion in favour of people and vice versa. The acknowledgment and sheltering of plurality need solidarity.

I definitely do not want to represent the opinion that mission amounts to nothing more than solidarity. Instead its task is to speak through solidarity about the one who is the only saviour of the world and of all future, who will be perceived the more universally and radically as the witnesses lend a face to this God's gift through their own commitment. Thus, the mission goal is not alone social welfare work but the propagation of Christ through what he was in Jesus' history and what he will always be in history: an authentic connection between word and deed. Wherever we comprehend mission as this dynamism, it will be the "balance spring" in the "time-work" of the Church: meaning not only to exist but also to pro-exist in a universal and radical way and thus to almost reach the goal of its existence, namely to perceive itself not only as assembled but also sent and not to forget this missionary dynamism in the pastoral service.

---

2 See 29.

2. *Mission as the Universalisation of Christian and Church Pro-existence (the Outside Aspect)*

First, I am concentrating on the universal responsibility to express in the form of "be-ing" human for/with the people (pro-existence) the fact that God loves all people even before they have changed. Christianity can refer to its own long history of misinterpreting God's universality which has cost millions of people possibilities of living, freedom and finally life itself. Religion inhibits solidarity whenever it restricts God's love to one's own area and considers all those who don't belong to one's own faith as not worthy of solidarity. On the other hand, religion always accelerates solidarity if it does not resent God's love for all people and nevertheless experiences the own limited area as a learning field where turning the inwardly directed solidarity turns towards the outside.

Every religious chauvinism applies God's mercy only *to itself*, rendering itself universal in relation to others, thus completely losing sight of God's mercy for all her creatures. Universalistic and thus integralistic strategies form the sharpest contradiction to removing one's own borders against the background of the only existing universality, namely God himself. This though imposes a specific dynamism on the Christian existence, namely not to render oneself universal but to detect God's grace in the world and to help shape it. The problem "inward-outward" has never stopped being a problem. Sometimes even inside the churches people have been "graded" despite the common baptism. Thus, white Christians in South Africa knew how to legitimise their policy of Apartheid against black co-Christians with the help of relevant Bible texts, which they interpreted in a racial and chauvinistic manner. The letter of the Bible alone does not save people from a religiously entitled withdrawal of solidarity, only the spirit and the intention respectively with which the Bible is read, namely that dynamism expressed in the Bible itself towards a more merciful God and a more universal inter-human solidarity.[3] The Christian creed thus coincides with human rights.[4] This *per se* is missionary dynamism.

Everything thus depends on a "globalised" understanding of grace within the horizon of a radical theology of justification and a radical solidarity with all

---

3 As an example I refer here to that dynamism of *Entgrenzung (dissolution of boundaries)* which Paulus allows himself against the Jewish people who have not turned to the faith though he is otherwise quite careful with such *Entgrenzungen* of the mutual conditional relationship between faith and salvation: see Rom 9–11; see also O. Fuchs, Die Entgrenzung zum Fremden als Bedingung christlichen Glaubens und Handelns, in: ders. (Hg.), Die Fremden, Düsseldorf 1988, 240–301, 269–280. Zu den Kriterien der Bibelhermeneutik vgl. ders., Kriterien gegen den Missbrauch der Bibel, in: Jahrbuch für biblische Theologie Band 12 (1997) Biblische Hermeneutik, Neukirchen-Vluyn 1998, 243–274.

4 See H.-J. Sander, Macht in der Ohnmacht. Eine Theologie der Menschenrechte, Freiburg i. Br. 1999.

people. This unconditional grace gives strength for unconditional solidarity. In our world-historical context it is absolutely necessary to promote this dynamism as a globalisation of solidarity. For only within it does God's grace relate to all people in such a way that solidarity with all people is possible for those who believe in this God. In Vatican II the Catholic Church made first steps in this direction[5] by qualifying itself regarding God and the truth in the world, and so putting itself in constructive relations regarding God and the truth outside itself. The theological basis is the picture of a factual universal presence of salvation in the world, actually not present all over but possible all over, in an ever different brokenness during the total history of people and cultures and in their ever own worlds of faith. But those too who do not say the truth, and those who are not good stay in God's unconditional love. Their right to life has to be secured in the same way as that of the others. They in particular will not fall out of God's salvation. Even if one's misery is the result of one's guilt, the divine right to help and salvation is not forfeited. This is true from the very beginning: Cain is marked not to get killed.

The neo-liberalistic and capitalistic globalisation which pushed already more than one billion people below the poverty line and largely into absolute misery, and which has not only sharpened the gulf between North and South but also crosswise between the poorest and the richest,[6] has to be countered by all powers of good will, namely globalisation of a solidarity which embraces all people and all nations.

It will have to be a solidarity which is not based on egotism but includes also the renunciation of own advantages. This global solidarity has to be implemented in time before wars of thirst and hunger force rich countries to do that, or respectively what will be more probable, before states with military and economic strength fall into the terrible temptation to close their borders

---

5 But also already previously as in the judgement on a rigorous interpretation of the statement by Cyprian: "Extra ecclesiam nulla salus" by Pius XII. in 1947 (DH 3866–3873).

6 I do not claim to be able to analyse the globalisation processes in detail but restrict myself to say that they are in any way ambivalent, not only for the countries of the Southern hemisphere but increasingly also for the classical countries of the so-called First World. For, globalisation speeds up the process of social change too, namely the fact that cutbacks in the social security systems are unavoidable because financing them overtaxes public finances for a long time. The growing international competition puts pressure on the social market economy with its networks and its endeavour to safeguard as many incomes as possible. There should be more preparedness to accept risks but one should first clarify who will carry the risks in failure. Whoever is not able to cope with private means will here as well as worldwide quickly fall below the poverty line, particularly in the countries with a majority of poor people. For the discussion of globalisation in the social context see: A. Wenig (Hg.), Globalisierung und die Zukunft der sozialen Marktwirtschaft, Berlin 2000; die katastrophalen Auswirkungen der wirtschaftspolitischen Globalisierungsprozesse in Lateinamerika bringt J. Comblin auf den Punkt: Lateinamerika in der Globalisierung (Vortragsmanuskript Münster 2000).

exposing millions and most likely billions of people to death from thirst and hunger. Whoever does not want to share now will have to kill later on![7] Then, as Carl Amery put it, the selection ramp of Auschwitz would become the anticipation of a global selection ramp in the twenty-first century.[8]

In order to motivate people towards this and to open people's view one needs relevant fields where solidarity is experienced within the more comprehensible area of one's own social forms and societal life. What is not learnt there cannot be realised for the outside and the future. But the opposite is also valid. Where people in missionary institutions, in missionary congregations, third-world groups and partnerships care for the poor and distressed in the countries of the Southern hemisphere, they learn to consider also more critically their own social areas and to meet the local victims of the situation with greater solidarity. For the sake of the universal option for the poor and oppressed, a mutual global networking of solidarity[9] is needed between inside and outside, between near and far. Structurally this should be realised in stronger networking between relevant institutions and initiatives,[10] because even in different contexts, the problems are similar. There is a kind of structural analogy between the places of crisis. They should therefore communicate their problems and hopes. This mirrors the future of our Christian and at the same time interreligiously constructive identity.

3. *Mission as Radicalisation of Christian and Church Existence (the Inside Aspect)*

Though helping and deliberating encounters with people who are poor and in distress are never a one-way street, but are encounters in which those who help and practice solidarity but also those who preach God's freedom and grace

7 See O. Fuchs, Die „Zukunft des Bürgerschaftlichen Engagements". Einige Anmerkungen zum Bericht der Enquete-Kommission des Deutschen Bundestags, in: Orientierung 66 (2002) 22, 244–248.

8 Cf. Carl Amery, Hitler als Vorläufer, Auschwitz – der Beginn des 21. Jahrhunderts, Darmstadt und Neuwied 1998.

9 Regarding this "new Catholicity" between globality and locality see R. J. Schreiter, Die neue Katholizität. Globalisierung und die Theologie, Frankfurt 1997.

10 Regarding the relationship between Christian faith, networking in parity and solidarity with those far away see: P. M. Zulehner u. a., Solidarität. Option für die Modernisierungsverlierer, Innsbruck/Wien 1996, 215ff. This paper proves in examples that fundamentalistic-exclusive concepts of faith and social forms (e. g. those which regionalise God's grace to the own area) are not able to develop solidarity with those far away. On the other hand: Religiosity which breathes the freedom of God's universal grace forms the humus for that solidarity to those near *and* far which is so decisive for our society, for the survival of democracy and the whole globe.

are enriched in their own life, they generally experience that such encounters are not free but cost courage, the courage to stand up and risk facing one's own discrimination. His revelation and solidarity with people cost God the earthly life and the cross of his own son.

3.1 Mission in "Martyrdom" (*Martyrium*)

Whoever transmits God's grace and thus God's justice to the people in word and deed knows that they will never fall out of this grace but also knows that this handing over of God's and the people's justice and charity may cost them much in ungraceful and graceless contexts. It is an integral part of the experience of God's grace that it still carries on even if human witnessing of God's grace approaches powerlessness and thus long- and short-term martyrdom, be it the "*martyrium fidei*" or the "*martyrium caritatis*". Here, the elementary necessity to spell out social- and faith-pastoral together presents itself once more so that the former does not end in resignation or violence,[11] because, in the face of a threatening lack of meaning and success, faith preaches that it is never in vain to work toward in justice and mercy even if it does not seem to make sense. The Gospel contains the eschatological message that only mercy and justice are the realities which fulfil God's Kingdom on earth and which will find eternal realisation in God's Kingdom. The option for the poor is not a programme of success but provokes additional experiences of powerlessness and failure in particular for those who take it seriously. To be able to believe that God (in the meaning of Romans 8:26) helps carry this powerlessness and "co-sighs", that he, in the co-suffering Christ, does not exclude himself, is that consolation of the Christian message which strengthens action and perseverance.

Since the beginning of Christendom something like the epistemological axiom that the identity of Christian and Church existence can be decisively learnt from the male and female martyrs of the Church has existed. They should not be forgotten. The Church Fathers of the first centuries knew this and saw this remembrance as the heart (*or core*) of the Church. To believe that they reveal forces for the shaping of one's own life was not in the least the consequence of the structure analogue remembrance of Jesus Christ, of his self-abandoning in life and death, the belief in this fore-martyr in the deepest sense of the word. Thus, God allows himself to be drawn into the history of humankind and willingly becomes a victim for the sake of the victims. A Church that forgets its martyrs forgets itself because it ultimately also forgets its roots in *the* martyr, Jesus Christ.

[11] See O. Fuchs, Für eine neue Einheit von Sozial- und Glaubenspastoral!, in: K. Gabriel u. a. (Hg.), Zukunftsfähigkeit der Theologie, Paderborn 1999, 93–112, 102ff.

Particularly in his texts at the turning of the millennium, John Paul II calls on the Church and the local churches not to abandon the remembrance of the global and local martyrs but to deepen and shape this memory, not only in regard to the first and last centuries but also mainly the ending century. In his apostolic letter at the occasion of the turning of the millennium and the Holy Year, he recalls programmatically that the Church originated out of the blood of the martyrs when he writes: "This is a testimonial which must not be forgotten."[12] Naturally, this sentence is also valid for the martyrs of all of history as well as the present. In this Church tradition an attitude shows through which has always been alive: The length of life is not the last value in life; the quantity of life is not the highest goal. In "*Incarnationis Mysterium*" (1998) the Pope names the key meaning of the relationship between the Church and recollection of such overexertion in martyrdom: "The faithful who has seriously considered his Christian calling for which martyrdom is a possibility already announced in the revelation cannot exclude this perspective from the horizon of his life."[13]

In this connection John Paul II refers to a newly detected "ecumenism of saints" in all Christian churches.[14] If people risk something, much, sometimes even everything, in order for others to experience mercy and justice or a redeeming transcendental relationship respectively, which lifts them up and does not destroy them, then this is a gift of God's grace to the faithful so that they may find in it encouragement and strength to enter into this dynamism of giving oneself, which is, depending on the situation, connected with the option for the poor and/or for the other, the discriminated and the confession for Christ. In this text the Pope makes one feel something which is elementary for the future of the churches: Their mission for the world will never again happen in the form of blanket conquests (be they of a military or a propagandistic manner), never again with any form of violence and freedom-destroying force. The faithful will have to learn (and this would be the relevant mission "towards

---

12 Johannes Paul II., Tertio Millennio Adveniente Nr. 37. One meets this consideration quite frequently in the Pope's texts. It would certainly be important to more closly analyse the Pope's theology of martyrdom, particularly in its ecclesiological and ecumenical valence. Martyrs seal an ecumen which happens on the base of this active self-devotion not independent from the background of the respective faith but in such a way that the decisive basis is not the faith consensus but this radical self-abandon. It seems that the Pope counts all persons who self-sacrificed for the sake of people to that circle of the ecumenical Christianity: See Johannes Paul II., "Incarnationis Mysterium" (Verlautbarungen des Apostolischen Stuhls 136), Bonn 1998, 17ff. (Nr. 13).

13 Johannes Paul II. „Incarnationis Mysterium" 18.

14 Against this background it becomes clear that martyrs are an "elite" of the Church, which is accessible to all people, to priests and lay people, the Lutheran and Catholic Christians, etc., to present a way that gives possibilities of identification to others. See: E. Kock, Beter, Täter, Zeuge – Nikolaus Groß, Paderborn 2001; J. Aretz (Hg.), Nikolaus Groß. Briefe aus dem Gefängnis, Mainz [3]1998.

the inside") to put up non-violent resistance in the representation of Christian options and thus themselves endure violence and do not to reply with destructive counter-violence. From this perspective, and if Christians don't want to give up God's mercy in a merciless world but preach and realise it, the coming century will mean following the cross for them: Jesus has not paid back in his own coin "the mendacious judgement and the violent attack but turned the intensified evil and gave it back as doubled love".[15] One should not fool oneself and others: Every step towards a solidarity which extends beyond the present borders and towards further poor and discriminated ones brings massive structural and individual counter-forces into the arena. The declaration of a limitless year of God's mercy cannot take place without meeting these borders *and* penetrate through them. It is then a special mercy of God in history if people accept risks for this.

There are situations and moments during which it is more important to be faithful to oneself, to others and to God than to survive. On account of the self-commitment to solidarity, there was and always is the self-commitment for the sake of this faith. Worldwide mission history is, particularly also in Asia, a history of martyrs in *favorem fidei* and only secondarily in *favorem caritatis*. Many have killed missionary men and women not because they did not show enough solidarity but because they came with another faith which was not understood or which was suspected to mean danger. Only at first sight does there seem to be less claim for this martyrdom out of faithfulness to Christ in a world with a plurality of religions. It remains nevertheless a real possibility within the context of fundamentalist and theocratic forms of religions, which are more likely to increase than to decrease in numbers.[16] In the so-called post-modern societies too, lack of understanding and possibly also disadvantage are growing for those who, in the face of people with different views and different beliefs, stand up in an un-egalitarian manner for the claim that their own faith is truth. A hard battle is necessary to counter the religious departures in society towards trivialisation and banality, the super-quick fulfilment and thus obstruction of transcendental yearning.[17] Finally, it is the relationship with Christ itself which breaks through any effort to remove plausibility from martyrdom even if it is well meant and justified by charity. At any time and even today

15 R. Schwager, Jesus im Heilsdrama. Entwurf einer biblischen Erlösungslehre, Innsbruck 1990, 146.

16 As the experiences of the "Shelter now" Organisation in previous Taliban Afghanistan have shown.

17 I am thinking mainly of the martyrdom of the Christian monks in Algeria (see O. Fuchs, Von der Empathie zur Solidarität, in: F. Weber, u. a. (Hg.), Im Glauben Mensch werden, Münster 2000, 75–83). In a Muslim environment they lived a Christian existence of prayer and solidarity in their convent without any attempts of "mission" in the old sense of the word but just so with a high degree of missionary strength regarding genuine Christian existence in this country.

there are reasons to prevent such radical overexertion with soothing arguments.[18] The charitable removal of plausibility from martyrdom is not new,[19] but is met already in the story told by Mark immediately prior to Jesus' passion: Jesus is sitting at the table in Simon's house. A woman enters with costly oil in a precious alabaster vessel, breaks the vessel and pours the oil over Jesus' head. Some of his disciples are displeased and find an argument to rationalise their indignation by quoting Jesus' charitable teaching. What a luxury: One could have given the money which was spent for these precious objects to the poor. But Jesus, who always supports the poor, protects the woman and states that she has done a good deed and justifies it thus: "The poor are always with you, and you can always do good to them as often as you want but you do not have me always." In this moment he stands up in favour of the wasteful instead of the charitable use because we have here a precious moment of a deep encounter and commitment which will not return and should not be gambled away. Such moments of giving oneself away without doing any calculations whatsoever are not at the expense of the poor, do not want to shame them, but are the experience of that depth of life in which people learn that sensibility and receive that strength which render them unconditionally capable to exert themselves for others.

In this story Jesus hits the context if he states shockingly and bluntly: "She has anointed my body in advance for the funeral" (see Mark 14:3–9). Wastefulness and self-abandonment to the extreme meet here symbolically and realistically in one single act. The cross demonstrates both: the "wasteful" mercy of God for our life in a wasteful self-abandonment in death. The self-abandonment in death counts for life. For Jesus the cross was the sealing of his integrity, namely his agreement in life and death with his teaching. Thus, he remains faithful to himself, to the people and to God in the very face of death, and he does not want to hurt this faithfulness through a longer life.

Hopefully, all this is not so dramatic in our present situation in Western Europe, at least not usually. But, as the term "*martyrium*" indicates, between the meaning of being witness up to real martyrdom, for the whole dynamism from the smallest testimonial to dramatic martyrdom, the following applies: Everything, also martyrdom, prepares itself in "its small coin" or, to use a biblical picture, in a small mustard seed which can reach full maturity very quickly in an emergency. This may happen in the readiness to confess to a merciful and just God; in the readiness for action in the context of assistance to and solidarity with the troubled nearby and far away; and in particular in the readiness to

---

18 See H. C. Zander, Warum ich Jesus nicht leiden kann, Reinbek 1992, 103–106.

19 Incidentally as little as the removal of pastoral plausibility of missionary dynamism; see O. Fuchs, Neue Wege einer eschatologischen Pastoral, in: Theologische Quartalschrift 179 (1999) 4, 282ff. It cannot be discussed in detail here in how far the dynamism of mission and that of eschatology belong together.

risk not abandoning such actions if one's own disadvantages and discriminations have to be accepted. Everyone among us knows relevant challenges in our own lives and where one can go *one step further* than up till now: deputising for many who do not manage to have this readiness to act or who cannot do so respectively out of consideration for others.

In their commitment to the lives of others, Christians, women and men in many countries go so far that this "overstepping of borders" costs them their lives. Faith without remembering them is like preaching resurrection without the cross. The female and male martyrs are an example that the ultimate consequence of Christian life can be to receive from God and to be dispossessed by people.[20] Whoever stands for God's de-limiting justice for the sake of those who are excluded must be prepared to be restricted and excluded in his or her own life chances.

3.2 Mission in Unfanatical Devotion

In his impressive description of a visit to Albert Schweitzer in 1932, Stefan Zweig precisely hit the quintessence of his thinking and acting when he writes: "For his highest action, for his hospital which he founded and established alone and without any government assistance in the tropical forest of Africa, purely as a humanitarian sacrifice, in order to atone for an European debt, for this unique and exemplary self-surrender everybody who knows about the human nature, loves and admires him, all those whose idealism appear great only when it surpasses the spoken and written word, and becomes deed through self-sacrifice."[21] Albert Schweitzer goes to Africa because the poorest of the poor and the most abandoned of the abandoned are to be found there. This alone is said to be lunacy by his friends and relatives. Why doesn't he stay in Europe where there is also a lot of misery? Stefan Zweig mentions another of Schweitzer's reasons, which he calls a "mystical thought": "And then—mystical thought—this one human being will in his own person atone this outrageous, unspeakable injustice which we Europeans who claim to be the cultured white race have committed to this black continent since centuries ... Thus, this one religious person wants to pay a minimal part of this immense debt through committing himself and founding a mission hospital in the tropical forest—finally somebody who does not go to the tropics for the sake of his own profit, his curiosity but solely to render humanitarian assistance to the most unhappy

20 Regarding the relationships between grace respectively life and martyrdom see L. Weckel, Um des Lebens willen. Zu einer Theologie des Martyriums aus befreiungstheologischer Sicht, München 1998.

21 S. Zweig, Unvergessliches Erlebnis, in: Ders., u. a. (Hg.), Albert Schweitzer. Genie der Menschlichkeit, Frankfurt a. M. 1961,9–19, 11.

under the unhappy ones."[22] To do this, he sits in lecture rooms in Paris together with young students and studies medicine under circumstances which are anything but easy, he, who had become professor of theology at the age of 30, because he wishes to be enabled to help where he will be from 1930 onwards: in the hospital on the Ogowe River in Lambarene.

The motives of overexertion and atonement interrupt the continuity of his previous life, and it is this very interruption whose plausibility can be hardly conveyed to his friends and relatives. Albert Schweitzer reveals in his own existence the dynamism of subjective self-sacrifice, also against prevailing plausibility and comprehension, even if it is perceived as lunacy (as formulated by Stefan Zweig). Without difficulties one can draw an analogy between what Schweitzer thinks, states and does in this context and the "foolishness of the cross"; one has to do so with care, but not as if it would not be fitting to look for and find this *Theologumenon* in human existence.

Thus, from the perspective of normal rationalisation each act of extreme testimony is perceived as not at all understandable and as utterly unnecessary. However, the affected know: This is needed in this very moment although they are often not able to rationally catch up with this need. Dietrich Bonhoeffer experiences this in 1939 in New York. Without being able to explain to his friends and even to himself but out of an existential evidence which is finally unfathomable but prepared through the depth of his faith, he feels compelled to leave the USA and to return back to Germany[23], although previous plans had actually been quite different. After having refused to stay on in New York, Dietrich Bonhoeffer writes on 20 July 1939: "For me this has probably more meaning at the moment than what I am able to see clearly. God alone knows. It is strange, in all my decisions I am not really clear about the motives. Is this a sign of lack of clarity, inner untruthfulness or is it a sign of the fact that we are led beyond our knowledge or is it both? In the end one is more likely to act from a level which remains hidden...At the end of the day I can only pray that God judges this day and all decisions mercifully. It is now in his hand."[24]

God's in history experienced "transcendence" means an unconditional challenge which in the end can be caught through neither argument nor through any calculation because one can also find good ethical arguments, justifiable in Christian faith, for remaining in New York. Thus, an existential decision is finally needed which has talked through all arguments and which does not think little of the rational level—but which it finally penetrates because it is no longer able to justify itself but puts its appreciation of the truth

---

22 Zweig, Erlebnis 12–13.

23 In his Christology Bonhoeffer finds that Christ's presence in those who suffer which renders compassion the decisive sense organ of Christian activity; see W. Kallen, In der Gewissheit seiner Gegenwart. Dietrich Bonhoeffer und die Spur des vermissten Gottes, Mainz 1997, 158–164.

24 D. Bonhoeffer, Gesammelte Schriften I, München 1958, 303–304.

with confidence into God's hand. Dietrich Bonhoeffer exposes himself to that happening and, without thinking that he could model his life self-determinedly, subordinates it under his own availability.

Something peculiar, totally antifundamentalist, presents itself here: namely the strict connection between absolute self-devotion and non-claimed absolute truth regarding this decision which totally affects the own self. Bonhoeffer hopes that his decision is the right one, but does not know if it is, not regarding his mental capacity or his relationship with God. He puts the validity of the truth of his ultimate decision in God's hand. Within such a relationship with God, which leaves it to God to judge the validity of one's own decision even if this decision is ultimate for one's own existence, prevents that fatalism and fanaticism, which often appear in the very radical self-abandonment as temptation, namely to claim for oneself and for others God's ultimate truth in the quality of the finality of a decision which affects one's own existence.

Bonhoeffer makes it very clear: In no decision, even one of great consequence regarding his own Christian identity, does he claim God's absolute truth. Otherwise, even in this moment, the great temptation would lie in waiting to make God an idol through one's own divinisation based on the claim of a radical self-devotion. In Jesus' cry on the cross (see Mk 15:34), asking why God has abandoned him, this elementary dialectic is expressed: In the stress between the final self-abandonment into certain death and the uncertainty of how God actually sees it: Truth is always an eschatological reality. This dialectic is not solvable up until death although it can be bridged again and again in hope and prayer. The inter-human need cannot be projected in a linear manner in respect to the divine truth, even if utmost solidarity approximates God's subjective truth, which appeared in Jesus Christ. Anyway, the latter may be intensely believed and hoped for.

4. *Result and Outlook*

Based on these reflections one can develop something like a critical hermeneutic of Christian martyrdom, in particular within the present actual context in which the term martyrdom is publicly mainly used in connection with suicidal terrorists. Not in the least from that latter aspect, a new also theological debate about Christian martyrdom is needed. The criteria are clear. The devotion must not take place against people but only for them, and in principle for all of them, for justice towards them, and for their redemption from poverty and suppression. It must not become dissociated from these criteria of the Gospel; longing for death alone is not martyrdom, which can always only happen as a consequence of a life and an identity measured against the life of Jesus of Nazareth who did not sacrifice others but himself.

Such a spirituality is not the over-challenging consequence of an "ultra-ego-legality"; it can never be made a duty or demand but grows out of a lively relationship between people and the love of God, and is thus expression of gratuity, of grace. It is a grace in which people know themselves recognised in their existence and their value by God, steadfastly, faithfully and for all times. Also beyond death.

We have not yet realised the dark "sign of the time" concerning the fundamentalist Muslim suicide martyrs: For we Christians have not yet reached the same level of self-abandon for the sake of others' lives they reached in their devotion against the lives of others. What Christians consider absolute in their own existence (because it is the will of the Absolute, God, to be at the side of the oppressed), they accept as the radicalism of their testimonial. After centuries of Church mission during which Christianity's claim to absoluteness often went against the others and also negatively affected them and their lives a million-fold, from now on Christian have to put this claim on themselves. There is no other form of mission for spreading the gospel: Christianity exerts itself for the sake of human dignity, the dignity of all people, and strives to do this in a radically unbeatable manner in order to so present that the own truth is unbeatable.

Christian martyrdom must not be tempted to claim divinity for itself as if this unconditional self-abandon would entitle one to unconditional access to God's will. Even in martyrdom the human being remains what she is, needing redemption and being sinful.

Through the testifying of a humankind exceeding transcendence of God, being ready for utmost martyrdom (regarding their previous continuities and rationalities) the "diaconia" for the poor and the option for the others won't be impaired but radicalised to the depth of its secret, namely God himself, and here radicalised to the depth of self-abandon.

The acceptance of their perspective (of the distressed) becomes a "*being* perspective "as those engaged become themselves distressed and victims, acknowledging the plurality of life in such a substantial way". Such an "ethic" is not the over-challenging consequence of an "ultra-ego legality"; it can never be made a duty but grows out of a lively relationship between people and God and the dynamism of the "semper major" (always more and greater) set by God for her people, and is thus an expression of gratuity, of grace. It is a grace in which people know themselves recognised in their existence and their value by God, steadfastly, faithfully and for all times. Also beyond death. The fear of dying is thus not taken away but may be made transcendent in the hope to be given a life beyond.

If Fr. Lunkenbein engages for the Indians, then this service may end in the absolute, namely the total loss of life, but also in meeting absolute life out of Christian hope. What he considers absolute in his own existence (because it is the will of the Absolute, God, to be at the side of the poor), he sees as the radicalism of his testimonial. After centuries of Church mission during which Christianity's claim to absoluteness often went against the others and also negatively affected them and their lives a million-fold, Fr. Lunkenbein puts this claim on himself. There is no other form of mission for spreading the Gospel. From now on at the latest, nobody can be canonized who spreads the faith by force and at the expense of others respectively. Christianity has grown out of religious children's shoes and fundamentalist puberty during which faith was spread in the form of an ideological philosophy of life which aimed at blanket coverage and conquest: into the freedom and strength of a faith in God which does not claim any other plausibility for itself, and which does not look for any other effect but that of a universal respect for people and a radical service of God.[25]

The many witnesses who through the centuries and particularly during the last century combined in their existence the *Martyrium fidei* with the *Martyrium caritatis*, and thus represented in their own life the content of this faith in God, reveal in their last consequence the imitation of the life and the cross of Jesus. In his succession Christians may dare to proclaim that Christ co-carries and co-endures the fate of this world not only for the Christians but also for all who suffer. They then present basically, and without craving integration, the annunciation of the universal compassionate presence of Christ in the whole history of humankind.[26] Thus, one will be able to at least accept the existentially radical authenticity of what they claim universally. Out of such an existence, Christians may also dare to expose in other cultures and religions all that to criticism that is damaging people' lives, the criticism of every religious attitude which sharpens the un-solidarity with others.

Through such an over-exertion of Christian and Church mission against the background of the faith in our being equipped with God's gift of unending grace in this life and beyond, Christianity brings into the future its own, particular contribution to the debate about the potential of religions to humanise or de-humanise a contribution which will be the more credible as it can be "studied" in the Christian and Church existences themselves. Thus, Christianity somehow takes seriously the polemic request from the Berlin philosopher, Herbert Schnädelbach,[27] to step down from history's stage and to dissolve itself. This means in our perspective to step down from history in a very particu-

[25] These radicalisation and universalisation can show itself mainly in the dynamism of reconciliation, namely as self-devotion in the direct encounters between previous victims and actors for whom it is infinitely difficult to ask forgiveness and to give it respectively, but who nevertheless go, and, in the common celebration of the Eucharist in the community meet God's infinite reconciliation and justice and in it meet themselves (as in the Christian reconciliation work in South Africa).

[26] See O. Fuchs, Kontextuelle Christologie im Horizont unbedingter Solidarität, in: M. Görg/W. Langer (Hg.), Als Gott weinte, Regensburg 1997, 162–202.

[27] See H. Schnädelbach, Der Fluch des Christentums, in: Die Zeit 20 (11. Mai 2000) 41–42.

lar form[28], namely the hitherto used form of "blanket coverage" spread of faith, with the simultaneous risk of hurting people's dignity, and to replace it by a new way of being which is much nearer to the core of Christianity's identity. This means that the old way of being is replaced by one in which Christianity exerts itself for the sake of human dignity, the dignity of all people, and strives to do this in a radically unbeatable manner in order to so present that their own truth is unbeatable only in this way. Plurality is an ambivalent word, if there is not a power which shelters those who are left into the lurch in their "plurality", caused by the fact that they do not live in a reciprocal way like the others, who have all resources to enjoy their plurality.

28 See in this context the feministic perspective K. Heidemanns, Schritte auf dem Weg zu einer feministischen Missiology, in: H. Waltz u. a. (Hg.), Als hätten sie uns neu erfunden. Beobachtungen zu Fremdheit und Geschlecht, Luzern 2003, 81–97.

II. The Role of Religion in the European Constitution

1. *The Problem*

The question to be explored in what follows is this: how is religion relevant not only to people's "private" beliefs, but also to the social and political arrangements people create for themselves? At the beginning of the latter half of the nineteenth century, among sociologists and social philosophers as well as the wider populace, the view had gained hold that as the secularisation of the various spheres of life and work progressed, the relevance of religion was going to be restricted to the private sphere of the individual: particularly to what is called "coping with contingencies"—the personal spiritual and psychological coming-to-terms with the experiences of disappointment, failure, suffering and death that we encounter in the course of our lives. But this concept does not accord any significance to religion as such in the independently operating areas of economics and politics. However, this version of the secularisation thesis has long since been abandoned: *on the one hand* because of evidence of intense and widespread religious re-awakenings in European societies; *on the other* because the fact must not be overlooked that people's political and economic actions are always linked to their religious contexts and convictions, even if, in such cases, they no longer become explicit in religious language games.

But *the most important point* is that most religions, according to their self-understanding, are not concerned with reducing their remit to coping with contingencies. Their vision always includes the world and society as a whole, and their own traditions include explicit references to the economic and political order. This is true for the prophetic tradition of Christianity and Judaism as well as corresponding traditions in Islam. At the very most it is esoteric religiosities, and esoteric elements of the religions, that may be limited to the purely personal sphere, but here too close scrutiny is required.

2. *The Preamble: Memory and Re-shaping*

The discourse about the preamble of the European Constitution featured this very problem: how to address these issues, undeniably real as they are, and what the shape of any future arrangement should be. At the same time the question arises of how to integrate memory—that of the history and heritage of the European countries—on the one hand, and normative ideas for their future, on the other.

Such is the function of a preamble: to take account of the current situation as the product of an evolutionary process and to extend that process into shaping a vision of the future. A preamble is "a foreword or introduction that precedes the actual text. Preambles are found especially in foundational texts such as constitutions or international treaties...In the preamble, the normgiver explains the reasons guiding the composition of the ensuing legal text and the purpose of the regulations that follow...The preamble...does not give the rules but the reasons."[1] The preamble serves to integrate and anchor the ensuing legal arrangements within a heritage context and an overarching value framework, which makes them more easily accessible and intelligible. What is said in the preamble delineates the contextual framework within which what follows gains validity insofar as the regulations themselves translate those premises into legal factuality—such, at least, is the underlying principle. Now, the respective frameworks of remembrance and justification which those responsible for making the law seek to enter into and ground themselves in are the results of conscious decisions. Historical facts on their own do not suffice: the preamble articulates one's *relationship* with the facts of one's own history and present. This concerns specific attitudes towards human and social reality: for instance, an attitude of social responsibility, an attitude of religious humility, or one of *advocatio dei*, the prayer-like appeal to God himself.

Thus, the preamble of the German constitution acknowledges a religiously grounded relationship of responsibility: "Conscious of their responsibility before God and man...the German people...have adopted this Basic Law." The Irish constitution couples the appeal to God with human humility: "In the Name of the Most Holy Trinity, from Whom is all authority and to Whom, as our final end, all actions of both both humans and states must be referred to, We, the people of Éire, humbly acknowledging all our obligations to our Divine Lord, Jesus Christ, Who sustained our fathers through centuries of trial..." The Greek preamble adopts a similar formulation, and so does that of Poland: "We, the Polish Nation...both those who believe in God as the source of truth, justice, good and beauty, as well as those not sharing such faith but respecting those universal values as arising from other sources...beholden to our ancestors for their labours, their struggle for independence achieved at great sacrifice, for our culture rooted in the Christian heritage of the Nation and in universal human values..."[2]

---

1 Matthias Triebel, Gott in der Diskussion um eine Europäische Verfassung, in: Theologische Beiträge 36 (2005) 254–266, 255.

2 Cf. Triebel, Gott 255–256.

In France the situation is different: there, the separation of state and Church has been in place since 1905—by law. While freedom of worship is granted, there are no longer any recognised religious communities. Religion is a wholly private matter. In practice, however, the situation is often different: religious communities may assume a special status in French jurisdiction, especially where the Church's charitable institutions are concerned. And while religious education as a subject is not part of the state curriculum, it is offered by private faith schools, 90% of which are funded by the Catholic church, with the state refunding the bulk of the costs. A similar situation exists in Portugal and the Netherlands.

All in all, three models of the relationship between the state and the churches can be identified: first, there is that of the *established* or *state church* (in place in almost one third of European Union countries, for example, Great Britain, Greece, Finland, Denmark, Ireland). The second model is that of a strict *separation of church and state* (at least in theory), and finally, that of a *legally regulated cooperation* between state and church (as in Germany, but also in Italy, Luxemburg, Austria and Belgium, where the churches and other religious communities cooperate with the state and society in certain areas, particularly in the areas of charity, education and pastoral care. In this way they have obtained a special status; in Germany they take the form of "statutory corporations").

3. *Taking Account of the Critique of Religion*

These various ideas and arrangements from individual countries provide the background to the discussion about the preamble of the European Constitution.[3] The issue featured already in the preparations concerning the church-state relationship in the 1997 Amsterdam Treaty. This was the outcome at the time: "The European Union respects and does not prejudice the status under national law of churches and religious associations or communities in the Member States. The European Union equally respects the status of philosophical and non-confessional organisations." Unsurprisingly, all EU member states were able to agree on this text, as it does not interfere with the various models of the relationship between the state and the religions. The text constitutes, as it were, the lowest common denominator of this question.[4]

In this debate, the two main Christian churches in Germany, along with politicians from nearly all parties, have advocated an explicit reference to the

[3] Cf. on this Felix Bernard, Wie steht es um Gott und die Kirchen in der Europäischen Union?, in: Pastoraltheologische Informationen 23 (2003) 2, 13–26, 14ff.

[4] Cf. Bernard, Gott und die Kirchen 20: This formulation can be found in an explanatory note on the final proceedings of the Amsterdam Treaty.

European countries' shared religious roots in Christianity. In making this proposal within the objectives of a preamble, there is a decision in favour of a specific historical memory and a particular future-oriented re-formulation of this memory and the responsibilities it holds; this is what gives legitimacy to all future legal regulations.[5]

The proposal is this: "Conscious of humanity's responsibility before God, and conscious too of other sources of human responsibility, the peoples of Europe are determined to work for a peaceful future. Taking into account its intellectual, religious and moral heritage, the Union is founded on the indivisible, universal values of human dignity, freedom, equality and solidarity."[6]

But France in particular has objected to the reference to God in the preamble, so that in the end a compromise was settled on: "Conscious of its spiritual and moral heritage, the Union is founded on the indivisible, universal values of human dignity, freedom, equality and solidarity ..."[7]

It has to be remembered that, while in languages other than German the word "spiritual" is included, in the German version this is translated as "geistig-religiös" [*intellectual-religious*] because the word "spirituality" could be misunderstood in German.[8] Thus, there is no direct religious reference in non-German versions. However, in light of the text as a whole, the term "spiritual" includes clear religious elements, as the preamble to Part II of the constitution shows in its final 2004 version:

"Drawing inspiration from the cultural, religious and humanist inheritance of Europe, from which have developed the universal values of the inviolable and inalienable rights of the human person, freedom, democracy, equality ..."[9]

Thus, while the preamble to the charter of basic rights talks of an *intellectual-religious* (in fact, spiritual) inheritance, now the religious elements of the term "spiritual" are clearly brought out: The English and French texts openly use the word "religious" as well.

In appealing to a religious inheritance in the context of this value orientation, it is evident that this religious inheritance is remembered with a very specific validation: namely in so far as it has endorsed, supports now and will promote in the future the inviolable and inalienable rights of the human person, freedom, democracy, equality and the rule of law. The memory invoked in

---

5 On these elements of a preamble, see Gerhard Luf, Richard Potz, Brigitte Schinkele, Gott in der Verfassung? Zur Frage der Erwähnung der religiösen Dimension in der Präambel des Vertrages über eine Verfassung für Europa, in: Österreichisches Archiv für Recht und Religion 49 (2002) 1, 353–360, 356.

6 Quoted in Bernard, Gott und die Kirchen, 21.

7 Quoted in Stefan Ihli, Die Grundlagen des europäischen Religionsrechtes, in: Richard Puza, Stefan Ihli (Hg.), Kirchen und Religionsgemeinschaften als „Motoren Europas", Münster 2007, 117–218, 126.

8 Cf. ibid. 127.

9 Quoted in ibid. 130.

this preamble, then, is limited to *these particular* elements of religion and thus implicitly rejects all those aspects of the religions which violate people's rights, obstruct freedom and destroy the welfare of particular groups of people. Here the modern democratic state asserts a responsibility to be critical of religion—for the sake of the humaneness of the religions.[10]

The same concern is explicit in the limits of religious freedom in the 1950 Convention for the Protection of Human Rights and Fundamental Freedoms: here the limits of freedom of religion and worship are set by the democratic society and linked to public safety, law and order, public health and morality, and the protection of the rights and freedoms of others.[11] Thus, a license to stop others changing from one religion to another or to threaten violent reprisals in such cases is not part of the concept of religious freedom.[12] Here again, the religious inheritance invoked does not include those parts of religion that would entrench themselves in violent and destructive ways vis-à-vis other religions and lifestyles. This does not, as we might be tempted to think today, refer only to fundamentalist Muslim strands. Rather, a distinction is made within the Christian heritage itself between destructive and constructive elements, because of the repeated violation of the freedom of people of other faiths, including their discrimination, marginalisation and even destruction, which is part of the history of Christianity in Europe. Thus, there is something "foul" about the Christian roots of Europe.[13] But this could be said about any strand of heritage. The real problem, rather, lies in the initial commitments that determine how this contradiction between "foul" and "clean", between a rejected practice and one allowed to influence the future, is charted and received in these areas of heritage. With this approach, the numerous victims of the violent implementation of liberty, equality and fraternity will not be deleted from the memory of the French Revolution. After all, the preamble and the laws themselves are written with a view to a societal reality which is never "clean" but needs those very texts and commitments to become more humane and avoid falling into inhumanity, as has happened often enough.

4. *An Explicit Reference to God?*

The same set of issues in and between the religions has also beset the discussion about an explicit reference to God in the preamble. Which concept of God

10 Cf. to this the thematic journal Concilium (D) 18 (1982) 5: Das Menschliche, Kriterium christlicher Existenz?

11 Cf. Ibid. Grundlagen, 135.

12 Cf. Ibid. 132.

13 Cf. Walter Bayerlein, in Verantwortung vor Gott und den Menschen, in: Stimmen der Zeit 232 (2005) 389–400, 391 (Bayerlein is quoting the Italian journalist, Gentiloni).

should be envisaged here if it is not to exclude non-Christian faiths and non-believers and their communities but rather to point to something that can be relevant to all? Alas, what has been said about the ambivalence of the religions applies to the concept of God too: it has been abused to legitimise crime and destruction. Yet this cannot in itself be a reason to abandon the concept of God because otherwise many of our values would have to be treated in the same way: the concept of human dignity (when defined unilaterally by those in power) or that of democracy (when practiced as a mere formality and thus contrary to its actual meaning). "To prohibit future use because of past abuse has always been a fallacy, both in legal theory and in practice. Our responsibility before God includes vigilance against all tendencies of life being made a means to an end and of totalitarianism. The constitution of the European Union should adopt such sensitivity and intellectual coordination."[14]

Let's call to mind again the purpose of a preamble: here is a decision, a careful selection of memories that look from the past towards the present and future, critical of all abuses of religious and state power and, thus, with an implicit commitment in favour of the real and potential victims of such abuses. Established value concepts are not abandoned but rather adopted, and whichever of their aspects are relevant to the future are articulated, even if this entails a fundamental criticism of past religious realities and a categorical rejection of their future recurrence. This applies to the memory of the Enlightenment (because of the Enlightenment's ambivalence) as well as to the Greek, Roman and Arab heritage within Europe itself: there were marginalising and destructive aspects contained even within the cultural and humanist heritage that fed into the Enlightenment and the French Revolution. Hence, the memory invoked in the preamble is not a straightforwardly positivist one that includes the whole of the reality of religion, European culture, etc.; rather, it refers to specific values which played a part in the realities remembered, often a dominant one, but often a minor one or none at all.

Given this insight, and given the religious re-awakenings and the multi-religious nature of a unified Europe, it seems all the more desirable for the concept of God to be treated in a similar way as the concepts of spirituality, religiosity, the cultural, etc., that is, for a specific meaning of the term to be applied as a basis for Europe. How can this be done?

---

14 Johannes Friedrich, Anker der Menschenrechte, in: Zeitzeichen 8 (2007) 5,12–13,13. In terms of "tendencies" Friedrich is thinking of the practice of what is called euthanasia against life allegedly not worth living in the Netherlands – which is purportedly done in the name of human dignity! (ibid. 13).

5. *God Supports Justice and Compassion*

As was done with the notion of our religious inheritance, the appeal to God, too, can be subjected to a hermeneutics of suspicion and scrutinised for ambivalences. The reason for this lies in the blatant historical contradiction that there were people who appealed to God in destroying others, but also people who appealed to God and gained the strength to devote themselves to serving others; crucially, people have turned to God in situations of extreme need to lament, but in lamenting did not abandon their relationship with God. Jews and Christians in the Nazi concentration camps grappled with God in this way. If the memory of past relationships with God carries this contradiction into the future, if there is a clear commitment in shaping a future Europe to take seriously humanising relationships with God and the relationship of the oppressed and suffering to God (and thus to put into practice the responsibility not to forget but to achieve justice for those who have done good and for those who were the victims of evil), then the reference to God will be unequivocal and not so open to abuse. After all, it was the appeal to God which provided the reason for freedom of religion and also for the attitude that would at all costs prevent others from being discriminated against or harmed because of one's own religion.[15]

This is the point where agendas meet: the political agenda to anchor the future of a tolerant Europe in a specific memory of God and the agenda of church people to present their own memory of Jesus Christ as a criticism of a use of God that marginalises and discriminates. The reference to God could allow what has been called the "soul of Europe" to shine through, especially with a view to the terror of the worst catastrophe of the twentieth century: "The reference to God in a European constitution could function as a reminder to Europeans. Let's not forget that the name of God was appealed to a million times in Auschwitz. Do we see these cries to God as a million private affairs? Or was not the appeal to God in Auschwitz a final appeal to a future humanitarianism, to justice and freedom in the Name of God?"[16]

From this perspective, the omission of a reference to God in a European constitution would indeed be an "alarming signal". Whenever there have been political attempts to delete God from the collective memory, this has been bound up with contempt for freedom of religion and tolerance. The reference to God points out that one of the rights to be protected categorically is the right not to believe in God. The reference to God is an indispensable foundation for human rights, which include especially freedom of religion and opinion."[17]

---

15 Cf. Luf, u. a., Gott in der Verfassung 357

16 Bernard, Gott und die Kirchen 21.

17 Friedrich, Anker 13.

This reference would be of benefit not only to Europe, but also to an adequate processing of European memories because it would mean that, whether good or evil, no memory would be overlooked or suppressed. The victims of the appeal to God as well as the offenders would be remembered, and from these criteria can be distilled ways to limit the occurrence of such offences in Europe, to encounter the victims with as much compassion as possible and to fighting for justice for those being discriminated against in terms of both the moral courage of citizens and the structures and laws of states.

And let's not forget: this memory is not just carried by state officials; rather such a preamble makes a critical tool available to the citizens and the people to scrutinise political and economic practice, and legal practice as well, when it comes to changing existing legal structures with a view to gaining greater justice.

6. *God: Mystery of the World*

There is another equally important argument for establishing such a responsibility through a reference to God. This concerns the belief found in all religions that "God is greater than humans"[18], that God is an infinite mystery to humans and not accessible to them, not through magic or reason. God remains this mystery even in her revelations, infinitely beyond that which has been revealed in the Torah, the Bible or the Qur'an. In Christianity, the Fourth Lateran Council talked about the fact that in the revelation and in everything humans think, say and do there is always more dissimilarity than similarity compared with God.

Referring to the mystery of God, what the religions refer to is the fact that it is in this very transcendence that surpasses all that is human and worldly that his divinity reposes. The precondition for this is that neither human beings nor religions put themselves in God's place but, through their revelations and worship, open up a particular pathway towards this mystery. They may claim that their truth is "fuller" compared with that of other religions or denominations, but they must never deny that other faiths, or other people's lives, are also rooted in the mystery of God and that this mysterious God has a relationship to them that is not accessible and controllable from human vantage points, for it is from the mystery of God that the creation of the world and of all people arises.

This is what the Catholic theologian, Johann Baptist Metz, has in mind when he suggests that the reference to God may be captured in the image of

---

[18] Cf. Karl Lehmann, „Gott ist größer als der Mensch" (Der Vorsitzende der Deutschen Bischofskonferenz Nr. 20), Bonn 1999.

the "empty seat of power". "This empty seat is not available for political use; but as long as this seat is left where it is—there, in the centre of the room, its emptiness looming with a certain pathos—the political protagonists have to take account of its presence."[19] Thus, the explicit reference to God stands as a placeholder, as "a warning and a reminder of the limits of human reason and human creative will".[20] In this way, a reference to God becomes a symbol of admonition regarding the danger of political or ideological powers usurping God's place and declaring themselves divine to force their own lifestyles and thought upon others. Reserving all absoluteness for God serves as a caution against might and power being made into "false absolutes".[21] Rejecting any self-apotheosis precludes "promethean megalomania" and expresses a rejection of "the marginalization of the individual by society or the state" as well as of "the idolization of the individual and his deluded belief to be responsible only to himself".[22]

The German legal theorist, Horst Dreier, writes in his commentary on the preamble of the German Basic Law: "If understood correctly, the reference to God in the preamble appears to be a kind of acknowledgement of humility ... The point is not to transcendentalise the constitution as an at least indirectly God-given text but, rather, to emphasise the worldliness and, hence, the immanence, finitude and fallibility of a democratic constitution. The state as a this-worldly order that can never be perfect and can never claim absolute truth; the state as the work of man and hence flawed—the historical situations in 1949 and in 1990 called strongly for an emphasis on these facts. The preamble constitutes a clear rejection of totalitarian models of state of any provenance."[23] He continues: "In so far as the reference to God in the preamble is seen, according to a widespread reading, as a denial of the absoluteness of the power of the state, this 'gap' is 'necessary for freedom.'"[24] This is where the concerns of the legal scholar and the theologian meet: in the understanding of the reference to God as a code for *this particular* political insight into the nature of humans and human social constellations.

Therefore, in 1977, the committee of experts tasked with revising the Federal Constitution of the Swiss Confederation justified the reference to God in the preamble thus: the reference to God, they said, was "an acknowledgement of the relativity of all political power", showing "that the Swiss people did assign an ultimate status to its state but recognized a divine task to realize a

---

19 Quoted in Christoph Konrath, Vermittlung und Erinnerung, in: Österreichisches Archiv für Recht und Religion 51 (2004) 1, 189–211, 194.

20 Konrath, Vermittlung 195.

21 Cf. Lehmann, Gott ist größer 8.

22 Bayerlein, Verantwortung 393.

23 Quoted in Bayerlein, Verantwortung 394 (in speaking of 1990, what is in view is the fall of the wall separating East and West Germany and the new shared future).

24 Quoted ibid. 394.

humane way of living together. As a symbol of a responsibility that transcends the realm of the purely human, the phrase should be acceptable even to atheists...This way of introducing the constitution should not promote a particular world view but was intended simply to express a certain attitude, namely that humanity and the state do not wish to found themselves upon themselves."[25] The German legal scholar, Böckenförde, has always emphasised that the liberal modern state is based on prerequisites that it has not itself created.[26]

The explicit reference to God raises this basic insight and attitude as relevant to the future of Europe: the rejection of any attempts to make political and economic power—indeed, any power—into absolutes.[27] The fundamental social critique of religion (see above, section 3) is thus paralleled by an equally fundamental religious critique of society in that religion also employs a hermeneutics of suspicion to criticise political power.

7. *God: Not a Shared Basis?*

Interestingly, opposition against an explicit reference to God in the preamble has come, and continues to come, not only from secular quarters, but also from firmly Christian circles as well. In view here are those sections of the Christian denominations, especially of the Free Churches and the Charismatic movements, who wish to limit the validity of the notion of God to their own revelatory texts. The assertion is more or less explicitly that, whenever the concept of God is used outside their own respective faction of Christianity, it is actually being abused by people who do not believe in their truth for purposes not sanctioned by their revelation.[28]

The suggestion that the reference to God may by be accepted by a range of people, faiths and worldviews as a symbol that prevents any human self-apotheosis against others is regarded in those circles as "God-talk light" be-

---

25 Quoted ibid. 395.

26 Quoted in Christoph-E. Palmer (Hg.), Europa in guter Verfassung, Stuttgart 2006 12f.

27 Cf. Matthias Triebel, Gott in der Diskussion um eine europäische Verfassung, in: Theologische Beiträge 36 (2005) 254–266, 258.

28 Cf. on the Protestant side Martin Stöhr, Zwischenruf, in: Junge Kirche 65 (2004) 2,13; Norbert Kotowski, Thesenpapier, in: homiletisch-liturgisches Korrespondenzblatt 21 (2003/04) 76, 81, where the author argues in favour of a reference to God in the preamble but makes clear that this can be articulated only from a Biblical Christian standpoint. This is the view that one's own concept of God applies universally. The Protestant theologian Dietmar Lütz: Gott ist in keiner guten Verfassung, in: Zeitschrift für Theologie und Gemeinde 10 (2005) 44–53, is also against a reference to God (with reference to Bonhoeffer. The fact that this position is argued particularly by Protestants may be due to Luther's doctrine of the two kingdoms and also with a secondary Barthianism where the realm of the Gospel is clearly distinguished, even separated, from that of secular affairs).

cause their own Christian doctrine of God is no longer explicit,[29] for only one's own God is the true God. Hence, God is unsuitable for functioning as a basis shared with those who believe or think differently. Therefore, there should be no reference to God in the preamble as it would be theologically dubious.[30]

Such attitudes shield from view those parts of the Christian tradition that see God as a universal God, one who relates to each of the world's realities in unique ways that cannot be controlled by Christianity. This is true from the perspective of the theology of creation as well as from the doctrine of the infinite mystery of God. The Christian concept of God is here rooted in the universal concept of God, representing this universality not in integralistic terms (as though all had to convert to Christianity) but as a God-given and God-assured recognition of other people, lifestyles and faiths. This recognition includes their appreciation and protection. Only then, and only on this basis, are critical dialogues and debates possible.

Strict opposition to a reference to God in the preamble has also come from France and Belgium because of the laical traditions of those countries, that is, the strict separation of church and state. However, some might wonder why even a Catholic such as the former president, Valéry Giscard d'Estaing, has taken this view. But his lack of enthusiasm for this matter becomes understandable if it is pointed out that he is close to, or even a member of, the right-wing conservative Catholic movement "Opus Dei". This strand of the Catholic church is concerned not only to claim the concept of church for themselves and deny it to other Christian churches, but also to accept only their own understanding of it as valid. The Protestant Free Churches have taken a similar line.

A fundamentalising attitude can be seen at work here: only the God revealed in one's own revelation (Bible or church tradition) is the God who created the world, the universal God who will judge all at the end of the world, basing His verdict mainly on whether people have believed in him in a very particular way. Those of this bent of mind cannot wish to see the concept of God included in a political-social preamble: for this would require allowing people of other faiths to worship the same God as one's own communities do.

The issue is familiar from the debate about the ecumenical prayer in Assisi: should a Catholic Christian be allowed to pray to God together with Muslims and people from other faiths, given that only his or her God is the true God? There is a parallel problem with believers of different faiths in a society referring to one God in a preamble, because they all have a different understanding of that God, each circumscribed to a degree that makes any *rapprochement* impossible. Any coming together would be possible only if those of other faiths were to become integrated in one's own domain, in other words, if they con-

29 Cf. Triebel, Diskussion 261.

30 Ibid. 266.

verted, thus establishing an identical understanding of God's truth. The political version of this strategy is a theocracy, where political power belongs to a particular religion or is at least significantly influenced by it. This blending of religion and state is always experienced by those who believe differently as a loss of rights, prosperity, sometimes even a loss of life, except in cases where, because of historical conditions of economic necessities, the presence of people of different faiths is tolerated in certain areas or ghettos.

8. *So What about Palestine?*

As far as the question of a constitution for the future Palestinian state is concerned, I see no possibility to avoid either religious issues or the reference to God: almost all groups within the population are in equally strong ways rooted in their faith and their particular denomination, their religion. To banish this religious dimension from the constitution would be to disrespect the collective memories of the various groups in that country whose lives have always been bound up with a very specific relationship to God.

It will be necessary—and this is what could be learned from the European debate—to reach an agreement about which aspects of the different denominations and faiths are important for the future of the country. Agreement must further be reached about the criteria according to which these memories of relationships with God and religious practices should have an influence upon the creation of the future of the country. The European debate has shown that whenever any given denomination or religion fundamentalises itself, unbridgeable divides open up that make any shared religious reference, let alone a reference to God, virtually impossible—unless the marginalisation and subordination of minorities are casually accepted. Hence, the crucial question is whether a concept of God can be agreed on that can be shared with other faiths and denominations as a basis for all religions: as a reference to a transcendence that criticises power and governance idolising each other and thus forms a basis for solidarity between all.

As far as I can see as an outside observer, the foundations for this approach already exist in this country: especially in the work of the al-Liqa' Center and the dialogues initiated there among Christian, Muslim and Jewish believers.[31] It will be necessary in this context to direct greater attention to the resources available from the traditions of the various faiths and denominations and to mobilise them in the service of mutual solidarity. In view here is the prohibition against creating images of God, even within one's own religion, at least not

[31] Cf. on this point Ulrike Bechmann, Vom Dialog zur Solidarität. Das christlich-islamische Gespräch in Palästina, Trier 2000.

irrevocable images. This is part of the Christian and Jewish tradition, especially the mystical traditions of those faiths. Similar traditions must surely exist in Islam as well in terms of God's absolute divinity that defies appropriation by humans and belongs to God alone.

If this is not achieved, or if a religious reference is avoided completely (because of a failure to reach consent already at the stage of the preamble to a future constitution), then such shared ground will not be available as a point of reference in future inter-religious conflicts.

Let me finish with a deep-felt wish for the constitution of a Palestinian state. May a foundation be found for mutual solidarity and justice that is accepted by all faiths—for a rich future for this country in peace and security.

III. The Churches' Responsibility for the Media

1. *The Kingdom of God as a Theological Point of Reference*

The positive theological point of reference for the relationship between the Church and the media (like any relationship of the Church to its own environment) is given by the fact that the Church responsibly indicates the initial realisation of the Kingdom of God in history: in word and action, in proclamation and diaconia, in symbols of transcendence and in actions of love for neighbour. However, this realisation of the Kingdom of God is not limited to the Church, just as there is much in the Church that has little to do with the Kingdom of God. In its actual presence, what on the basis of revelation the Church can call the Kingdom of God, giving hope and encouragement, transcends the Church—not only in the actions of love and justice performed by many people, but also in many religious and non-religious symbolisations, in so far as they maintain hope in situations where there is little hope and put the options of justice, freedom and love into practice even in situations where there is a threat of meaninglessness and risk.

A basic question about the future of the Church is how it determines and shapes its relationship to the Kingdom of God outside itself and how honestly and courageously it tackles that within it that is incompatible with love of God and neighbour. Any black-and-white contrast between "inside" and "outside" leads to the ghettoising of the Church and prevents an inculturation on the basis of an exchange.[1] The more Christians and church social forms deal disinterestedly (in terms of maintaining their institutions and recruiting for them) with other people and spheres of life, the more convincing, inviting and attractive they will be for seekers. Offers of this kind of experience and aids towards orientation which are the no longer open to the suspicion of indoctrination and recruitment will play their part in encouraging interest in the Church among people who have come of age.

The time of "all-or-nothing" pastoral work is finally over. Perhaps we should really learn from that pastoral work which is increasingly possible and necessary in the major cities,[2] the "*pastoralia* of the passer-by". The churches

---

1 Cf. in detail O. Fuchs, ‚Kirche und Medien auf dem Weg zum Jahr 2000. Anmerkungen zu einem römischen Textentwurf', *Stimmen der Zeit* 106, 1991, 411–421.

2 Cf. W. Simon, *Kirche in der Stadt*, Berlin 1990.

represent themselves and their concerns in the form of "personal offers" at various central places of human life and experience, in the meditation in a city church, in an hour's conversation with someone who may then go away again, in the media in high-quality religious broadcasts. In all these examples it is no longer possible to calculate what is "coming out" of them and who is "returning". What the church authorities are understandably fond of defining as pastoral success, namely the degree to which their own work also makes some contribution to their own organisations (from church attendance to active presence in key communities), may need to be qualified and supplemented by another attitude: any increase in hope and humanity which is made possible and advanced by religious and church initiatives is a work of the Kingdom of God in this world (even if those addressed do not come into the inner sphere of the Church) and thus falls essentially under the responsibility of the Church. Like the Kingdom of God, so too the pastoral work of the Kingdom of God points far beyond the maintaining of its "own shop".

This also relativises the constant question about the meaningfulness of church broadcasts on the media, whether they reach those who are remote from the Church and whether they serve to bring the audience back into the Church. More important is the question of whether broadcasts sponsored by the churches take such a form that those who have become distanced are reached so that their *own* capacity for hope and humanity is built up, in other words, if they feel, "Here we aren't being got at, but something is being given to us." To use a church symbol: here they are being given bread for life (and not sweets to attract them).

2. Forms of Religious Presence in Secular Products

The question of religion in the media prompts the question: which religion? For religions, too (measured by their power to humanise and heal), are completely ambivalent entities. In the name of religion people can build one another up and destroy each other. Human nature can be confirmed and legitimated to a gigantic degree with the concept of God, but so too can its shadow side. We know such experiences not least from the history of Christianity. We must not lose sight of this ambivalence even in the various manifestations of Christianity in the media.

The explicitly religious element in secular productions

First, I want to discuss secular entertainment products in which religion appears in one form or another (comes off well or badly), not least also because such religious components even have an entertainment value for the public and serve as a form of identification. I am thinking on the whole of non-religious (i.e., "secular") broadcasts with religious settings, i.e., with language and content that one knows from the Church. Sometimes the curiosity and entertainment value of religious worlds is so great that whole series are devoted to them—for example, soap operas are constructed round the figure of a pastor.

Let's look at such a secular religious programme in more detail. I remember a scene in Ingmar Bergman's film *The Serpent's Egg* (1976). The film is set in Berlin at the height of the inflation of late autumn 1923. Anxiety about violence and the future dominates people's feelings. Against this background Bergman sets a "religious" scene which at the same time is one of the most human images of this film, indeed of any film that I know. Manuela goes into the sacristy to an elderly priest after mass: she feels or knows that she is guilty of the suicide of her husband, whom she had left. At first the priest turns her away (he has to get on with the next service as quickly as possible, but then he starts a conversation with her in the sacristy and feels her deep spiritual need). When he suggests that they say a prayer, they both kneel down. She asks, "Is it a special prayer?" "Yes, yes, yes, be quiet," he says, and after a pause he continues, "We live so far from God that he probably cannot hear us when we ask for help. So we must grant each other the forgiveness that a distant God fails to give." Then he puts his hand on her head and says, "The death of your husband is forgiven you; you need no longer feel guilty." After a pause he continues, "I ask your forgiveness for being so remote, so forbidding; please forgive me." Somewhat amazed, she looks up, now puts her hand on his head and says, "Yes, I forgive you." "We cannot do more," says the priest, breaking off the conversation quickly to get away as soon as possible, so as not to offend his superior.

So in the midst of this bad time, when already (like the reptile in the transparent serpent's egg) the monster of later National Socialism is visibly incubating, this utterly inter-personal encounter of reconciliation in the sphere of religion, for all its brokenness, and a faith which in the face of what people are doing to each other can "experience" God only as the one who is utterly remote, but nevertheless holds to him, can give content to that inter-personal reconciliation with its silence. In this broken situation the unbroken assertion of the nearness of God would only have seemed inhuman and the expedient of a church official. But not only these words are impressive; so is their combination with the attitude and the faces of the pair. The priest also kneels, and both individual's eyes show pain and liberation at the same time.

The penitential scene offers a welcome contrast to many films in which the Church and the clergy do not come out well: because as functionaries of the church powers they are blind to human needs; because they act on the side of the rulers; because they treat non-believers in an inhuman way; because they cannot cope with the sexual-erotic dimension of love or, if they can, because they do so only with a secret dual morality. Even if the increasingly naïve and brash clichés of such productions, which in part are despising of the Church and in part are just trivial, get on my nerves, it cannot be disputed that there, too, sometimes in a fair way and sometimes in caricature, religious reality is disclosed in its perverse manifestation which is so humanly destructive. Proud defensive and injured retorts are not much use here, where we are talking (like the confessor mentioned above who kneels and asks for forgiveness) about where religion itself has been and is guilty.

Implicit Christianity in secular products

However, there are also secular productions which do not translate religious and Christian concerns into religious language and forms of communication (or in negative instances get in their way and destroy them), but adopt as it were an anonymous, yet nevertheless realistic, approach. This happens when (in positive instances) the option of humanity and justice, of mercy and reconciliation, is put forward or dramatised in a series of images (for example, in reports or scenes which draw attention to social problems, in films and series in which solidarity, tolerance and conflict are lived out).

From a theological perspective, anything that strengthens and builds up mercy and justice between human beings has to do with the praxis of the Kingdom of God.[3] Here the Christian criticism of the media has the same task as Christian proclamation to contemporaries who are remote from diaconia, namely to appreciate their action and to learn from them for its own praxis. In our world there is more expression and realisation of humanity than talk of God. If churches and pastorates and their sphere of influence are not to turn into the opposite of this, they must pay attention to this practical "strange prophecy" which can provide stimulation for imagining possibilities of realising the Kingdom of God outside themselves.[4]

The presence of the Church in the media

In these two forms of the presence of religion in the media, it is not the Church which uses the media as a means of expression for its concerns. Here it is those responsible for the media themselves who explicitly or implicitly include religion and Christian elements in their secular broadcasts. More attention will be paid to such forms of the presence of religion in the media if the media are not used as instruments for church interests but there is co-operation with those who work as producers and artists in a way which builds up relationships that

3 Cf. O. Fuchs, Heilen und Befreien. Der Dienst am Nächsten als Ernstfall von Kirche und Pastoral, Düsseldorf 1990.

4 Dorothee Sölle has developed the concept of 'realization' for defining the theological relationship between secular literature and its religious and Christian content: 'Realization is the secular concretion of what is "given" or promised in the language of religion', and 'Theology and literature here stand in the relationship of tradition and concretization, of promise and realization', *Realisation. Studien zum Verhältnis von Theologie und Dichtung nach der Aufklärung*, Darmstadt und Neuwied 1973, 29, 48.

bring mutual recognition and enrichment. I would argue emphatically not only that the presence of Christian content in the media should be seen and organised from the perspective of church initiatives and institutions but also that a structure of encounter should be built up which is as constructive as it is critical (on both sides)—one which is not active on behalf of the Church and perhaps also "outside" it, but one which is intrinsically connected with what the Church calls the Kingdom of God. If this is clear, then it may also be said that the Church has a right to be represented in the media and to put forward its own concerns.

So there are the quite explicitly religious broadcasts which are predominantly made by the church editors in broadcasting organisations. They arise from within the churches and in their interest (structurally this also applies to broadcasts which are critical of the churches). Here the level of interest can be very different depending on the area: from rulings by the church authorities to the free work of Christian journalists. The public for such material probably consists largely of church insiders and to a lesser degree of those who are neither close nor distanced, those who are still interested and already distanced and to a very small degree those who are remote from the Church—here the nature of a broadcast and its imagery can also address the latter to an increasing degree. Research into individual instances will have to clarify how much this is then the case.[5]

Church broadcasts can also be divided into two groups: programmes explicitly concerned with proclamation, the assurance of faith (like the German programme "Wort zum Sonntag") and the symbolic communication of the content of faith (Sunday mass on television) and programmes in which praxis of Christians and congregations—and their activities in society and the world—are looked at to bring them into a positive or critical connection with the values of the Gospel (explicitly or simply because a particular broadcast takes place in the affirmative context of a church radio station). One example might be the presentation of a social initiative in which Christians and those remote from the Church act together for people in need or those suffering under injustice.

3. *Learning to Hear and See*

The topic of how the Church deals with the media relates to two large groups of people: the many who work in the media, who produce and are responsible for broadcasts, and all those who hear and see the results of this work on radio

5 Cf. H. Bogensberger, ‚Das Publikum kirchlicher Medienverbund-Programme', *Diakonia* 17, 1986, 6, 422–424.

and television. Whereas so far we have been particularly concerned with how the church authorities deal with the media, with what aims they produce them and how they relate to non-church products and producers like artists, now we shall be mainly concerned with the question of how the public deal with the media, how they become competent critics of the media and where the criteria for this competent criticism come from.

This aspect of the church's use of the media is often overlooked. But the Church has a social and ecclesial responsibility not only for its own appearances on the media but also for seeing that those who receive the media are not manipulated and belittled but find that the media strengthen their powers of being and communicating themselves. In that case we are not just dealing with professionals who represent the Church on the media but with church people as the subject of dealing with the media. In other words, we are dealing with how the churches as the people of God use the media.

What in particular can the social resources of church communities do so that people are not presented with all kinds of information and entertainment together with the value orientations which are more or less explicitly conveyed in them, and in addition presupposing every possible kind of religion, but rather are offered help in distinguishing between what is useful and what is damaging, between what is un-Christian and what is Christian? It is the task not only of media pedagogics but also of pastoral work, in order to help Christians to come of age (and this is a theological option according to the Vatican II theology of vocation), to encourage the active creativity of the viewer in church and society.

Accordingly, it is necessary for people to be able to classify the products of the media in terms of importance. The apparatus, professionalism and technical perfection of media products suggest (as does the printed word in the sphere of books) an objective general validity which transcends the individual, which these media cannot have because in each case they are always human products that are no more or less valuable and can no more or less be valid than their recipients. The solution is not to stop reading or looking at the television but to be able to relativise the significance and scope of such products in the same way as the material of interpersonal communication. As audio-visual messages usually have a more marked emotional impact on the psyche than what is read or heard, this postulate applies above all to television and videos. Make no mistake about it; this is not because they are worse (certainly there is also a lot of bad printed matter), but because even if they are bad, they can be very effective (above all where there is a combination of sex and crime).[6]

---

6 Cf. M. Kundczik, *Gewalt und Medien*, Cologne 1987.

There is a real danger that people do not take their own "direct" experiences as seriously as the "secondary"[7] media experiences. The empirically demonstrable contradictions between public opinion and everyday experience brought out by sociology are illuminating in this context: whereas marriage and the family are losing significance in public opinions as expressed by the media, in questionnaires the generally positive experience of families and a high opinion of them come through almost intact. The public assessment of divorce as a relatively trivial matter contrasts with the general experience of depression among divorced persons (including their constant longing for a successful partnership and in part also for a family). "Many people mistrust their own experiences and values and do not think that they can be capable of generalization although they are demonstrably shared by the majority."[8] In such a double climate of opinion with its split between personal experience and public assessment, people evidently find it difficult to assert their own individual experiences over against the images communicated by the media. Here in fact something like a public marginalisation of important personal experiences takes place.

4. *Not Flight, but "Walking Upright"*

The media have become a source of everyday experience that has to be thought about. There are hardly any spheres now which are free of the media unless one goes into an anachronistic ghetto, and in that case one also cuts oneself off from links with the central processes of exchange in present-day society. Furthermore, a general defamation of those active in the media, which is inherent in this reaction, does not do justice to these people or to their product.

A black-and-white ideologisation of "secondary" experiences over against "primary" experiences is also not tenable; it distorts the insight that the former can be very constructive and the latter very destructive. There is no unambivalent sphere of human life, society or the media that does not have both negative and positive possibilities. However, it is important for the public to have some self-awareness, to regard what does not appear on the media as important and real, and also to promote values which are passed over by the media. Conversely, I can remember excellent programmes which (for example by broadening horizons) point to charitable and political needs and in so doing identify values which have been lacking in everyday public awareness.

---

7 For the possibility and problems of this term cf. O. Fuchs, *Kirche - Kabel - Kapital. Standpunkte einer christlichen Medienpolitik*, Münster 1989, 108–114.

8 R. Köcher, 'Familie und Gesellschaft', in: E. Noelle-Neumann and R. Köcher, *Die verletzte Nation. Über den Versuch der Deutschen, ihren Charakter zu verändern*, Stuttgart 1987, 83.

In short, what needs to be done is to break down hierarchical relationships and to build up relations of parity between the different subjects and institutions in society.[9] Of course this is a question of power, not just socio-political and structural enabling but also of that psychological enabling which has made the various social forms flourish for individuals. This insight immediately raises a question within the churches: are our congregations such that people in them can develop strong selves and empower themselves? Are they communities in which adults are questioned about their creativity, their personal faith and their practical activity?

How important it is to strengthen people against the influences of the mass media also emerges in families which have problems of communicating because the television has not just become an additional "member of the family" but in fact is the dominant one.[10] Here it is of no use for church representatives to accuse families of a lack of Christian socialisation if at the same time the social forms of the Church do not help to strengthen and build up what is important to parents for *their own* faith und life, for example enabling them to open their mouths in the community even when they are going against the stream, without the inconvenience that they cause being punished by pressure to fall into line or by expulsion from the community. Parents are relatively helpless concerning their growing children unless they can learn to speak about their own faith (and their own doubts), for young people will hardly be convinced about the faith by mere formulae of assent and catechism answers. It is better if they can experience identity here, and perhaps also honest questioning and helplessness, from their parents. But if that is to happen, parents must first have learned to deal honestly with themselves and their own weaknesses in encountering others and God.

A meaningful and effective *pastoralia* of the media will aim at two goals: a lowering of the quantity (of consumption of the media) and an increase in the quality: media economy and media coming of age. The two are connected, for where time and energy are taken up with too much media consumption there can no longer be any mature reactions, because these need time for reflection and discussion.

5. *Economy and Coming of Age*

If the capacity to keep a distance and select from what one encounters is a function of human coming of age, then it is vital to call for a reduction in the flood of images so that concentration and the investment of time in a good film

9 Cf. in more detail Fuchs, *Kirche* (n. 7), 152–170, 192–217.

10 Cf. R. Merkert, 'Der Bildschirm als Familienmitglied', *Communicatio Socialis* 15, 1982, 3, 167–92; Köcher, 'Familie' (n. 8), 77–78.

is again possible. The danger in the excessive amount of audio-visual material that is on offer is not that it wastes time but that it wastes energy. That there should also be some social time in addition to working time and media consumption time should be a very important concern for the culture of family, community and social encounter. Social time is that time in which we are primarily involved in taking up and cultivating social relationships and the social forms that have value in themselves.[11]

For believers, the concept of social time also has another dimension, that of encounters with God. Where there is no time for resting, for solitude and for prayer, spiritual interruptions of everyday life hardly have a chance. "Prayer is resistance to the banality which threatens our lives, to the total focussing of our life on a society of exchanges and needs."[12] The more space is actively sought for social time, and especially time with God, the more economic and selective we shall have to be in dealing with the media. This does not exclude the possibility that the mass media can also communicate encounters with God, for example, in broadcast meditations, in conversations, services and so on, but these will always be surrounded by more sensational and more spectacular material, unless we have already learned in the sphere outside the media to long for the more peaceful image and the capacity to see behind it.

Here it becomes clear how much the Church not only does a service to society but also makes possible its own proclamation of God when it develops alternative forms of shaping leisure time in family and community, for example, in groups in which people meet regularly that cut right across stages of life or specialist interests, to discuss particular broadcasts or films and exchange views about them, possibly also for a time of rest and reflection, to experience and encourage their own creativity and competence.

The detachment and criticism made possible in communicative forms of reception also lead to the discovery and development of a sense of detail, a feeling for the small and unobtrusive features that are to be found in the background of good media productions. Productions will be linked with human experiences and need not be consumed privately at home and remain undiscussed (as they often are in the family). In the attempts at a community-orientated media, associations are being made in the parishes.

Initiatives could increasingly be connected with this in which a community's own products made with whatever media means are available (above all by video), either local documentaries or plays, are produced and discussed. Here it would be an advantage for the churches to learn from alternative political and social video groups and associations how "proclamation from below" might be possible in the media. It is at such interfaces between technical media material and its use in spheres of dialogue encounters that citizens and Christians who

11 Cf. P. Spescha, *Arbeit - Freizeit - Sozialzeit*, Frankfurt a. M. 1981.

12 J. B. Metz (and K. Rahner), *Ermutigung zum Gebet*, Freiburg i. Br. 1977, 35.

have come of age will make some decisions for the future (of the politics of both the media and the Church). The "domestication" of media techniques and products from the context of the mass media in interpersonal encounter gives an experience of dealing with the media, which can then also have some effect on the wider reception of the mass media. Church institutions and forms of community are increasingly resorting to such a network of media and personal communication in theological faculties, adult education and community work, in the various specialist groups and age ranges and in the connections between them.

E. Responsibility in Church Offices

I. Pope Benedict and the Perception of Reality

1. *What Is at Issue ...*

According to Karl Popper, Plato hated "the individual and his freedom no less than he did shifting, discrete experiences and the multifariousness of the mutable world of perceptible objects."[1] What Popper is saying here about Plato—and he is certainly simplifying and not being fair to him—could better be said of the Neo-Platonists, Plotinus especially (at whose feet Augustine sat no less than did Joseph Ratzinger, who, after all, wrote his doctoral thesis on Augustine's ideas concerning the house and people of God[2]). Ashamed as he was at even having a body at all, Plotinus experienced in his own flesh—literally—that the supreme realities are not material but spiritual.

Elmar Klinger, the Würzburg-based fundamental theologian, has cited Popper's analysis of Platonism as what lay behind the dispute over the theological qualification of the Second Vatican Council.[3] By "conceiving positively of the individual in terms of human vocation", by coming down on the side of freedom and human rights, by advocating not a top-down, or "assistentialist", approach to helping the poor, but a bottom-up one instead, in which decision-making was predicated on first having entered in dialogue with those affected by the decision,[4] the Council overcame Platonism in the Church. That this is so can be clearly seen by comparing the first chapters of both the ecclesiastical

---

1 Karl R. Popper, Der Zauber Platons, Munich ³1973, 148. Author's note: The English translation is from the German translation of a text originally written in English. This practice has been generally adhered to below.

2 Cf. Anthony Grafton, Reading Ratzinger. Benedict XVI, The Theologian, in: The New Yorker, July 25, 2005, 42–49, 44.

3 Cf. Elmar Klinger, Armut. Eine Herausforderung Gottes. Der Glaube des Konzils and die Befreiung des Menschen, Zürich 1990, 280–287.

4 Cf. ibid., 285.

and the pastoral constitution of Vatican II.[5] The assertion that the Church is the outward sign and instrument of God's love of humankind (LG 1) comes with a quite definite shift of focus, namely to develop from human experience itself, and with human help (GS1), that which consists of the experience of God's love in history (and the narratives woven around this). Between assertion and reality, however, lies a gap; to close it requires that all things human should "resonate in the hearts of the faithful" (Pastoral constitution 1). The Latin expression used is "*resonet*": Thus, what is being asked of the Church's pastoral mission and leadership is that it demonstrate an ability to resonate in the face of human experience, especially that of the suffering and the afflicted. Here, the theology of the Second Vatican Council is not hard to discern: it binds the authority of ecclesiastical office strictly to a quite specific function, freeing it from the misunderstandings of authoritarianism by respecting the human dignity of all, including the faithful.

Resonance and relevance are two sides of the coin. To refuse to confront concrete circumstances as they are in the real world, to carry on as if they do not exist and that one's definitions somehow possess greater reality, is to abuse reality by projecting onto it one's own "ideas" (for which read abstractions). According to Theodor Adorno, we can recognise an ideal-typical ideology by its propensity to "glorify reconciliation in the midst of the unreconciled as [if it were already] accomplished"[6] and to construct syllogistic connections that cannot be undermined, or dispelled, by any experience, no matter how catastrophic.

Not that we do not need a discourse about conceptual issues and identifying the principles at stake. The latter are all the more indispensable for alerting us to two things: one of these is Adorno's insight that knowledge itself cannot escape from the "spell of being" and "is entire in the same deformed and threadbare nature it would escape from".[7] The other is that such thinking must not succumb to the temptation of supposing the link between thought and reality to lie in deduction—or, when deduction is institutionalised in a system of rule, in subsuming individual fates under a then generalised concept. Rather, the proper relational mode is one of encounter, under conditions of mutual respect for cognitive insights (which will always vary at the best of times) and for often highly differential experiences and/or situations.

This much is clear: while Platonic ideologies and theologies barely take seriously the world as it really is, they do exert, especially in combination with

[5] On the texts of Vatican II and their most recent commentaries cf. the five-volume work by Peter Hünermann and Bernd Jochen Hilberath (eds.), Herders theologische Kommentar zum Zweiten Vatikanischen Konzil, vols. 1–5, Freiburg 2004 to 2006.

[6] Theodor W. Adorno, Gesammelte Schriften vol. VI (ed. by Rolf Tiedemann inter al.), Darmstadt 1998, 382.

[7] Theodor W. Adorno, Gesammelte Schriften, vol. IV. (ed. by Rolf Tiedemann inter al.), Darmstadt 1998, 283.

dominance hierarchies, an enormous influence on the human worlds we *do* inhabit. Within the Church, reactions to this take two forms: believers either integrate themselves into the hegemonic ideas and institutional structures or they drop out.

2. *Spiritual Generalisation of Social Reality*

In this very horizon the interpretation of a passage from the Bible, to which the Pope in his book on Jesus devoted seven pages—the parable of the rich man and poor Lazarus (Lk. 16:19–31)" —illustrates well how Ratzinger's mind operates when linking biblical texts to certain realities of life.[8]

I venture the following thesis: the manner in which Ratzinger relates to the reality narrated in Lk 16:19–31, can, in certain respects, be compared—and also identified—with the manner of operating that Theodor W. Adorno has described in his analysis as the "jargon of genuineness (Eigentlichkeit)".[9] This similarity poses, from my perspective of course, no less a critique than what Adorno intended by analysing this self-same jargon as a critical undertaking against Heidegger. In my case, this critique is linked to my concern not to so "meditate" biblical texts that the reality they narrate is stripped of its "objective" status and dissolved into the thin air of a language of genuineness: genuine in the sense there is something more authentic, original, important and real behind reality than simple reality itself.

First let me describe the problem: The parable of poor Lazarus turns, as Ratzinger tells us, on the crisis of faith experienced by an innocent sufferer, ultimately in this case Lazarus, in his "truth" and "authenticity"—in other words, Christ, that "great sign of God", whom the parable would lead and invite us "to believe in and follow".[10] The social problem is turned into a problem of faith, and the judgement meted out to the rich man in the afterlife is meted out only to those that are without faith.[11] The rich man's demand that the dead be

8 Cf. Joseph Ratzinger, Benedict XVI. Jesus von Nazareth. Erster Teil. Von der Taufe im Jordan bis zur Verklärung, Freiburg i. Br. 2007, 252–258.

9 Cf. Theodor W. Adorno, Jargon der Eigentlichkeit. Zur deutschen Ideologie, Frankfurt a. M. 1964.

10 Ratzinger, Jesus 258, cf. also 254.

11 Pope Benedict XVI would seem to have "moved on" from the older text by Joseph Ratzinger in his Jesus book. In his Encyclical "Spe salvi" (from 2007) he makes clear that the possibility of hell does not indeed depend on faith or lack of faith, but on the gulf separating good from evil. He speaks of "those that have lived out their hatred and have trampled on love ...There is nothing left in such persons that could be healed, the destruction of any good [in them] is irreversible: this is what is meant be the word 'hell'" (no. 45). How the coming judge of humankind will react is, therefore, not primarily coupled to faith, but to that which Matthew 25 is at pains to make clear, namely the extent

sent to warn the living to mend their ways, allowing his rich brothers to escape his own fate, is now transmogrified, albeit with a certain admixture from St. John's Lazarus, into a signal test on whether one believes in the Crucified and Resurrected Christ. All of this might be acceptable if this same faith was, in turn, linked to a quite specific social practice, namely that of the narrated and narrating Jesus that Luke has given us.[12] But not a bit of it! Adorno, had he had this text in his sights, would probably have glossed it as elevating "the Ascension of the word over the realm of the factual, the constrained, the controvertible".[13]

In his vehement Heidegger critique, Adorno picks up on a remark once made by the philosopher[14] in which he speculates about the "housing shortage" as one of the major problems of the time: "Where housing falls short ... is not in there not being enough housing. Where housing really falls short ... is that mortals first have to learn what it means to have a house over one's head."[15] Thus, we are told, behind the de facto housing shortage lies another and deeper shortfall, namely "that man has lost his own essential nature and so cannot come to rest".[16] Adorno's comment: "What is being got at in thus dilating on the housing shortage is more serious that some posture of existential gravitas—the dread of joblessness, a dread that slumbers in all those inhabiting advanced capitalist countries, kept at bay administratively and thus nailed to the stars above us in a Platonic firmament."[17]

A similar spiritualising of a real economic contradiction can be laid at Ratzinger's doorstep, as when he writes that "the rich man was even in this world a man with an empty heart, who took to debauchery to hide his inner emptiness".[18] Adorno would see in this a mind set given to "sublimating as metaphysical suffering, which cuts off those so afflicted from the real suffering it causes".[19] We might also say that what Ratzinger is doing is "ignoring the

---

to which we, in our lives, have shown compassion for others or have vented destruction on them: "For I was hungry, you gave me food ..." (Matt. 25: 34).

12 Let alone that the socio-political intentions and consequences of his practice would feature.

13 Adorno, Eigentlichkeit 13. I venture no opinion as to the truth of what Adorno is saying, namely that this Ascension is orchestrated in an "authority-addicted" way.

14 Cf. Adorno, Eigentlichkeit 31, here in connection with Otto Friedrich Bollnow, Neue Geborgenheit, Stuttgart 1956, 170.

15 Cited in ibid. 31.

16 Cited from Bollnow, ibid.

17 Adorno, Eigentlichkeit 31. Cf. in this connection Hermann Häring, Jesus – logischer gemacht?, in: LIT-Verlag (ed.), „Jesus von Nazareth" kontrovers [unklar was mit kontrovers gemeint ist], Berlin 2007, 109–120, 124f.

18 Ratzinger, Jesus 256: Here we see the great ambivalence of a canonical Biblical exegesis that would view certain passages through the lens of others, glossing them in a direction that extinguishes the intrinsic value of the compared text.

19 Adorno, Eigentlichkeit 35.

objective meaning of the words".[20] That the rich man is rich in the sense that he is unwilling to still Lazarus's hunger, and that it is precisely in having the good things of life and in exercising power over others that he takes his pleasure and his derives meaning, is now given a novel twist, or—to vary the metaphor—has a superstructure added on, within a new language game, in which he, the rich man, is suddenly made into the victim of having an empty heart.[21]

Here the linguistically objective description of a rich man (and the catastrophe that befalls him) is being made the point of departure for a new meaning in a different semiological system, namely a system of faith and the lack of faith. But if that were all there were to it, there would be no problem, for language always has two sides to it, going under various names: description and reflexion, denotation and connotation, perception and evaluation, reality and myth. Crucial, however, is how they relate to each other, especially whether it is the case that the denotative meaning still figures in the connotative one or whether pondering the meaning of things has not become so divorced from the way things really are as to dissolve in a puddle of excessive speculation.[22] "In language worthy of the name, both sides come across."[23] When exegesis uses its knowledge of how things really are only as a stepping stone to its own self-rotating dynamic of interpretation, this lures us it into a false consciousness of this self-same reality, draping a veil over its very nature—which is, in the highest degree, ignorant, however elaborately it may be worked out.[24]

Taking as our fundament the two semantems of the rich man and poor Lazarus as the principal concepts in the syntagma of the narrative, we find Ratzinger erecting pillars of paradigmatic substitution upon them, affording a synoptic insight into the loss of reality:

20 Ibid. 51. On the relationship between denoted objective language and connoted or even mythological, secondary language and on the different ways in which these can relate to each other, cf. Ottmar Fuchs, Sprechen in Gegensätzen, Munich 1978, 70ff. and 54ff.

21 Cf. Ratzinger, Jesus 255.

22 Cf. on this point Roland Barthes, Mythen des Alltags, Frankfurt a. M. ^{3}1974, 83ff.

23 Adorno, Eigentlichkeit 51.

24 Cf. ibid. 49.

paradigma		
p	The rich man is actually the one without faith	True Lazarus is Christ Himself
a	A hollow generation clamouring for signs	True wisdom
r	Who have an empty heart and Choke	Those who are awakening
a	back their emptiness	and are faithful
d	The fools	Those who are full in their hearts
i	Those who are full with material goods	with truth and true greatness
g	The hostile nations	Who are free of envy
m	The cynics and the mockers	The suffering Just
a	Who do not believe in God	The slaughtered Israel
	The rich man	*The poor Lazarus*
		S y n t a g m a

In his introduction to the bibliography of his Jesus book,[25] Ratzinger speaks of his project, which is to set before us "a reading that is of a decidedly theological kind". In so doing, he places himself "above" historical-critical exegesis, since he proposes to "transcend" the latter to achieve the former. Ratzinger has recourse to an allegorese to table a Biblical interpretation "that, transcending the literal, uncovers a deep-seated theological dimension in the text".[26] An allegorese, of course, can always "speak differently" (than the text itself does), inasmuch as the person resorting to it is satisfied that he or she has successfully inserted this deeper-lying symbolic dimension into their own interpretation. But this uncoupling from the text has a downside: the narrative dimension is stripped of its grounding in practical theology, such as this may be.[27]

Then, too, the urge to realistically face up to one's responsibilities in the real world diminishes or even disappears. The need for social responsibility, which Luke communicates so well, appears only at the margins of the papal meditation. Presumably Adorno would say: "Mere conviction, without a willingness to intervene, only strengthens that from which it recoils. Bridging irreconcilables is a task beyond reflexion, yielding only to the imperatives of how things really are."[28]

To be blunt: whether someone is rich or not is, for Ratzinger, actually not so important; what *is* important is that the rich, too, should be "awakening", as is indeed the case with Nicodemus and Joseph of Arimathea.[29] What matters, therefore, is not to change the social order (this being a mere accident); what matters (and this he sees as a point of substance) is to be awakened into a faith grounded in truth.

25 Ratzinger, Jesus 409.
26 Cited from the glossary to ibid. 420.
27 Cf. Häring, Jesus 118ff.
28 Theodor W. Adorno, Eingriffe. Neun kritische Modelle, Frankfurt a. M. 1963, 8. On the aspect of practical intervention cf. also Adorno, Eigentlichkeit 139.
29 Cf. Ratzinger, Jesus 255.

Of note is the great likeness this author's text (and others from his pen) bears to statements made by the now canonised founder of Opus Dei, José Maria Éscriva de Balaguer, who made no bones about his belief that a priest had no business "treating secular, time-bound issues. These belong in the temporal and civil spheres ... I also know that the priest must turn his back on, and avoid, a narrow-minded collective spirit, that when he opens his mouth it should only be to bring souls to God, to His Saving Grace, to the Holy Sacraments endowed by Christ, and to the inward life which brings us closer to the Lord ..."[30] And again: "I do not abuse my priestly office when I say that anyone wishing to interpret the Kingdom of Christ as a political programme has not understood the supernatural direction of faith."[31] And finally: "The Lord abhors injustice and condemns those who perpetrate it; but he refrains from intervention, because He respects the freedom of the individual. God does not cause the suffering of His creatures, he only tolerates it, because it belongs through Original Sin to the human condition."[32]

3. *The Papering over of History and Politics*

When Pope Benedict XVI, speaking before the Latin American bishops conference marking the opening of CELAM's general assembly, began by saying "The promulgation of Jesus and the Gospel did not, in any sense, involve an alienation of the pre-Columbian cultures, nor did [the fact of] occupation by, and imposition, of a foreign culture",[33] then what he was conveying was a "distorted image of reality".[34] The Church's teaching that Christ is humankind's Redeemer takes on what we might call a Platonic or ideological character, unless it takes a hard look at that which is not redeemed and makes this its yardstick. The Christian salvational scheme has no meaning unless it delves deep into human misery and affliction. To speak of Christ's redemption without naming its historical and human apparitional form in concrete terms is a retrograde step, tantamount to denying the Incarnation itself. Christian faith says that Christ is our Redeemer, but it also says that the experience of his redemption becomes an enabling factor, a source of power, so that, even in *this* life, a maximum of misery and affliction can be eliminated or forestalled.

30 José Maria Éscriva de Balaguer, Christus begegnen. Homilien, Bonn 1977, 418.
31 Ibid. 421, cf. also 258f, 308f.
32 Ibid. 375.
33 Cf. Benedict XVI, opening the 5th general assembly of the Bishops Conference for Latin America and the Caribbean that was held in Aparecida, in: L'Osservatore Romano (2007) 20 (18th May 2007, 5–6.
34 Franz Helm, Der verstellte Blick auf die Realität, in: Tiroler Sonntag 27th May 2007, 12.

Criticism from the downtrodden was not long in coming: Luis Evelis Andrade, representing Columbia's indigenous peoples, had this to say: "We cannot accept that the Church does not recognise its responsibility for the destruction of our culture and our identity."[35] The Innsbruck-based professor of intercultural pastoral theology, Franz Weber, spoke of a trivialisation and a belittlement of the wounds of history and of a papering over of historical fault lines.[36]

If, then, the Pope several days later, following his return to Rome—and clearly stung by the storm of protest his speech in Brazil had touched off—signalled that he had not been making a historical but a theological statement—this only points us again to the root problem: there is, and can be, no theology that does not, when speaking of God, also, and always, speak of human beings and their history or histories. Otherwise, we might as well give up on revelation and all that the Bible claims in this regard, for here faith in God is experienced in the histories of individual people.

In his critique of the Pope's speech in Latin America, Weber regretted that in it neither the small Christian communities nor liberation theology rated a mention. While the "option for the poor" did get one, it was also detached from the shock of social frictions and spiritualised into being a component of faith itself: "In this sense, the 'option for the poor' is already implicit in the Christological faith in this selfsame God who has made Himself poor for our sake, so that we may grow rich through his poverty."[37] Christology trumps sociology, instead of honing our ability, as it should be doing, to recognise social aberrations for what they are.

It is not as if the Pope is indifferent to justice, but—as he sees it—it is the state's role, and its exclusive purview, to ensure that justice is done; private persons have no business here, nor do the faithful. Responsibility for ensuring just outcomes cannot, and evidently must not, be pegged to acts of resistance of a kind that claim to enforce justice and seek its furtherance through organised demonstrations and other acts. All that is possible, according to the papal take, is a committed participation in the social discourse on justice. The issue of the Church's political responsibility is reduced to the discursive power of

---

35 Cited in Franz Weber, „Das ist ein Rückschritt", in: Tiroler Sonntag, 27th May 2007, 12.

36 Ibid. – In a speech given in the Auschwitz concentration camp, which was not otherwise lacking in intensity or a sense of what was called for in this place of death, the Pope, nevertheless, played down the responsibility borne by the German people for the Nazi regime, almost as if the Germans had not flocked in their millions to adulate Hitler. The pontiff described the latter "... as a son of the people, over whom a band of criminals had gained power through mendacious promises, through promises of greatness...with the promise of prosperity, but also through terror and intimidation, so that our people was used and abused as an instrument of their lust for destruction and domination." For an opposing view cf. Lucia Scherzberg (ed.), Theologie und Vergangenheitsbewältigung, Paderborn 2005; Rainer Bendel (ed.), Die katholische Schuld? Katholizismus im Dritten Reich – zwischen Arrangement und Widerstand, Münster 2002.

37 Benedict XVI, in his opening speech to the conference, 5.

argument, all the while ignoring the issue of what is to be done if, say, discourse is no longer more helpful and acting is required.

The Pope had already argued along these lines in his Encyclical "*Deus caritas est*". When society is unjust, then the Church, for its part, is permitted "in the struggle for justice not simply to stand by. It must commit itself, using the means of argument, to the battle for reason; and it must awaken the spiritual forces, without which justice, which invariably has to settle for less than perfect outcomes, cannot be achieved and cannot thrive."[38] The first part of this sentence, which is further elaborated on elsewhere, peddles the Socratic (and by derivation also the Platonic) folly that deliberately perpetrated injustice can be done away with by rational discourse. The latter part is referring, when it talks of spiritual forces, to individual persons, and to these it would delegate the responsibility for settling for less, for waiving maximal demands—this in the interest of securing justice and just outcomes for all. Here we see a curiously dislocated notion of the Church's mission at work, leading us to ask: Are these same persons not the Church? Does the Pope consider the Church merely to consist of its top echelon of leaders?[39]

Just as he did in his first encyclical, Benedict XVI, addressing the Latin American bishops, did not speak a word on the martyrs of the small Christian communities in that continent or on the theology and practice of liberation. This much is clear: if he is determined not to see this theology and this practice, then he will surely not see any martyrs either! There is no escaping the fact that the voice of these martyrs has so far not been heard in Christian social teaching or its consensus-oriented discourse. By establishing a counterweight to liberation theology, we lose sight of a practice that is not only predicated on purifying the *ratio* of human justice by passing this through the sieve of the Christian social teaching; it is *also* predicated on using the direct encounter with human suffering, injustice and mortal imperilment as a stepping stone to another direct encounter, this time with Christ—a Christ who, in Matt. 25:31–46, identifies with the downtrodden and the losers of this earth. Thus, the Pope is, in all he writes, visiting (and then revisiting) the same front already opened up in his *Instructio* against liberation theology.[40]

---

[38] Benedict XVI, Encyclical "Deus caritas est" (Proclamations of the Apostolic See 171), Bonn 2006, no. 26.

[39] The Roman Bishops Synod had in 1971 (Gerechtigkeit in der Welt, Rom 1971) a contrary view: "Here the faithful generally take the initiative in acting ...; to a certain degree, however, the Church shares some of the responsibility too, as they are its members."

[40] Cf. Congregation for the Doctrine of Faith, Instruction concerning Certain Aspects of "Liberation Theology" (Proclamations of the Apostolic See 57), Bonn 1984. John L. Allen (Joseph Ratzinger, Düsseldorf [2]2005, 119) writes in this connection: "Ratzinger silenced liberation theology precisely at the moment when in Latin America globe-spanning capitalism gained the upper hand. By the end of the 1990s, so-called 'neo-liberalism', which by then had more than a decade of proliferation behind it, ... had unleashed impressive economic growth, from which relatively few profit but *through* which inequalities are

4. *Leadership Guided by Principles that "Trample on Corpses"?*

Nowhere is the gap wider between "pastoral care by day" and "pastoral care by night" than in the battle against HIV-Aids, and this not least in the African countries, where women especially are at risk of infection.[41] If the men would accept using condoms, the infection rates could be drastically lowered. Here we see, in a nutshell, the cutting-edge nature of a pastoral care that would respond to suffering humanity not with abstractions but with help where help is wanted; a pastoral care that is not some "compromise" or other, some watered-down version of "real" pastoral care, but which is, literally, the only one that will do under the circumstances. Clearly, the problem of the sexual exploitation of women will not be solved through the use of condoms. But the most pressing and important goals can be achieved, namely the prevention of infection. Additionally, acceptance of condoms by the men can be the first step towards sensibilising them to their wives' plight. To talk of a technical solution, as some have done, is to overlook the social dimension in which this first became possible.

Or is the intention perhaps that people should not escape contracting the disease if they refuse change their sexual habits? Is it perhaps intended, in what would amount to a secret complicity with the disease—a complicity as eagerly exploited as it would be explicitly denied—that the Church's preferred moral-theological principles be implemented and made binding?[42] The price of rigidly forbidding the use of condoms is simply too high, as it must be paid for in human lives. Here we see the difference between an unconditional, diaconical pastoral care and one that is only conditionally diaconical, but comes saddled with a plethora of ifs and buts, such as that the persons in question should "not sin" in certain respects. Sadly, the Pope, judging by the record of his statements to date (including those made during his time heading the Congregation for the Doctrine of Faith) has tended to agree with those who condemn

considerably exacerbated, contributing to what some observers have called 'social apartheid'. This is only speculation, but Latin America might wear a very different face today if the Vatican, instead of silencing and hindering them, had thrown their full weight of support behind the liberation theologians, appointing bishops who were willing to heed their cries for justice, or if Vatican officials had sat down with members of the Christian basic-communities or touched base with those striking for their rights. But no, the Catholic Church in Latin America, despite the efforts of individual bishops and theologians, could not have distanced itself further from playing such a transformative role. That this was so is due largely to Joseph Ratzinger."

41 Cf. Simon Lindorfer, Sharing the Pain of the Bitter Hearts. Liberation Psychology and Gender-Related Violence in Eastern Africa, Berlin 2007, 75–95, 419–429.

42 Cf. on this point Francis X. D'Sa, Jürgen Lohmayer (ed.), Heil und Liberation in Afrika. The Kirchen vor der missionarischen Herausforderung durch HIV/AIDS, Würzburg 2007.

the use of condoms, even in an HIV context and especially, one might say, in an African context.[43]

But precisely herein lies the cause of what I will call Diaconia Denied. Related to this I would oppose a vision of a pastoral care willing to run the risk of guilt, if only to stave off an outcome that is even worse. In seeking the lesser evil, it is willing to let the comparative of alleviated suffering trump the superlative of sticking by one's principles. In such complex situations, pastoral compromise *is* the indispensable core of pastoral care. By fleeing into the peaceful waters of Platonic principle no doubt one can keep one's vest clean, having kept the world's misery at a decent remove; but this will be to overlook dirt of a grimier kind, the kind that adheres in the form of guilt: the guilt one acquires as a result of having refused help where help is due. A pastoral care that is willing to take on board the travails and incongruities, the limitations and the dark spots, of people as they really are, can never be free from guilt, can never hope to attain "purity". Being pure is the lot of those unwilling to descend into life's lower depths.

The problem with such a reading of the true and the pure is that no room is left for discrepancies, not just in the ecclesiastical domain but also in the encounter with God. Neo-Platonic theology involves a top-heavy Church insisting on top-down solutions, a spirituality without the freedom to contradict—all these go hand in glove. For a drastic example we need look no further than to "*Deus caritas est*". The spirituality of lamentation and of holding God to account is disavowed with what is surely a cheap shot: it vaults humankind into the position of "judging God".[44] But this is to completely overlook the fact that the spirituality of lamentation is itself situated in the Bible. Moreover, this spirituality is precisely the prayerful consummation of the confrontation with God in the face of God's experienced remoteness and incomprehensibility.[45] The pontiff's spiritual cluelessness in this matter, as displayed in these two numbers of the Encyclical, screams to high heaven; as if *that* were not enough, the Encyclical evidences a woeful ignorance of the theological and spiritual publications on the prayer of lamentation that have appeared during the last thirty years.[46] In the biblical spirituality of lamentation (not excepting Psalm 22, recast in the

43 Cf. Grafton, Ratzinger, 49.

44 Benedict XVI, Deus, no. 37. A small addendum: this text dismissing the spirituality of lamentation cannot have stemmed directly from the papal pen, given that in his Auschwitz speech in the summer of 2006 he himself takes up the lamentation of suffering Israel, citing Psalm 44:20, 23–27 and joining with Israel in posing the question: Why Auschwitz?

45 Contrary to ibid. no. 38.

46 Cf. the collection of essays on the topic of lamentation published in Jahrbuch für Biblische theology no. 16 (Neukirchen-Vluyn 2001).

words of the crucified Jesus) we may discern in all clarity that truth in our relationship to God can also be manifested in difference, an insight not without eschatological implications.[47]

5. *Not Inculturation, rather Integration in a Specific Catholic culture*

Paulo Suess, remarking on what he calls the "historical project of impoverished others",[48] has analysed the problematic of a hegemonic and exclusive culture of Christianity fixated on its own origins and what this means for radical recognition of other cultures. The fact that Christianity was suffused, right from the very start, with cultural elements is to be radically interpreted in the sense that the source, or originary, identity of the Gospel, when the latter is transplanted into another culture, does not dispossess it. The specific cultural form of an historical era, even when that form is believed to have had a deep impact (e. g., Hellenism and early Christianity), may not be allowed to subordinate other cultural identities in the manner of a generalised transculturalism or, if you will, a leading culture. Under conditions of a normative Christian culture, there can be no inculturation of Christianity among cultural others, given that "others [too] have a culturally and historically rooted identity to defend".[49]

When Joseph Ratzinger seeks to replace the concept of inculturation with that of interculturation, he is being guided by the not implausible insight that the process of incarnation cannot be repeated by dissolving the nexus between inculturation and Christ and putting a different [inculturation] in its place, or, as he puts it, "that we time and again, as it were, strip Christ of his flesh and offer him another flesh instead".[50] But the thing about inculturation is that it is not about replacing Christ's own inculturation with another; what it *is* about is leaving Christ's incarnation in Israel intact and truly encountering it on the intercultural plane in such a way that the new Christian existence, in effect, does not have to be plucked from its own cultural context. What it is *not* about is replacing the target identity with the originary identity of the Gospel; central, nevertheless, is the encounter between the former and the latter. Multiple inculturation and the capacity for intercultural relationship are two sides of

---

47 Cf. Ottmar Fuchs, Das Jüngste Gericht. Hoffnung auf Gerechtigkeit, Regensburg 2/2009, 77–109.

48 Cf. on this issue and what follows: Paulo Suess, Ein gewisser Exodus. Zum historischen Projekt der armen Anderen, in: Jahrbuch [für?] politische Theologie 1 (1996), 206–222.

49 Ibid. 217.

50 Joseph Ratzinger, Der Christian Glaube vor der Herausforderung der Kulturen, in: P. Gordan (ed.), Evangelium und Inkulturation (1492–1992), Graz 1993, 9–23, 20.

one coin.[51] To be sure, it is indispensable that each instance of an extra-Judaic inculturation of Christianity should engage in a constant interchange with Christ's "first" incarnation in Israel. But the condition for this happening is precisely *not* that Christ be dispossessed of his own inculturation; rather, he *is* a facilitator for such an encounter

There is certainly something to the notion that the Church in all cultures has, among other things, what Ratzinger calls "a cultural subject of its own",[52]since it is a fact that in each culture it acquires something in the nature of a "sub-culture", which may, at some specific points, rub against local mores and lifestyles. The only thing to do then is to make sure the points of variance, of difference, are correctly drawn. This will *not* mean that Church is entitled, *a priori* as it were, to parade its own "cultural subject" slap bang through all the cultures. (For the record, the Church's "cultural subject" is chiefly characterised by a certain dominant, and correspondingly universalised, inculturation in the Hellenistic world[53] and, later on, in Western Europe). The benchmark, rather, consists in the theological distinction between the powers of sin and death on the one hand and the powers of life, of reconciliation, of justice, of conversion, of the Resurrection on the other.

To engage in this way, we need inculturation into the various living cultures to meaningfully explore these boundaries for the benefit of all humankind. An intercultural monolithic culture in the Church would, on the other hand, leads to a relative self-ghettoisation of the Church within its living cultures and would allow the boundary between Church and periphery to become a more important boundary than the one between the powers of destruction and the powers of divine life. Then, the Church would no longer exist in devoted solidarity with the world: only, at the worst, in solidarity with itself or, at best, in a condition where solidarity with the world is extrinsic and accidental and solidarity with itself is intrinsic and essential.

This is not just an aspect of the freedom other cultures have in their commitment to Christ; it is also a necessary aspect of their right to be different, even in having differing incarnations of the living Christ in his Church and in having a reciprocal right of correction between the inculturated local churches. No expression of Christianity's historical presence, not even the Jewish, Hellenistic or Western ones, is free from ambivalence. According to Ratzinger, it is incumbent on the various cultures to integrate into the Church's own true Culture, which in its essence is transcultural (and whatever cannot be integrated falls, of course, outside its writ). Thus, Ratzinger did not mince words in

---

51 Zur christologischen Vertiefung dieser Überlegungen cf. Ottmar Fuchs, Praktische Hermeneutik der Heiligen Schrift, Stuttgart 2004, 321–356.

52 Cf. Ratzinger, Glaube, 19.

53 Nowhere more than in stressing and imposing the Hellenistic inculturation of the Gospel (including its neo-Platonic segments) as the Church's defining culture does he sanction and immunise his Platonising abstractions, rooted in Hellenism as these are.

contradicting Walter Kasper, who had insisted on the autonomy of the local churches from the Bishop of Rome, thus entering a plea for horizontality *among* the local churches and for greater horizontality *with* Rome. This is an object lesson in how a neo-Platonising neglect of the on-the-ground facts underpins Rome's proclivity for authoritarian generalisation: generalisation and centralisation are the twin faces of Janus.[54]

Ratzinger is of the opinion that values, despite falling outside the Church, can only be allowed to have an impact internally on how the Church sees the world if they have first been appropriately purified and corrected. What is required, therefore, is to integrate these cleansed values into the Church and its view of the world. The Cambridge-based historian of the Catholic church, Earnon Duffy, has vehemently rejected this as a deculturated value orientation. Values are not spiritual identities that can be dislodged from their cultural contexts, or, for that matter, from their intellectual, social, political and economic contexts, which, indeed, flesh out values with a sense of the lived reality from which they emerged. "They are not tablets that can be swallowed painlessly, although one needs to be careful to get the dosage right. In reality, what incorporating the best values of the culture of freedom means is that the Church agrees to involve itself in whatever deep-structural transformations are afoot."[55]

And if it is true that one cannot simply detach the contemporary value of human dignity from its socio-political context to then "cleanse" it for internal Church use, this must also apply, no less, under the postulate of both men and women being endowed with equal human dignity, to the issue of changing the admission requirements for ordination. From this perspective, we can see what Ratzinger is doing: mounting a broad-based defensive strategy against the likes of Hans-Joachim Sander, who, as an annexe to the pastoral constitution adopted by the Council, suggested an approach to interacting meaningfully with the "signs of the times", an approach that is as open-minded as it is critically alert. Indeed, there is no shortage of challenges in the various cultures, challenges that have it in them to deepen the Church's own sense of identity, rendering this more explicit, even inducing the Church to so reposition itself as to renew, and to revitalise, its mission in a particular culture.[56] Thus, in all probability, Ratzinger would say that the ordination of women, being an issue of the Church's own culture, cannot be recast as an issue of gender equality in the

---

[54] Cf. on this dispute between Cardinals Ratzinger and Kasper, Ottmar Fuchs, Ortskirche – Weltkirche – Romkirche. Eine praktisch-theologische Verhältnisbestimmung im Kontext heutiger Globalisierungsprozesse, in: Albert Franz (ed.), Was ist heute noch katholisch?, Freiburg i. Br. 2001, 227–265, 261ff.

[55] Cited in Grafton, Ratzinger, 48.

[56] Cf. Hans-Joachim Sander, Theologischer Kommentar zur Pastoralkonstitution über die Kirche in der Welt von heute, in: Herders theologischer Kommentar zum Zweiten Vatikanischen Council, vol. 4 (Freiburg 2005), 581–886.

society's culture, so that a refusal to have women in the priesthood on theological grounds is no infringement of equal dignity for men and women. Note that the question of the extent to which the exclusion of women from sacred office is itself theologically sacrosanct is not even posed. We may take refuge in what Klinger said in a different context: "When a German Vicar General alleged that, once ordained, a priest forfeited his human dignity, he was speaking Platonically."[57]

6. *Generalising from One's Own Biography?*

What has always fascinated me about the Anglican church is its concern, and incidentally also its ability, to keep and retain within the fold directions, groupings and whole communities of faith which square off against each other to the point of open warfare (figuratively speaking)—discharging their tensions from time to time in heftily waged controversies, they always know when to step back from the brink. This is not to deny that the parties do not suffer from their differences; they do, but they never seem to undermine their sense of belonging to the same church. What makes this possible, of course, is that the groupings know they are parts of a single ecclesiastical edifice, meaning they are willing to grant to other groupings the same dignity they claim for themselves, rooted in their spirituality, that not they themselves will have the last word, but only God him/herself.

The Pope's decision to lift even that part of the excommunication of the bishops of the Pius Brotherhood covering the dispensing of the sacraments and holding high clerical office served to make clear, if it had not been clear before, just what kind of minister—and, by implication, what kind of ecclesiastical leadership—he wishes to rehabilitate and make prominent within the Church. To be sure, these bishops caricature though their extremes the Pope's own more moderate stance. "The Pope sees the Church's crisis of acceptance in the modern world and believes that in winning back deeply traditional circles lies the future of the Church."[58]

When one contemplates the rising receptivity, reflected in an explosive growth in numbers in almost all the Christian churches, for fundamentalist longings and whisperings, one is almost tempted to say that the Pope has not erred too far wide of the mark—only in terms of successful religious politics—in deciding to offer a scaled-down version of religion, shorn to the maximal extent of complexity in its parcelling up of the world (and world to come), this presumably as an anodyne to the lack of transparency, the hustle and bustle,

57 Klinger, Armut, 285.

58 Peter Hünermann, Excommunicatio – Communicatio. Versuch einer Schichtenanalyse der aktuellen Krise, in: Herder Korrespondenz 63 (2009) 3, 119–125,125.

the rapid transformations to which modern life is heir, both on the home front and between societies.[59]

Sympathetic as the Pope has been towards the Pius Brotherhood, his tone has been altogether different in recent years when dealing with liberation theologians worldwide, not to mention the local churches (which have not hesitated to follow their own—authentic—identity in such matters as liturgical inculturation). What niggles is the lack of any sense of fairness in this "distribution" of God's mercy. The Pope takes his office and himself to be one and the same thing, and he uses his office to implement, nay to ram through, a theology of his own making, whose roots lie in his own biography. It would seem that, in doing so, he is instrumentalising his office to drive through his own brand of theology and his notion of where the Church should be going.

Benedict practically put an end to the theological dispute with Walter Kasper (to cite a particularly prominent case) concerning the relationship between Rome and the local churches, and he imposed it with such gusto that the Austrian bishops, in their pastoral letter of 16 February 2009, felt the need to write: "The faithful rightfully expect that the procedure of searching for candidates, of giving consideration to suggestions, and of communicating the final decision should be handled carefully and with pastoral sensitivity. Only thus can it be ensured that bishops are appointed not *contra* but *pro* a local church." When a pope is as determined as this one plainly is to impose his own school of theological thought by pursuing a rigid policy of appointments—thereby confusing his person with his office—he will not think twice about dropping all pretence of pastoral sensitivity when it comes to hearing what the local churches are saying based on their experiences. Hierarchy here has transformed into a hierarchical system, creating its own top-down version of reality.

There is no greater task facing our church leaders than to do justice—and I am talking globally about the local churches (down even to the smallest Catholic communities) —to the various charismatic manifestations and personalities that have emerged, have been thrust forth, as signs of the times. Not only must they learn treat them justly; they must also get them to relate to each other in a spirit of mutual respect (nobody, of course, is above criticism) in which no one needs to avert their gaze. What I mean, especially, is that when some segments of the Church think differently from those in high places, there is a particular need, in such cases, to tread cautiously and sensitively in dealing with them; they too have a right to be protected and appreciated.[60] Paul VI, to take the case of an earlier pontiff, in his decisions (whether appointments or mat-

---

59 Cf. on this point Ottmar Fuchs, Religionskritik in praktisch-theologischer Verantwortung, in: Joachim Kügler, Ulrike Bechmann (ed.), Biblische Religionskritik. Kritik in, an und mit biblischen Texten, Münster 2009, 48–77.

60 Cf. dazu Ottmar Fuchs, Gestaltendes Amt in einer missionarischen Kirche, in: Johannes Kreidler, inter al. (ed.), Zeichen der heilsamen Nähe Gottes, Ostfildern 2008, 216–234; ders., Identität des priesterlichen Amtes, in: Pastoralblatt 56 (2004) 5, 131–139.

ters of substance) was always careful to keep those affected by his decisions in the loop; because he operated through networks and accepted dialogue, he has a claim to be the first modern pope—if by that we mean that dialogue, as well as the ability to listen, is no longer peripheral to, but at the heart of, the task for anyone proposing to mount the Throne of Peter.[61]

Benedict XVI has evidently succumbed to the official ideology that not only his own person, but also his personal biases in matters of faith and Church politics, have been ordained—co-ordained, if you will—and that the latter are to trump the various charismatic manifestations arisen of late, not to mention what the faithful actually think, every time. The very fact that he was chosen to be pope seems to him the ultimate expression of this ideology. But ordination, whether to the priesthood or the office of bishop or even to the papacy, does not mean the enthroning of one's own charisma. When a priest is raised to the priesthood, this is a sacrament in its own right, involving the bestowal of a unique Grace of Office[62]—and this is not to be identified with one's own charisma; rather, it places the latter in the service of the clergy's mission of leadership within the Church, in which all charismas, including those of the "others", are protected and encouraged and brought together in a spirit of community. The charisma of office harnesses personal charisma, not the other way around!

To be clear: the problem is not that every theology, being biographically enabled, is mediated and one sided, nor is it that Joseph Ratzinger is not at liberty to articulate whatever he likes on some issue of theological discourse. The problem lies elsewhere: when one's biography is detached from its singularity, its context of origin, and imbued with general relevance; when a theology of one's own devising is loosed from its biographical moorings and elevated to universal significance; when this proclivity is conjoined with the great temptation to use the papacy to make one's standpoint on the theological issues into a peremptory yardstick for the entire Church; when, furthermore, one is not just tempted, but actually uses one's power to push through this programme—then we have to say that this manner of interacting with one's own biographical history is "platonising" the other way around, in the sense that a thing historically enabled and constrained is advanced as the idealistic banner under which the whole Church is expected to march.

Biographically, this strategy may well have its roots in events a Tubingen professor called Ratzinger experienced traumatically "during the disturbances of 1968", as Pope Benedict XVI recalled in an address he gave to the College of

---

61 Cf. on the point Peter Hebblethwaite, Paul VI: The First Modern Pope, London 1993.

62 Cf. concerning the laying-on-of-hands as an authentic sign of the bestowal of the Grace of Office (1Tim. 4:14) Ottmar Fuchs, Das Presbyteramt in ökumenischer Perspektive, in: Herders theologischer Kommentar zum Zweiten Vatikanischen Council, vol. 5, Freiburg i. Br. 2006, 229–238.

Cardinals and the members of the Roman Curia on the occasion of the Christmas reception on 22 December 2005.[63] Clearly, Ratzinger had seen the actions of the students as a—from his perspective—entirely unwarranted and, for him personally, menacing questioning of what he had presented in his lectures. That the students were not interested in locking horns with his arguments within the parameters of principled theological discourse, but were themselves determined to make a practical point through their disruptions, was evidently so irritating to the professor that he quite failed to see that the political point extended to his own professorial responsibility (after all, it was not as if the students, in opposing America's presence in Vietnam, were not taking a stance that was theologically relevant). Why, then, did the students react sceptically to theological principles? It was not to overthrow them, but to actually see what they amounted to in the fire of reality! It would seem that Ratzinger's failure to discern a potential clash between reality and theology set him on a pathway from which he has not subsequently deviated.[64]

7. *God's Wholeness as Grace?*

Big generalisations spanning the whole of humankind, covering every shred of our existence, rightly make us suspect that the importance of singularity is being played down. Adorno speaks of a sacrality of jargon, by which he means the language of "an invisible kingdom existing solely in the surreal sullenness of the silences in the land".[65] It is a sacrality that orchestrates itself in big generalisations, words promising purity and inwardness, even as they order them and, in doing so, coerce the subject into self-abnegation.[66] In his reception of Heidegger, Adorno takes issue with philosopher's basic problematic: "Philosophical banality arises when universals are thought to possess a magical participation in the absolute."[67]

---

[63] Published in the Proclamations of the Apostolic See, 172, Bonn 2006, 19.

[64] Cf. on this point Allen, Ratzinger, 57–59. After Ratzinger's departure from Tübingen to Regensburg (1971) he "continued to argue that the enthusiasts at the Council, with their passion for reforms, had been carried away and no longer saw the 'Church as a whole'; they no longer saw the wood for the trees; they were like villagers who think they know best about the affairs of state." Ratzinger will, from now on, of this we can be sure, be representing a theology of the whole Church; where his preferences lie about woods and trees is a known quantity.

[65] Adorno, Eigentlichkeit 61.

[66] Cf. ibid. 63.

[67] Adorno, Eigentlichkeit 46. Cf. concerning the Nazis' success in orchestrating a collective release of emotion, Rainer Bucher, Nietzsches Mensch and Nietzsches Gott, Frankfurt a. M. 1986, 101–122.

But there are generally valid truths that sustain, rather than subordinate, human life—for example, the specific *and* universal reality of God that rejects if-then trade-offs with their implication that God is the ruler of humankind, preferring, instead, to conceive of God as *the* unconditional source of enabling and empowering human life, human freedom and human survival beyond the grave.[68] Grace may be the source of genuineness, which does not destroy authenticity, what is unique about persons, nations or identities. When the general is received by human beings not as a command, but as a sustaining and freedom-bestowing enablement, then it is all-sustaining, without depriving this "all" of its unfathomable multiplicity and contradictoriness.

So what we are left with, finally, is sacrality of a different kind, or, to be theologically more precise, sacramentality, in the sense that sacraments are always the place where God's love is unconditionally made manifest, in ways that speak dramatically and symbolically to our senses. That we find a deep symbolic dimension in all narratives, including the biblical narratives, does not invalidate the singularities or their meaning, which is anchored in God's own infinitude. Nor is it, as many biblical episodes show, a grace that is left dangling in the air or only availed of for its own sake; rather it is a grace that, by facilitating deeds of justice and compassion,[69] restores us to what is truly real.[70] We are called on to strengthen the resource of being-loved[71] to free up the capacity to love.

---

68 Cf. on this point Fuchs, Hermeneutik 213–249.

69 "Concrete political and social orders are therefore part and parcel of "immediate sacrality" (*contra* Joseph Ratzinger, Die Geschichtstheologie des Heiligen Bonaventura, Munich 1959, 151). Along with the necessary rejection of theocratic-universalistic system, it is important not to also reject concrete political responsibility for putting in place just structures Cf. on this issue Horst J. Helle, Der Gott des Papstes, in: LIT-Verlag (ed.), Jesus 143–150, 149ff. Helle comes to the conclusion that Ratzinger sees in Jesus a "medium" leading to God (i.e., not so much a "medium" leading back to human practice).

70 Cf. on this point Fuchs, Jüngstes Gericht 137–146.

71 Cf. Ottmar Fuchs, Predigt als Gnadenerfahrung, in: Theologische Quartalschrift 186 (2006) 4, 313–335.

II. Pope Francis and the Grace of Preaching

1. *Heart to Heart*

The following text explores the homiletic remarks made in the third chapter of *Evangelii Gaudium.* As homiletic options there are the sacramental quality of words, the homiletic quality of a homily, the a priori character of preaching as grace, freedom and creativity, maternal attitude and speech, preaching focused on inculturation, the message as empowerment, a method of delivery motivated by a theology of grace, hermeneutical responsibility with an awareness of the difference between humans and God and homiletic "time off".

In his Apostolic Exhortation *Evangelii Gaudium* (The Joy of the Gospel) Pope Francis devotes slightly less than twenty pages to preaching, but these pages really pack a punch![1] Without claiming to do full justice to the text, I would like to highlight ten distinct yet related major perspectives which, given my own homiletic options, are very close to my heart.[2]

Pope Francis focuses on the liturgical proclamation of the word of God, especially in the Eucharistic assembly (137). In doing so he brings two mutually reinforcing dynamics into play. *First,* there is confidence in the *power of preaching*, as it is God himself who "displays his power through human words" (136). Hence, the word itself has what might be termed its own salvific efficacy.[3] *Second*, there is an analogy with the *sacramental celebration*,[4] in which preaching is

---

1 Cf. Apostolic Exhortation Evangelii Gaudium (The Gospel of Joy) of the Holy Father Francis, sections 135–159, http://w2.vatican.va/content/francesco/en/apost_exhortations/documents/papa-francesco_esortazione ap_20131124_evangelii-gaudium.html, 24.04.2015. The title is a reference to the Apostolic Exhortation of Pope Paul VI, Evangelii Nuntiandi (8 December 1975), the publication of which ten years after the Second Vatican Council sent out an important signal. This parallel was undoubtedly intended, and Evangelii Gaudium contains numerous references to Evangelii Nuntiandi.

2 Numbers in brackets refer to the sections of the Apostolic Exhortation. As many of Pope Francis' ideas on homiletics have also been the focus of my own publications and match my own thoughts, I will point out connections wherever they exist. Additional publications can be found in the various articles quoted here.

3 Cf. Fuchs, Ottmar, Die Predigt als möglicher Beitrag zu einem kommunikativen und herrschaftskritischen Lebensstil – Homiletische Perspektiven, in: Englert, Rudolph, et al., Christlicher Glaube als Lebensstil, Stuttgart 1996, 107–124, on Karl Barth's autonomous impact of the word – cf. Ibid. 16ff.

4 Cf. Fuchs, Ottmar, 'Unbedingte' Vor-Gegebenheit des Rituals als pastorale Gabe und Aufgabe, in: Theologische Quartalschrift 189 2, 2009, 106–129.

included as "part of the offering made to the Father and a mediation of the grace which Christ pours out during the celebration" (137).

In this context, preaching God's word not only shares in the "mediation of grace". It also has a distinctly "sacramental" quality[5] inasmuch as it has its own way of functioning as an effective event of grace[6] and therefore needs to be handled by the preacher accordingly. Otto Semmelroth developed the salvific efficacy of preaching in analogy with the sacraments and characterised both in conjunction with one another.

To ensure that a homily takes place within a sacramental theology of grace, preaching must not be "purely moralistic or doctrinaire, or one which turns into a lecture on biblical exegesis". In either case, such preaching "detracts from this heart-to-heart communication which takes place in the homily and possesses a quasi-sacramental character" (142).

It is a thetic homily if it ensures that the aforementioned is spelt out, i.e., that the individual is unconditionally desirable and loved. The thetic element consists in the fact that, through God's justification of sinful humanity, divine love becomes in itself a legitimate entitlement even before the person has changed.[7] In other words, it is not primarily a matter of specifying a demand, a law or moral code. Rather, it is given unconditionally and as such cannot be disposed of or limited either democratically or monarchically. After all, it is impossible to vote or decide on whether God is love or hate and whether Christ is present in the sufferers or in the perpetrators.

The aspect of grace also means that a homily should be a loving dialogue with the listening members of the community—an event in which people's burning desire for God is understood by the preacher at a deeper level and where it meets with the same yearning on his part (137). It is a question of heart-to-heart communication. Anyone who preaches must have listened a lot. "If we wish to adapt to people's language and to reach them with God's word, we need to share in their lives and pay loving attention to them" (158). And: "The preacher must know the heart of his community ..." (137).

Preachers are neither owners nor masters of the message they proclaim, nor are they rulers over their audiences. Any sermon that aims to score points is bound to have an undermining effect in the long term, even if it is delivered with great expertise and rhetorical skills.

---

5 On the wider discussion of the sacramental character of the word cf. Fuchs, Ottmar, Predigt als Gnadenerfahrung – Aspekte einer indikativen Homiletik in: Theologische Quartalschrift 186 4, 2006, 313–335, especially 313–316.

6 Cf. Semmelroth, Otto, Wirkendes Wort, Frankfurt a. M. 1962, 182, 207ff.

7 Cf. Fuchs, Predigt als Gnadenerfahrung, 316–319.

A homily of this kind reverts to its "established" setting within the homiletic process. After all, the concept of homiletics and its underlying meaning (*homoios* = equal) presupposes a dialogue between believers on an "equal" footing.[8] It focuses on the way they relate to one another against the background of the "same" (equal) faith, entering into dialogue, supporting and upholding one another. The background of faith manifests itself specifically in the calling to mind of the stories and messages of the Bible and the Church's traditions. Hence, the concept of homiletics has both a synchronic and a diachronic dimension. It involves not only interaction between the faithful here and now, but also with those who have gone before us and who speak to us through the Bible and through history.

Within this dialogue preaching has a dual function. It ensures that not an iota of the old stories is lost and that those who are alive now enter into dialogue with them and with one another. Although preaching takes the form of a monologue, its function is to express and encourage dialogue.[9]

By listening to that love which is proclaimed to God's people, they "will sense that each word of Scripture is a gift before it is a demand" (142). Without this unsentimental, heart-to-heart kindness—which in itself means an ability to empathise and to renounce rhetorical violence—any proclamation of God's grace would lack an anthropological basis.[10] "The preacher has the wonderful but difficult task of joining loving hearts, the hearts of the Lord and his people" (143).

However, a preacher can say nothing genuine or authentic about God's love and grace or indeed interpret a given passage in this light unless he himself seeks this experience: "What is essential is that the preacher be certain that God loves him, that Jesus Christ has saved him and that his love always has the last word" (151). Significantly, "the Sunday readings will resonate in all their brilliance in the hearts of the faithful if they have first done so in the heart of their pastor" (149).

Preachers thus mediate between the inspiration of Scripture and the inspiration of modern-day people who, borne by the spiritual gifts of baptism and confirmation, put their faith in the Gospel and bear witness to it in their lives.

Francis quotes *Evangelii Nuntiandi* in this context: "The Holy Spirit, who inspired the word, 'today, just as at the beginning of the Church, acts in every

---

8 The Greek word *homileo* is based on *homoios*, meaning "same" or "equal".

9 Cf. Fuchs, Ottmar, Gotteswort und Predigt – Je dichter am biblischen Text, desto näher am Leben der Menschen – ein homiletisches Prinzip!, in: Ortkemper, Franz-Josef; Schuller, Florian, Berufen, das Wort Gottes zu verkündigen – Die Botschaft der Bibel im Leben und in der Sendung der Kirche, Stuttgart 2008, 85–104, 85ff.

10 OWT Vol. 7 (Evangelii Gaudium) 283 pp. 5.25x8.5.indd 151 8/28/15 8:45 AM 152 The Proclamation of the Gospel.

evangeliser who allows himself to be possessed and led by him. The Holy Spirit places on his lips the words which he could not find by himself" (151).

2. *Given and Giving in Freedom*

At the same time Francis emphasises the necessary relationship between freedom and creativity: "The Lord wants to make use of us as living, free and creative beings who let his word enter their own hearts before then passing it on to others." Therefore, he continues, "Christ's message must truly penetrate and possess the preacher, not just intellectually but in his entire being" (151).

The freedom and creativity with which the preacher can approach and refer to tradition will thus also influence the relationship he has with his audience who "want someone to serve as an instrument and to express their feelings in such a way that afterwards, each one may choose how he or she will continue the conversation" (143). Manipulative and inflammatory rhetoric is just as much out of place as is any form of argumentation aimed at scoring points.[11]

As preachers we must "offer ourselves and all our abilities as instruments" (145). This means not just bearing witness to our understanding of Scripture, but also testifying to any possible lack of understanding or resistance, using all our skills which enable us to respond to a piece of Scripture or indeed to any other reality (145).[12] What matters is not just the conceptual meaning of a biblical text, but also the impact and significance that is intended. On this basis the preacher must enter into a similar relationship with the present, unlocking not just the meaning of a text, but also its significance (147).[13] After all, "one of the defects of a tedious and ineffectual preaching is precisely its inability to transmit the intrinsic power of the text which has been proclaimed" (148).

Although historically it is not totally uncontroversial to see the Church as a mother, Pope Francis nevertheless associates this ecclesiological description with the essential qualities of a mother, "knowing that the child trusts that what she is teaching is for his or her benefit, for children know that they are loved. Moreover, a good mother can recognise everything that God is bringing about in her children, she listens to their concerns and learns from them."

---

11 On such rhetoric cf. Fuchs, Ottmar, Von Gott predigen: Anleitungen – Beispiele – Überlegungen, Gütersloh 1984. 57–67; ibid, Zu Gert Ottos Predigtverständnis, in: Gert Otto, Rhetorisch predigen – Wahrheit als Mitteilung: Beispiele zur Predigtpraxis, Gütersloh 1981, 107–140, 110ff.

12 Cf. Fuchs, Gotteswort und Predigt, 86ff.

13 Cf. ibid, 88ff.

This ecclesiological understanding is rooted in the theological hope that God himself has a motherly side and that all people are longed for, desired and loved by God from birth. This pre-sacramental identity as God's children right from birth is something which has always been at the focus of preaching, the sacraments and the Church itself, seeking to make it part of people's experience, so that they can derive strength from it and so that they can celebrate this identity. It means that the Church and its preaching recognise this human identity in a major way, in the same way that they recognise God's creation, calling people into existence by his love. In fact, there is nothing God seeks more ardently than that his love should be appreciated by his people (139).

Calling upon preachers at the Eucharist—preachers who are still largely male—Francis exhorts them to be motherly in their approach and to use "a kind of music which inspires encouragement, strength and enthusiasm" (139). In terms of hermeneutics this is the practical key to a "mother culture", opening both sides to one another—God in his motherly character, on the one hand, and, on the other, an experience of God through a Church that is motherly in this sense as well as through the sacraments and through preaching.[14]

In this way preaching magnifies the source that loves us, and so Francis touches upon the same root of the issue that was formulated by Theodor W. Adorno: "Everyone nowadays, without exception, feels insufficiently loved, because everyone can love too little." Such love cannot be preached prescriptively because "it already presupposes a different character structure than the one we wish to change".[15] Demands are ineffective. "As soon as we demand that children should be given more warmth, it becomes artificial and is thus negated...The encouragement to love—perhaps even in the form of an imperative, as something one *ought to do*—is in itself part of an ideology which perpetuates coldness. Characteristically, it then becomes compulsive and oppressive, counteracting a person's ability to love."[16] Adorno had an inkling that it was a decisive and "major...stimulus of Christianity to redeem that all-pervading coldness. Yet the attempt failed, probably because it had no impact on the social order which produces and reproduces coldness."[17] Theologically speaking, the message of God's universal and unlimited love—a love that always gives first and thus empowers people and does not wait until certain conditions are met—has not sufficiently carried, reached and changed the real lives of people. This is because, over the centuries, this love has always been associated too closely with all too human and inhuman conditions and with people's lives, neglecting pressing principles. In his homiletics Pope Francis redresses the balance!

---

14 On the unlimited intensity and scope of motherly love, cf. Fuchs, Ottmar, Eine Liebe, die die schlimmste Grenze überschreitet, in: Diakonia 45 (2014) volume 2.

15 Adorno, Theodor W., Stichworte – Kritische Modelle 2, Frankfurt a. M. 1969, 98.

16 Ibid., 99.

17 Ibid., 99.

The method of delivery that is used in preaching must therefore be based on precisely the premises I have just outlined. After all, preaching is not merely a matter of communicating a truth, but "truth goes hand in hand with beauty and goodness" (142). Moreover, "far from dealing with abstract truths or cold syllogisms, it communicates the beauty of the images used by the Lord to encourage the practice of good" (142). The way Jesus used contemporary imagery of nature and culture to proclaim the Gospel must also influence the way in which a homily today enters into synthesis with our own contemporary images, with examples of familiar everyday references and with people's aspirations, narratives and experiences.[18] When Francis speaks of a "synthesis", he means that preaching must refrain from conveying mere "ideas or detached values" (143).[19] Furthermore, "an attractive image makes the message seem familiar, close to home, practical and related to everyday life. A successful image can make people savour the message, awaken a desire and move the will towards the Gospel" (157).

To prepare a homily in such a way that the edifying and robust parts of the Gospel can genuinely be "savoured" and that the audience becomes aware of God's gift of love is something that generally requires more work and dedication than the preaching of mere demands and of abstract arguments (144).[20] The way we talk therefore has its own theological quality which is just as important as the message we preach. Biblically and homiletically, the focus should be above all on imagery and narratives, i.e., on narrative forms of expression with which the audience can identify. Narrativity itself is a rhetorical experience of something given and therefore also of grace.[21] But lucid reflection, too, can be experienced as a gift of theological literacy.[22]

In the same context Francis also highlights the need to speak positively. The focus should be less—and not primarily—on what people ought to do, on what they are failing to do or on what they are not allowed to do. Instead, it should be on the way God's Spirit is already at work within them and on how something that is already there can be done even better (159).

Again and again, we can see the fundamental principle of his homiletics, viewing the fragmentary nature of life as more important than the victory of platonic idealism over all realities[23] and experience as more important than

---

18 Cf. Fuchs, Ottmar, Die lebendige Predigt, Munich 1978.

19 Fuchs, Gotteswort und Predigt, 93–97.

20 See the example of an "experience poem" used by Theodor Storm Fuchs, Predigt als Gnadenerfahrung, 322ff.

21 Cf. Fuchs, Predigt als Gnadenerfahrung, 325

22 Cf. ibid., 323.

23 Cf. Fuchs, Ottmar, 'Plötzlich so viel Schmutz', Papst Benedikts apotropäischer Jargon der Reinheit", in: Meyer-Blank, Michael, et al., Sündenpredigt, Munich 2012, 302–321.

abstract arguments. Significantly, therefore, an entire chapter in *Evangelii Gaudium* bears the title: "Realities are more important than ideas" (231–233).

3. *The Message as Empowerment*

For example, Francis emphasises the need to consider not only the message and the what, but also the how. He quotes *Evangelii Nuntiandi*: "The obvious importance of the content (...) must not overshadow the importance of its ways and means" (156). This is how Francis talks about the precarious relationship between knowledge and power: If knowledge is believed to be good and necessary for people, how does it reach them? Does it conceal an unacknowledged but nonetheless powerful desire for domination over others, or does knowledge lead to empowering others, enabling them to give free rein to their own creativity, and does it give them freedom in handling that knowledge?[24]

Francis takes a very clear position. Preaching requires a spiritual attitude of conveying knowledge through the speech act of God's love which is given to us and of our love for others—a love which we are enabled to give because we have received God's love. If this spiritual attitude is lacking—and I think even a yearning for this attitude is sufficient—then knowledge in matters of faith may be interesting but it does not constitute any proclamation of the Gospel. Rather, we are "a resounding gong or a clanging cymbal" (1 Cor 13:1), without conveying any of God's or the preacher's empathy (156).

If preaching is rooted in, and derives its energy from, the fountain of God's love and from sharing that love, then we have established a link between preaching and pastoral care. This link between the message of Scripture and a human situation is a concern which "has nothing to do with shrewdness or calculation; it is profoundly...pastoral" (154). This is in fact the essence of pastoral care, and, as Francis puts it with reference to *Evangelii Nuntiandi*: "Fundamentally it is a 'spiritual sensitivity for reading God's message in events'" (154).

Preaching, says Francis, always involves a non-negotiable tension: on the one hand, "we should never respond to questions that nobody asks" (155) and, on the other, we must not "look for excuses to water down the clear meaning of the text" (153). It is important to beware lest we "make the text say what we think is convenient, useful for confirming us in our previous decisions, suited to our own patterns of thought" (152). Although our own experience can indeed open up a Bible passage, we must not make this the main criterion for a homily. Passages should therefore also be preached upon that are difficult for the preacher—and indeed out of solidarity with the audience who often feel

---

[24] Cf. Fuchs, Predigt als Gnadenerfahrung, 324–329.

the same about it. Although God relates to our experiences, God is never defined by them.

When it comes to delivery, Francis is also concerned that preaching should not draw too much attention to itself, e. g., by being too long. Although it does function independently, it must serve its intended purpose, which should also be accessible through brevity. This means that it must not be too strenuous or indeed merciless towards the audience on account of its length (138).

Pope Francis speaks of "an intense and happy experience of the Spirit" which can occur through a homily as a "constant source of renewal and growth". And, looking at the Pope's own preaching style, he clearly means not merely the preacher's preparation, but also the actual delivery, with sermons that are unscripted and which give the Holy Spirit space to do its work of renewal and even to disrupt a prepared speech (135, see also 151).[25]

What is needed is not rhetorical perfectionism or impeccable sermons, but inspiration by the Spirit of love, which then nourishes and carries any bright ideas the preacher might have, whether in terms of content or delivery. Both in his talks and in his written output Pope Francis dares to "fascinate" his audience with his "patchiness" (as a colleague remarked so appreciatively at a conference). This is partly because he has the self-confidence to interrupt any systematic stringency with narrative reminiscences and with impressive imagery from culture or nature. When it comes to dogmatic and the text types that currently form part of dogmatic, the ordinary Magisterium presents us with a rather exciting challenge. If we refrain from using mandatory compact packages, we enter an open terrain which lets us breathe and gives us freedom.

Jesus' parables give people their own options of identification and thus the freedom to develop their own thoughts and theological creativity. Such preaching is no longer opaque, i.e., it is no longer obsessively condensed in its argumentation and use of language. It no longer instrumentalises language, the faithful and even God himself (as it is no longer a sermon we can only reject it completely or totally integrate into it). Theologically, non-coercive preaching is rooted in God's own infinite mystery which does not allow for any final and complete access to the mind of God.

Pope Francis points out that God "does not demand a full response if we are not yet ready". Rather, "he simply asks that we sincerely look at our life and present ourselves honestly before him" (153). Full of understanding, Pope Francis therefore says: "Even if the homily at times may be somewhat tedious, if this maternal and ecclesial spirit is present, it will always bear fruit, just as

[25] Cf. Fuchs, Ottmar, Glaubenswissen im Horizont der Gnade – Plädoyer für eine indikativische Homiletik, in: ibid, Von solcher Hoffnung kann ich leben ... Predigten, Luzern 1997, 185–207, 187ff., 205ff.

the tedious counsels of a mother bear fruit, in due time, in the hearts of her children" (140).

Pope Francis also indicates that, although it has always been the Church's doctrine that the Bible must be taken as a whole and that it is inspired as such, it does contain different types of texts and in fact texts that may even be disproved elsewhere in Scripture. The Bible is not a harmonious whole nor is it an innocent book. Nevertheless, the truth remains "that the Holy Spirit has inspired not just a part of the Bible, but the Bible as a whole" (148). There are biblical texts which serve as beacons, compared with which others appear far from exemplary, not to say startling. But even the negative parts of the Bible (e. g., texts that are full of violence) are necessary. Their inspiration lies in the unveiling of such negativity, as they indicate and make us aware that God should *not* be instrumentalised and used against others.[26] Inspiration is not identical with textual affirmation or fundamentalist hermeneutics that encourage imitation. Instead, it is a critical, Spirit-inspired process between the Bible and the Church.

Everything else in the Bible must be read with critical discernment, from the perspective of the Suffering Servant in Isaiah and Christ's death on the cross. People's understanding of God's will may have grown in various contexts compared with others, in both the history of the Church and the present day (148).

The Pope warns against "using something sacred for our own benefit ..." (152). Such an attitude would destroy our doxological capacity, which involves acknowledging God's word as greater than our own and recognising the infinite difference between humans and God when we approach God in worship. It is of course true that God speaks to us through other people and that this produces a certain clarity. Yet what remains is the infinite and unfathomable mystery of the universal God, a mystery that goes much further. Even in preaching, the word is merely a small island that floats on the sea of a divine quality which we hardly know at all: God's unfathomable character, which always and totally puts a limit on our preaching.[27]

Nevertheless, it is possible for us to speak of and with God, because he has spoken to us and enabled us to enter into dialogue with him and about him. Without this dialogue God's mystery would be utterly inscrutable and ultimately meaningless—at least for humans.[28]

---

26 Cf. Fuchs, Ottmar, Praktische Hermeneutik der Heiligen Schrift, Stuttgart 2004, 438–461.

27 Cf. Rahner, Karl, Erfahrungen eines katholischen Theologen, in: Lehmann, Karl, Vor dem Geheimnis Gottes den Menschen verstehen, Freiburg i. Br. 1984, 105–119, especially 106ff.

28 Cf. Rahner, Karl, Von Gott muss geredet werden, in: Orientierung 53 (1989) 6, 91.

Considering that God's love and acceptance of humanity came first and indeed as a free gift, the reality of God and an experience of him are reflected in the behaviour and spirituality of the preacher who freely gives his time to preaching and to the preparation of homilies. Pope Francis argues that a sufficiently long time should be spent on preparing one's homilies and that this should be prioritised "even if less time has to be given to other important activities" (145).

It is, as it were, time outside one's normal pastoral work and therefore "time off". "To interpret a biblical text, we need to be patient, to put aside all other concerns, and to give it our time, interest and undivided attention" (146). In this way a preacher freely responds to God's free gift of grace. Pope Francis continues by saying that "preparation for preaching requires love. We only devote periods of quiet time to the things or the people whom we love; and here we are speaking of the God whom we love, a God who wishes to speak to us" (146).[29]

This grace dynamic involves two "embraces" by our heavenly Father: first, his embrace at birth and baptism and, second, the embrace of our merciful Father at the end of our life and at the end of all time (144). It is the function of a homily to apply this dual grace to people's entire life spans, so that they can derive strength from both "embraces"—their origin before the beginnings of time (their pre-birth "time off") and their future, their memories and their hopes.

4. *Theological Background: Indicative Preaching*[30]

Forgetting is one of the worst things (especially according to the Old Testament) that can happen to a community or a person when matters are concerned that are vital for life and that stay alive merely by means of memory. When a subject is not constantly discussed and is made current in togetherness

---

29 Cf. Fuchs, Predigt als Gnadenerfahrung, 329–335.

30 In spring 1991 I received an invitation from the University of South Africa, Pretoria, to spend several weeks as guest professor at the Department of Practical Theology to give lectures on the topic "The diaconical dimension of the church". I accepted the offer gladly and went to Pretoria in autumn of the same year. During these weeks the colleagues of the Department of Practical Theology at the University of Pretoria kindly invited me to debate the question of how a homiletic conception should be when it constitutes itself in the horizon of diaconia. With the following text I opened the discussion, which I appreciated and enjoyed very much. I am very grateful for this brief but intensive exchange of ideas and viewpoints.

(and if it is not being related to a direct reality) then it gives way to the creeping loss of relevance and becomes marginal.[31]

The sermon is a decisive institution of remembrance within the Christian and ecclesiastical community, to act against such forgetfulness in its constant work of remembering and thereby maintaining the *memoria*. Regarding the contents of their memories, Christians rely on the stories from the Bible, in particular the story of Jesus Christ. The biblical stories substantialise for them a characteristic relationship, which is manifested in constantly new occasions of experience: the relationship of God with the people and the people's relationship to God. In this "theological horizon", encounters within humankind also take place, become important there and become possible and necessary in their humanity.[32]

This formulation of a "theological horizon" is obviously very approximate and open and requires a more precise definition, in particular the most essential: this divine area of humanity has itself the structure of encounter, of a realistic relationship. This is often explicitly discussed and remembered, for example, in the stories of vocation, in the texts of prayer and particularly in Jesus's relationship to God. The related dialogues between God and people have a character of interaction where both partners make use of the word (in calling or prayer). YHWH, the God of Israel and Abba, the God of Jesus, is a God who wants, creates and maintains relationships. The related dialogues between God and people have a character of interaction where both partners make use of the word (in calling or prayer) whereby they are completing "speech acts"[33] and whereby they initiate actions.

There is not only a non-arbitrary relationship between faith and its social praxis within our daily lives, but also within the faith itself, between belief and its spiritual praxis, between the word of God and its liberating experience within our existence. Speaking of the diaconical dimension of the Church, we should not forget the diaconical dimension of the Christian message of God itself. Preaching God's presence in the word and in the world is a part of this theme, because talking of diaconia one must not only think of the inter-human relationship of justice and help. It is rather an integral part of the subject of diaconia, that the first deacon in Christian life is God himself, his love and help for humankind. To speak of this love of God towards us has to be regarded as one of the most important tasks of Christian preaching, which wants to convey

31 Cf. C. Westermann, Lob und Klage in den Psalmen (Göttingen 1977) p. 192. Cf. O. Fuchs, Die Klage als Gebet (München 1982) pp. 216–230.

32 Cf. in detail O. Fuchs, Von Gott predigen (Gütersloh 1984).

33 Cf. J. R. Searle, Sprechakte. Ein sprachphilosophischer Essay (Frankfurt a. M. 1971), (Speech Acts 1969).

God's unconditional acceptance to the people: towards an indicative and facilitating speaking of God in the church.

That is the theological horizon where the relationships within humankind have their place, their value and are facilitated. It would not be a good theology to talk here of the horizontal and vertical dimension of biblical interpersonal reality or spirituality. Both these areas of communication are (undivided and unmixed) "meshed" together, namely, in the fact that they explain each other, recognise and deepen each other and identify one another. When one speaks of God's redeeming encounters with humankind, one implicitly speaks of the encounter of the people amongst themselves, which becomes possible because of this given relationship with God. When one encounters people in a benevolent way, one realises implicitly the structure of communication of God with humankind. The modality of the discourse is however different. When one speaks of God's encounter, one speaks mainly in the indicative; when one speaks of the relationship of people amongst themselves, in the horizon of this God, one speaks in the imperative so long as the Kingdom of God has not fully arrived, so that its constantly new comparative to the present is to be put forward.

The indicative of the relationship granted by God is something given and offered, whereby this "being given" already reveals itself in its form of conveyance, in the remembrance of the corresponding examples which are given in the biblical stories. For telling stories conveys narrated interactions and is therefore open to spontaneous identifications. Listening to and understanding stories takes less effort than do lectures or even sermons (if they do not tell stories or parables, use metaphors, etc.).

Thereby these stories that are committed to memory are not only valid for the narrated people within these stories themselves, but carry—in the horizon of Gods lasting love—the promise within them to be valid for ever, so that the process of memory simultaneously proclaims its validity throughout history and makes itself and God's grace behind it present. Such is the biblical understanding of "*zkr*" (the Hebrew word for "*memoria*" or "remembrance") insofar as the stories become true and real, become substantialised by means of telling and believing them in a community. Precisely this indicative should not be forgotten in Christian preaching: the "giveness" of a God who wants encounters with humankind and encourages humankind to enter into communication with him (even beyond death and the end of the world). Such a desire for encounter on the part of God also has a slight imperative part: God offers him/herself for encounter, but humankind also has to involve itself to succeed. This imperative is, however, the result of an indicative that can be realised, as the offer of a unbreakable friendship, that wants to make friends, to allow friendship to be experienced! The biblical literature of prayer and the richness of the speech act of praise and thanks, lament and bidding clearly shows how central the lively dialogue with God expresses and interprets human life within such a relationship. There is nothing in human life that should be excluded from this vital encounter with God and the diaconia God has shown to the people.

When Christian preaching takes the fact seriously that this process of interaction between God and humankind makes real encounters possible, then God cannot only be spoken of as a cypher, a word for more humane communication, but also so that the concrete human relationship with God becomes a subject itself and a reality on its own. If God were only an idea in the biblical tradition, an abstract, an absolute, a neutral, an ideal, an idealistic and intellectual dimension, then one could quite rightly say: "God—that means that we are good to each other". But then the biblical God becomes forgotten in his concrete nature and personality, in her anthropomorphous partnership with humankind. Accordingly one must say; "God—that means that He is good to humankind and also shows this!" Only such an indicative makes the imperative possible and releases it from obeying the laws and humankind from the craze of achievement or despair and resignation.

This subject also has biographical roots within my own life. In the first years of being minister in a parish I always pushed (like my contemporary colleagues) to change the world, especially for the Christians to become more effective in their actions for freedom and justice, their actions for the sake of others. I interpreted the biblical stories mostly as ethical imperatives, until, through the criticism of people and of talks with my colleagues, I realised that such a preaching is only half of what we have to say; yes, such a continual imperative preaching reminds the believers of the facilitating possibility to love and help one another, which is the redeeming relationship with God himself.

5. *Against "God" as a Term of Achievement!*

We have to be careful about transferring the talk of God to the talk of humankind too quickly, for example, in such sentences as "Mercy: that means that we have to treat each other with mercifulness!" "Resurrection means that we should not fall, but always get up again!", etc. In such sentences concerning God him/herself, the connection with interaction is extinguished. But only this interpersonal connection makes up the point of reference and context in the framework of its validity and possibility. This point is: Mercy means that God is merciful to you; with such an experience of belief, a human being can also be "merciful". Resurrection means that God resurrects a person who has died for the love of humankind and for the sake of its liberation and thereby continues her life further and legitimises it; with such an eschatological deed, it is also possible for a human being to risk a similar life "for no reward" against a lack of success and the suspicion of senselessness.

Where God is not constantly discussed in homiletic discourse, preached in sermons and addressed in prayers as the personal communication partner of the people, then their actions reduce themselves mercilessly to obeying laws of the exemplary. To present Jesus only as an example of benevolence is the personified law-making of the Christian message and thereby is a hopeless overtaxing of human beings, inasmuch as Jesus's God and his own relation to him, which has made such a life possible, are omitted.

The depersonalising of God leads to the moralising of humankind! "God" is supercharged with directions for actions which humankind has to do itself. Think in this context of Lk 11:46: "And Jesus said, 'Woe to you lawyers also! For you load men with burdens hard to bear!'" God is preached as a term of achievement and not as the communicative facilitator of the possibility for more humane life and history. That is a distressing conforming to the structure of achievement of late capitalist and highly industrialised societies and their fantasies of total power, even to the attitude that God could be at our disposal by means of ethics. That is a kind of atheism within Christianity. The belief in progress in a complete and saved world which is to achieved by humankind has already provokes violence or resignation in many places.

Many modern sermons are not much different in their structure than the old casuistic and moralistic way of preaching, even though the purposes have changed. In both cases theological issues become too quickly directions for action; the interpretation of God is functionalised and fades to the religious-argumentative legitimation of what one has to say to humankind as the imperative. This is also true of attractive contemporary sermons even if their form of address does not display any direct commands or laws, but is characterised by dream-filled, aesthetic and poetic images and stories which, although they allow more freedom than direct demands, still interpret God as the area of action of the good people. Biblical theology, on the other hand, claims that the talk of God is not a mythical statement of purely human qualities, hopes and actions, but that the biblical myth presupposes the reality and reality of encounter about which it talks.

Such a "boomerang preaching", which throws the vector of the human relationship to God back to the relationship of the people among themselves (prayer as a conversation with oneself) and with others (God as human benevolence), can only be based on sporadically used sections of the Bible with the help of short-sighted and naive hermeneutics. This is true for example of the story of the two sons, where one of them says "yes", but does not go to the vineyard, and the other says "no", but goes to work there after all. In its message, the story does not annul the relationship-orientated "yes" to the Lord; it has as its aim to not let this "yes" stand on its own, but to fill it with the corresponding practical and humane meaning (cf. Mt 21:28–32).

The difficult and precarious question about God cannot be answered by simply creating identities: "God is identical with benevolence"; "The confession to Jesus Christ is basically identical with living as Jesus lived as far as our fellow human beings are concerned". Such identifications do not solve the "problem" between humankind and God; they destroy it. Simultaneously such an identity of humankind with God destroys God as a real encountering partner.

Contrary to many trends of individual moralising (with regard to marriage and the family) as well as socio-political moralising of the biblical horizon of God, we must try to realise God as an independent reality of partnership and thus to respect her as the meaningful place of relationship from which such activities for the sake of humankind and its society become possible even over long distances in distress (and at the same time are to be criticised by the liberating character of God's deeds). Thus, Christians can involve themselves to the point of the courage of sacrifice for peace in different areas of life and between peoples and show solidarity with the appropriate movements. At the same time, with their belief in God, they bring the necessary condition to have patience and stamina for long distances and also in planning stages as well as to bring up the corresponding theological criticism of human activities.

How then should preachers speak? That this is homiletic "hard work" is already known by preachers who endeavour to verbalise the theological indicative of our faith, insofar as a sermon can do it. My plea for the indicative "talk of God" should not be euphorically or charismatically misunderstood, as if one could overcome the problem when one speaks pathetically and conjures up the reality of God by asking for special experiences of vocation against which most listeners would be helpless. The sermon which is meant here should not transfer the work it has to do to the listeners; the sermon has to do the work of remembrance itself with the help of the biblical texts, with whose narrative and spiritual (especially concerning the Psalms) hermeneutic power similar encounters of God can be made possible, as they are found in the stories. On the other hand, the sermon should do this work listening to the listeners, to the baptised believers and their experiences of God (which include the lack of such experiences, too), correlating them in an encouraging way with the biblical events. Doing this, the sermon can be the bridge between the inspiring stories of the inspired Bible and the inspiring experiences of the inspired Christians. Talking of God thus provokes an extremely sober and realistic work preaching, concerned with the experiences, situations and memories of the people, both past (in the tradition) and present (in the Church).

III. Diaconate Between Title and Implementation

1. *Diaconia Is Rooted in the Gospel*

Jesus said that "the whole Law and the Prophets" are down to the two commandments about the Love of God and the love of one's neighbour (cf. Mt. 22:37–40). If the nature of the Church refers to Jesus Christ, then, historically and concretely, it follows Jesus and thereby attains the Christological quality in which it historically embodies the spirit of the Risen One. This includes both types of real presence of the Risen One in his Church: in the preached words and celebrated signs of remembrance and in meeting Christ in the naked, sick and homeless (cf. Mt 25:31–36) and in suffering people in general (cf. Rom 8:26). The Church knows that it serves this real presence of Christ among people in favour of the reality which is constantly in the heart of Jesus Christ, namely the reality of the Kingdom of God in our age: as a faithful hope in God and as solidarity with people.

The nature of the Church can, accordingly, be defined thus: the proclamation of God's love (as comfort of the love of God to the people and as the corresponding answer of the people to God) and of the requirement of love towards people (made possible by the above)—proclamation of God's salvific acts, in words, rituals and encounters and in the practice of interpersonal and interethnic justice and mercy. Martyria and diaconia therefore constitute fundamental dimensions of the Christian and ecclesial self-realisation which one can no longer do without. How these dimensions are realised in the concrete ministerial or even just functional missions in the areas of evangelisation, rituals, community work and solidarity service and between them is not a matter of secondary importance, but flexible according to each challenge that might appear.

In the Second Vatican Council, the Church remembered in a new and intense way that evangelisation, ecclesial communion and liturgy are not the only essential elements of its self-realisation, but that also the diaconia (in the contemporary sense of the word) pertains to the essential vocation of the Church. This is defined, first, by the Pastoral Constitution[1], in which the notion

---

[1] For this reason, I agree with Hans-Joachim Sander when he says that the explicit connection between the diaconate and the Council's Pastoral Constitution has to be observed, cf. Hans-Joachim Sander, Diakonat – die heterotrope Dimension des kirchlichen Amtes, in:

of pastoral is extended to include diaconal action, namely to the salvific action of the Church in today's world. The practical realisations make manifest the fact that the Church is a sacrament of salvation for the world. Diaconia transforms the soteriology (doctrine of salvation) of the Church's evangelisation into soteriopraxy (practical ministry of salvation) which can be experienced interpersonally. Margit Eckholt also starts from the same essential dimension of the Church, as expressed in charity and states that the diaconia "in conjunction with leiturgia and martyria is an expression of the fundamental sacramental structure of the Church, as posited by the Second Vatican Council"[2]. Both are done "*in persona Christi*" and therefore have a sacramental character: the proclamation and celebration of the Paschal mystery in the Eucharist and the equally really present meeting with Christ in the poor and suffering, for he meets us in the lowly ones with an authority that is all the more necessary.[3]

Richard Hartmann, Franz Reger & Stefan Sander (eds.), Ortsbestimmungen: Der Diakonat als kirchlicher Dienst, Frankfurt a. M. 2009, 38–58, 47, Note 13; cf. Hans-Joachim Sander's commentary in Gaudium et Spes in: Peter Hünermann & Bernd-Jochen Hilberath (eds.), Herders Theologischer Kommentar zum Zweiten Vatikanischen Konzil, Bd. 4, Freiburg i. Br. 2005, 581–887. About this relationship to the world in solidarity and love cf. also Karl Bopp, Wozu braucht die Kirche ein diakonisches Amt? Praktisch-theologische Perspektiven für die zukünftige Gestalt des Diakonats, in: Richard Hartmann et al. (eds.), Ortsbestimmungen, 209–217.

2 Margit Eckholt, „In uns vollzieht sich das Sakrament der Liebe" (Madeleine Delbrêl). Der Diakonat der Frau und die ekklesiologische Grundlegung einer diakonischen Kirche, in: Richard Hartmann u. a. (eds.), Ortsbestimmungen, 123–143, 135.

3 My intention in the beginning more than a decade ago under the impression of the very attractive conceptual and practical definition of the diaconate in the Diocese of Rottenburg-Stuttgart, was to give a theological clarification of this diaconal (in the narrow sense of the world, i.e., social service) orientation of the diaconate against the backdrop of exactness this ecclesial practice, and in this way to accompany theologically this ecclesial development in the diocese. With this focus of mine, I have not disavowed other realisations of the diaconate, as Rupert M. Scheule reproaches me, and if I somehow gave this impression, I regret it very much. Cf. Rupert M. Scheule, Ja zum wahren Amt, Apologie eines offenen theologischen Selbstverständnisses Ständiger Diakone, in: Richard Hartmann et al. (eds.), Ortsbestimmungen, 70–77, 71. In other publications, I myself elaborated on and defended the diaconal diversity (in the broader sense). On the different areas where the diaconal ministry is realized but always from a specifically diaconal perspective cf. Ottmar Fuchs, Im Innersten gefährdet. Für ein neues Verhältnis von Kirchenamt und Gottesvolk, Innsbruck 2009, 69–92. Therefore, I took this very ecclesial self-realization in Rottenburg-Stuttgart very seriously even then, also as a gift for which one should be grateful to the Lord (cf. Scheule, Amt, 73). Precisely in this context Scheule would most likely concede himself that exposing an ecclesial self-realisation to criticism, in order to avoid that its normativity grow immeasurably, does not solve either the problem, or the responsibility. This was impressively demonstrated primarily by Sander in his criticism of the *societas perfecta* vision cf. Sander, Diakonat, 58. The fact that the Church is gifted by grace must not lead to their legitimising self-immunisation. It is not correct that the Church not have also an "ethical-normative" project: against Scheule, Amt, 74.

2. *Dual Developments*

Therefore, quite early in the post-New Testament time of the first centuries, Church ministry was also understood as a dual one: expressing the love of God and in the love of one's neighbour; it could, however, be differentiated in all the practices of the ecclesial existence (as well as in different connections between these practices). As to the liturgy, there was, already in the early Church, the elementary connection between the preparation of the altar gifts and the ministry to the poor. "It is from the charity work, especially from the contact with the gifts from the donations to the poor that their (the deacons'– O.F.) liturgical participation in the preparation of the gifts and the distribution of the Eucharist to people who were absent and sick arose..."[4] But it is not all about this dual structure of the nature of the Church and its ministries; it is also about seeing the love of God and the love of neighbour as being on the same level of value. For Jesus qualifies the commandment of loving one's neighbour as "like" the one about the love of God. He didn't have to stress this only to the one who raised the question at that moment. This emphasis is one that cuts critically through the whole history of the Church and regards not least the essential structure of Catholic ministry. For the equality between love of God and love of neighbour should be reflected by the equality between the hierarchical grades of presbyterate and diaconate. However, up to this day, this is not the case, with the exception of the first centuries, when male and female[5] deacons had a well-defined and powerful position. If in the early history of the Church the presbyters were the guarantors of tradition, in the same way, the deacons, female and male, were the guarantors that, in the Christian communities, the poor were never humiliated. As such, they had, even compared with the presbyters, great prestige and (because they administered property for the benefit of the poor) were a big influence in the community.[6]

Through the "hierarchical anchoring of the community's charity work" in the deacons[7] what happened was that "the individual needy person, through the charity of the community, escaped the arbitrariness of individual handout and obtained an entitlement to help from the community..."[8] This observation shows the Ordo-structure of the diaconate: it must make sure that the relationship with those needing help is not left to the whim of the faithful (let's say of

4 Ernst Dassmann, Kirchengeschichte I. Ausbreitung, Leben und Lehre der Kirche in den ersten drei Jahrhunderten, Stuttgart 1991, 172.

5 Cf. Peter Hünermann et al. (eds.), Diakonat. Ein Amt für Frauen in der Kirche – Ein frauengerechtes Amt?, Ostfildern 1997, Dorothea Reininger, Diakonat der Frau in der Einen Kirche, Ostfildern 1999.

6 Cf. Dassmann, Kirchengeschichte, 163–175.

7 Cf. ibid., 171.

8 Ibid. 250 cf. also 244ff. and 248ff.

their majority) but that it belongs, from the word go, to the very essence of the Christian community.

What we have here is a precondition that is imposed from outside ourselves (*extra nos*) to the Church's existence, presupposing a very specific kind of witness, even if necessary in contradiction and counteraction to the circumstances in the Church and society. The sacramental character understood in this sense is based not on spiritual community leadership and on presiding over the Eucharist but rather on the immediate proximity of Christ to the one attacked and beaten up, who is cared for by the Samaritan who in turn represents the wounded one, the present and helping Christ. The diaconal encounter is a personal encounter with the suffering and solidary Christ who becomes incarnate in history in both the suffering and the solidary. One can't get more Christological or, in better words, Christopractical than that!

The Second Vatican Council explicitly says that the deacons[9] are not ordained to priesthood but to a ministry of service[10]. This is a peculiar contradiction, which needs some explanation (see subchapter 5). In any case, it is the extra "*nos*" of the being-there-for-the-others of the Christian existence. Such a ministry has an animating and multiplying quality, therefore a quality of leadership. But it does not have to be a spiritual leadership.

3. *Contextual Meaning of the Titles*

It follows that with the works of Anni Hentschel and John N. Collins we find ourselves by no means in a crisis of legitimation of diaconia and the diaconate, as assumed by Raja Scheepers when she says, in her review of Anni Hentschel

---

[9] My explanations always speak of the deacon, because the Catholic Church to date has only allowed men into the diaconate. But this limitation does not apply to the theology of the diaconate. Everything written here will hopefully also apply sometime in the future to the diaconate for women cf. Eckholt, Sakrament deiner Liebe. Zur Möglichkeit des Frauendiakonats in der katholischen Kirche aus kirchenrechtlicher Sicht, cf. Bernhard Sven Anuth, Frauendiakonat in der katholischen Kirche. The present state of the issue and perspectives from a canonical point of view in: Thomas Schüller & Martin Zumbult (eds.), Iustitia est constans et perpetua voluntas ius suum cuique tribuendi (Festschrift für Klaus Lüdicke), Essen 2014, 37–85.

[10] Cf. in this regard, Peter Hünermann, Theologische Argumente für die Diakonatsweihe von Frauen, in Hünermann et al. (eds.), Diakonat, 98–128, 119. Bernd Jochen Hilberath as well assumes the necessity of a sacramental ordination of the diaconate, because it represents the "not from itself and not for itself" fundamental dimension of the Church (cf. Hilberath Dogmatische Fragen zum Diakonat der Frau, in: Peter Hünermann et al. (eds.), Diakonat 212–218, 217). Cf. on this discussion about the possible or rejected differentiation between the diaconate outside of clerical community leadership and the diaconate at a priestly level, Reininger, Diakonat, 167ff.

on the notion of diaconia in the New Testament,[11] that with those works "invoking the supposed biblical roots (of diaconal action, O.F.) was demolished",[12] for the argument in terms of the essence is not dependent upon such semantic analysis.

Further on, the reviewer expresses the following opinion: "The New Testament roots of the institutionalized form taken by Protestant charity are, therefore, to be found elsewhere, not in the realm of what was later termed 'diaconal'".[13] One should be reminded at this point that, also in the latest semantic investigations, the New Testament diaconal mission does not rule out those areas that are considered diaconal in today's sense. It entails—and that is its very nature—both aspects. With the loss of the New Testament title of "deacon" as foundational figure for the modern ecclesial diaconia or charity work, we stand to lose nothing, because its foundation is to be found in the whole Christian Gospel. It has always been inadequate for the theological discourse to focus on the ministerial divisions in the New Testament rather than on Christian mission in general. It is much more appropriate to analyse the ministerial segmentations in the New Testament in the same light of Christ's mission and submit them to criticism from this perspective, just as we do with the present ones. If, in some attempts to legitimise the hierarchical grades, one refers to supposed deacons (in the modern sense of the word) in the New Testament, one misses the mark in this regard and totally, not just "semantically", because the result should be measured in a constructive way against the original mission. One can, therefore, have a concretion of the Christian mission in the present time that is totally adequate theologically and ecclesiologically, whilst its legitimising arguments making reference to the title of diaconia might be exegetically incorrect.[14]

What we know now, in any case, on the bases of Anni Hetschel's and John N. Collins' research, is that we must give up, at least partially, this line of legitimisation, but keep the practice which came out of it, because it is ecclesiologically essential and necessary.[15] And the research on the "diakon-lexeme" in the

[11] Cf. Anni Hentschel, Diakonie im Neuen Testament. Studien zur Semantik unter besonderer Berücksichtigung der Rolle von Frauen, Tübingen 2002.

[12] Rajah Scheepers, published on Anni Hentschel, Diakonia im Neuen Testament, in: H-Soz-Kult, erschienen am 28.08.2009, available at http://hsozkult.geschichte.hu-berlin.de/rezensionen/2009-3-167,column 1.

[13] Scheepers, Besprechung, column 5.

[14] A wonderful example is the close relationships between Lutheran diaconal institutions in the writings on the semantic field of diakonia in "Kittels Theologischem Wörterbuch", cf. Klaus Kießling, Dienstbares Aufwarten an den Tischen oder missionarisches Dazwischengehen?, in: Diaconia Christi 46 (2011) 213–217, 215.

[15] In my own articles on the topic of the deacon and diaconia in the Catholic Church I have never made use of the title of deacon in the New Testament as for as the theological basis of this area and its hierarchical development. Cf. Ottmar Fuchs, Der Diakonat als Ferment einer diakonischen Kirche, in: Diaconia Christi 25 (1990) 1, 2–8; Wer ist der Diakon? Seine

New Testament corroborates precisely this connection between normativity and concretion, between task and fulfilment, between mission and being sent, between the person of Christ and representation. For they create the necessity for the diaconal action or diaconal leadership in a Christian community/parish to see itself as commissioned to do the mission of Christ and to be responsible for this mission. This responsibility also entails that it really benefits people. The commissioning to mediate is inseparable from the experience of service.[16]

When it comes to the time-conditioned concretions of the one dual mission, it should be said that they have their own theological quality even faced with the concretions that we find in biblical texts. Diachronically, other times may provide different concretions. And most importantly: in the ecumenical concert we have even now, synchronically, a plurality of such concrete forms. One should not, therefore, think of it as a tragedy if there is a difference regarding the concrete forms. Imaginative lexical transfers to the biblical concretions can very well be adopted. This does not diminish the situational necessity of the concretions in the horizon of the normative mission.[17]

The semantic analysis of the New Testament material (primarily of the Epistles) does not, therefore, provide any proof that henceforth the ministry of charity and solidarity must not constitute the specific of the diaconal ministry. For this specific does not stem from the New Testament conceptions of the diaconal ministry or the diaconal function, but rather from the mission as described by Jesus himself in the Gospels and as discussed in other texts as well at a conceptual level. Consequently, diaconia is also not eliminated from the New Testament-founded diaconal mission but is part and parcel of this mission. Bettina Eltrop gave an interpretation of the biblical results in their diverse and interrelated development.[18] In so doing, she emphasises that the New Testament understanding of diaconia comprises both aspects: the "lowly" waiting on tables and the authoritative commissioning to a certain, comprehensive

Berufung, seine lokalen, überregionalen und globalen Aufgaben, in: Arbeitsgemeinschaft Ständiger Diakonat in der Bundesrepublik Deutschland (ed.), Dokumentation 18 – Jahrestagung 2001 (Gemeindeentwicklung und kooperative Pastoral), Mömbris-Würzburg 2001, 47–61; Das diakonale Amt als Sakrament der Kirche für die Welt, in: Klaus Kießling (ed.), Ständige Diakone – Stellvertreter der Armen? Projekt Pro Diakonia. Prozess – Positionen – Perspektiven (Diakonie und Ökumene, Bd. 2), Berlin 2006, 67–91; Dienst am Volk im sakramentalen Diakonat, in: Karl-Werner Goldhammer (ed.), Vielfältig dienen. 40 Jahre Ständiger Diakonat in der Erzdiözese Bamberg, Bamberg 2010, 180–193.

16 This is indicated by Kießling, Dienstbares Aufwarten, 214.

17 But, for this dialectic of freedom and obligation in the understanding of biblical texts a personal reflection a practical biblical hermeneutics cf. Ottmar Fuchs, Praktische Hermeneutik der Heiligen Schrift, Stuttgart 2004; same author, Praktische Theologie in und mit der konturierten intertextuellen Bibellektüre, published in: Jahrbuch für Biblische Theologie 31 (2016) in press.

18 C. Bettina Eltrop, in: Biblische Grundlagen zum Diakonat, in: Richard Hartmann et al. (eds.), Ortsbestimmungen, 91–99.

mediation work. One must therefore insist that all the services which are part of this mission are of the same value, even the so-called "lower" ones. They are also part of the official commissioning and mediation. Waiting on tables also mediates between the space of cooking and the space of meals; without it, there can be no eating.[19]

"In Collins' and Hentschel's works", according to Eltrop, "the aspect of charity, of the works of mercy, of the Jewish works of love is insufficiently considered; moreover, the difference between the Gospels and the Pauline tradition is not sufficiently reflected. For in the Gospel tradition, *diakonia/diakoneo/diakonos* essentially refer to waiting on tables and supplying activities. The social aspect is also often underscored in the biblical texts."[20] However—and this is an important observation, to my mind—charitable action in itself constitutes such a mediation; it is an activity instituted clearly by the authority of Jesus and thereby possesses a high-ranking value in the proclamation of the Gospel as well as an experience of God's closeness and love.[21] Charitable action and evangelisation "both belong, according to biblical witness, to diakonia"[22].

4. *Challenges which Lead to Progress*

The exposure to the New Testament ideas about the diaconal mission provides a good opportunity to relate to each other evangelisation and charity, liturgical and social ministry, spiritual leadership in evangelisation and spiritual leadership in the social field in the horizon of the notion of diaconia which encompasses all these activities and to do so also taking into account their interdependence and potential to develop.

The New Testament-based diaconal mission has both the relationship to God and the relationship to one's neighbour as pre-conditions. To call this gift and this task generally "diaconal ministry" makes sense also from a theological point of view, because what takes place in both areas is diaconia, the diaconia of God to the people on the one hand and the diaconia of people to people (and to a certain extent also to God, cf. Mt 25) on the other. I see as the most exciting challenge for us today to understand, in a perichoretic way, the relationship between evangelisation and social ministry, of *martyria* and *diakonia*, and that one of them always makes the other present without replacing it and without losing its independence.

---

19 Cf. Kießling, Dienstbares Aufwarten, 215.

20 Eltrop, Grundlagen, 93. In detail on the service character of diaconia in the Gospels in a critical confrontation with Collins, cf. Kießling, Dienstbares Aufwarten, 215–216.

21 Eltrop, Grundlagen, 93.

22 Ibid. 99.

Therefore, there is a diaconal responsibility in the evangelisation as well, to the extent that God's diaconia to us is highlighted therein and can be spoken of as the horizon in which the interpersonal diaconal action is enabled; also through the fact that one can already see where people treat each other with justice and mercy to gain the courage and hope necessary to do it ourselves (so that the proclamation of love for one's neighbour not be suffocated by postulates and eventually discourage). Every activity in the area of evangelisation, whether it is situated in the area of the proclamation of God or in the area of human relationships, is a form of the overall diaconal relationship of the Church in the world. The Church serves the world by means of its ministry of the Word and ministry to people. In this way, diaconia becomes a key for the clarification of the Church's mission, including of the proxy task of the Church until the Lord comes again.[23]

Both gain, in the perspective of the commissioning which is necessary for both, an authority that they don't have by themselves, but from the one who gives them the mission to carry it out. To boast about it oneself is, therefore, not correct and also not necessary. For the authority in these circumstances is a gift of grace, not of self-righteousness.[24] The fact that the new research underscores this aspect is something to be explicitly saluted. Against the background of the semantic results we should also think about the fact that in the area of today's diaconia/caritas, it is possible to have a spiritual leadership in a diaconate that resides over the Eucharist.[25]

5. *In the Art of Networking*

Starting from the general notion of diaconia, the deacon can really be seen as "a specialist for the undefined", because diaconia may refer to all the forms of ecclesial self-realisation, from the liturgy through evangelisation up to social service and community building, and each of these forms can assume a specific responsibility.[26] Michael Hochschild sees the specific of the deacon in a civilian

---

[23] Cf. Gertrud von Le Fort, Hymnen an die Kirche (1924), München 1961, 53f. On the theology and spirituality of proxy, cf. also Klaus Kießling, Spiritualität der Stellvertretung, in: Klaus Kießling (ed.), Diakonische Spiritualität. Beiträge aus Wissenschaft, Ausbildung und Praxis, Münster 2009, 36–55. J. Christine Janowski, Bernd Janowski & Hans P. Lichtenberger (eds.), Stellvertretung. Theologische, philosophische und kulturelle Aspekte, Neukirchen-Vluyn 2006.

[24] Cf. Ottmar Fuchs, Die andere Reformation. Ökumenisch für eine solidarische Welt, Würzburg 2016, 13–14.

[25] Cf. Fuchs, Im Innersten gefährdet, 72–75.

[26] Cf. Michael Hochschild, Individualisierung – (De)Privatisierung – Professionalisierung. Der Diakon im Bermudadreieck seiner Berufung, in: Richard Hartmann et al. (eds.), Ortsbestimmungen, 144–160, 150.

profession in the fact that "in the social network of the Church in our times, he ties knots towards the exterior while maintaining the connections in the interior".[27] I personally would assume the same characteristic for the deacons working full time for the Church, also because we are talking about married deacons. In this way, the diaconate represents "a resource-sparing capacity to connect to the world of today and within it".[28] But this does not express the specific contents of mediation.

This specific is formulated in a systematic-theological perspective by Hans-Joachim Sander, who sees in the diaconate a key to keeping the Church from isolating itself from the world, helping it to strive to share life and the conditions for life, to share the gift of life and of the Gospel "because it provides the evangelization with a different place among people and ensures its heterotopic qualities". That is to say: "the diaconal work in social focal points make the whole structure visible; in such places the social divisions form which people suffer become visible. The diaconate does not avoid them, nor does it accept them in any way...If the diaconal ministry does not avoid heterotopically marked places and spaces, the message of diaconal sharing becomes a discursive force against that determining order of things which is ruled by a 'divisor'[29] i.e. which isolates, marginalizes and divides." In a similar way, Klaus Kießling connects the motif of the "go-between" to Jesus, who as "Lord of the Kingdom of God...ministers voluntarily and therefore, as in the scene of the washing of the feet (Jn. 13) turns human hierarchies upside down".[30]

The networking aspect can pervade even the liturgy if sacraments and rituals are celebrated not only as central points of churches and communities, but on the frontier between inside and outside and as a mediation between the respective inside and the respective outside.[31] Therefore, one of the specific responsibilities of the diaconate could be to discover aesthetical spaces and encounters in which such a community-building capacity can be lived, that can sustain difference and prevent the explosion of violent conflicts.[32] Within the context of Christological reflection, one can state: "The deacon outlines for the

27 Ibid. 154.

28 Ibid. 160.

29 Hans-Joachim Sander, Diakonat, 58 and 57.

30 Kießling, Dienstbares Aufwarten, 216.

31 Cf. Ottmar Fuchs, Sakramente – immer gratis, nie umsonst, Würzburg 2015, 30–48. Cf. in this regard my research project in the Erfurt Theological Research College on the topic of Hybrid Rituals: On the Interreligious and Interdenominational Potential of Ritual. A publication on this is in preparation. On the deacon in liturgy, cf. also Stephan Winter, Der Diakon in der Liturgie. 'Randbemerkung' in liturgie-ästhetischer Absicht, in: Richard Hartmann et al. (eds.), Ortsbestimmungen, 190–206.

32 Cf. on this topic Ottmar Fuchs, Poesie als empathische Imagination interreligiöser Freiheit – am Beispiel Goethes West-östlichen Divans, in: Francois-Xavier Amherdt, Mariano Delgado & Salvatore Loiero (eds.), 50 Jahre Dignitatis Humanae, Tagungsband des 7. Freiburger Forums Weltkirche, Freiburg/Schweiz 2017, 131–157.

Ordo the kind of worldliness which corresponds with the kenotic representation of Christ to which the ministry is called."[33] It is the peculiar dialectic which turns normal reality (where the richer and more powerful person will have more justification for her life than the poorer and less powerful) upside down. It is the order of things spelled out in the Magnificat in which the lowly are raised up and the mighty lose their lordly legitimisation. This provision has an effect on both the area of the clergy and the Ordo as a whole and on the corresponding relationship between the Church and the world. It is not just any kind of being-in-the-world but the particular being-in-the-world of the self-emptying for others on the basis of the gift and grace given in the Sacrament of Holy Orders as an enabling strength for this self-giving.

However, it is hard to see why there shouldn't be, precisely within this grade of the hierarchy, a faculty of spiritual leadership. For to see as the specific of the diaconate the fact that it purportedly is a subordinate ministry thereby excluded from the leadership faculty assumes that the leadership task of a priest or of a bishop would be a faculty expressing a kind of lordship not in agreement with the Magnificat. For the faculty is already bound to an inversion, i.e., obliged to make room for the dominion of the Gospel over any other dominion. The arguments according to which one should speak of the diaconate as being a subordinate ministry and to declare it a particular form of self-giving as opposed to the other grades of the hierarchy, whilst there other grades have a faculty of leadership—coming from presiding over the Eucharist—which entails an all the more radical kenosis[34] are quite shallow. On the contrary, the diaconate must not duck but rebel if anyone within the Ordo should attempt to eliminate the charity component. The rebellion component contained in the Magnificat is to be thought of, in the case of the diaconate, as its prophetic component. Within this dialectic, the hierarchy in the Ordo must always think about the inversion thereof, i.e., that the powerful are all the more meant to serve.[35]

Regarding this relationship with the world, one should not think by any means that the form of life of the deacon (i.e., married life or having other professions) is of more importance as if other forms of life wouldn't be connected to the world just as intensely but differently. All forms of life may be extremely ambivalent in this respect: they can be positive in matters of net-

[33] Scheule, Amt, 76. Cf. on this constitutive self-giving dimension of the Ordo; Fuchs, Im Innersten gefährdet, 961–963; same author, Einige Aspekte zu Wesen und Vollzug des Weiheamtes in der Gegenwart, in: George Augustin & Günter Risse (eds.), Die eine Sendung – in vielen Diensten, Paderborn 2003, 71–93, here 83–84.

[34] Contrary to Scheule, Amt, 77.

[35] Cf. Fuchs, Einige Aspekte, 76–80.

working possibilities or negative because of the exclusion of other areas of life and other persons.[36]

All situations are different, but not necessarily with regard to the intensity of their relationship to the world[37] (as we can see for example in the case of the "working priests" living in celibacy[38] or of Father Rudolf Lunkenbein[39]).

---

36 Regarding the ambivalence of family, cf. Ottmar Fuchs, Familie und Gemeinde, Vertrauensquellen überbrückender Liebe?, in: Theologische Quartalschrift 191 (2011) 1, 25–45.

37 Anders Scheule, Amt, 76.

38 Cf. Theologischer Kommentar zum Dekret über den Dienst und das Leben der Presbyter. Presbyterorum ordinis, in: Peter Hünermann & Bernd-Jochen Hilberath (eds.), Herders Theologischer Kommentar zum Zweiten Vatikanischen Konzil, Vol. 4, Freiburg 2005, 463–465.

39 Cf. Ottmar Fuchs, Die andere Reformation. Ökumenisch für eine solidarische Welt, Würzburg 2016, 2/2017 Reformation, 148–154.

F. Spiritual Traces

I. "Priest Mothers" and "God Mothers"

1. *Qualitative Empirical Approaches to the Image of God*

What human beings think and say, what they hope and believe, what they suffer and do: to perceive and make sense of these in their theological implications has always been so important to Johannes A. van der Ven that he developed an entire branch of theology, that of empirical theology, in which this process of apperception (*Wahr-Nehmung*, literally "truth-taking) has been raised to a complex scientific level. Behind this undertaking is discernible a rigorous ethical choice, namely to use a methodologically framed distancing to inquire into the deeper reality behind so-called first impressions and as a way of counteracting the tendency to incorporate the other into one's own wishes and stereotypes. Contemporary empirical work honours the potential difference and foreignness of the other, so that we can say: the more objectively this reality is perceived the greater the likelihood that communication about it will do justice to the subject.[1]

Anyone who looks into the face of humanity with such open and inquiring eye sees darkness and light, heights of reason and abysses of unreason, the whole ambivalence of human and social existence. The human (in the generic sense) countenance is not necessarily human (in the valuative sense) und hence the topic of the title "The Human Image of God" may prove fraught with ambiguities and conflict. Is the countenance of humanity so humane that it can be called an image of God? If so, when? Is the inhuman face of humanity also an "image of God", albeit a paradoxical and negative one? Conversely: Do human beings experience God as "human" or "inhuman"? Regardless of how one an-

---

1 The same impulse has shaped also van der Ven's reflections on the formation of the moral self: Van der Ven, J. A. (1998). *Formation of the Moral Self.* Cambridge.

swers these questions, one thing is certain, namely the pragmatics that flow from the semantic assumption that humanity is the image of God. For much depends on whether we treat one another as though we were made in God's image or, more precisely, on whether we believe that we all are made in God's image and that therefore the *other* is also the image of God. Inasmuch as the whole of human existence, as blighted and sinful as it may be, remains nevertheless in the image of God, it possesses that infinite dignity that is evoked by the idea of the divine.

The communicative value of this attitude is apparent, since this apperception and appreciation of the dignity of human existence opens up a means of bringing about an experience of self-worth in the communication partners that affirms in them the belief that they too possess such a dignity. It is such experiences of receiving the gift of acceptance[2] and appreciation that activate the resources within people which enable them to sense, to discover and to develop in themselves the image of God. And those who act as the channels for this acceptance and appreciation also prove themselves to be human images of God because they represent *God's* infinite acceptance of human beings. This acceptance is illustrated in many biblical stories in which God takes human beings, in all their ambivalence, seriously as partners in communication, never abandoning that communication, even when the face of the human partner is distorted or disguised.

The phenomenon has not only personal aspects but also cultural ones, inasmuch as human cultures also bear traces of the image of the face of God face in this world—although here again that reflection is not without ambivalence.[3] While it is surely right to discern in suffering peoples and oppressed cultures the face of the God who suffers in solidarity with them (cf. Mt 25:36ff.), in a peculiar dialectic to this one cannot entirely deny the sinners, the perpetrators of suffering and oppression, the dignity of being made in God's image, especially since from the perspective of *Rechtfertigungstheologie* God includes even—and particularly—sinners in the infiniteness of his salvation.[4]

In this article I propose to restrict myself to examining the *how* of the communication that takes seriously the dignity that is rooted in the human image of God. Such communication appears to be a precondition for unlocking people's ability to discover and share human images of God. Therefore, I would like to pursue the ethical impetus of empirical theology and perhaps also to expand on it by reconstructing this dignity at the level of the methodologically reflected and justified encounter with the empirical "subjects". The narration

---

2 On the importance of the problem of acceptance in the contemporary context cf. Honneth, A. (1992). *Kampf um Anerkennung. Zur moralischen Grammatik sozialer Konflikte.* Frankfurt a. M.

3 Cf. Rosner, E. (1993), *Gottes Indiogesichter*, Mainz.

4 Cf. Fuchs, O. (1999), Neue Wege einer eschatologischen Pastoral. In: *Theologische Quartalschrift* Vol. 179, No. 4, 260–288, 279ff.

of benevolent God images in such encounters and the rejection of destructive ones becomes a special consequence of this quality. Specifically, these themes will be examined in relation to two works that have sought to achieve both of these aims: the construction of a special relation with people within the course of a research project and the examination of the nature of the God images that are drawn on, yearned for, feared or desired by the subjects of that research.

2. *Empirical Social Research and Theological Choices*[5]

Analogously to the exegetic disciplines, which are concerned with the textual analysis of testimonies of faith as found in the Bible, an important aspect of Practical Theology consists of documenting in the textual form the experiences of contemporary believers and reconstructing the contents of the resulting texts in a painstaking work of textual analysis. Theologically such an undertaking is motivated by the dogmatic insight that it is not only the testimonies of biblical revelation that are inspired, but that also the spirit of God may be manifested in the testimonies of present-day believers. This is a datum not only of sacramental theology (especially with respect to baptism and confirmation), but also an ecclesiological one. For the *sensus fidelium* is the sphere in which the Church realises its mission, and for that very reason it is also a *locus theologicus*, one whose tidings must be picked up by Practical Theology and rendered fruitful for both the theological discourse and the praxis of the Church.[6]

If should be noted that the term "*sensus fidelium*" denotes a highly complex reality, in both practical and theological terms. First, it must not simply be taken as synonymous with "*consensus fidelium*". A glance at the Bible, including the writings of the New Testament, suffices to show clearly that consistency cannot be one of the historical names of God.[7] Thus, the *sensus fidelium* will

---

5 For an overview of recent discussion of the concept of God image in the Bible and in contemporary society (particularly with respect to its contrast and ambivalence) cf. *Bibel und Kirche* Vol. 54, No. 1 (1999), special issue on God images.

6 Cf. Grözinger, A. et al. (2000). Empirische Forschung als Herausforderung für Theologie und Kirche. In: M. Bruhn; and A. Grözinger (eds.), *Kirche und Marktorientierung* (13–32), Freiburg/Schweiz, 18ff. In Catholic theology this relationship, which was characterized by Schweitzer, F. (1993) as the "reciprocal construction of Christian tradition and contemporary experience" (Praktische Theologie und Hermeneutik. In: J. A. Van der Ven; and H.-G. Ziebertz (eds.). *Paradigmenentwicklung in der Praktischen Theologie* (19–47). Kampen-Weinheim (1993), 31), was worked out in Vatican II, which holds that dogma and pastoral theology also develop in a relationship of reciprocity: cf. Klinger, E. (1984). Der Glaube des Konzils. Ein dogmatischer Fortschritt. In: E. Klinger; and K. Wittstadt (eds.), *Glaube im Prozess* (615–626). Freiburg; cf. also Fuchs, O. (1990). *Heilen und Befreien*. Düsseldorf, 75ff.

7 Cf. Fuchs, O. (1990). *Zwischen Wahrhaftigkeit und Macht*. Frankfurt a. M.; Wiederkehr, D. (ed.) (1994). *Der Glaubenssinn des Gottesvolkes*. Freiburg i. Br.

comprise not only the efforts at consensus, but also those efforts that do not abandon communication even in dissent and hence create a space for difference and contradiction. Nor should the "*sensus fildelium*" be understood in perfectionistic terms: Belief will always exist in a context of partial unbelief, so that belief itself, at least in its concrete form in human beings and their social constructions, will exhibit a variety of dominances and selectivities. Therefore, it is essential for the various believers, church groups, congregations and local churches to be aware of one another, to illuminate each other's blindnesses and in this way to represent in approximate fashion the whole of the faith of the Church.[8] The exchange in and among communities of the Church consists above all in telling—to one and about one another—stories about the meaning of belief and its existential importance, where challenges to belief are to be experienced, in what ways it may serve as a foundation and support, and above all how it occurs in the vital and uncircumventable experiences of joy and suffering, be it as faith or the breaking through of faith.[9]

We therefore consider it a specific responsibility of pastoral theology to perceive the truth, in the deepest sense of the word, of the narrative community and communities of beliefs as well as their communal forms and to contribute, within its own discipline, to insuring that this narrative process is not broken off but on the contrary becomes ever deeper and broader.[10] In keeping with its own diaconal identity and responsibility, to the extent that these are oriented towards the message of the Gospel, pastoral theology will turn its attention above all to those groups whose competence perhaps has not yet, or not fully, been apperceived by the prevailing *sensus fidelium* as well as the *sensus fidei* of the ecclesiastical creed. *Which* segment of reality empirical-theological research will concentrate on is therefore determined by a *theological* decision in the context of certain preferences for those who have in the past remained unheard and hence disadvantaged: in favour of a Practical Theology that qualifies itself as diaconal-pastoral on *its own academic level.*

Practical Theology thus becomes a school for the apperception of a particular social reality in the church or society. The apperception in turn must establish contact at the scientific level with the human sciences that serve to particularise it and make it intersubjectively verifiable. Exegesis found apposite partners in discourse in the human sciences that deal with textual analysis and historical criticism; in the quest for the perception of social realities in the present we must turn to the sociological methods.

8 On the relation of belief and unbelief in belief cf. Metz, J. B. (1965). Der Unglaube als theologisches Problem. In: *Concilium* Vol. 1, 484–492.

9 Of course one must not forget that the narrative community in and between the social forms of the church also encompasses the sensus defunctorum, that is the religious sense their failures, be it in the biblical or the ecclesiastical traditions.

10 In speaking here of the community in and between the churches, in other words the Christian sphere, I do not claim for it an exclusive but rather a generative importance.

Analyses of this kind are necessary in both disciplines because one aspect of the theologically founded subjective quality of these texts, whether past or present, is that they (can) not be overly hastily inserted into one's existing framework of ideas and prejudices but form a true subject, another, that may also appear alien. What is true in diachronic terms (e. g., for biblical texts) is true also synchronically: to insure that believers, either individually or in groups, not become victims of prejudices *about* them, it is important to listen, or observe, for a long time in order to do justice to their experiences of life and of faith in a fair encounter.[11]

To apperceive the truth of the social and personal reality of the present, Practical Theology is therefore dependent on an intensive collaboration with the quantitative and qualitative empirical social sciences. At the same time, it must critically examine the latter's methods against the background of—in particular—the theological anthropology that stands for the non-pervertability and non-objectification of human beings within the horizon of the divine. This rules out empirical approaches which deny the subjects of the study a say with regard to the method and results. To be favoured are those empirical approaches in which the intersubjective encounter between reaching and researched subjects is not broken off and replaced by an instrumentalisation of the researchee.[12] This basic problem of the empirical sciences should not, however, be summarily identified with the conflict between quantitative and qualitative social research. The subject orientation of the research activities that precede a study and that subsequently interpret the results in a subject relation is possible in both cases and in the context of Practical Theology requires a separate discourse in each case. This is best engaged in within the framework of a concrete project to avoid its becoming dissipated in abstractions that in any case can only be verified or falsified in concrete terms. In the following I will concentrate on two empirical studies in the field of Practical Theology that have discovered and developed special subject orientations in their qualitative approaches and have inquired into the nature of God images in the process.[13]

---

11 On the distancing function of exegesis *in* the context of the diachronic encounter see Fuchs, O. (1997). Kriterien gegen den Missbrauch der Bibel. In: *Jahrbuch für Biblische Theologie* Vol. 12 (Biblische Hermeneutik) (243–274). Neukirchen-Vluyn, 246–251.

12 Cf. Fuchs, O. (1988). Krise der Theologie: Krise der Theolog(inn)en? In: I. Cremer; and D. Funke (eds.). *Diakonisches Handeln* (56–71). Freiburg i. Br.

13 Körber-Hübschmann, B. (1997). Priestermütter. Expertinnen in Kirche und Theologie. Bamberg; Hoyer, B. (1999). Gottesmütter. Lebensbilder kinderloser Frauen als fruchtbare Dialogräume für Pastoral und Pastoraltheologie. Münster.

2.1 Priest Mothers

Barbara Körber-Hübschmann's book *Priestermütter* (Priest Mothers) concerns itself with a very specific group of believers in the Church, namely the mothers of priests. Within the Church, the "priest mothers" as a group are especially liable to be the "victims" of clichés and prejudices, and this from quite different theological directions. This is reason enough for the author not to develop theories *about* this group, but instead to meet with actual mothers of priests, listen to their stories and, through a conscientious analysis of their words, to preserve their experiences, attitudes and teachings in all their authenticity. In the ecclesiological context this particular group proves to be highly competent in their perception of conditions in the Church and the possibilities for Gospel-oriented change. Their "position" in life as mothers of priests allows them to be aware of events and *aporias* that others do not see, but also to express ideas that others are not able to articulate as precisely. This positive prejudice bestows on the mothers a certain status as experts in ecclesiological realities and theological insight.

The author begins by setting out the theological foundations of the study, in particular the need to apperceive the *sensus fidelium* and to take it seriously as a factor in the development of the Church. Within this theological perspective she then embarks on the quest for potentially convergent sociological concepts that will, in their content as well as their methodology, adequately respond to the theological question of the study. A theology that ascribes to the priest mothers religious and ecclesiological relevance will demand a sociological theory that similarly endows a particular social reality and develops methods suited to interpreting those realities. The author therefore explores the insights of sociological research, feeling her way step by step through the entire methodological field in a series of choices justified always on the basis of the stated research interest. Homing in on the target in this way she arrives at Meuser and Nagel's data collection and analytical method of the open-ended "expert interview" on a particular theme, which she proceeds to further concentrate and modify with a view to her own textual material.[14]

The steps of the process are dictated by this method: transcription of the recorded interviews, a first condensation of the text material through paraphrasing and the addition of headings, content-led selection and classification of text material into one of four thematic areas. From this relay point between vertical and horizontal analysis (the former the analysis of individual interviews, the latter the analysis of common themes), it is now possible to carry out the *thematic* analysis. The researcher's highly intentional interests are ex-

[14] Cf. Meuser, M.; and Nagel, U. (1991). ExpertInneninterviews – vielfach erprobt, wenig bedacht. In: D. Garz; and K. Kraimer (eds.). *Qualitativ-empirische Sozialforschung*. Pfaffenweiler. Cf. Körber-Hübschmann, *Priestermütter*, 26–49.

plicitly and consistently incorporated into this analysis. Her intent is especially to highlight those messages that have special significance for the identity of the Church: the *image of the priest*, the *image of God*, the *image of the Church* and the *priest mothers' perception of themselves as women*. The transition from vertical to horizontal analysis corresponds among other things to the desire not only to take the women seriously as individuals but in sociological terms, also to treat them as an expert group. This discipline-specific conceptualisation is followed by the comparative step of theological generalisation, in which the statements of the respondents are compared and contrasted with the "theories" and prejudices about them.

The author conduced and analysed ten interviews. Although the nature of her research interest dictated that she use qualitative methods of social research, this number can also claim a relatively high quantitative representativity (at least for the Archbishopric of Bamberg where the interviews were conducted). The corpus of transcribed interviews comprises 261 pages (an average of 26 pages per interview). These were submitted as part of the doctoral thesis and can be requested from the Bamberg University Library for purposes of verification. The publication itself contains only the paraphrased versions of the interviews, with characteristic passages quoted. Each interview begins with a brief biography and concludes with a description of the circumstances of the interview.

This is the first academic monograph to concern itself with the mothers of priests as a group.[15] The manner in which the interviews were conducted, as seen in the complete transcripts as well as in the paraphrased version, reveals a strong communicative sensibility. In interviewing and listening to these women, the author learned that this listening is itself a pastoral activity, because a good proportion of women experienced this interest in their own experiential knowledge and personal faith as a form of respect that is rarely, or not readily, accorded the in other situations. The principal themes are pursued carefully but also firmly to yield in the end a corpus that is highly meaningful with respect to the theological categories.[16]

With a captivating stringency, the author moves from her theological research interest into the discourse with the social sciences and, through ongoing selection and modification, arrives at the aforementioned social-scientific

15 A small booklet was published by the same name several decades ago, but it must be considered as belonging to the literature of spiritual edification of the time.

16 A small methodological inconsistency (attributable to the selected sociological method and not to the author) would appear to be that the relationship between the principal theme and the substantive categories is not fully clarified. Nonetheless it is certainly true that the principal theme implicitly contains the categories which are established subsequently. In any case, despite the very different questions on the main theme, in the course of the interviews groups of statements crystallize out very precisely. These are then readily assigned to the categories of God image, Church image and so on.

method that is convergent with the theological intent. The human partner is not instrumentalised as an auxiliary to the research methodology, but is affirmed as valuable in her own right (here in the category of expert). This approach represents a valuable contribution to the tools available for theological research, while conversely the suitability of this qualitative social-scientific method for theological research lends additional credibility to this sociological project.[17] Theological concerns are identified within the sociological aggregate, and sociological means are evaluated within the theological field of exploration. The theological choice to affirm the relevancy of the experiences of this group corresponds to the sociological insight that the most interesting experts in a particular field will not be encountered at the top levels of institutions but often in the middle range.

What impresses about the author's work is the matter-of-fact, pragmatic tone of this interdisciplinary research project, honest in its assessment of its own limitations and all the more precise and clear because of it. In the analyses as well as in the concluding evaluations, the author never claims *more* in the way of results than what is actually covered by the interviews. Step by step, she presents, succinctly and precisely, the attitudes and views of these mothers in relation to the image of the priest, the image of God, the image of the Church and their own self-images. They indeed prove themselves to be experts who, sociologically speaking, offer correctives for the social system, just as, in ecclesiological terms, they possess a theological competence about how the Church should shape itself, a competence that up until now has been not much utilised, because the mothers of priests have been regarded only in terms of this specific function and have generally been buried under a mountain of stereotypes. What they have to contribute to our understanding of the images of priests, the Church, God and women in the Church serves as a corrective not only to the relevant *ecclesial praxis* (as concerns the treatment of the others of priests) but also to the largely empirically unfounded assumptions that have been made in the *theological research* itself (as for example in E. Drewermann's book about the clergy[18]). The work represents a gain in empirical apperception as well as a critical gain for the treatment of these women in theology and pastoral work. It establishes an empirical foundation from which past prejudices and stereotypes can be effectively countered.

The view of these women in many cases corresponds with currents in theological thinking that, although entirely in keeping with current theological assumptions and concepts, have not, up till now, been associated with this group of people in the Church. Certain "solidarities", for example, arise be-

---

17 On the interdisciplinary concept of Practical Theology and the social sciences see Mette, N.; and Steinkamp, H. (1983). *Sozialwissenschaften und Praktische Theologie*. Düsseldorf.

18 Körber-Hübschmann, *Priestermütter*, 205; Drewermann, E. ²(1991). *Kleriker. Psychogramm eines Ideals*. München, 269–653.

tween the theory-based praxis of the priest mothers and the praxis-based theories of theology. Vague theories filled with prejudices against priests and mothers of priests are unerringly unmasked by Körber-Hübschmann as not in accordance with the reality. In the end, therefore, we can fully agree with the author when she states that it is essential for the future of practical theological research that she "declare herself the advocate for the discernment and recognition of the theological competence of the people of God and its range of very different individual and collective subjects, including those who, by reason of their own self-assessment or an outside judgement (or prejudice) are generally not felt to be experts in theology and the Church."[19] What is at stake is the dignity of these subjects, a dignity which constitutes one of the building blocks of the Church itself.[20]

2.2 God Mothers

What Barbara Körber-Hübschmann discovers and reflects in her empirical work, namely that the empirical encounter itself takes on pastoral and pastoral-theological qualities, Birgit Hoyer also discovers and examines in depth in her work on childless women. She defines the lives of these women in her subtitle as "fertile spaces for pastoral and pastoral-theological dialogue". The methodological form of this encounter occurs in the context of a qualitative-empirical research project. It too makes explicit the theological foundation of its empirical activity, which is that the experiences of human beings form an essential source of knowledge in theology and especially pastoral theology: in the theology of Vatican II concerning the fundamental importance of humanity's vocation for theology and the Church, as well as the concept of the Church's pastoral responsibility, both inward and outward, toward Christianity and the whole world.[21]

As part of the effort to understand childless women as subjects of pastoral work, she modifies the *available qualitative social-scientific methods* to be consistent with the specifically pastoral-theological paradigm of the *pastoral interview.*[22] Behind this stands the hypothesis that empirical studies that do not depart from the basic concerns of pastoral work but rather are realised *as* pastoral activity in a dialogue with the methods of the human sciences are entirely

19 Körber-Hübschmann, *Priestermütter*, 211.
20 Ibid., Note 158.
21 Hoyer, *Gottesmütter*, 13ff.
22 Ibid., 28–31 (also drawing on the North American „pastoral counselling" movement of the 1970s).

justifiable from a practical-theological point of view.[23] In this methodological interweaving of pastoral work and Practical Theology, the work contributes in a creative manner to insuring that Practical Theology is able not only to *assert* its contextuality but also to actually manifest it in the course of the research process. The women for their part experience the interviews as a pastoral interview in a protected space in which they can relate and report things that they are rarely or never asked about in other situations. The author is engaged in a continuous "accompanying dialogue" (begleitender Dialog)[24], which she does not abandon in the subsequent interpretation process but rather establishes as the precondition for it. As part of the research process itself, she concerns herself with the experiences and problems of childless women, thereby engaging in a pastoral activity at the modern epistemological level of openly declared bias and methodological reflexivity.[25] In this way science and daily life are linked, solving the fundamental problems of those scientific disciplines that define themselves explicitly as contextually meaningful. The author also makes thorough use of the feminist literature relevant to the research concern. This literature too is tested for its relevance to real life. Ideological shadowboxing that abstracts itself from and subordinates the issues of real life is foreign to Hoyer.

Form a theological perspective the author thus develops a specific method for realising the theologumenon that human beings with their individual experiences are important for the faith and for the Church. Her approach compromises an aspect of *apperception* and an aspect of *action*: first, to listen to the experiences and problems recounted by the women and then to develop ideas

---

23 It is of course a tricky question whether in fact the research situation and the pastoral situation can or should be one and the same. There is no doubt that they can be kept separate, just as there is no doubt that they may be related to one another if (as was evidently the case here) the research situation is experienced by the participants as something that is identifiable with pastoral work in the broader sense. By pastoral work we mean the broader definition as developed in Vatican II, especially in the Pastoral Constitution, insofar as the term refers to Christian and ecclesiastical experience and action as a whole and is not reduced to the concept of counselling or even therapy. This does not exclude the possibility that a research situation could in fact be experienced as therapeutic. Perhaps the situation can be situated thus: Every empirical study (in the field of practical theology) derives its impetus, from a Christian perspective, from the wish to reconstruct the dignity of human experience in both the content and the methodology of the process. In this sense every empirical study is pastorally relevant. The more this is experienced by the participants themselves in the course of the research process, the more one can speak not only of pastoral relevance but of actual pastoral work. Stated negatively: No researcher should seek to develop research sets that fall outside of the pastoral value orientation (in the sense of an affirmation of human dignity).

24 Ibid., 47 and 55.

25 On the relation of bias and science cf. Fuchs, O. (1998). Wie verändert sich die universitäre Praktische Theologie, wenn sie kontextuell wird? In: *Pastoraltheologische Informationen* 18, 115–150.

about how to relate to these people from the perspective of the Gospel. For this purpose the author selects, in a dialectic with the childless women on whom she will focus, the basic concept of "motherliness". *Motherliness* is presented as the central pastoral-theological category within which people actively shape the processes of life-giving and life-sustaining, especially as a bridging of destructive oppositions and the breaking out from restrictive roles.[26] This thematic orientation broadens an overly narrow concept of "motherliness" and at the same time posits it as a dimension of study that is as productive for theology as it is for pastoral work. That childless women experience motherliness in this sense would enable these women to restore the sometimes deficient view of their own existence—a view mediated by societal as well as ecclesial judgements—towards an increasingly positive understanding of themselves.

The author also draws heavily on feminist theology in her closer interpretation of the concept of motherliness, particularly in her focus on the power of relationship as a force for the sustaining and nourishing of life, in a protected space in which it is safe to show hurt and sorrow and in which crises are opportunities for life renewal. The social space in which these are permitted and encouraged is the space that constitutes the direct concern of pastoral work and the object of reflection for pastoral theology. At the same time it is the space that opens onto the other who is inherent in and at the same time transcends it: *onto God, who is conceived as the primeval ground and the transcendental condition of life-giving and life-sustaining motherliness, above all in relation to the biblical images of God as mother and the model offered by Jesus in his care, his listening and his healing of body and soul.* In this way the childless women are accorded that very quality that now, set free from biological fixation, can lend to their lives the dignity they yearn for, but that is usually not given them by society or the Church.

What is touched upon by the concept of motherliness is manifested in the methodology itself, especially in the pastoral interview that establishes the framework of the planned encounter and in the discussion of subjectivity, intersubjectivity and objectification in terms of symbolic interaction research. Based on the insight that objectification does not consist in an abstraction away from the subject but rather in a positioning of the subject within a context of communicative certainty, Hoyer focuses on qualitative social research (including biographical research) and opts for the data-gathering method of the *problem-centred interview.*[27] This decision is in keeping with her research interest: namely to encounter these women from the basis of a very particular thematic preconception and then to interpret the data from the point of view

[26] Hoyer, *Gottesmütter*, 286–296.
[27] Ibid., 50–51.

of this same preconception, with the help of the categories of *childlessness, life-form, socialisation* and *religion*.[28]

With respect to interpretation the author opts for a process of gradual generalisation: from the transcripts of the full interviews[29] to the first condensation into "portraits"[30] and the interpretive "overview" of the life stories. From there she proceeds to the interpretation of thematic cross-sections *among* the portraits, in which commonalities, differences and basic tendencies are filtered out and discussed within the context of pastoral work and pastoral theology. The book begins with the portraits. The "personal overview" that follows each of the portraits summarises (in the interpretive language of the author) the key issues of socialisation, life form, childlessness and religion. The book contains 27 of these portraits—empirically verifiable and comprehensible representations of the women and their stories. Each portrait begins with a motto that summarises, in the words of the woman herself, the essential aspect of each of the interviews.

The work then proceeds to operate on two different and yet interrelated levels of dialogue: first the level of *pastoral work* and then that of *pastoral theology*. At the level of *pastoral work*[31] the situations, experiences and reactions recounted by the women are tied in with the literature relating to these situations and experiences in theology and the human sciences (medicine, for example) in society and the Church. Personal and general insights are contrasted and compared, not in order to amalgamate the singular experiences into the generalisations, but as a way of lending even more weight to (and where necessary against) them and creating a complex public space in which the narratives are brought into relationship with societal circumstances and tendencies.

At the level of *pastoral theology*[32] the central theme of motherliness is taken up as a specifically pastoral-theological topic, within which the author gathers together elements for a conventional and praxis-related theology of motherliness, under the headings of tradition, relationship, creation ("Zur-Welt-Bringen" or "bringing into the world"), hospitality and security. These are followed by the women's various experiences and images of God, including those which occupy a not unambivalent position between shadow and light. The author then focuses on the social aspects of religion, particularly the women's experiences with the Church, and on the visions of "motherly" social

---

28 Ibid., 56f.

29 The thick volume containing the transcripts of the interviews (as the empirical basis of the dissertation) is also available for review at the Bamberg university library.

30 The authenticity of these concentrations can be verified by comparison with the transcribed texts. One of the reasons these texts are not published is to safeguard the subjects' anonymity.

31 Hoyer, *Gottesmütter*, 162–283.

32 Ibid., 284–330.

forms within the Church, with the corresponding avenues of hope and complaint, vitality, crisis and mourning.

3. *Avenues of Future Research*

3.1 God Images

In the pastorally relevant and qualitative-empirically grounded interviews, the *priest mothers* articulate the centrality of trust in God's work in their lives. At the same time, He is the one who breaks through all human limitations of place, time, situation and low. God is available to all people at all times. "The image of a threatening God is rejected."[33] This religious content leads to a very particular communication of tolerance towards other people. What is clearly shown here is that the more inclusive and non-sanctioning the person's notion of and belief in God, the more inclusive the relationship to the divine.[34]

Birgit Hoyer summarises the God images of the women she interviewed thus:[35] A God who knows no mercy cannot be accepted. God is interwoven with the individual's entire existence, in a loving and supportive but also powerful way. He is the good friend, the All powerful, in whom is placed absolute confidence. He is the eternal truth—tangible, moving, helping, a haven that is always accessible. He is the foresighted, knowing maker of the way. He is inextricably interwoven with one's own life, eternal, incomprehensible, the centre that leads to one's own centre. He the One who gives, to whom praise is due. He speaks to us, lives with us, plans our lives, the only Power and the All powerful. He is fleeting, to be experience in human relations. He is the One who saves us from damnation, the ground of life. He is our motivation to be good, a confiding confidant, benevolent supporter, like a mother, accepting freedom, caring, the source of permanence and value. He is transmitted through people. He is warmth. He I one who lets go und looks ahead, soft and still, open to relationship, sensitive, a generous lover.

God's ambiguities are also expressed by the childless women, but with an entirely different emphasis than is seen in the responses of the mothers of priests. He is the arbitrary giver of life and bringer of death, an unpredictable creator of incontrovertible will; He is distant and uninterested, One who is doubted, who abandons and wounds. He is goodness and curse. He is a jerk, condemned, cursed, hated, One who refuses to take responsibility, who excludes and deserts, rejects and selects, and in this sense both adversary and

33 Körber-Hübschmann, *Priestermütter*, 193.
34 Cf. Concilium Vol. 5, No. 2 (1999) (special edition on „Grenzüberschreitungen").
35 Hoyer, *Gottesmütter*, 306–322.

lover. He is One who forgets and shows no concern, who will not do even the smallest favour, whose will alone counts, a dispenser of arbitrary punishment, a source of strength for the submissive. He is experienced as a stern and reproachful judge, a diabolical enemy of the body, as fate, as inaccessible. One woman speaks of God as boring, unknown, unconnected, powerless, out of touch with life and artificial.

All of the contrasts found in biblical texts dealing with the experience of God are found here also with the same force.[36] The fact that the women were able to speak so openly about their relation to God, and in some cases their contempt for God, once again affirms the special communicative quality of the research process.[37] Here we see clearly that it depends to a significant degree on the pastoral quality of empirical research whether the subjects will feel sufficiently secure to bring up their experiences and conflicts about God so openly. Perhaps one could even conclude that the more "pastoral" the design of the research set, the greater the chance that not only the ongoing and socially acceptable topics will be raised, but also the often conflict-ridden and unacknowledged elements that lie below the surface—what Herman Stenger has called the "stowaways".

3.2 The Communicative Method of Empirical Research

The distinguishing feature of both of these works is the flexibility that allows the methodology to be closely adapted to the empirical subject of the research. Methodological decisions are gauged according to how they promote respect for the subject. The authors elucidate the pastoral content of this process by setting up the empirical inquiry as a pastoral encounter. With a view not least

---

36 Cf. Baumgart, N. C. (1999). Unaufgebbar. Die Spannung in der Gottesrede. In: *Bibel und Kirche*, Vol. 54, No. 1, 10–17.

37 It would appear to be due to the differences between the groups of women that the mothers of priests do not express ambivalence as a basic theme of their relation to God or that it appears only indirectly (for example in the experience of the ambivalence of church structures). These mothers are less likely to venture to ascribe to God direct responsibility for such experiences. Perhaps they also did not dare to admit the shadow sides of their thoughts either to themselves or in conversation. On this subject see also the review of Priestermütter in Journal of Empirical Theology (1999/1) by G. Heinemann, who also suspects that the "stowaways", or private, unadmitted motivations, are not sufficiently expressed in the interviews. What Heinemann argues with respect to unacknowledged motivations, which in some cases are similar to the analyses of Leist, Rey and Drewermann, could also be applied to conflicts with or about God that are not acknowledged or only indirectly acknowledged.

to the theological connotation that the cultural practice of hospitality holds in the Bible, Birgit Hoyer considers herself a "host", one who affords the women the opportunity to reveal themselves in conversation without being instrumentalised. This situation of the academic discipline of Practical Theology taking the form of pastoral action results in a pastoral theology that Hoyer calls "motherly" and that Körber-Hübschmann describes as anticipatory of content and respectful of the subject. This is not a case of a special theology for a particular group. Rather, these examples, these empirical and theological loci, may serve as generators of practical-theological methods applicable to other pastoral situations as well.

The interactivity of qualitative social research has itself pastoral and pastoral-theological relevance. This connection, particularly in the explicitness with which it is implemented here, will doubtless be important for future research as a thematic and structural generator. It is obvious that the two processes (pastoral interviews and qualitative social research) critically complement each other by helping to expand and deepen their respective disciplines. Social research is enhanced by not objectivising human beings and degrading them to mere research material and by developing its communicative instruments in the direction of a reciprocal rather than asymmetrical research communication. The pastoral interview benefits from being viewed no longer from a privatist perspective, becoming part of a larger context via the theological discourse with the relevant societal factors and the human sciences (sociological as well as psychological). In this way the *content* of the pastoral interview gains from theological and human-scientific as well as ecclesiastical and sociopolitical generalisations and hence takes on supra-individual significance.

In theological terms this integration of pastoral work and empiricism corresponds to the dignity of human beings that is rooted in God's general will for salvation, their right to qualified attention and finally in the diaconal postulate that people who have been little heeded in the past be accorded pastoral and scientific consideration. In the combination of interviews and social research, the *distance* between researcher and subject becomes more clearly defined, as does the preexisting perspective of the researcher or research bias. Within the framework of their thematic interest, the authors maintain a distance between themselves and the women. They want to find out something from them, and the women know this. This is not a therapy session, but rather a situation in which a (female) researcher sets out to learn about the women for academic purposes. This does not exclude the possibility that the women may indirectly feel that the experience has been therapeutic because in the process of being heard they have learned something about themselves. They remain the preeminent experts on their own lives. Through the process of academic research they are simultaneously revealed and "published" in their critical capacity vis-à-vis society and in their prophetic capacity vis-à-vis the Church. The authors thus avoid the trap of turning their subjects either into clients or empirical objects. By preserving an empirical distance they steer clear of empathetic overload, but also avoid any kind of cold and unempathetic analysis.

That the subjects are taken seriously is seen above all in that both authors make extensive use throughout of direct quotations of varying lengths to express relevant topics, results and insights in the women's own words. This lends weight to the individual experiences and affords them exemplary depth and documentary force by comparison with the generalisations. These passages are at times dismaying, distressing and shocking.

The results point to a number of pastoral and pastoral-theological options: for a pastoral theology that engages with life and acts in a subject-specific manner, in other words with respect for human beings and their lives especially in the turning points in these lives and the upheavals and transformations associated with them, and not least also (as Birgit Hoyer notes) for subject-specific rites and rituals. Inasmuch as the authors conceive of Practical Theology itself as a locus of pastoral dialogue, their work sets the standard for future analogous pastoral-theological undertakings in the spirit of a methodologically reflected contextualisation of Practical Theology. They set standards also in the sense that they view the sphere of pastoral activity as a broad continuum, ranging from the human body to the society as a whole, entirely in the spirit of evangelisation theology, which holds that no area of human existence can be divorced from evangelisation.[38] The project of the human image of God is eschatologically a universal process. Christian living, pastoral action and theological research all aim to reveal and make the human image of God present everywhere in our lives.

[38] Cf. Paul VI., Evangelii nuntiandi of Dec 8, 1975.

II. The Pastoral Meaning of the Marital Rite

Victor Turner (1920–1983), the grand old man of ritual studies, holds that "the study of ritual [holds] the key for understanding the inner constitution of human societies".[1] Rituals "express hidden values ... In rituals people express their deepest motivations, and because they are conventionalised and obligatory forms of expression, rituals reveal group values ..."[2] With this in mind, the question raised by the Christian marital rite is this: which are the profound hidden values which it expresses? How does it address people's motivations? Which Christian group values does this ritual express? What is the understanding of the inner constitution of marriage which it reflects?

Following Van Gennep, Turner distinguishes three phases in rites of passage: separation, liminality and reaggregation. The separation phase facilitates people's release from everyday activities into the realm of symbols; the liminal phase marks a pause in the ritual process itself, and during reaggregation people move back into the domain of everyday life, equipped as a result of the ritual with renewed hope and vigour[3]. This does not mean that the ambiguities of existence disappear from everyday life, but the ritual provides a new horizon for engaging with them, enduring and tackling them.

1. *Ritual as "Liminal"*

To begin with, the marital rite expresses through drama and symbol a turning point in life which began with a couple's first encounter and now includes the hope of, as long as possible, a relationship in the future and (normally) of a family with children. However, the ritual is not only an expression but also an interruption of this relationship: the pause marked by the ritual attributes to the relationship a significance which, though incorporating a personal dimension, is related to an "objective" framework of meaning. The "group value: involved here is that of a set meaning which is not inherent in the relationship. Rather, it derives from a separate *a priori* that reminds us that the relationship itself depends on a particular different, transcendent reality.

In the sphere of religion, what is in view here is the way God and a particular relationship to God are "givens", are "pre-givenesses". Thus, the Christian

1 Victor Turner, Das Ritual. Struktur und Antistruktur, Frankfurt a. M. 2005, 13.

2 Ibid.

3 See. Turner, ibid., 94; cf. Arnold Van Gennep, The rites of passage, London 1960.

ritual is "liminal" in that it raises a particular turning point in life up to the threshold of encounter between humans and God. From here, the couple return to their everyday relationships to each other and to other people. As a result, the norms and values that used to govern these relationships are rooted in a deeper reality or overridden or even abandoned by its otherness. For Turner, such a ritual is "accompanied by an experience of unprecedented power".[4] Theologically, this involves a kind of "status reversal"[5] in that the couple's relationship is no longer linked only to their own responsibilities and thus their own achievement but, basically and crucially, to God's responsibility for this bond.

Thus, pausing in this ritual space "betwixt and in between" the ritual itself amounts to a transition during which another world enters or breaks into the couple's world.[6] The ritual offers, as it were, a theological "meta-commentary" on a couple's relationship[7], but one that is experienced not in an idealist way, but through symbol and drama and thus "through the body". Those undergoing this ritual enter a liminal state that triggers a transformation and is capable of sustaining and carrying the everyday reality of this relationship in the future. It is this connection of symbolic drama and everyday pragmatism that raises crucial questions for practical theology: What are the longings with which people approach this liminal state? What hopes, enablings and empowerment for the future do they gain from it?

Religion may lapse into an outsized if-then framework that ascribes to humans either subservience to or mastery over God (in that they have certain claims or even rights as long as they meet certain conditions) or religion may take seriously the Christian message that God wants humans to walk upright and accepts humans unconditionally into liberating support and love even before they have changed. The latter option gives the connection of the marital relationship with the relationship to God a radical significance for and a deep meaning concerning the theology of grace. If we take seriously Turner's notion that a liminal ritual involves the imposition of antistructure upon the conventional structure of human institutions, the we are dealing here with the contrast between achievement and grace, between doing and receiving, between planning and mystery, between contingency and infinity, activity and passivity.

Would it be taking the case too far to associate this liminal state, this symbolic drama of pausing and inhaling, with the passivity and humility which Turner perceives in his ritual analyses? Standing before God, humans are "naked", so to speak, they no longer have to offer any achievements or hide any-

---

4 Ibid., 125.

5 See ibid., 180f.

6 On this point see Silvia M. Schomburg-Scherff, Nachwort zu Turner, Ritual, ebd., 198–206, 201f.

7 See ibid., 205.

thing from God, who loves even their shadow aspect or, as Paul puts it, loves them as sinners.[8] This can indeed amount to a reshaping, equipping people with new powers that enable them "to come to terms with their new situation in life"[9] for a new and altered life.

2. *The Pregiven Set Format of Ritual as an Experience of the Unconditional Absolute*[10]

The pregiveness and relative continuity of a ritual—in other words, it does not need to be made or achieved—provides a basis in anthropology and in the theory of symbols (in the sense that "*gratia supponit naturam*"—"grace presupposes nature"), which seems especially appropriate to provide the medium for expressing the givenness which in the theology of grace and justification is believed as the divine love given to sinners even before humans have to achieve something or change themselves.

While in Protestant thought the significance of that unconditional grace is reflected in the central position of the theology of justification, the similar point is reconstructed on the basis of symbols in the Roman Catholic theology of sacraments: in the doctrine of sacraments, a sacrament is an effective sign of grace instituted by Christ. A sacrament does not contain the grace that it signifies in a mechanistic way, but bestows and grants it because Christ, the cause of grace, has bound himself to this symbolic medium of unconditional grace which is the sacrament. "The presence of divine grace in the sacrament depends neither on the holiness of the one who administers it nor on the holiness of the one who receives it. For the cause of grace is not humans and their achievements, but only God and Jesus Christ. The teaching therefore is: the sacrament is effective *ex opere operato*, that is to say: once the sacramental rite has been executed and the holy symbols have been placed, Jesus acts and comes into our midst."[11] This we may surely believe in and trust in God's promise.

New thinking within the Church in the latter half of the twentieth century has pointed mainly (merely) to the danger of an objectivist understanding of the sacraments and of ritualist praxis that lacks a connection between ritual and experience. However, with the emphasis on believers' performance and participation in church activities, a new misunderstanding has taken root, struggling to appreciate the constructive "objective" content of the sacra-

---

8 Cf. on the foregoing analyses Turner, Ritual, 94ff.

9 Ibid., 95.

10 Cf. Ottmar Fuchs, Sakramente – immer gratis, nie umsonst, Würzburg 2015.

11 Leonardo Boff, Kleine Sakramentenlehre, Düsseldorf [2]1978, 95.

ments: the suggestion here is that the sacrament loses not only its meaning, but ultimately its efficacy without human participation, without particular performances involving preparation for the sacraments, attempts to understand them and specific if-then formulas regulating morality and acceptance of the church's authority. This kind of attitude lacks any openness for God's action beyond human action.

Indeed, in this regard, the faith of those who attend church only for the official life ceremonies (baptism, first communion, confirmation, marriage, funeral) possesses in a certain sense greater "added value" than that of regular churchgoers in that it is not bound up with their own understanding or their meeting certain conditions. The notion of "added value" derives from empirical research which revealed that such *casualia*-focused Christians, such "marginal people", approach ecclesiastical rituals with expectations that transcend their own achievements or capabilities.[12] Their instinctive feeling tells them rather certainly that the rituals of the Church belong to them in the sense of God giving free blessings, cost-free gifts, to humans so that they may live and act in the knowledge that their existences are firmly supported—particularly at turning points in their lives.

A considerable number of the *casualia*-focused Christians surveyed state clearly that their use of the rituals makes a difference in their lives. It becomes meaningful as everyday life is invested with a transcendent quality that gives them something to hold on to, sustains them and facilitates particular actions. Hence, there is no doubt that the rituals of the Church, including the marital rite, must not be lightly denied to anyone and, in particular, must not be instrumentalised as a tool of exclusion.

3. *Marriage and Pastoral Care: Between "Inside" and "Outside"*

Church rituals are not only the focal points (for example, of initiation) of a believing community in its innermost centre, its core community, but their position is also one "at the margins" between the inside and outside, between those who are close and those who are at a distance. Rituals are the locus for connecting the Church gathered and the Church dispersed, for connecting organised communities and those who experience the gift of these rituals in their own lives beyond direct institutional affiliation and outside the controlling power of church officials. Rituals serve two purposes—social concentration

[12] See Johannes Först, Joachim Kügler (Hg.), Die unbekannte Mehrheit. Mit Taufe, Trauung und Bestattung durchs Leben? Eine empirische Untersuchung zur „Kasualienfrömmigkeit“ von KatholikInnen, Münster 2006.

and social "delimitation" (transgressing and dissolution of boundaries). Both of these open up a particular orientation towards transcendence, which in both cases is a gift that is not manmade: the gift of God's pregivenness through ritual in any case.

Thus, individuals experience the representatives of the Church as people who are able to engage in "double speech": "Personally I'm against you marrying in the church. Your motives are not sufficient. You don't know enough about it and you don't seek to be part of a regular church community. Yet: it is not for me to decide, personally. I am in charge of a reality which surmounts my objections. I hold this position in the church to represent, not myself and my own 'hang-ups', but the mystery of God's infinite love which defies my own understanding, too. Thus, my hope is that the experience of the sacrament of marriage triggers something within you of which I know nothing, but to which you will be able to open yourself up. I can't see that there is any point in it for you, but I don't know the meaning of the gift God wants to give to you in this way."

Of course, such a pastoral approach is open to abuse: but here those responsible in the church are in excellent company—that of Jesus Christ himself. The steadfastness of a loving relationship to God, reflected as it is in the continuity of the ritual, does not depend on its being understandable or on its leading to social affiliation. The symbolic content does not merge into it; it is a reality in its own right set over and against these processes.

Let us draw out the implications for the pastoral aspects of the sacrament of marriage. If, for example, young people query whether and why they *are required* to marry in church, the first aim of pastoral counselling must be to convey that the sacrament is not a "requirement" but rather God's powerful affirmation of their bond. *God* supports their "yes" to each other; the foremost assurance of their bond is not their own achievement but God's own confirmation of their wedding vows to each other. Thus, God frees them of the fear that they should have to secure their wedding vows by clinging to each other, which they will never be able to do because the future is not within their control. Thus, the sacrament is an experience of relief and liberation: the couple can breathe easy in the knowledge that the marital bond rests safely upon the ritual and through it in God. They can rely on it.

This is particularly important in relation to the transition marked by the wedding: the transition from a "private" encounter to a long-term institution even with bureaucratic ramifications. Notwithstanding the joy and delight of this situation, there is also the anxious wish that the vitality of the couple's love not be lost in the face of down-to-earth, everyday necessities. The kind of trust described provides a backdrop against which the couple will be able to forsake compulsive clinging, dominating behaviour or mutual put-downs[13];

---

13 Cf. Max Frisch, Biographie: Ein Spiel, Frankfurt a. M. 1985.

their trust and acceptance will enable them to release each other into an open and shared future. Their vows to each other are guaranteed, not by the couple themselves, but by God in her infinite love and trustworthiness. Herein lies the spiritual and pastoral meaning of the ritual for the couple's life.

This belief will, furthermore, enable the couple to make it through the tough times that run counter to that symbolic experience. Rather than splitting up when the first conflicts arise, they will be able—sometimes "counterfactually", that is, in contrast to the way things seem—to continue to believe in the power of that which is being symbolised: their belonging together on a more profound level, in God, even when accessing that experience of togetherness is not easy. Small problems can be kept in perspective, and there is a chance for big problems to be solved or endured together. If mutual trust is rooted in a shared trust in God, a liberating sense of humour can arise, a sense of serenity that makes all fixations obsolete because it allows the "otherness" of the partner to be and to grow. The couple know their differences, they respect them and suffer them, but they laugh about them as well. They can get along with each other, come to terms with each other and bear each other.

In this way the ritual will have an effect in the couple's life. Those acting on behalf of the Church may hope, and, because of their own theologies of grace and of the sacraments, rest assured in the certainty of faith that such a ritual and the experience of grace through it will be effective. These effects can be guides and signposts that can be pointed towards against the backdrop of grace even in the initial pastoral consultations. The indissolubility of marriage is first and foremost a gift and only in the second place a task. Those who hastily rush into talking of duty destroy not only the ritual, but also the Christian message of a God who comes alongside people in their lives.

4. *A Plea for a "Sell-out"*

The pastoral aspects of rituals concerning official acts in general and the pastoral aspects of marriage in particular challenge those active on behalf of the Church to acknowledge the priority of grace in their pastoral activities—that is to say, to avoid incorporating their own limits of knowledge and influence into the boundaries of grace. Ultimately, there is no justification for refusing a sacrament other than the ones that seem indispensable in extreme cases. And those confronted with cases of the latter kind will not be able to emerge satisfied at having got it right, but will be aware of their guilt in having failed to reflect God's unconditional grace in their pastoral care. Extreme cases do exist where it is necessary to avoid becoming a collaborator with evil in history. The excommunication of a Holocaust-denying member of the Pius Brotherhood is probably such an extreme case. Exactly which cases fall into this category between necessity and unconditioned pastoral care is an issue that warrants a separate discussion. The key point is surely the extent to which, by tolerating a course of action, one becomes complicit in something which runs counter to the identity of the Church as a whole. For example, in a historical context where millions died, excommunicating Hitler would have been as necessary historically as it would have been culpable in terms of the theology of grace.

It goes without saying that those who take advantage of the rituals offered by the Church do not constitute such extreme cases. It is their expectations that should guide those officially entrusted with pastoral care: that power will not be exercised to exclude some and that God's grace and power will override subjective judgements passed on a person's level of participation. Those who trust the ritual and the divine grace that it bestows more than the set of conditions they might want to lay down subjectively will exemplify trust in the efficacy of God's grace as well as hope on behalf of those who receive the rituals. If someone wants to receive the ritual in the face of grave concerns uttered by those charged with administering it, even then the church officials have no power to exclude him or her, at least according to the theology of grace.

Hence, my plea for a "sell-out" of church rituals applies both internally and externally in the spirit of Isaiah: "Come, all you who are thirsty, come to the waters; and you who have no money, come, buy and eat! Come, buy wine and milk without money and without cost ... Give ear and come to me; hear me, that your soul may live. Surely you will summon nations you know not, and nations that do not know you will hasten to you, because of the LORD your God, Holy One of Israel, he has endowed you with splendour" (Isaiah 55:1–5).

5. *The Spirituality of the Gift*

If the pastoral context of the marital rite is conceived along the lines indicated, a specific spirituality is envisaged on the part of those who undergo the ritual. This is a spirituality which does not answer primarily to the conditions of integration into the Church, to moral standards, the precondition of understanding and similar imperatives, but allows the objective "givenness" of the ritual (as a representation of the objective givenness of God's unconditional love) to impress and impact as directly as possible upon the subjectivity of those involved.

In modern ritual studies, much attention has already been given to the change in the understanding of rituals away from a combination of collective values (especially concerning initiation) towards a private and individual appropriation of church rituals and ceremonies that creates effects in the personal and social sphere.[14] Even in Turner's own approach, the emphasis is

[14] Cf. Martin Engelbrecht, Pforten im Niemandsland?, in: Först, Kügler (Hg.), Unbekannte Mehrheit 55–76, 63ff.; Roy Rappaport, Ritual und performative Sprache, in: David Krieger, Andrea Belliger, Ritualtheorien – Ein einführendes Handbuch, Wiesbaden 1998, 191–211.

shifted from the function of ritual symbols within the collective onto the meaning of these rituals for the individual. This should be a challenge for pastoral care in the Church to likewise realise its own rituals not only in relation to its own collectives, but to set them free, moving them towards the margins or the interface between inside and outside, building up open and accepting communications, even if they don't last very long: God is looking for the volatiles, saving loose contacts (Eccl. 3:15). In this we bear in mind that the "outside" is always relative anyway: for in the theology of sacraments even marginal, only *casualia*-focused Christians are part and full members of the Christian churches in that they have been baptised.[15]

The antistructure represented by the ritual is characterised theologically by the notion of rest and relief (cf. Matthew 11:28–30) in a "world" that is no longer focused exclusively on achievement pressure and relations based on exchange and possessions: in the anarchic, unpredictable space of grace, all if-then frameworks have been abolished.[16] This space is an "untidy" one, which is dynamic in a quite different sense than "ordinary" space is.[17] Such a liminal space creates an awareness in those who enter it of "another" dimension not only in this space itself but in the realm of ordinary life as well. The liminality experienced here will no longer be ignored in everyday life either. The latter is now perceived as holding gifts, as enabling, as triggering memories of the ritual and thus as confirmation of the truth of the ritual within the structure of daily life. If this is the case, the dimension of grace, of gifts and gratefulness will enter into everyday life in the same way in which Tuner describes the growth of liminality, which "enters through the gaps of structure, in the form of marginality on the edges of structure and inferiority below structure".[18]

Hence, the churches are well advised to exercise the pastoral care of marriage not as one of the few forms of power, not as one of the last strongholds over others still available by setting conditions for admission and excluding those who do not meet them. Rather, the key is to connect people's longing for God's blessing with the givennness of the ritual as supported by the theology of grace—relinquishing all conditions as far as possible, enabling people to perceive and experience the unconditional nature of human relationships here as well as in life generally. To what extent those who take advantage of the ritual will adopt the Church's social forms must be left up to God.

There must be no limits to the performative power of the ritual in the pastoral context. The gift-like nature of the ritual is to be made clear, rather than obscured, in the way it is carried out and, in particular, in the performa-

---

15 For Turner does not understand the notion of *communitas* in a collective sense but, rather, as sustained by vital, unpredictable and initially unstructured individual relationships, cf. Turner, Ritual 96f., 105f., 122f., 134f.

16 Cf. Turner, Ritual, 105.

17 Cf. Schomburg-Scherff, Nachwort, 205.

18 Turner, Ritual, 125; cf. also Schomburg-Scherff, Nachwort, 204.

tive passages of the marital liturgy. In this sense, the encouragement to wear the ring as a symbol of love and faithfulness, for example, is connected with the name and thus the blessing of the triune God: "In the name of the Father and the Son and the Holy Spirit." The couple's faithfulness is sustained by God's faithfulness. God's constancy is not merely a model to be emulated in terms of achievement and performing his example but, rather, the enabling factor, the gift which makes the fulfilment of this task possible.

The confirmation of the marital bond expresses this concept: "God, who called you to marriage, is faithful. He will stand by you and bring to fulfilment the good things he has begun." And the witnesses of this bond are called on to witness not only that humans must not separate what God has joined together (understood as a command), but that humans cannot and do not need to do so because God brings and holds them together from the first moment. In analogy to the Ten Commandments being introduced with an act of grace on the part of God—I am the Lord your God who led you out of Egypt! (cf. Exodus 20:2)—every Christian ritual is part of a doxology: always allowing God's grace to transcend our own capabilities and incapabilities.[19]

Facit: The Christian marriage rite possesses a definite meaning that needs to be made clear both theologically and pastorally. Since marriage is considered by Catholics to be a sacrament, this suggests a theological interpretation that radically emphasises God's grace in the rite. Such an interpretation then makes possible a new pastoral relationship to those who "only" request the ecclesiastical sacraments while otherwise keeping their distance from the church as a social reality. For all who participate in it, whether distanced from the church or remaining near, the sacrament of marriage is to be understood pastorally not as a condition-filled requirement, but primarily as a place where the unconditional grace of God may be grasped in God's promise to support, to develop and to enable the covenant of marriage. This view has clear implications for both the spirituality of the married couple and the spirituality of those who perform the church's pastoral rites.

---

19 Cf. Ottmar Fuchs, Gott in Dunkelheit erahnen. Die biblische Verbindung von Lob und Klage, in: Bibel und Kirche 63 (2008), 22–27.

III. Christian Eschatology and Pastoral Care

1. *Survival in the Context of Christian Eschatology*

Fragility and destruction, experienced by victims or caused by perpetrators, are out of reach of our care of souls, like many people we cannot reach in the present time. But if we speak of survival related to the Christian faith, we consider two kinds of survival: survival before and survival after death. In combining both for the sake of the present care of souls, I would like to find my approach to our theme.

Hardly another passage in the Bible links human justice so closely with divine justice as the Last Judgement text in Matthew 25:31–36. Here, the judicial actions of the coming Christ through his own person are connected with the actions of people when faced with those affected by need and injustice: "I was sick and you visited me". This is not only a "metaphorical" statement, but also a real, present and fundamental association of Christology and diaconal work.

Here, the culture of amnesia with respect to past suffering and averting one's gaze away from present misery is countered by another culture, namely the urgent complaint of suffering people (like in the psalms of lamentation, Job, Jesus on the cross, cf. Mk 15, and all suffering persons) as well as God's will to live in solidarity with suffering humans. In the persona of his son, God does not turn her back on human history and stories. Rather, in the manner of Paul Klee's Angelus Novus as an angel of history, as described by Walter Benjamin in the midst of his theories on history[1], God faces the rubble of history with shock on her face and is constantly catapulted forward through history right into the events of the last days. In the Last Judgement, the storm of history, which prevents the angel from doing what is necessary, that is, to give salvation, suddenly abates. For the angel of history the time now comes to gather up the rubble, which, with his eye on the storm, he has seen, and he has noted its position. Then, something like a new storm begins, contrary to that of history: the angel chases through the course of history in the opposite direction, to its beginnings, and collects absolutely everything, not forgetting anything. That is the messianic, the eschatological day that stops at all points in the past to raise the dead and piece together that which is broken. Whenever people dare to turn around to see this viewpoint of history, then they may be successful in already

[1] Cf. Walter Benjamin, Über den Begriff der Geschichte, in: Illuminationen, Ausgewählte Schriften, Frankfurt a. M. 1972, 251–263, 255 (IX. These).

seeing the rubble now in the storm of history, in anticipation of the Last Judgement, and be able to piece it together, to save other people and to reconcile them. If such a turning around takes place, then Benjamin's dictum can be experienced: "The Day of Judgement is the present turned backwards."[2]

I will first refer to several features of the existential substance of Christian eschatology.[3] In their mirror we may detect what God means for human beings faced with fragility and destruction.

1) The cry for salvation and justice

In the face of the immeasurable suffering which people bring upon others, the question of God is fundamentally combined with the question of whether the victims are lost forever or whether the perpetrators can triumph forever[4]—furthermore, whether there is a God who will intervene and who does not allow things to develop "indifferently", but who rather creates a turning point in which the victims are saved and heard and in which the perpetrators are accused and called to account.[5] Should such a divine Judgement not exist, then a life after death would only have to be bought in the end at the price of the derision of the victims and the subsequent legitimisation of the perpetrators. From the perspective of justice, such eschatology could be compared to atheism, which must also assume that there is no solution for the historical aporia of suffering and injustice.

2) Accusation against God

The fact that there are suffering and victims in history is not only a function of perpetrators but is due above all to the aporetic condition of the world, not only in the suffering caused by violence and cruelty, but also in all the pain which cannot be attributed to human causes: catastrophes, illness and death.[6]

---

2 Cf. Walter Benjamin, Gesammelte Schriften Band I, Frankfurt a. M. 1974, 1232.

3 Cf. Ottmar Fuchs, Das Jüngste Gericht, Regensburg 2007.

4 The extreme category between victims and perpetrators naturally refers to the tip of the iceberg of the fact that it occurs in everyday life in minor offences and neglect. It should be remembered that the victim-perpetrator scheme cannot be observed with the same degree of distinction as in the extreme area.

5 From the perspective of the theory of original sin, one could say that we are not at all able to distinguish between victims and perpetrators at this stage, that is, between good and evil, because this power of distinction in itself is highly ambivalent. However, one must do so with a greater extent of dialectic for the sake of the victims and justice, even with the danger of being guilty of making precisely this distinction again and again. The Sermon on the Mount is clear proof of this. This pressure to act stood in its time in the dialectic that the final truth has to be left to the decisive action of God.

6 In the psalms of lament, the people also accuse God, although he is never declared guilty at any point. Whenever the accusation implicitly contains accusing, then this is an intersubjective utterance on the part of humankind and not an objective statement about God.

According to the spirituality of lament in the Bible (e. g., Job, Psalm 22 and Mk 15), God has to be held responsible for this in accusation and lament, or already for the fact that there are such things as sin and death in the world. Christian belief thus consists of the fact that in the eschaton our lament becomes a "lament which is heard".[7] But for this to happen, this lament also has to be brought forth in the Last Judgement by the person broken as a result of suffering and sin: with the great hope that God can indeed justify him/herself not below the level of his compassion and in the bearing of human suffering. Thus, the eschatological event will bring out the final revelation of God's historical solidarity with humankind. It is only as such that a possible "meaningful answer" from God can be accepted.[8]

3) The cry for the reconciling God

Perpetrators who are willing to gain insight into their deeds desire satisfaction and reconciliation. The fact that they are also acknowledged in their human dignity and ability to embark on an alternative future and, if this acknowledgement is refused them, that they themselves do not become victims of punishing violence focuses theologically on the question of the reconciliation of God with sinners. From the point of view of the theology of justification, reconciliation is offered to them in the belief in the salvation offered by Christ. The eschatological "justification" will have a particular effect on the part of the perpetrators without which they cannot experience and accept this act of reconciliation in its quality referring to both the victim and God.

4) Pain in the horizon of unending Love

I am reconstructing this "reaction" of the perpetrators on the horizon of the eternal grace of God's reconciliation in the form of remorseful suffering. The power of God's reconciliation frees them from impenitence and opens their eyes to what they have done to other people (and to God). It allows them to see suffering in relation to God's eternal love, and this seeing shows them precisely what the demand for justice contains: that, through grace, they see so clearly what they have done that they experience remorse with the same intensity as the suffering they have caused, or not prevented from happening. In the area of human relationships, they will show remorse in the quality of the reflection on inflicted suffering. In their relationship to God, they will show remorse in the shame they experience when faced by sympathetic solidarity and God's endless power of reconciliation. This is because nothing about inflicted suffering can be simply "given". Suffering can never achieve satisfaction if it is less than the suffering itself.

---

7 Cf. O. Bayer, Erhörte Klage, in: NZSTh 25 (1983), 259–272.

8 Cf. O. Fuchs, Das Jüngste Gericht, 77–109.

5) Anticipation of the eschatological judgement in penance

The Christian penance rite can then also be defined from such a vision of hope of the eschatological judgement so that the "not yet" of the Last Judgement already finds its beginnings in the "already now" in the stories and in the history of humankind. It is apparent here that the topic under discussion as a whole extends into the centre of the ecumenical conflict. As a Catholic theologian, I can easily combine these previous considerations with the theology of the sacrament of penance which considers satisfaction and judgement as integral parts of the process of reconciliation between people and God. A new discourse is long since overdue with regard to the extent to which there cannot be a "reconciliation" between a theology of justification and a theology of judgement and the satisfaction which happens within both. To face the anticipated judgement and to accept satisfaction already now, and particularly satisfaction which benefits sufferers here and now, would at the same time also be an anticipation in the sense that it favours a reduction in the suffering of remorse on the Day of Judgement.

6) Eschatological pastoral

What is true for the rite of penance in particular has to be "democratised" for the pastoral as a whole: in anticipation of the Last Judgement. The parish becomes a type of community of remembrance for the injured and those who cause it, for accusation and lament, for concessions and compensation, where those people who seek and make judgement encounter each other on the level of their common faith in God's reconciliation: towards a mutual, brotherly and sisterly correctio between the criticism of others and themselves.

7) Between dogma and pastoral

Methodologically we are dealing here with a chapter of practical theology which (after decades of fruitful self-reflection on biblical texts) now has to be questioned more frequently concerning what value for life and development systematic-theological or dogmatic formulations have and what value they are able to develop further. This new approach of practical theology towards systematic theology does not take place any longer in the ancilla paradigm of applied science but in the brotherly and sisterly paradigm of mutual perception, development and criticism. This approach can be related to the epistemological conception of the pastoral constitution of the Second Vatican Council, which can be considered as revolutionary for theology, in which dogma has a substance of principles and existence which both develop each other on the horizon of very specific signs of the times. In the face of the "selection ramps" which are threatening worldwide between useful and useless humans, but also in the face of increased potentials for global justice and reconciliation, a new critically motivating and hope-inspiring topicality regarding the dogma of the Last Judgement is required in the Christian sphere.

With regard to eschatology, there is something in the nature of a vacuum in the church's preaching which is filled and compensated for by free-floating religious offers. The motives and causes for this vacuum are various. One motive is certainly to be found in the universal reluctance to take God's "dark side", his wrath and his judgement, seriously. Rather more quickly than in homiletics, religious education, in particular through direct encounters with young people and their apocalyptic conceptions, has reacted to this deficit and has demonstrated independent, new eschatological teaching in connection with this situation.[9]

2. *On the Level of a Theology of Justification*

At first sight, one could have cause to fear that, in the light of these theses, an "old" dissent between Catholic and Protestant theology will break out, as the question of judgement and reconciliation cannot be discussed outside the respective theology of justification. However, this does not have to be the case. Because it remains true: In the sense of Paul's theology of justification, the sinful person is forgiven, is loved by God unconditionally, without any justice through works. Remorse is not the condition of grace but the result of it.

From the perspective of the definition of justice, the question arises here as to how just it is that this grace of justification applies in the present as well as eschatologically to all sinners to the same degree, no matter if they are the worst sort of perpetrator or "only" people who are normally liable to sin. And it raises the question as to what effect this divine justification has on the part of people, particularly on the part of the perpetrators; that is, whether the justice is realised in the different effects of the grace of justification in that the acceptance of this grace turns out to be more painful on the part of the perpetrators than for the others.

What remains incontrovertible is that if one takes Paul's theology of justification seriously, then it actually applies to all people: they are all "*simul iustus et peccator*", which applies to the godless and the believers and applies to the worst perpetrators as well as to those who have done their utmost for justice and against violence. As "unjust" as this may seem, God's justice, which cannot be obtained by human categories of measurement, is very much constituted

[9] Cf. A. Biesinger and J. Hänle, Zwischen Horror und Erlösung. Gerichtsvorstellungen Jugendlicher als Herausforderung an religionspädagogische Theorie und Praxis, in: ThQ 178 (1998) 3, 209–228. In 1991 already F. Rickers pointed out in a lecture the eschatological dimension of the question of God in religious education: Gott in der Schule, in: J. Heumann (ed.), Freiheit und Kritik. Beiträge zu einer ideologiekritischen Religionspädagogik, Oldenburg 1992, 45–63.

within it. Nevertheless, the question of justice still remains, not as a distinguishing feature within the theology of justification, however, but as a distinguishing feature in *experiencing this blessing*. For reasons of justice, but also for reasons of communication, there will be something in the nature of a response in the justified sinners: with regard to justice inasmuch as the grace of justification is experienced according to the degree of their guilt manifesting itself in those who receive it as something which affects them deeply and painfully with respect to their past. I can think of no other words to use here than "the pain of remorse". With regard to communication, the grace of justification is not perceived as an answer to be experienced in the receiver and thus does not constitute the intended communication (between God and humankind) if the person who is supposed to receive it is not open to this encounter and for this justice. In any case, what takes place in the answering field of justified sinners will correlate with what they have done and thus correspond with the grace of justification which is experienced in it and which is all the more unconditional and radical.[10]

Thus, in the similar way as the sufferers have wounds (analogous to the stigmata of the resurrected Christ with which he became part of the Trinity), the perpetrators carry the wounds of their deeds tattooed onto them, after having experienced reconciliation, as wounds[11] of remorse at whose lowest point the judged person is judged for eternal life. Thus, heaven is not a place which has been bought by amnesty and amnesia, by mere absolution, or even through pure mindless disregard. In the new world, the memory of the old one is preserved in the wounds of the sufferers and the wounds of remorse of the perpetrators as remembrance after reconciliation; they are a scarred or "transfigured" remembrance of the old world and its suffering.

In particular, an acute apology of this Easter message, the Easter hope is required in opposition to reincarnation: at one with the impersonal God in the world, this symbiosis, which only at first sight seems comforting, between humans and God in nature, history and the universe reduces itself to an incestuous cycle which degenerates humans and God and in which the hungry al-

---

10 To emphasise this point once again: salvation does not happen through feeling the pain of remorse, but the latter is the consequence of salvation. The pain of remorse is not in an "if-then" relationship to salvation.

11 The term "wound" should be taken here as a representative term for the fact that the experiences of this world are never forgotten, not even in heaven. In contrast, there is certainly the notion that it is somewhat uneasy and that it could damage salvation as a whole if heaven is combined with the term "wound". Perhaps this is not the appropriate word, even if it attempts to refer to the wounds of the resurrected Christ, who, with these wounds, did not only rise from the dead, but returned to the "heaven" of the Holy Trinity, too. One should rather consider more closely the meaning of the term "transfiguration" in this context.

ways remain hungry and the cruel can always wreak destruction. The godhead experienced in ourselves in the symbiotic feeling of unity with nature and the cosmos may be conceived as "eternally" spherical, but is reduced in the end with respect to humankind and history only to the prison of its possibilities and impossibilities and to the dialectic of its constructive and destructive urges. And with regard to God, she seems to have degenerated here to the stage of an unconscious single-cell organism with the level of motivation of an amoeba. I can happily concede such a belief to people if it helps. But with the best will in the world I cannot muster more sympathy than that. This is because such a perception does not take God seriously as the real God who, beyond that which is given, can still be God and who has not sealed up "judgement" as the decline or increase of reincarnation in the immanence of the world, which would result in evil and suffering being made eternal. Judgement mutates to the stabilisation of the deficient aeon, whereas it has the potential to form its beginning and opening into a new aeon if one allowed God to be God beyond it. If there were not universal judgement and the hope that everyone will open themselves deeply in freedom and in their own will to the pain of remorse, one must say: whoever does not open herself to judgement may then be born again for ever and ever into an old world which becomes more and more hellish. In the perverted reception of reincarnation in the West (which in its religious sources is a curse and not a blessing, and is transcended by the belief in being redeemed from it), this prison is redefined as a market for ever-new opportunities, whereby in the Western world orientated towards fulfilling positive experience, one hardly ever thinks that one could be reborn as someone infected with HIV in the slums of an African city.

But people themselves are also not taken seriously; not the wishes and the rights of the victim, not only that their status as victims comes to an end and culminates in a coming life free from suffering and cruelty, but that the wrongfulness of the existence of suffering itself can be lamented, which cannot be justified by any means, not even by a real or presumed assumption of having become guilty. Suffering cannot be "offset in the category of exchange" in this way. In the end, the existence of the wandering soul remains an ego trip which only has itself at its core and not the solidarity with others for their own sake.

Paul argues (see 1 Corinthians, 15): the resurrection brings down the veil between immanence and transcendence, shatters the cycle and raises humankind into a completely new dimension of existence. Jesus will return, but not in the preserve of this world, but as the one who will burst open this world into a new one where the vicious circle and the eternal reoccurrence of inner-historical retaliation and reward, of life and death, suffering and well-being will be broken: towards a world without suffering, retaliation and death.

3. *Meaningful Consequences*

The Christian faith assumes a God who has given and gives this world a history limited in time and who with his future Judgement supports the necessity mentioned above and who thus gives it a messianic meaning referred to himself. Those who do not utilise the historical time reserved for them, but who waste it, are subject to Judgement. There is a time limit for whether someone (in this case, a person, social form or epoch) uses his or her talents or not. When the Lord comes, the time has run out. Even if the "Naherwartung" (immediate expectation) has become obsolete (although it can become real for everyone at any time), there is still a new and indispensable modus to combine limitation and the message of Judgement with each other! Thereby, the eschatological dynamism cannot dissipate not even into the pure knowledge of belief and cannot only be discussed as a problem of belief, but has to be freed as a driving force to organise this life better with regard to the future as a whole.[12] Important signs of the times are to be identified with respect to their eschatological quality: the fact that, ecologically speaking, the Earth is on its last legs as a matter of secular urgency takes on an additional dynamism on the theological horizon. It is God who will lament and punish the destruction of creation.

At a time when religious issues are being separated from ethical ones, their mutual deepening and intermingling are an increasing concern, without reducing their respective autonomy, that is, without allowing them to reduce each other. Accordingly, one may assume a synergy effect between secular and eschatological urgency. The more seriously Christian and church existences take on their own eschatological dynamics of time, the more sensitively they will be able to perceive the "secular" urgency of the signs of the times, too. To keep the eschatological meaning of our living and caring secret or to neglect it would certainly be a loss of that Jewish-Christian identity apparent in so many passages of the Bible.

I know how delicate a reintroduction of the "Judgemental God" into the care of souls (of the ones who care as well as of their clientele) is after preaching; particularly in the past decades it has more or less refrained from doing so as this idea of God quickly becomes too closely identified with the threat of Hell. Therefore, every opportunity must be seized to avoid the old combinations of Judgement, Hell and fear clicking into place. But, in light of the urgent

12 Accordingly, one must reflect more carefully from the point of view of systematic theology that there is not only a systematic-theological prioritisation of the truths of belief, but also an eschatological one which makes these truths important with regard to a very specific crisis and urgency, which has to be qualified eschatologically so that the eschatological dogma, if it is taken seriously, concretely applies a corresponding time-based index to all other truths of belief.

necessity of global solidarity for the benefit of many marginalised people not only in the southern, but increasingly also in the northern half of the globe, Christian teaching and preaching cannot take on the function of a "softener" that finally allows everything to culminate painlessly in the positive ending of a banally good God. It is high time to speak of judgement in a new way, no longer in connection with the Hell afterwards, but with the threat of Hell beforehand. In this regard, the "baby" of the fear of God may not be thrown out with the "bathwater" of the fear of Hell. For this, the dangers that the Earth will become a Hell for more and more people are much too great. Relevant passages from the Bible cannot be avoided or rendered harmless; it is moreover important to work one's way through them.

Thus, I advocate a kind of eschatologically orientated "anticipatory socialisation".[13] In social work this term is applied to preventative learning to better deal with future crisis situations through an appropriate readiness to react. Something in the nature of an anticipated crisis is dealt with: transferred to our context, this is a judicial intervention and a provocation of crisis. In such an eschatological "anticipatory socialisation" what is also involved, amongst others, is to fill the old term of "*ars moriendi*" with life to become "*ars vivendi*", namely in the ability to live according to the great sentence by a Jewish rabbi of the Chassidim: "Be converted one day before you die!". The anticipation of death and Judgement in life adds depth to life.

> The preaching of judgement is to be seen in the sense of a "democratisation" of prophetic preaching (as already encountered in the Old Testament, for example, in Joel 3, 1–2). In a similar way, it is important to establish domains of encounter in which people already learn to regret things, not only in the private sphere of the confessional booth, but also in protected public rooms in the parish. These are encounters where also those who have suffered remember what they have suffered.
> What happens in the sacrament of penance as a presentation of the last judgement would be something that could be considered and created as a real encounter in the social form of the parish in which those seeking justice and those who dispense it encounter each other on the level of their faith in the coming Lord: towards a mutual, brotherly and sisterly correctio in which I perceive my own miserable situation when faced with the other and when I accept criticism from others as self-criticism and take the appropriate steps in the opposite direction.

This would be a culture of encounter in which the injuries of others and one's own injuries could be expressed openly, a culture of *parrhesia*[14] (free speech) in which we tell each other something true about ourselves and hear something true about us from others. Such processes often cost us a great deal. But without them we will not attain the fundamental level of eschatological anticipa-

---

13 Cf. M. Lechner, Theologie in der Sozialen Arbeit, München 2000, 126–152.

14 On the term "parrhesia" cf. K. Rahner, Schriften zur Theology Band VII (Schriften zur Theologie des geistlichen Lebens), Einsiedeln 1991.

tion. If present forms of community organisation want to qualify themselves on the horizon of the future Judgement, then they will anticipate the eschatological Judgement in the fact that it is already here now by means of lament and confession, in reconciliation and conversion between "perpetrators" and "victims" in their different shapes. Precisely this is the sense of the Judgemental speeches of Jesus, namely, to direct and organise present life *now* from the perspective of the coming Judgement (cf. Luke 16:19–31).

In addition to this, we have to set out on the search for rituals and symbolic acts in which the future Last Judgement will be dramatised and experienced as an act of mimesis, beyond the mere remembered words. An eschatologically orientated pastoral lacks its symbolic experience of depth without an eschatological liturgy.
In doing so, a reactivation of the eschatological character of the Eucharist or the Last Supper would also come about. This is due to the fact that, with regard to the celebration of the Eucharist, too, the idea that it has something to do with the parousia (return) of the Lord until he comes again has disappeared from the consciousness of most people involved. In contrast, Erwin Keller has shown that in early Christian and patristic times the eschatological dimension was intrinsically present and celebrated in the Eucharist.[15] The response of the congregation "... until he comes again!" is today simply cited more often than it is experienced in its meaning. Thereby, particularly in the relationship between the Eucharist and eschatology, on the level of the sacrament there is an analogous structure to be seen to that which I would like to claim for the relationship of corresponding present experiences and the eschata in the realm of everyday life, providing the corresponding experiences become eschatological symbols, that is, signs in the present time in which something significant is happening for the eschata. In the fact that the Eucharist is celebrated as a prefiguration of the coming world, particularly of the coming heavenly wedding feast, as proven by Keller for the time under consideration, then I see it pointing the way for a practical theology of eschatology as a whole providing it embarks on the search for such prefigurations in the experiences of humankind and interprets these as being symbolic for the future event.

4. *The Sinful Character of Guilt as a Liberation for Change*

This combination of care of souls and the theological-spiritual horizon of eschatology is not only a question of the relationship of the Christian activities to the "outside", but also a question of this outside concerning our society. What Jürgen Habermas has to say, on the level of social and cultural philosophy, about the relationship of secular and religious language games applies to the correlation between, on the one hand, guilt and therapy, and, on the other,

[15] Cf. E. Keller, Eucharistie und Parusie. Liturgie- und theologiegeschichtliche Untersuchungen zur eschatologischen Dimension der Eucharistie anhand ausgewählter Zeugnisse und frühchristilicher und patristischer Zeit, Freiburg/Schweiz 1989.

between pastoral care and sin. This is a challenge for the plural constructions between inside and outside, in and between persons and communities, too.

Christian belief has no other "transcendence" than the remembered one. How can the different personal and societal beliefs of transcendence be opened for this semantic of God? Or is this endeavour not necessary at all? For example: Is it appropriate to support people in converting guilt into sin? How can the theology of grace be connected with the achievement of professionalism? How can the meaning of a profiled practice (narrated in the Bible) be saved from being forgotten, the worst sin in Israel? How can the situation in which many pastoral areas and communications—for the sake of possible spiritual and diaconical results—cannot speak explicitly of their Christian roots and motives be connected with the solidarity of the other pastoral areas?

In his much-noticed speech in Frankfurt's St Paul's Church (2001), Jürgen Habermas, cautiously but insistently held before the liberal state the possibility that "given the religious provenance of its moral foundations...in the face of utterly new challenges" it should beware of "failing to measure up to the level of articulation of its own historical development".[16] What is at stake here is not only the capability of religious language to communicate itself to secular language. Habermas also stresses the responsibility of the secular realm to relate itself to, and express itself through, religious language, expanding and intensifying its own discourse in this process. Thus, the task of undertaking this kind of "translation" and transfer is not allocated solely to the religious realm as though it were the perennial responsibility of religion to reconstitute itself within the rational paradigms of secular discourses. Neither is Habermas' concern restricted to a call for secular rationality to catch up with its own historical development in the sense of a hermeneutics of understanding. He is also concerned with valid suspicions about its validity, in other words, with a critical debate and at least partial acceptance of certain claims to validity that memory makes for the present and the future.

In this way, Habermas shows how the secular realm is interested in, or at least alleges that it may gain from, such communication both in reflexivity and in its ability to deal with pluralism (for example, in the mutual translation among narrative, mythical and conceptional ways of expression)[17] and with the societal problems of decreasing solidarity. Along these lines, in his later publications Habermas indicates the necessity to translate the linguistic forms and reflexive processes of the religious realm into the modes of secular terminology and reflection.

---

16 Jürgen Habermas, Der Riss der Sprachlosigkeit, in: Frankfurter Rundschau (16. Oktober 2001) Nr. 240, 18.

17 Cf. Ottmar Fuchs, Praktische Hermeneutik der Heiligen Schrift, Stuttgart 2004, 203–252, 416–422.

The crucial point is that this necessity is argued to be rooted in the need to safeguard that which is essentially human. Without the religious dimension the linguistic resources for accessing and activating resources and motivations for the human condition at a deep level that go beyond mere feasibility and instrumentalisation wear thin. If the secular language of modernity eliminates the religious dimension of its origins, it deprives itself of the resources for transcending itself and for making us conscious of the ambivalence of secularisation and its ability to outperform itself.

As far as the subject matter of the present paper is concerned, Habermas puts it like this: "Something was lost when sin was converted into guilt. For the wish for forgiveness goes hand in hand with the unsentimental desire to make undone the suffering inflicted upon others. The irreversibility of past suffering is even more unsettling for us—the injustice that has been suffered by those abused, humiliated and murdered innocently and goes way beyond any human capability for reparation. The lost hope for resurrection leaves a palpable emptiness."[18]

Against this background, the central concern is twofold: on the one hand, it is important for humans to be aware of their history of guilt and sin[19]; on the other, it is important that this does not paralyse and diminish individuals but, rather, opens them up and creates a capability for self-integration in grief, reconciliation and solidarity. From a Christian perspective, this twofold insight—both historical and theological—is fundamental: guilty before each other and sinful before God humans undoubtedly are[20]; God bestows the grace that does not diminish sinners but accepts their existence unconditionally[21]—that is, in their very state of hostility towards God and humans—so that from this acceptance they may draw the strength for "*metanoia*"—a reform that does good wherever good can be done and repairs where reparation is possible.

---

18 Habermas, ibid.

19 The awareness of guilt and sin in view here is not of the kind prone to cause defensive attitudes, self-justification and obduration of the heart in people. Any bad conscience that is externally imposed and thus apt to cause embarrassment simply increases the reverse dependence not to have been guilty and not to want to be guilty. Rather, what is in view is the category of guilt and sin as a place for sober insights into the dark side of both history and one's own existence, accepting this darkness as one's own so that through guilt a relation is established between the dark aspects of history and personal responsibility.

20 Concerning this principal perspective cf. Jürgen Moltmann, In der Geschichte des dreieinigen Gottes, München 1991, 74–89, with the respective consequence for the practical hermeneutics of biblical texts: Ottmar Fuchs, Praktische Hermeneutik der Heiligen Schrift, Stuttgart 2004, 416–422.

21 Cf. Ottmar Fuchs, Die andere Reformation. Ökumenisch für eine solidarische Welt, Würzburg 2016, 2/2017.

5. *Pastoral Care in the Horizon of God's Grace*

This God-oriented concept of sin aggravates inter-personal sin while accepting the sinner. The acceptance in which the sinner is, according to St. Paul, "made just" or justified is received gratuitously but not without a call to pass on the gift through deeds of love. But this duty results from the gift and is to be fulfilled out of it[22]. Hence, "it is the *Spirit of God* which enables individuals to live according to the will of God and calls on them to do so"[23]. Against this background, something was indeed lost when sin was converted into guilt: the possibility to live out of the dialectics of faith, to face the guilt of humanity as well as one's own without having to repress or downplay it or drown it in self-justification. In this process, it is a quite specific relationship to God that keeps us from falling into despair. It is one which, on the basis of the unconditional gift of our own existence and its acceptance by God, enables us to embark upon an ongoing journey of repentance in the hope of doing good or repairing something through our own life with the help of God.

For centuries, believers have experienced the proclamation that we are sinners as a self-humiliation, and many today have grown tired of such defamation of humans. But evidently this proclamation has suppressed at least partly the other aspect of the Christian message, namely that this characterisation, though realistic, also means that we are not forlorn and alone but accepted by God as we are. We are liberated again and again for a new life in the Spirit of God coupled with the hope that, hand in hand with the human capability for reconciliation, something may be realised of that reconciliation which, in unimaginable ways, God will effect in the Judgement at the end of the world and beyond.

The precondition, however, for accepting the set of theological arguments just set out is to tie the awareness of guilt strictly to the sensitivity for suffering. Paul does this by linking life in the Spirit of God with the highest virtue, i.e., love (1 Cor 13). The experiential centre of guilt and sin is lack of love, the extreme being a lack of compassion for those who suffer, or even worse, the active causing of suffering to others. Therefore, any God-oriented concept of sin must not be formalised or isolated to the degree that it can no longer be found in lack of love between humans. Crucially, the causing of suffering must be bound up with a notion of sin that describes and delineates on the part of the wrongdoers what they have done to others. The power of definition here lies with the victims and those who suffer, or else those who speak on their behalf historically. It is more than necessary that the perpetrators accept this "objective" guilt subjectively and are willing to atone and make reparation.

---

22 Cf. Michael Theobald, Der Römerbrief, Darmstadt 2000, 227–258.

23 Ibid., 242.

Otherwise, not only would Paul be misunderstood thoroughly if justification by faith were taken to replace atonement and reparation, but the action-related aspects of justification by faith would be omitted too. In that case, the theological discourse of guilt and forgiveness would indeed "protect the offenders"[24].

Von Kellenbach exemplifies this problem with Protestant pastors who did "soul care" with Nazi perpetrators during the Nuremberg Trials. The result of her research was: The Protestant theology of justification led to a separation between the reconciled relationship with God on the one hand and of their destructive deeds against the victims on the other hand. The grace of justification was not realised as a power giving the facility of *satifactio* in doing good again or in reparation (German: *Genugtuung* or *Wiedergutmachung*), at least in feeling empathy and remorse concerning the victims. This soul care mentality certainly was one of the reasons why there was nearly no openness for a victim-orientated remembrance (and in realising the present victims especially in the Vietnam War) in Germany till the student uprising in 1968. Of course the clients of the contemporary soul care are not perpetrators of such a calibre, but they are not innocent either, and mostly they know it even if they refuse to acknowledge it at first. According to the theory of knowledge given to us by Walter Benjamin, the extreme cases reveal what is going on under the cover of normality and what can become our dreadful possibilities.

Against this background, the realistic as well as theological insight that no one is without guilt and sin must not be de-individualised and subsumed under the collective. If pastoral care is concerned with people in need of such care, theologically this need lies not only in their own suffering, but also in the guilt/sin that did not prevent or actually inflicted suffering and which in turn causes suffering by being unable to cope with one's behaviour. Pastoral care addresses both (just as Jesus healed and reconciled) people's roles as victims and perpetrators, which are integrated differently in each person.

In this, and this is an important kind of transcendence, the theological perspective cannot be limited to the amount of awareness of guilt that those "in need" already have. Rather, it triggers a step that goes way beyond the so-called therapeutic by bringing to light as yet unconscious, repressed guilt: The guilt under which the victims suffer but not yet the perpetrators, especially in the area of structural guilt or lack of solidarity. At the same time, feelings of guilt that go "over the top", take on pathological features and cannot be

---

24 Katharina von Kellenbach, Theologische Rede von Schuld und Vergebung als Täterschutz, in: Id./Björn Krondorfer/Norbert Reck (Hg.), Von Gott reden im Land der Täter. Theologische Stimmen der dritten Generation seit der Shoa, Darmstadt 2001, 46–67. Here is the oppressive example of a very specific ideology of justification, which understands the 'gratis' nature of grace not as an empowerment to reparation, but as its replacement, whereby at the same time an action-related connection both with the past and with the present victims is destroyed from the outset.

shaped in realistic terms need to be corrected. Hence, if in pastoral care the focus is not only on the victims but on the offenders too, the "solidarity of guilt" in view here should not be understood as something in which individual sins dissolve: "Incomprehensible and unatonable. Where everyone is guilty, no-one can be held to account."[25] Rather, the insight into into the ubiquity of being driven to suffering and of the causing of suffering and of guilt means that all of us are implicated in it, each carrying their own share, so that no one will be able to say: I don't want to be involved with this sinful world! Each and every one of us is involved in their own way.[26] In both history and the present, there are outbreaks of horror that bring home to us what humans can do if sanctions are lacking and the mantle of civilisation wears thin.

6. *Grace as Motivating Resource*

In what follows, I align myself especially closely with the thoughts Katharina von Kellenbach presented in her article at the symposium: "The Reformation criticism of the Catholic doctrine of penance and especially the *satisfactio opere* makes it extremely difficult to hold the offenders accountable towards their victims. But it seems to me that the third step of the Catholic doctrine of penance, the *satisfactio opere*, provides a way of allocating a role to the victims in the Christian process of reconciliation."[27] This insight, which is strikingly contrasted with pertinent counter-effective cases of forgiveness towards Nazi offenders, corresponds with the desire to see one's own sin "over and done with" not only in one's relationship to God. Rather, it is this relationship of God to the sinners which enables and requires them to establish a relationship to those who suffer or, if this is no longer possible, to live out this commitment—made possible and triggered by forgiveness—for the benefit of those who suffer now, orienting their atonement towards the present. Reconciliation with God is not a way of getting around "reparation" but actually gives its reality. As Ernst Käsemann put it: "Grace that does not become active is an illusion!"

Incidentally, the positive appraisal of the Catholic doctrine of penance von Kellenbach offers from a Protestant perspective can also open up a new perspective for the Catholic theology of absolution, where the set of issues just outlined is at stake[28]. Moreover, the Christian possibility must be considered that penance can be lived and done vicariously, on behalf of offenders who

---

25 Cf. von Kellenbach, ebd., 55.

26 Cf. ebd., 64.

27 Cf. Katharina von Kellenbach, Schuld und Vergebung. Zur deutschen Praxis christlicher Versöhnung, in: B. Krondorfer u. a. (Hg.), Mit Blick auf die Täter, Gütersloh 2006, 227–312.

28 Cf. Ottmar Fuchs, Die Buße im Horizont des Jüngsten Gerichts – ein vergessener Zusammenhang, in: Anton Bauer (Hg.), Doch bei dir ist Vergebung, Ostfildern 2000, 13–34, 35ff.

have not made atonement, who have died and are no longer able to atone. Just as in the case of satisfaction, such atoning action is possible only on the basis of the Christ event "*pro nobis*", where we are not let off for something we could repair or atone for ourselves, but through which we are enabled to do so[29]. Finally, a specific eschatology of judgement (analogous to the sacrament of confession as the anticipation of the eschatological judgement) emerges: the reconciliation offered and given by God can be effective only if it is met, on the part of the sinners, by something that corresponds to the suffering they have caused. In addition, in encountering the victims they must embrace the necessity—unimaginable as it is for us—to expose themselves to the victims' equally unimaginable willingness for reconciliation—sustained by God's infinite power of reconciliation and in a way that is absolutely not collectivist but includes the most differentiated of memories[30]. *Satisfactio* is not a precondition of forgiveness, but if it does not occur it falsifies the latter's efficacy by grace. For "he who, lacking salvation, turns the Gospel of Salvation upside down...must be considered the anti-Christ."[31]

Such a radicalisation of attitudes of solidarity by a pastoral care motivated by Christian religious attitudes must be in the interest of the state and society too; this means the existence of not only a therapeutic or reason-orientated, but also a Christian approach to pastoral and soul care. This view from the outside corresponds to the long-standing Christian inside view of pastoral care as integrating anthropology and theology or, in practical terms, as integrating the person and the situation on the one hand and the memory and the Gospel on the other. This includes the dialectic, according to which the biblical relationship between God and human has meaningful parts, but it also often surpasses human reason as well.

Not every pastoral process has to embody the full spectrum of religious and secular language, of explicit Christian remembrance and helping, liberating, consoling encounter. This also applies to the institutional and structural modes in which pastoral care takes places and by which it is made possible. Now, in the face of pluralised forms of personal and social life and thought, how can we envisage a pastoral care which, while rooted in Christian remembrance, does not lessen personal and political solidarity and does not metaphorically dissolve the God-oriented Gospel (*martyria*) in inter-human service? What are the structural conditions that safeguard the diversity of pastoral modes as well as cross-links between them, not in the sense of simplistic inter-

---

29 Cf. Ottmar Fuchs, „Stellvertretung" - eine christliche Möglichkeit, in: Theologische Quartalschrift 185 (2005) 2, 95–126.

30 Cf. Ottmar Fuchs, Neue Wege einer eschatologischen Pastoral, in: Theologische Quartalschrift 179 (1999) 4, 260–288.

31 Gunter Wenz, Ekklesiologie und Kirchenverfassung, in: Reinhard Rittner (Hg.), In Christus berufen. Amt und allgemeines Priestertum in lutherischer Perspektive, Hannover 2001, 80–113, 102.

action, but with a normative view to fostering the thicker ropes that hold the net together, and, by this, the rooting of the diverse parts in a substantive common ground?

7. *Abandonment of Survival for the Sake of Survival*

1) Taking risks

Eschatological survival opens the unending field to collect treasures in heaven for the sake of human treasures in earthen vessels: for the sake of the solidarity concerning the survival of others (cf. Lk 6:20–23, 32–35 and Mt 10:1–16).

I want to highlight this certain attitude, which can be found within the Bible itself. Wherever someone accepts suffering violence in someone else's stead and does not respond with violence, we see the suffering servant in Second Isaiah, the suffering Son of God praying for his violent tormentors even from the cross (cf. Luke 23:34), returning the violence he suffered as love.[32] Both scenes presuppose a context of violence and destruction, which the social psychiatrist Horst Eberhard Richter put in these words: Those who don't want to suffer must hate![33] So do these texts seek to educate us about self-discrimination for the sake of others, even the perpetrators, in other words, to endorse martyrdom?

The Servant and Son of God inflict violence upon themselves, allowing it to be inflicted upon them, juxtaposing the non-violent force of their own bodies. The body is their resistance (which the opponents need to clear away before carrying on or, indeed, deciding to refrain from doing so). The "heroes" and protagonists here are not the subjects of violence (the perpetrators), but those subjects who non-violently rise against the violence wrought by others and who expose themselves to it (vicariously) for the sake of others, protecting the perpetrators rather than destroying them. After all, Cain was marked so no one would kill him without bringing down the sevenfold revenge of God (cf. Gen 4:15).

2) The path of Christian care

For this understanding and transformation to be firmly and plausibly established (against many of the plausibilities of church and society), a social context is needed that *sustains* this perspective through internal and external interaction.

---

32 Cf. R. Schwager, Jesus im Heilsdrama. Entwurf einer biblischen Erlösungslehre, Innsbruck 1990, 146; Ders., Gewalt als anthropologische Konstante? Auf dem Weg zu einer neuen Gewichtung, in: Concilium 33 (1997) 4, 555–564.

33 H. E. Richter, Wer nicht leiden will, muss hassen. Zur Epidemie der Gewalt, Hamburg 1993.

The Christian Creed can provide such a compass through its substantive dynamic of God's descent and self-emptying in Jesus Christ and his resurrection and the resurrection of humankind. However, the texts of the Creed possess a high degree of abstraction and need images that can be thought and visualised. The more God's people tell each other the relevant stories (or hear the stories about saints and exemplary figures past and present), the more the *willingness to delegate all violence, both current and eschatological, to God and to God only—conscious of the permanent danger and temptation of taking violence into their own hands*—will develop. The biblical message exposes our profound sinfulness, that is, our violence, and at the same time proclaims a God who accepts sinners back into her love and justice and, at least according to Paul's theology of justification, refrains from violent punishment. Those who in their proclamation and belief are able to join God in this unconditional love will from the very heart of their being no longer be driven to violence. Grace alone can conquer violence.

Once more, the social forms of the Church emerge as the external condition for the possibility (or impossibility) of this perspective on the Bible's texts. Social hermeneutics leads to biblical hermeneutics and vice versa. If Christian and ecclesial existence accepts discrimination for the benefit of the less fortunate in the name of God, rather than chasing their personal advantage, certain biblical texts (and their context) will disclose their meaning quite differently. People treat the Bible the same way they treat each other and outsiders.

The ancient fourth century depictions of Christ the Emperor prevailing over evil, treading on lions and dragons, do not add up. The underlying idea of the fight between the forces of good and evil probably remains valid in its portrayal of what is called a fight and what today, within a different linguistic framework, we call the permanent dialectic of history, its worst contradiction, that between perpetrator and victim. But the category of eschatological time, too, must be applied to this. Ultimately, Christ will prevail over evil upon his return. But wherever today someone thinks they can accomplish through their own violence what Christ does not presently through his (just as Jesus did not), the picture is misread. In this eon, God's power over history unfolds differently, namely according to the dynamic of a particular image: that of the lamb bound and readied for slaughter. And is not the shepherd carrying the lamb both the person who found it and the person who delivers it to slaughter, in other words, to the sacrificial altar?

Can we find "plausibility" for this in our faith and proclamation? It would be high time, so that a millennium of mainly violent Christianity can be succeeded by a millennium where Christian existence embraces surrender and "vicarious" existence rather than the subjugation of others, empowerment rather than the exerting of power.

We derive the strength for this not only from the hope that God's ultimate power over history and the secular forces will one day be manifest, but also the fact that even now God accompanies us on our ongoing path of blocking and reducing violence; just as on the cross God walked this path right to the end, so God will walk and endure it with us. That is the root of God's credibility: he will eventually exert his power for the benefit of justice and mercy because even now he gets involved in the necessity of justice and mercy and its consequences. If God does not intervene now, if she did not interfere on the cross, this does not mean she is not able to interfere. The reason why in the present he intervenes in the form of the one who bears violence and sends back love remains hidden from us. But one thing is made plain by this: God does not sit on the fence and does not abandon humans in their violent actions, but gets involved himself and, in doing so, indicates how to deal with them.

3) Confronted with our own fragile existence
Our care of souls always bears the mark of personal relationships in our own lives, of constraints placed on our freedom of action. We are likely to come out for *those* persons in distress to whom we have, in one form or another, cognitive ties (we know them or know *of* them) or affective ties born of empathy or shared resistance.

In the teeth of this inevitable *factual* constraint, there is a need, on the level of *principle*, to go further and recognise that, even beyond our own radius of knowledge and emotionality, there are victims no less deserving of help, even if their deserts are such that we cannot feel them because of prior identifications in our lives. But we have to acknowledge these limits, too. The least we can do is to keep up this tension and not get into a situation where victim is ranged against victim, in competition for our sympathy; none will then be beyond the pale of commitment born of solidarity.

Although we often cannot prevent our solidarity from disadvantaging other victims than those it was aimed at helping, we can indeed, by recognising that they are in principle no less deserving, prevent them from becoming wholly indifferent or from experiencing that solidarity extended to the one is just code for suffering aggravated in all the others. When solidarity for the one is a zero-sum game where the others necessarily have to lose, positive and negative discrimination are two sides of one coin. With its limited resources, church development aid for poor countries constantly runs up against this problematic of flipping the coin, of deciding which victim to assign priority to over the other; dissonance and injustice are a permanent feature of such work, as aid workers well know.

We are not Gods in our care. And even God's care in this history has its limits. What is at stake is therefore not only human ambivalence, but the negative dialectic in God's liberating actions and in our relationship to God, indeed the ambivalence of our images for, encounters with and experiences of God. Odd things will always remain here and we will have to bear with God in his strangeness, her ineffability and hiddenness, both in suffering and in violence, in solidarity and sinfulness. For what continues to be fatal and incomprehensible about the pertinent biblical texts is the fact that God's intervention is experienced not only as the power of authority but indeed as naked violence. God's intervention for the benefit of the Israelites is experienced as brutal destruction by the Egyptians. God continues to owe them their salvation. Within the mess of history, God commits lovingly to someone or to his people while at the same time inflicting injustice or violence on others. On the cross God had dispensed with violence within this world. This is our way, too. Ultimately, it is hoped, God's love will bring about the kind of violence that will universally create a new world without suffering and death, where neither God nor humans desire to cause injustice and no longer have to.

8. *Conclusion: Easter – A Tremendous Victory of Love*[34]

It is a great suffering that with Christ's birth and resurrection almost nothing has changed in human history, not even through Christianity itself, when one perceives the horribly dark side of its history. That is why Jesus, the Coming, said that there is still much to be done, that he will come again: at the end of our stories in death and at the end of human history. Here Christian believers are in a similar expectation as Jewish believers who are also waiting for the Messiah who is yet to come.

The first coming of God into this world constitutes the second coming, in which all that Jesus promised is accomplished. But why is this taking so long? How does God himself endure that? Why does God allow people who start wars, to rape, murder, torture and defile children? God still owes us the answer.

Jesus also does not receive heavenly hosts. Therefore, the attitude that God can never intervene becomes too easy. That this is a deception is what the raising of Jesus from the dead stands for. Here God's power prevails over the destruction of love. In other respects too, the biblical texts of God's mighty intervention prove to be memorabilia, never to forget that God can intervene and will certainly intervene once and for all, with an unimaginable violence, as described in the last book of the New Testament in impressive images, which uncompromisingly sweeps away all existing destructive violence and thus destroys the violence of injustice and evil. Without this intervention of God at the end of history, we would have no hope of justice, and people would be lost forever in the terribly beautiful universe.

[34] Cf. Ottmar Fuchs, Das Jüngste Gericht. Hoffnung über den Tod hinaus, Regensburg 2018.

1) Violence of love

The Messiah will come again, but then no longer in the impotence of love, but with a power of love that no longer lets anything that is without love into the new world. The faithful have always associated both fear and hope with it. Therefore, the whole Bible ends with the cry "Maranatha", our Lord, come!

What kind of violence is this that will prevail? It is not a violence that destroys people, it is another violence in which God meets people "powerfully". In 1946, after the terrible catastrophes of the Second World War, Reinhold Schneider expressed hope for the Second Coming of the Lord incomparably more dramatically and intensively:

You're coming, my God. ...
You will tear down the mighty towers.
And any wall that still separates you. ...
We will fall
In your power. In the most terrible of courts.
Give us the most intimate violence of love...
But we ask: Come! O come soon.[35]

That love becomes "intimate violence"; now in a hope which, following the first coming of the Messiah, gives us strength to act in solidarity, and in the end, in the fulfilment of this hope, in the second coming of the Messiah, this is the heart of the Christian faith.

2) Nothing gets lost

God does not stand with his back to history in the Son of Man, but (like Paul Klee's Angelus Novus as the angel of history in Walter Benjamin's middle of his Theses)[36] with his frightened face to the debris field of history and constantly hurled forward through history into the events of the Last Days. The storm of history, which prevents the angel from doing what is necessary, namely saving, is ended in judgement. The angel now begins the time of the great gathering of the rubble, which he has seen all with the look against the storm and has noticed exactly.

Now something like a new storm, contrary to that of history, is happening: the angel of history is now chasing in the opposite direction through history to its beginning and will not forget anything, to collect everything. This is the messianic day that lingers in all places in the past, awakens the dead and brings together the broken. Where people dare to turn to this view of history, they may be able to see and assemble ruins in the storm of history in anticipation of

35 Reinhold Schneider, Apokalypse. Sonette, Baden-Baden 1946, 15.

36 Cf. Walter Benjamin, Über den Begriff der Geschichte, in: Illuminationen. Ausgewählte Schriften, Frankfurt a. M. 1972, 251–263, 255 (IX. These).

the Last Judgement, to save and reconcile people. This is what the first coming of God in Jesus stands for.

3) Justice in salvation

It is not a question of threat, but of that fear of God that is connected with the great hope that an inexhaustibly loving God will meet us in death and that in this encounter we will experience all the more painfully, or even with joy, what we have done or not done in each case. Therefore, it is about that double hope: on the one hand, that judgment does not mean God's withdrawal of love, that the Last Judgement takes place in this love and in it radically, and not outside love, and on the other hand, that it is precisely in this that all evil is accountable and in the horizon of God's inexhaustible love hurts bitterly.

Because love does not make everyone equal but intensifies the opposites from the perspective of love and lack of love, without withdrawing love from the lack of love. But she does not look at them with joy, but with horror and pain. Perhaps the human experience, which parents sometimes do not spare, helps: They experience how their sons and daughters go not only other, but also bad ways. Her parental love does not lose its intensity, but it is now changing: from joy to pain. From this experience, the cross can be understood as the expression of God's pain at the sufferings of human beings and in the face of their evil. And thus as an expression that God's love loses nothing of inexhaustible love in both directions.

4) Longing for retribution

When I hear about parents whose daughter was raped and beaten to death, I cannot bear my own compassion alone. There is a vital right of these parents to hate the perpetrator and not to forgive him, combined with the longing that the perpetrator must suffer and atone for it. This is what the biblical curse psalms stand for (cf. Ps 58), which call for God's revenge on the worst perpetrators, just as Rom 12,17–21 where, according to Paul, fiery coals are gathered on enemies by doing them good.

For people who have inflicted terrible suffering on others, there are appropriate punitive systems in societies, but they are not enough because they are external to what has happened, because they do not reach the heart. Even traditional hell is an external punishment that remains external to what has happened. It does not reach the heart of what has been inflicted and suffered. This can only happen in the horizon of what has been deeply hurt here, namely love itself, a love that is then unimaginable for us because it is inexhaustible, which in itself covers everything that was loveless with an infinite pain in God. The victims longing for retribution; will be inexhaustibly fulfilled in the Last Judgement, because the perpetrator is concerned with his innermost marrow.

The dogma of eternal fire remains valid just as the biblical statements about the furnace of fire, where weeping and gnashing of teeth will take place (cf. Mt 13:42), but even more radically than this was previously thought of as "hell". In the excessive love of God and in the face of those to whom suffering has been inflicted, pain does not calm down, not because it is imposed from the outside, nor because it is a condition to be experienced for this love, but because this divine dynamic of inexhaustible love makes exactly this explodingly possible. It is a pain within bliss itself and within a reconciliation that never ceases and in which, in the grace of coming to good with the past, infinite bliss is experienced.

5) Heaven in the sign of judgement

Our often flat notions of heaven are often also shaped by the fact that the blessed are equally blessed. On the other hand, there are also those pictures in tradition in which the heaven is thought of as pyramid-capable, with different gradations from bottom to top. Even in Dante's Divine Comedy, heaven has gradations. This reflects an inkling that the blessed are not equally blessed, that there are differences depending on how they lived.

With Dante there are nine spheres which bring one up to and ever closer to God and into ever more perfect bliss. It is interesting to note that over all nine spheres the highest heaven is at the same time a heaven of fire, which reaches into infinity and thus into the unlockable. Light and fire are mutually dependent and not only the light but also the fire never ceases. This is a revealing perspective for the difference and lasting quality of the fire experience in the heavenly area. Fire and light are the metaphors for the inexhaustible being loved, which applies to all, but which does not make them equal, but does justice to every human being in a highly different way. The image of graduations must therefore be corrected to the effect that these are not hierarchies, because they are all loved with the same infinite power and this is precisely what makes them different.

Therefore, the consequences of the Last Judgement reach into heaven and are reflected there. A criminal who has taken the life of others cannot be blessed in the same way as a person who has worked to the extreme for the lives of others. Blessedness does not flatten differences through lack of traces, but expresses them more intensively. For inflicted suffering can never be undone, not even by forgiveness. Forgiveness overflowing with suffering does not do justice. Rather, forgiveness is the condition for being able to perceive this suffering all the more intensively in the horizon of this love of reconciliation. It's not about an excuse. It's about being sorry for inflicted harm.

6) The wounded heaven

As the suffering have their wounds (analogous to the wounds of the Risen Lord with which he was received into the Trinity), so those who have inflicted suffering bear the atonement wounds of their deeds, not as senseless pain but as wounds of repentance gone through reconciliation, but in a transforming and transformed form, namely as the Bible call it "transfigured" (cf. Mt 17:2; 1 Cor 3:18). The pain of repentance is transformed into the happiness of its enabling out of God's love. What was thought of as eternity outside the love of God in relation to the fire of hell is now regarded as the fire of love and repentance within the love reference. Judgement is the one fire, the eternal fire, which is God Himself, and which suffices for heaven, purgatory and hell.

The concept of the wound may be assumed here as a remedy for the fact that even in heaven the experiences of this world are never forgotten. On the other hand, there is certainly the idea that it is somehow uncomfortable and could damage the entire salvation if heaven is connected with the term wound. This dialectic cannot be dissolved in human speech. God's inexhaustible love itself will bear its contradictoriness and lets us experience it as love as we cannot imagine. In any case, it is a sign that this world cannot be perfumed away by the heaven.

But in all this, all these helpless speech attempts are only a straw against the unimaginable, what will really happen.

G. Translations

I. Poetry as a Deep Experience of a Different World: Goethe's West-Eastern *Divan*[1]

Literature creates an imaginative space where acts of identification with other realities become possible. On the one hand, the literary text is a blueprint whose characters and stories guide our emotional reactions, but on the other, much space is left for us to elaborate them creatively within our own affective setting in ways that enrich our imagination. Patrick Colm Hogan suggests that different cultural expressions are rooted in an emotional constitution shared universally by all humans: "Reading literature and philosophy from other traditions is not...a matter of looking at different icons, at other selves and social relations. It is the same icon all along, the same human self and the same human relations. But through the various traditions, that icon is loosed from its fixed place, lifted from behind a glass, as if I could now turn it in my hand and examine it from a different angle."[2] For either is true and both must be discovered: "Emotions have a universal dimension. And: Emotions are also shaped by our cultural context (particularly by education and upbringing)."[3] Hence it follows naturally that "intolerance is the consequence of forgetting our shared humanity".[4]

If that literature comes from other religions and cultures, from unfamiliar social strata and personal backgrounds, there is a correlation, and a mutual enrichment, between literary competence and intercultural competence. "If we empathize with a fictional character, we at the same time empathize with

1 Delivered in the Department of English Language and Literature – Sultan Qaboos University, 3rd International Conference on Language, Linguistics, Literature and Translation: Connecting the Dots in a Globalized World, November 3–5 2016, Oman.

2 Patrick Colm Hogan, The Death of the Goddess: A Poem in Twelve Cantos, Preface.

3 Christa Knellwolf King in her lecture at Oman University on 9 February 2016.

4 Ibid.

the cultural community represented by him or her. Empathizing with a real or fictional person is a means of inhibiting aggression and violent responses."[5]

This way of accessing the Other breaks down the biogenetic fixation on one's own pack, family and descendants, and the concomitant hatred of strangers—other people, tribes and nations. This happens within an aesthetic context or conversation where we do not feel threatened and engage in the transition playfully and imaginatively.

Because it operates poetically, Goethe's "West-Eastern *Divan*" can be considered an excellent role model for intercultural learning, centred on training in empathy, so to speak. The path offered here is that of imitation, or taking on a role or attitude by imitation through a play, acting or stage drama, analogous perhaps to experimental archaeology. To understand the meaning of the Muslim prayer position as a physical expression of reverence for God, we must experience it through our own bodies.

1. *Mahomet: a Genius*

Currently, questions about the possibility of shared spaces enabling intercultural and inter-religious co-existence are of great importance, and here Johann Wolfgang von Goethe's *West-Eastern Divan*[6] is interesting to me in two respects: first, because of its poetical hermeneutics of an alien world; second, because of how it deals with what it finds in that alien world—in terms of both what is appreciated and what is rejected.

Goethe's first attempt at tackling the Mahomet material dates from 1773. Many years later, looking back as he is writing his *Poetry and Truth* in 1814, he talks of his intention of using the example of Mahomet to explore the general patterns of a great character and a great mind: "What is heavenly and eternal becomes embodied in earthly intentions and is swept away towards a transient fate."[7] Goethe writes: "thus grew in me the intention of using the life of Mahomet, who I had been able to regard as a fraudster, to depict in dramatic fashion those ways which I had studied so keenly in reality, and which lead not to salvation but to perdition. Just prior to that, I had taken a great interest in, and done much reading about, the life of the oriental prophet, and thus I was fairly well prepared when the thought occurred to me ... Everything that genius can do to humans by way of the character and the mind was to be depicted, and all the ways it gains and loses in the process."[8]

5 Ibid.
6 See Johann Wolfgang von Goethe, West-östlicher Divan, München 1982.
7 Johann Wolfgang von Goethe, in: Klaus-Detlef Müller, Aus meinem Leben, Dichtung und Wahrheit, Text und Kommentar (3. Teil, 14. Buch, 1814), Frankfurt a. M. 1986, 685.
8 Ibid., 685 and 687.

In opposition to the Enlightenment's preference for rationalisation, Goethe enters here the "storm and stress" of empathy, feelings and emotions, of a world that reason cannot comprehend.[9] Thus, he has Mahomet say: "Do you not see him? In every still spring, under every blossoming tree I encounter him in the warmth of his love. How grateful I am: he has opened my breast and softened the hard shell of my heart, so that I can feel his approach."[10] The importance of this particular image to him is shown by his wish, articulated in a 1772 letter to Herder: "Oh may I pray like Moses in the Qur'an: Lord, create a space in the tightness of my breast"[11] (see Sura XX).

The God experienced by Goethe's Mahomet is manifest in genius, in the person of genius, in the "stream of genius" that flows from the spring in the rock, complete with all its tributaries, into the ocean of eternity.[12] "Neverending creativity takes the genius (including the religious genius) into a realm where boundaries are transcended, into the divine infinity, symbolised in this instance by 'father' ocean.'"[13] Thus, Goethe focuses on the charismatic prophet Mahomet and claims him as an example of a person of genius that is particularly impressive, not least due to his intriguing otherness. This situates him in the context of the genius debate of his time.[14]

2. *The Debate about Mahomet*

Here, the negative elements are construed in terms of the genius failing because of adverse circumstances, which negates any purely negative connotations. This allows that which otherwise may be viewed as criminal, unscrupulous or fraudulent to be integrated into the pattern of a person of genius whose life is headed towards perdition rather than salvation.[15] In this way, a counterargument is developed addressing the established prejudices of one's own world (Mahomet the fraudster). This is achieved by adopting an accepted contemporaneous discourse (about genius), which thereby acts as the hermeneutic key for understanding of what is alien about Mahomet. Having been trans-

---

9 Vgl. Gerhard Sauder (Hg.), Theorie der Empfindsamkeit und der Sturm und Drang, Stuttgart 2003.

10 Johann Wolfgang von Goethe, Mahomet, Fragment (1772), in: Gerhard Sauder (Hg.), Johann Wolfgang von Goethe. Sämtliche Werke nach Epochen seines Schaffens, Band 1.1, Der junge Goethe 1757–1775, München 1985, 517.

11 Quoted in Kommentar zu Mahomet, Fragment, Text und Kommentar, in: Sauder (Hg.), Der junge Goethe, 941.

12 Cf. Goethe, Mahomet, 518–519.

13 Mahomet, Kommentar, 943.

14 Cf. ibid., 943.

15 Cf. Goethe, Dichtung und Wahrheit, 685.

formed in terms of one's own understanding of the patterns of genius, he is now met with appreciation.

This manoeuvre yields an enormous gain in tolerance. Inter-religious boundaries and fixed categories are broken down by being understood and conveyed against the backdrop of the universal human drama of the genius. The Other, Mahomet and the actual Qur'anic text in its entirety contribute hardly any contrary suggestions or challenges to this game. Whatever does not fit the script of an omni-benevolent and all-loving God revealing himself across all cultures and religions through people of genius is excluded from this encounter. Goethe entangles the quest for God with the desire to experience an oriental culture.

From a structural-analytical point of view, we could say that Goethe appreciates in the Other what he admires in the familiar. Everything else, for example, the existence of a hell or the possibility that God's love might be conditional upon faith, falls by the wayside because against the backdrop of a generalised human-divine drama, it has to be rejected for the sake of inter-religious tolerance and the levelling of inter-religious boundaries. Thus, Goethe discovers what is good and familiar in what is alien and other, and he expresses his approval—the price being the Other's having to submit to this pattern. This, therefore, is the mechanism that facilitates a connection with a limited pluralism of people in diverse religions and cultures.

So we can appreciate the dilemma Goethe found himself in on being asked by his Duke Karl August, a big admirer of Voltaire's, to translate Voltaire's play "Mahomet" so that it could be included in the Weimar theatre's repertoire; this happened almost three decades after Goethe's Mahomet fragment. Goethe was indebted to the Duke and could not say no.[16] The challenge this translation presented was that Voltaire represented the opposite view, so to speak, supported by the majority of the intelligentsia of the time: namely that Mahomet was an unscrupulous religious and political power broker, a fanatic with violent, fraudulent and even criminal tendencies.

So Goethe had his work cut out in "purging all criminal and ambitious traits from the figure of Mahomet, and turning it into one possessed by a demon. The purely didactic elements are pared down, the direct and matter-of-fact content is adapted and lightened up ... his changes are ... targeted and intended to freshen up the material, and they are apt to convey his idea of what a resonant German language of the stage is. Where he intentionally diverges from Voltaire's vocabulary, it is because he seeks to mitigate the latter's

16 Cf. Johann Wolfgang von Goethe, Übertragung von Voltaires „Mahomet" (1799/1800), Text und Kommentar, in: Victor Lange (Hg.), Johann Wolfgang von Goethe. Sämtliche Werke nach Epochen seines Schaffens. Weimarer Klassik 1798–1806, München 1988, im Kommentar 918–924.

often ruthless and ideologically-determined tactics."[17] Thus, he talks of the seducer rather than the fraudster and of inner turmoil rather than outer rebellion.[18] Goethe's work is not that of translation but of transformation—remodelling what is unacceptable to him in line with the concepts he advocates.

The situation is very odd indeed: Voltaire and Goethe have a shared objective—namely, increased tolerance—but they pursue it in completely different ways. Voltaire makes no secret of his revulsion to fanatical religion and its violent demarcation of inner and outer boundaries—and to him, fanaticism is inherent in the very fact that the boundaries of the faith coincide with the limits of salvation and that non-believers are treated accordingly. The destructive antagonism between the religions, which to be sure is often supported by experience, is crystallised in Voltaire's image of Mahomet (and mirroring Goethe, he too fits Mahomet into a specific pattern). Goethe, by contrast, elevates Mahomet to the level of the ideal man, the genius; through his image and by means of his authority he summons the universal benevolent spirits, both human and divine, that transcend the religions and their boundaries. In this way, he re-enforces Mahomet (and this pattern) as a view of life, humans and God appropriate for his own culture. Both Voltaire and Goethe use Mahomet as a foil, either attractive or repulsive, for reflecting their own ideas and views.

3. *Poetic Appropriation*

The issues featuring in Goethe's dislike of Voltaire's image of Mahomet will resurface with a vengeance for the ageing poet when, in 1814, he encounters the *Divan*, the collection of poems by the Persian poet Hafiz, the German translation of which was published a year earlier.[19]

In encountering the Persian poet, Goethe enters into yet another new and different relationship with the Other: on the level of "shared" poetry. This is the hermeneutics of appropriation, of poetic empathy. Goethe now goes further than he did before: No longer does Mahomet serve as a foil onto which to project a European concept of genius; between 1814 and 1819 there occurs a kind of abandonment of one poet to another poet, with the encounter including elements of self-surrender. Conrady talks of a "creative event" in discussing the fact that "in the seventh decade of his life, Goethe produced such lyrical richness" and was able to develop a "new lyrical language".[20]

---

17 Ibid., 924.

18 Cf. Ibid., 924.

19 Cf. Katharina Mommsen, Goethe und die Arabische Welt, Frankfurt a. M. 1988, 194–238; vgl. in neuer Auflage dies., Goethe und der Islam, Frankfurt a. M., Leipzig 2001, 31–95.

20 Karl Otto Conrady, Goethe. Leben und Werk, Frankfurt a. M. 1987, II, 390.

Goethe's poetical path between two worlds is reflected in his explanation of three distinct approaches to translation: The first aims to familiarise us with a foreign country and "for this, a simple and prosaic approach is the best". The second approach involves "aiming to transpose ourselves into the circumstances of the foreign country but is actually just a grasping what is foreign and representing it in our own terms." The highest form of translation, however, occurs where "we seek to make the translation identical with the original, so that the one may stand, not instead of the other, but in place of the other. This approach was initially met with the biggest resistance, because the translator who commits himself firmly to his original virtually gives up his own nation's originality, and thus a third entity comes into being, and the masses need time to develop a taste for this."[21] To hear Goethe talk of the one taking "the place" of the other is at first slightly startling. However, he does not envisage the familiar replacing the Other; the dynamic he addresses is the reverse: namely, that the Other may live and flourish in the familiar that is given up. For the resistance originates from the fact that the originality of what is one's own is given up, so that a sort of surrender occurs of the familiar to the Other. This is what generates a "third entity", for which according to Goethe most people still lack a sense. However, "feeling" meaning in the Other is just what is at stake for Goethe.[22]

In 1815, Goethe writes about the strong effect Hafiz's poems had on him: "... and I had to respond productively to them for otherwise I would not have been able to withstand its force. Its effect was too powerful ... and so I had to find a way of taking part." So Goethe does not want to be simply a receptive reader; he wants to respond productively and take part in the Persian writer's poetry. The only way of doing so is through a poetic mirroring of his poetry, through an "imitation"—not in the superficial sense of the word but in the sense of a behavioural hermeneutics, analogous to a behavioural therapy where it is by way of behavioural change, and not chiefly via analysis, that understanding is achieved.

Thus, experience through imitation is not a superficial copying but a deep, emotional comprehension of another reality that encompasses our own existence entirely. Even what is not understood rationally can be the object of such

21 Goethe, westöstlicher Divan, Besserem Verständnis (Übersetzungen 1819), in: Goethe, Divan (Reclam) 280.

22 For this see also the translation theory of Rudolf Pannwitz and Walter Benjamin (Illuminationen, Frankfurt a. M. 1977, 59ff.; see also from the perspective of an intercultural conceptualisation of a diachronous hemerneutics between the Bible and the present: Ottmar Fuchs, Praktische Hermeneutik der Heiligen Schrift, Stuttgart 2004, 318ff.; and last but not least cf. Paul's idea of becoming a Jew to the Jews, see 1 Cor 9: 19–23. There is a functional and structural analogy between what poetry does for Goethe, and what becoming one in Christ is for Paul, see Gal 3:26–29.

imitation, in the sense of a physical "understanding", an embodied feeling of a reality. And this is possible at any age, with nursery-age children or with the mentally disabled. Some things cannot be understood, but can be intimated through action, and then reason may follow, as best it can. To understand the meaning of the Muslim prayer position as a physical expression of reverence for God, we must experience it through our own bodies. Life is like this: a gift through birth, it is not until later that it is understood; an experience of meaning, or of its opposite, occurs later in connection with the gift of embodied life.

In the same way, small infants have to take food and drink by blind faith to survive. The body needs itself prior to rational understanding and control. Every human being is dependent on this sense of basic trust to survive and live. There is no reason not to apply this principle of basic trust in other areas, for example, in empathising with others' experiences, cultural and religious customs, etc. The experience shows the same structure in each case, centred as it is around an unreserved embracing of a reality and being held in it.

The idea of promise can be applied here as well: we enter into something Other without a prior understanding or experience of it. Any inter-cultural or inter-religious encounter always involves such a deferment of gratification. This secondary transfer of our sense of basic trust should become a habitual advance, in analogy to a culture of hospitality where an openness is shown to the physical and spiritual needs of the visitor without knowing him or her beforehand.

It is a kind of experimental archaeology in that there is a putting-into-practice, through experiments, of ways of living and experiencing that stem from the past (in archaeology) or from elsewhere (in intercultural dialogue). To experience what life in a stilt house was like, a group may, for example, design an experimental set-up to try and live in such dwellings like people did centuries ago. This approach goes beyond digging up artefacts by reconstructing the lived context of such artefacts within our contemporary experience. Thus, Goethe writes in the Book of Hafiz, in "Imitation":

In deine Reimart hoff ich mich zu finden,
Das Wiederholen soll mir auch gefallen.[23]

In your rhymes' mode myself I hope to find,
The sound reiterated should please me well.

Where experimental archaeology uses reconstruction, Goethe's experimental poetic hermeneutics bridges exteriority through poetic empathy. It could perhaps be described as a non-colonialist, unselfish way of entering the inner

[23] Goethe, Divan 21–22. Translation by Edward Dowdon, London and Toronto 1914: https://archive.org/stream/westeasterndivan00goetuoft/_divu.txt (1.10.2019).

centre of an alien world, investing everything one's own world has to offer in an effort to experience, at least through *imitatio*, that centre as authentically as possible.

What is at stake here is therefore not a shallow idea of imitation that involves an integralist copying of literature by simply quoting it, but rather one that involves a deep experience of the Other through the Self. This relates to the concept of mimesis as discussed by Wolfgang Braungart, following the poetical dogmatics of Alex Stock[24]: a mimesis that leads us to an imitation of the resurrected one with his wounds and his light, and thus to a compassion in both suffering and joy.[25]

For Goethe, too, the poetical encounter is identified with specific tenets of the "Mohammedan religion", which his approach allows him to be very precise about: "unconditional surrender to the unknowable will of God, serene survey of ... earthly concerns, love, suspension between two worlds, all reality cleansed, dissolving symbolically". Surrender to the unknowable will of God is mirrored methodologically in symbolic dissolution, which cannot occur without a surrender of the self to the Other.[26]

4. *A Journey into Open Space*

Goethe is fully aware that this journey will be a long one. Thus, at the start of the *Divan* he has the poem "*Hegire*", the French term used in Goethe's day to refer to the *hijra* or Mahomet's emigration from Mecca to Medina. Goethe, too, embarks upon a journey of emigration, away from everything that has been: "The poet sees himself as a traveller. In an instance he has arrived in the orient. He delights in its customs, habits, artefacts, religious attitudes and views, and he does not reject the suspicion that he might be a Musulman himself."[27]

Goethe writes about this journey: "Above all, the author of these poems would like to be considered a traveller, deserving of some credit for taking a sympathetic reading of the unfamiliar, seeking to adopt its language and share its attitudes and customs. He may be forgiven for succeeding only to a certain extent."[28]

---

[24] Cf. Braungart, Herausforderung, 60; cf. Alex Stock, Poetische Dogmatik – Christologie. Figuren (Band 4), Paderborn 2001.

[25] Concerning the correspondent construction in the Gospel of Marc Ottmar Fuchs, Sucht ihn in Galiläa, in: Franz Kaspar / Dieter Zeller (Hg.), Predigten zum Lesejahr B, Mainz 1978, 48–52.

[26] Goethe in a letter to Zelter 11.5.1820, quotet in Goethe, Divan, Anmerkungen 134.

[27] Sic Goethe in his announcement of the Divan, in Morgenblatt 1816, zitiert in: Goethe, Divan, Anmerkungen 136.

[28] Goethe, Besserem Verständnis (Einleitung 1819).

Hegire[29]

Nord und West und Süd zersplittern,
Throne bersten, Reiche zittern,
Flüchte du, im reinen Osten
Patriarchenluft zu kosten,
Unter Lieben, Trinken, Singen
Soll dich Chisers Quell verjüngen.[30]

Dort im Reinen und im Rechten
Will ich menschlichen Geschlechten
In des Ursprungs Tiefe dringen,
Wo sie noch von Gott empfingen
Himmelslehr in Erdesprachen
Und sich nicht den Kopf zerbrachen.
...
Will in Bädern und in Schenken,
Heil'ger Havis dein gedenken;
Wenn den Schleier Liebchen lüftet,
Schüttelnd Ambralocken düftet.
Ja des Dichters Liebeflüstern
Mache selbst die Huris lüstern.[31]

Wollet ihr ihm dies beneiden,
Oder etwa gar verleiten;
Wisset nur, daß Dichterworte
Um des Paradieses Pforte
Immer leise klopfend schweben,
sich erbittend ew'ges Leben.

HEJIRA

North and West and South up-breaking!
Thrones are shattering, empires quaking;
Fly thou to the untroubled East,
There the patriarchs' air to taste!
What with love and wine and song
Chiser's fount will make thee young.

29 Goethe, Divan 5–6.
30 Chiser is the keeper of the source of life.
31 The Huris are the beautiful-eyed playmates of the blessed in paradise.

There, 'mid things pure and just and true,
The race of man I would pursue
Back to the well-head primitive,
Where still from God did they receive
Heavenly lore in earthly speech,
Nor beat the brain to pass their reach ...

In bath or inn my thought would be,
Holy Hafiz, still of thee;
Or when the veil a sweetheart lifts
From amber locks in odorous drifts;
Ay, whispered loves of poet fire
Even the Houris to desire!

Would you envy him for this,
Or bring despite upon his bliss,
Know that words of poets rise
To the gate of Paradise,
Hover round, knock light, implore
Heavenly life for evermore.

These lines make clear that the poet is able to reach deeper than thinking alone would allow. In these depths, the poet's words take us to the gates of paradise.

It is not only in the Book of the Cupbearer that Goethe links the exclamation:

„Hafis o lehre mich,
Wie du's verstanden!"[32]

O Hafiz, instruct me,
How seemed it to you?

with enjoyment, especially the enjoyment of drinking:

Und mit diesem Lied und Wendung
Sind wir wieder bei Hafisen,
Denn es ziemt des Tags Vollendung
Mit Genießern zu genießen.[33]

[32] Goethe, Divan, Im Schenkenbuch, ibid., 86.
[33] Im Buch des Sängers, Goethe, Divan, 13.

And with such winding of my lay,
Hafiz, once more we hear thy voice;
'Tis meet in each concluded day
*With the rejoicing to rejoice.**

In the Book of Ill Homour, Goethe directs his criticism at his own faith background:

„Was? Ihr mißbilliget dem kräft'gen Sturm
Des Übermuts, verlogne Pfaffen!
Hätt Allah mich bestimmt zum Wurm,
So hätt er mich als Wurm geschaffen.“[34]

What, lying priests, you take it ill, this storm
Of human pride and passion never sated?
If Allah had decreed me to be worm,
Belike a worm I then had been created.

5. *The Teaching Prophet versus the Poet*

In the Book of Hafiz, Goethe addresses the tension, and the contradiction, between faith and poetry, between Hafiz and the Qur'an: Thus, in "Indictment":[35]

Weiß denn der, mit wem er geht und wandelt,
Er, der immer nur im Wahnsinn handelt?
Grenzenlos, von eigensinn'gem Lieben,
Wird er in die Öde fortgetrieben
Seiner Klagen Reim' in Sand geschrieben,
Sind vom Winde gleich verjagt;
Er versteht nicht, was er sagt,
Was er sagt, wird er nicht halten.

Doch sein Lied, man lässt es immer walten,
Da es doch dem Koran widerspricht.
Lehret nun, ihr des Gesetzes Kenner,
Weisheit-fromme, hochgelahrte Männer,
Treuer Mosleminen feste Pflicht.

---

34 Goethe, Divan, 47.
35 Goethe, Divan, 19.

Hafis insbesondere schaffet Ärgernisse,
Mirza sprengt den Geist ins Ungewisse,
Saget, was man tun und lassen müsse?

Knows he, indeed, with whom he lives and moves
He all whose actions madness sways? He loves
With wayward passion, and its boundless stress
Drives him afar into the wilderness.
His tuneful plaints are written in the sand,
And by the wind are swiftly chased away.
He comprehends not that which he may say,
Nor to the word he says will dare to stand.

And yet his song men still allow its rule
Yea, though the Koran it should flout. But ye,
Skilled in the law, ye men of piety,
Wise, learned, be ye masters of the school,
For each true Mussulman, of duty strict.

Hafiz, in chief, has many a conscience pricked,
Mirza has plunged the soul in questionings vain.
Say ye what men should do, and where refrain.

This indictment is followed by the fatwa, or scholarly opinion on religious law.[36]

Hafis' Dichterzüge sie bezeichnen
Ausgemachte Wahrheit unauslöschlich;
Aber hie und da auch Kleinigkeiten
Außerhalb der Grenze des Gesetzes.
...
Denn Allah gab die Gabe jedem Dichter;
Missbraucht er sie im Wandel seiner Sünden,
So seh er zu mit Gott sich abzufinden.“[37]

in
FETWA

[36] Goethe's poem alludes to a scholarly pronouncement about Hafiz, written by Ebusuud Effendi, a famous 16th century mufti: "Hafiz's poems contain many settled and incontrovertible truths, but occasionally there are details that no doubt fall outside the boundaries of the law." quoted ibid., notes 138.

[37] Ibid., 19 und 21.

Hafiz, the poet, in his art expresses
Truth wrought and rounded, indestructible;
Yet here and there are certain little matters
Which overpass the limits of the law.

To every poet hath Allah given gifts;
Were they misused in sinful paths he trod,
Let him see to it and come to terms with God!"

The issue is addressed once again in "Open Secret":

Sie haben dich, heiliger Hafis,
Die mystische Zunge genannt,
Und haben, die Wortgelehrten,
Den Wert des Worts nicht erkannt.

Mystisch heißest du ihnen,
Weil sie Närrisches bei dir denken
Und ihren unlauteren Wein
In deinem Namen verschenken.

Du aber bist mystisch rein,
Weil sie dich nicht verstehn,
Der du, ohne fromm zu sein, selig bist!
Das wollen sie dir nicht zugestehn."[38]

"The mystical tongue" they have named you,
O Hafiz, our saint, nor to one
Of these scholars so learned in word-lore

The meaning of "mystic" is known.
A "mystic" because in your pages
Their silliest notions they hail,
And their own sorry vintage the tapsters
In your name, as true Hafiz, retail.

Pure mystic you are, and with reason,
For your meaning they never can hit,
You, while nowise the pious the blessed!
A fact they refuse to admit."

38 Goethe, Divan, 22.

Both the prophet and the poet have been seized by God, "but the poet squanders the gift bestowed on him in enjoyment in order to produce enjoyment"; he shies away from a focus on a single purpose, "seeks to be diverse and to show himself without boundaries in approach and presentation. The prophet, on the other hand, is focused on one particular purpose ... He wants to preach a set of teachings and to gather all the peoples through it and around it, as though it was a standard. All that is required is for the world to believe, so he has to become and remain unvaried. For the diverse is not believed, it is grasped."[39] Both Hafiz and Goethe, however, are poets and thus they represent, across all the cultures and religions, a peculiar quality in their mutual *rapprochement*, the feeling that they had "lived as neighbours".[40] Poetry thus becomes an "imaginative space for exploring intercultural balance".[41] The poetological empathy of world literature becomes a vehicle of intercultural communication.

In his notes to the Book of Love, Goethe characterises this book as lending itself to "symbolic digression, which it is hard to resist in the realm of the orient. A great mind, not content with what it is given, considers everything that is presented to the senses a disguise. Behind it, a higher life of the mind is hiding, cheekily and stubbornly, to draw us towards it and lure us up into loftier regions."[42] The image of the disguise is interesting because the same image is conveyed by another text, although using a different play on language: "What is called idea: whatever appears and therefore presents to us the law of all that appears."[43] Poetry, then, notwithstanding its diversity, uncovers whatever is "disguised" and at the same time holds it together within the remit of the poetic mind.

In 1827, Goethe writes: "Since many an aspect of our experiences defies straightforward statements and direct communication, I have for a long time been resorting to the method of revealing the deeper meaning to the perceptive reader by means of contrasting structures that are reflected in each other, as it were."[44] Goethe is fascinated by this freedom, achieved through reciprocal reflection.

---

[39] Johann Wolfgang von Goethe, West-östlicher Divan (hg. von Hendrik Birus, 2 Bände), Frankfurt a. M. 1994, (Noten und Abhandlungen zum besserem Verständnis des westöstlichen Divan, 1819), Bd. 1, 157; vgl. auch Johann Wolfgang von Goethe, West-östlicher Divan. Studienausgabe (Reclam), 287.

[40] Johann Wolfgang von Goethe, (Einleitung zu:) Thomas Carlyle, „Leben Schillers", 1830, VII.

[41] Quotation of Katharina Braungart, Tübingen.

[42] Cited by Goethe, Divan, Anmerkungen 139.

[43] Goethe in the Maximen und Reflexionen Nr. 1136, cited by Goethe, Divan, Anmerkungen 142.

[44] Goethe in einem Brief an den Orientalisten Iken vom 27.9.1827, cited by Goethe, Divan, Anmerkungen 134.

Something special comes out of Goethe's encounter with Hafiz: it no longer revolves around the identification of the self in the Other (as a condition of acceptance), but, *ab initio*, around absolute and unconditional acceptance in a shared poetical space. What is at stake is the freedom of diversity, of spirit and mind that is inherent in this; what is at stake is the process whereby the familiar is let go of, surrendered and offered up for the benefit of the Other, so that a space is opened up and empathy created for the Other within the familiar, allowing the Other to flourish and blossom.

6. *Removing Boundaries*

The search for deep experiences, analogous to poetry, that transcend boundaries—including boundaries of understanding—has considerable relevance today. Think for example, of the primary importance of shared everyday experiences with a view to the possibility and the necessary limits of understanding. "In a globalised world, everybody will never understand everything, regardless of how many attempts there are at dialogue. Therefore, understanding can never be a precondition of acceptance and peaceful co-existence. The existence even of that which we do not understand must not be threatened. We must practice accepting others as Other!"[45]

Here is a story I was told many years ago: two families, one Muslim, the other Christian, live side by side as neighbours, treat each other well, and are kind and helpful to each other. Then, one day, the Muslim woman says to her Christian neighbour: "I can't put up any longer with having to believe that you and your family won't go to heaven." The religions have made resources available that can be applied when such situations arise in welfare and social work.[46]

This kind of "behavioural therapy" is the complement to analytical therapies in that, through behaviour modification (which may be a prescribed behaviour modification), a modified way of life becomes possible. This is of value especially where there is limited time for taking an in-depth history or where sufficient capacities for "working through" memories are not available. Putting this in terms of inter-cultural and inter-religious relations: on the level of social politics, there may not be enough time for getting to know and understand the other side's history and situation thoroughly; there may be an urgent need to change actual behaviour so that disadvantaged groups are able to survive.

45 Ulrike Bechmann, Besprechung von Kuschel, Karl-Josef: Juden-Christen-Muslime, in: Theologische Revue 105 (2009) 4, 342–348, 347.

46 Exemplary: Ulrike Bechmann / Sevda Demir / Gisela Egler, Frauenkulturen. Christliche und muslimische Frauen in Begegnung und Gespräch, Düsseldorf [2]2003: cf. also the Innsbrucker Projekt: Daniela Kästle, Martina Kraml, Hamideh Mohagheghi (Hg.), Heilig und Tabu, Ostfildern 2009.

Understanding is important and necessary and may help create solidarity; but it must not become a pre-condition of the latter. Even what is not understood can be integrated into *mimesis*; what is not understood may open up, through *mimesis*, its own form of experiential knowing. Such inter-poetic *rapprochement* and appropriation will, of course, lead to some degree of relativising—of that which is familiar, but especially of that which, considering the prophet and faith, creates in/out boundaries and sets down sanctions.

This is a sort of "free intellectual trade"[47] unregulated through doctrine[48]. Instead, a hybrid is created, bridging contradictions on a new level and making surprising connections.[49] This discovery of inter-poetic similarities within cultural and religious differences generates a different understanding of time as well: there is an acceptance of what is ephemeral vis-à-vis what is permanent and of lasting structure. "There is a striking similarity between Hafiz's and Horace's views of life, which can be explained only by the fact that both poets lived in similar eras that saw a destruction of the certainties of bourgeois existence, leading people to limit themselves to fleeting enjoyments grasped in passing, as it were."[50]

"Goethe's piety found much to resonate with in the work of the Persian poet Hafiz (1320–1390): contemplation and worship of God through the countless manifestations and metamorphoses of his creation; ... religiosity, but of a wide-ranging kind not bound by the limitations of a particular creed."[51] In the *talismans*, at the start of the *Divan*, Goethe praises God in his one hundred names. "In essence, to Goethe, the image of Allah could be linked more firmly with an unencumbered joy of life than the God of Christianity."[52] Thus, Goethe "assimilates wisdom and insight wherever they present themselves."[53] Goethe's understanding of symbolic language, too, reflects this relationship of God and

---

47 Goethe to Carlyle VII.

48 Goethe, in the Noten zum besseren Verständnis, 456, cited by Goethe, Divan, Anmerkungen 134.

49 There are other texts by Goethe that show the same tendency to disassemble the boundaries of national literature and relate it to world literature. For example, he was not content with a national library limited to the German language. In 1808, he requested the following changes: "indeed, one would have to explicitly point out the achievements of other nations, not least because the books is intended for children, too, and especially in this day and age they have to be made aware of the achievements of other nations." Quoted in Conrady, Goethe II, 499. What is important for Goethe here is not only that which relates to the familiar, but that which contradicts it: "... thus it is to be expected that every (nation) will find in another something acceptable and something revolting, something worth copying and something to be avoided." Quoted from Thomas Carlyle, Leben Schillers, Entwurf; 12, 364, in Conrady II, 500.

50 Goethe, Besserem Verständnis (Künftiger Divan 1890), in: Goethe, Divan (Reclam) 268.

51 Conrady, Goethe II, 402.

52 Ibid., 402.

53 Ibid., 402.

diversity. In it, an intellectual contemplation occurs "wherein the phenomena adopt an allegorical character pointing beyond itself."[54]

While the *Divan*'s poems do "not lose sight of the typical and general", they mark the point at which "the entire diversity of phenomena may acquire an allegorical significance, where even the simplest manifestation may carry a symbolic meaning and become transparent to the realm of the mind and the spirit."[55] The phenomena are not the space for, or shadow of, ideas, but they are in themselves the places where the unknowable reveals itself. Through its very diversity, what is manifest is an infinitely effective revelation of that which is infinite, ineffable and unreachable.

7. *Depth Relationships that Undermine Belief Systems*

During the period of *Sturm und Drang* (storm and stress), great importance was given to the notion that history and nature, including the vital force animating human history, rather than being known, must be "felt as creative vitality, and can be understood only once it has been felt and lived."[56] It is through poetry, music and art that such revelations are discovered and made available to experience.

At this point, Goethe seems to foreshadow the path that others were later to take, with the focus being shifted away from the person of genius and onto the symbol as the locus for the revelation of the infinite.[57] In his novel "The Unbearable Lightness of Being", Milan Kundera formulates a similar longing for meaning and its resolution in music:

"... and suddenly he realised that since his youth he had done nothing but talk, write, lecture, concoct sentences, search for formulations and amend them, so in the end no words were precise, their meanings were obliterated ... And what he yearned for at that moment, vaguely, but with all his might, was unbounded music, absolute sound, a pleasant and happy all-encompassing, over-powering, window-rattling din to engulf, once and for all, the pain, the vanity and the futility of words. Music was the negation of sentences, music was the anti-word!"[58]

---

54 Ibid., 403.

55 Ibid., 404.

56 Rüdiger Safranski, Schiller oder Die Erfindung des Deutschen Idealismus, München, Wien 2/2008, 50.

57 Cf. MaryAnne Stevens, Der Symbolismus – ein französisches Monopol?, in Wilton, Upstone (Hg.), Symbolismus 47–63, 52.

58 Milan Kundera, Die unerträgliche Leichtigkeit des Seins. Roman, München, Wien 1984, 91.

The short-lived and ephemeral nature of such experiences, their resistance to structured planning, is due to the fact that their depth dimension is always temporary and difficult to repeat as an everyday occurrence. A memorable example is offered by Anke Bosse: the "West-Eastern Divan", Daniel Barenboim and Edward Said's orchestra that brings together young musicians from Israel and Palestine. There may be heated discussion there occasionally, but once the leader plays an A, all will tune their instruments accordingly. Joint music-making, rehearsing and performing allow the musicians and the audience to experience a connection for a limited time—the duration of the music. All differences other than musical ones are negated by this connection. Side-stepping and undermining cultural and religious differences, a new experience of community is created in a new and different fourth dimension, so to speak. However, this new aesthetic space in which everybody is held is bound to come to an end. But the experience gone through will illuminate everyday life and is not easily forgotten, and it may soften many a knee-jerk reaction that may previously have been part of attitudes towards the Other, thus opening up new possibilities.[59] Back in their mutually hostile home countries, many of these musicians have become actively involved in peace activism.[60]

Cultural politics will have to include both: Goethe's path of entering the Other's aesthetic space and losing oneself in it—in the most positive sense of the word—and then gaining oneself in a new and different way (a simple example being mosques and churches opening their doors, inviting people to enter into the space of their respective faiths and experience their aesthetics) as well as Daniel Barenboim's path of discovering and building new shared aesthetic spaces, where differences are transcended on the level of shared experience. These are all spaces that bypass established contrasts but themselves cannot be bypassed: on a new level of mutual recognition.

From this perspective, what is needed is a cultural and societal politics of new aesthetic spaces, asking: to what extent do the popular mass media, film and television, theatres and museums, art and music, literature and religion, open up infinitely wide spaces that act as sources of creative imagination? Are they by their nature able to fructify everyday life as well as all the minor and major political decisions in a way that sustains us and facilitates solidarity? In this view, literature, music and art are indeed "media", close to what went

[59] Cf. Anke Bosse, Interkulturelle Balance statt „clash of cultures". Zu Goethes „West-östlichem Divan", in: Etudes germaniques 60 (2005) 2, 231–248, 244.

[60] On July 7, 2001, Daniel Barenboim conducted Richard Wagner for the first time publicly in Israel. This reflects a difficult and oft-criticised attempt at rehabilitating Wagner and his music to create community and avoid remaining fixated on how he was instrumentalised by National Socialism to make the horror of exclusion and destruction aesthetically representable.

before, impacting everyday life, offering deep experiences and, therefore, ambivalent and with consequences open to criticism.[61]

Having been deeply influenced by the popular piety I grew up with (in the Frankonia region of Germany)[62], my first visit to a Hindu temple in Pune, India, somehow felt like coming home. I carried a lot of childhood empathy within me in relation to the status and images of saints, the multitude of candles and accompanying smells, and "transferring" it onto this place came easily to me. It found space to flourish here: in this environment with its many figurines of varying sizes, the many candles, the incense, the piety of the worshippers there and their ways of expressing their admiration and longing. I was especially taken with the elephant-headed Ganesh, a very popular Hindu expression of the divine[63], probably because a little more than thirty years ago a friend had brought a wonderful poster of Ganesh from her journey to India, wishing that this gift of wisdom would stay with me always.

In this context, I found myself thinking about Hermann Hesse. In his "Short Biography" and the autobiographical fairy tale "The Childhood of the Magician"[64], entitled "The Magician"[65], he describes a similar experience: "I was lucky ... in that among the people bringing me up was the god Pan, who sat in my grandfather's glazed cabinet in the form of a small dancing Indian idol. This deity attended to me in my youth, and long before I was able to read and write ... it took root in me to such an extent that in later life, every encounter with an Indian or Chinese sage felt like a coming-home."[66] Those who never knew this sort of popular piety in their own environment, and even more so those who sneer at it, will find empathy difficult when it comes to inter-religious experiences, or they might look down even more on similar phenomena in other religions. This prevents any "transformation of emotions" into what is unfamiliar.[67] What is at stake here are not diffuse "good feelings" but cognitively charged emotions that have a particular direction and are rooted in the body. What a person has experienced and "believes", they will feel: it is an entering into the phenomena, an authentic empathetic rapport and emotional concord. The "truth" of each faith is left untouched and transformed into a symbolic experience that transcends it, or put differently, is turned into a expansive

61 Cf. Ottmar Fuchs, Die Menschen in ihren Erfahrungen suchen, in: Rainer Bucher/Ottmar Fuchs/Joachim Kügler (Ed.), In Würde leben, Luzern 1998, 209–334; cf. Wolfgang Welsch, Grenzgänge der Ästhetik, Stuttgart 1996.

62 Cf. Rainer Bucher, Rainer Krockauer, Es geht nichts verloren, Würzburg 2010, 149–165.

63 Cf. Anneliese und Peter Keilhauer, Die Bildsprache des Hinduismus. Die indische Götterwelt und ihre Symbolik, Köln 3/1990.

64 Cf. Hermann Hesse, Kindheit des Zauberers, Frankfurt a. M. 1974.

65 Hermann Hesse, Sämtliche Werke, Band 12, Autobiographische Schriften, Berlin 2003, 23–45.

66 Ibid. 23.

67 Cf. Dominik Perler, *Transformationen der Gefühle. Philosophische Emotionstheorien 1270–1670*, Frankfurt a. M. 2011.

experiential dimension of what sustains all religions: namely, to use Dietrich Bonhoeffer's words, to be so wonderfully sheltered by a gracious power.

II. Sermons and Meditations[1]

1. *Christmas*

The Gospel of Christmas: we know this building of words like the front of a well-known house that we pass but seldom enter. We know the words; they remind us of the happy eyes of children, of past feelings of joy and excitement. But now this story has become old, not very exciting. And it has become difficult to realise that this story once was a message that brought the Good News to humankind, which was more exciting and surprising than a detective story. Because this Christmas story answers the most important human question: who is God? Why did God create the world, the earth and us ourselves? Is he a selfish God, who created us only for his own sadistic pleasure, watching us—as a German play writer puts it—like fish of pray in an aquarium who devour each other? Or did she create us for our own sake because she didn't want to be alone in her power, didn't want to love only herself, but to love others as well? Humankind has asked this question about God for thousands of years. And God has given the answer very often, but people have understood the answer only too seldom.

God repeatedly offered his freeing friendship to his people Israel. He sent leaders who freed the people from the slavery in Egypt. He sent prophets who spoke of YHWH as the advocate and protector of the poor and outcast. But nearly every time the people didn't understand this kind of God and forgot him very quickly. They couldn't understand him, because they always had an entirely different picture of God. God should be the mighty on earth, should come with glory and power to destroy the enemies, and should of course make his people powerful and mighty as well. But this picture of God is wrong and can't feel and sympathise with who God really is: love with all its disadvantages, with all its weakness. God's love is tender, affectionate, does not force, is free of pressure. Therefore, God is without pressing power on this earth, unless it is a power of love itself.

Therefore, two thousand years ago God undertook the last possible and unsurpassed attempt to offer his friendship to humankind: he came upon earth himself; he became a real man. He took his love, put it together and sent it to earth in Jesus of Nazareth. And again God's appearance of love is free of pressure, is without any power as people use and appreciate it. God came unsensa-

[1] Sermons in Buxton, St. Anne's Church, 1971, and in Ashbourne, All Saints Church, 1991.

tionally like a little child, unsheltered like a baby, in a powerless, helpless, tender and fragile way. I understand now what Luke says: "And this will be a sign for you: the baby and the manger, the helplessness and the poorness. Yes, this baby and manger are the signs of our God on this earth, the signs of his great and non-pressuring love. Here you find the sign for the fact that God does not share the human structures of power, that God does not take part in the human imagination of standards and images. On Christmas God undertakes an overturning of human values. The weak will be strong, the last will be first, the looser will be the winner, and so on." Mary praises God in her Magnificat because of this divine love.

This, dear brothers and sisters, is the joyful message of Christmas to all of us. God is your friend. And it doesn't matter what kind of past, present and future you have. God doesn't want to push you, but to love you, to tell you that you are desired as you are. During his whole life Jesus, whose birthday we celebrate tonight, offered his and God's friendship to all who met him. He offered not only something; he offered himself. He offered confidence and trust to all: to the poor and the rich, the sinners and the Pharisees, the established and the outcasts. Jesus shows us how God is and how the human being could be.

This is the Good News of Christmas: God is our friend. God never abandons us because we are desired by him. To be desired: I think this is the centre of every friendship. We are desired; let us therefore tell our God that he is desired as well: in our heart and in our life.

Today I refuse to say very much about our responsibilities which derive from the fact that God is like this. No morals tonight. Just one recommendation. We are used to giving Christmas presents to each other. I think the root of this habit is to show somebody that he or she is desired, that I like him, that without her my life would be poorer and duller. Therefore, I would like to encourage us to show each other, in our families and fields of life, that the other one is desired and necessary for us. In this way we give the Good News of Christmas through ourselves and the love of God becomes reborn in our life.

But before all invitations and responsibilities of ours God took responsibility of all of us, and God takes care of you. Before all our activities she has invited us to friendship and love. Therefore, let us rejoice tonight. Let us rejoice in the message of Christmas, which has been given to all of us, the story and Good News of God's great and indestructible friendship. This friendship gives our daily life a new quality, for beloved and desired people live in a new way of life. Then Christmas takes place in our days.

2. *Conversion of Paul (January 25)*

Conversion and vocation belong to each other, because conversion fulfils our vocation. And normally conversion lasts a whole lifetime: permanently trying to live out our Christian life. Paul had an extraordinary experience leading him to his conversion. Most of us have never had such an experience. But nevertheless we are called, too: by those sentences of the Gospel that strike us especially or by some words spoken by friends or foreigners, words that we can't forget.

May each of us now remember in silence a word, a sentence that we have heard recently from the Gospel, from the others today at this conference. Words that could be or become a very important road sign for our conversion, step by step, in patience and mostly without any wonderful signs.

This Gospel (Mk 2:18–22) is about the signs of the time. In Jesus's eyes his disciples acted according to the signs of the time if they didn't fast. Because it was the time when the bridegroom, the Messiah himself, was with them. And this is a time of joy, of celebrating, of eating and drinking. This is the time of listening to him to accept his message, to repent, to become a new wineskin, so that God's life is able to enter the disciples, so that we are open to God's gifts in our time.

You remember Martha and Maria. Maria listened to the Lord and by doing this she reacted correctly to the sign of the time.

It is one of the most difficult tasks and problems to see and interpret the signs of the time authentically. Indeed, this is one of the most important purposes of the Second Vatican Council: to look at our present time and situations very carefully. Otherwise, the Church would neglect and escape the life and sorrows of the people.

Sometimes the process that leads to the correct interpretation of what is going on can be rather twisted and surprising. In the morning, when the three bishops visited us, we could hear such an example: when the church in Zambia had to struggle against the strong influences of Scientific Marxism and Materialism, then the bishops not only reacted, but they also intensified the social responsibility of the church. Here you see how an atheistic movement outside the Church can detect a maybe hidden part of the Church's identity itself. The Church of Zambia has read these signs of the time, this challenge of the situation authentically, because it developed and enforced a necessary dimension of the Church: for the sake of humanity in the society. Only fighting Marxism would have been a relatively weak reaction to this situation and not done much for the sake of increasing humanity in the country. We need to pray continually for Christ's spirit to lead us to a practically fruitful reflection on the signs of the time.

3. *Ash Wednesday*

The Jewish rabbi Eleazar used to say: "Repent, return to the Lord one day before your death!" This sounds strange. How can we know whether the next day is the day of our death? The rabbi used to answer: "If you return every day of your life, then you can be sure that you will return on your very last day as well. Today, dear sisters and brothers, we remember the death, which will certainly be on the end of our lives, of mine and yours. Nobody can escape. The life is the beginning of death. Isn't such a life meaningless? No, I don't think so: death makes our life and every day of it very worthy and precious. Every minute we live is one minute less we will live.

But we are very successful in hiding this reality. Our society doesn't realise death. It displaces and represses it. Let me remind you of Evelyn Waugh's "The loved one" (German title: "Death in Hollywood"), in which the author describes our society's deep wish to repress death. Our time deals with dead people as if they were living, especially during the preparation for funerals, when they get their makeup. Thus, our time has forgotten to live with death in all its appearances: illness, sorrow, disappointments, frustrations and so on. We love the high life and do not realise that we miss and destroy real life if we do not realise death! For the anxiety, the dread of death we repress will arise in a horrible and uncontrolled way: in our dreams, in various mental illnesses and nervous breakdowns and in our relationships. For example, we shy away from the sight of handicapped people, the sight of the poor and the darker sights of life. This makes us inhuman, cruel to all, who have no high life at all, who taste death.

The liturgy of Ash Wednesday reminds us that death has a special meaning and message for us Christians: make your death worthy of your life. This sounds like a paradox, but it isn't: your time is valuable, every minute, therefore live in a valuable way. Turn away from everything that is nonsense, that is rubbish in your life and doesn't count in the eyes of our God: hate, power, to much property ...

We all know very well what is valuable in the eyes of God. There is no need to enumerate. We always need an overturning of our values to return to the values of God. We need such a return to a Christian life every day.

Let us tell each other that we are ashes and will return to ashes. Then our life will become valuable in intensity and quality. Yes, return one day before your death. Or as a rabbi put it: if not now, when then! Then we realise the Christian message: life is the beginning of death, but death is the beginning of life.

4. *Holy Thursday, Eucharist*

As you know, a little child in the first year of life wants to put everything in its mouth. The fingers, eyes and ears are not enough to feel, see and hear. The child rather wants to incorporate things, people and experiences into their small body. Especially during this period, in which the baby opens him/herself to the surroundings in such a way, the child's deepest connection to its parents arises, a relationship that will stamp and influence the future life of the baby decisively. What is visible during this period of human life so apparently remains one of the deepest human wishes for their whole lifetime: the longing for confidence, deep relationship and security. Behind these words there is the longing for life, the indestructible wish to live, the wish to destroy danger and death and restore and maintain life.

In Jesus Christ God wants to fulfil this longing for life, security, unity, trusting relationship and connection. And Jesus fulfilled this wish especially in his manner of dealing with people: he took a lot of time to eat and drink with hosts and guests. Therefore, his enemies called him a glutton and a drunkard, a friend of tax collectors and sinners (Mt 11:19). They didn't like his manner; they fought against his most striking habit. Whenever people sat down, ate something, ate bread and drank wine, when they could relax and were not forced to do something, when they could get food and new energy and were not forced to give energy, whenever people were in this relieving and redeeming situation, then Jesus had his great hour, then he could tell his redeeming message, so that his listeners could really experience and see his redeeming words within such relaxing situations. His listeners not only ate with him, but they, so to speak, ate the loving message of Jesus itself by eating bread and wine. They incorporated him and his message of his loving father, of his merciful and giving God. Because God loves humankind, he dines with us in Jesus Christ.

Finally, during his last supper with his friends, Jesus's eating with others reaches its highest point: the supper became, was sacrifice. The supper before his death celebrates his death for his friends as a hopeful and life-restoring event. This is a healing paradox: when Jesus was ready to leave his friends, so they could not feel his hands any more from the outside, Jesus wanted to be closer to his friends and disciples from the inside and became their deepest and most inner friend. Now he really became their food which gives everlasting life, which gives the community with Jesus Christ and through him the communion with God. There is hardly a deeper and more intense fulfilment of our original longing for unity, security and friendship on this earth than this holy mass, this Eucharist, this sacrifice and supper. Through this sacrament God wants to reach our deepest existence, our deepest roots. According to John: Christ is the true vine; we are the branches. Whoever remains in him, there Christ makes his home.

So we do celebrate the memory of the greatest feast on this earth. We celebrate the redeeming feast of God with us. And in this we celebrate our own future, our eternity in our presence, because in heaven God is going to be our host. Therefore, we also celebrate with all the beloved deceased who sit at the other end of this table. Through this heavenly feast all of us get the last fulfilment of our deep wish for life, unity and communion.

Therefore, let us rejoice; this last supper is not only an earthly meal, but it also represents our own future, it shows and guarantees what we are allowed to expect for ourselves and others: the resurrection, the victory over the death and its power. As St. John says: To have life, and to have it abundantly in overflow. God gives his life, his love to us. Therefore, God enables and encourages us to distribute this life and love to each other and treat one another in justice. Then we are able to bear fruit in plenty. Not because it is demanded but because we are empowered to do it. Like parents are able to say: For the sake of my child I would do or give anything, even my life. Not because it is a demand but because this solidarity comes out of a living and vital love and friendship. We all live in in such a friendship with God.

5. *Easter (with St. Francis)*

St. Francis lived in imitation of Jesus of Nazareth: That is the theme of Giotto's pictures in San Francesco. At first the life of Jesus and then parallel to this life the life of St. Francis was composed.

But what is the mystery of their lives, what made their life so fascinating to their fellow creatures? The answer is: they opened themselves to every situation and every person. That was their poorness and their richness, their humility and their greatness, their weakness and their strength, their humanity and their goodness.

Jesus and Francis continually ran the risk of presenting themselves to the nearest person who did (or didn't) need their help or criticism, their questions and answers, and above all their solidarity.

Mark put this reality of Jesus in words, and he did this in a unsurpassed way. Jesus is dying a terrible death, the death of a criminal on the cross. He cries in a loud voice: "My God, why have you forsaken me?" This was not only a death of his body, but also the death of his hopes. And Mark continues: when the centurion saw Jesus dying in such a way, he said: "Really, this man is the son of God!" Beyond his weakness and poorness, the human deepness, he is the real Son of God, and this was testified by a pagan.

What are the meaning and responsibility of this passage for us? I think it is: Run the risk of opening yourself to everybody. Open yourself fto the people, give love and confidence in advance. Yes, you will risk the cross, the passion in your own life. It's possible that your love will open you up also to your enemy, can make you naked, weak and poor. But this is the only way to live a meaningful life. And Francis did realise this kind of life: Jesus didn't abolish the cross from this world, but he erected a new one: the cross of kindness and love, of poorness and weakness for the sake of others. Such a cross is meaningful because it fights against the meaningless cross, where people hate and destroy each other for the sake of their own power and richness. And such a cross demands openness and poorness in reality and mind.

Finally, I present an example of such a risky Christian life, which St. Francis of Assisi has given us. One evening some robbers came to the little convent of Francis. Francis himself was not yet there. The friars tried to resist, but they were knocked down and the robbers took everything they could get. The robbers soon came again. But this time St. Francis was with his friars. When he saw the robbers, he opened the door and invited them to come in. He gave them all he had and invited them to spend the night with the community. Some of the robbers converted and remained as brothers.

Like Jesus who gave his "goodness" for humankind, Francis opened his doors and gave all he had. In what situations should we open the doors—without any calculations, whether we get a reward or not? What should the first step be?

There is a second legend. When St. Francis was dying, he wanted to be brought into his cell and asked the brothers to take off his habit because he wanted to die like he was born, completely naked. Such is our life and so it should be: a direct path from the poorness and weakness of our birth to the poorness and weakness of our death. The better you are able to be poor and weak for the sake of others, the better you are carrying the cross and passion for Christ's sake, the better you can say: *consummatum est*, my life is fulfilled. Therefore, we are allowed to celebrate this mass, this Eucharist, this thanksgiving, this memory of Christ's death. His death is our responsibility.

In this Easter mass we are trying to find a new law and way of life—not the law and system of the normal life and social system around us in which at least in the long run everybody is everybody's enemy and wolf. We try to develop a new system of life and hope, a life in simplicity in which we only possess what we give away to others. Knowing this in our heart, of what use can all our ambitions and longings for riches and power be?

In this way the deaths of Christ and Francis show us our responsibility to show real unselfish love, a love which risks even disadvantages and experiences of death. This is not too new for us, because we all know through our own experiences that true love includes sorrow and suffering. Our poets have realised this truth very well: remember Shakespeare's "Romeo and Juliet" and many other plays of this kind, also the modern ones like Erich Segal's very popular "Love Story". We ourselves have realised this experience in our own lives many times: There is never real love in this life without the cross, because love is God's own language in this world and therefore very often foreign, misunderstood and rejected. This is the reason why it is so delicate and difficult to speak and preach about love. But the Christian religion is simply the religion of love, of God's love of humankind, which God showed and proved on the cross of Jesus. God released and sacrificed his Son for the sake of his creatures.

Since that time we know that there is no true love in this life without sacrifices. And we have to preach and to realise this truth so that our church and its members will never become the source of hate, war and oppression (as happened sometimes in the past). Jesus is the personification and fullest realisation of this strong connection between love and cross. He has shown us what real virtue is, and therefore we have to follow him by imitating his life. He himself is love; this means that if we truly love our neighbour, then we are sincere followers of the Lord. In Jesus's life God shows us her will. Because in Jesus' resurrection God legitimates his life as the life according to his will.

This, dear brothers and sisters, is the crucial point: such a life open to all and for the sake of others is meaningful, full of sense, despite all the others who love only power, prestige and social success regardless of their inhuman consequences for the weak. This is the joyful message of Easter: Not the smallest piece of love is done in vain. But power and pressure are always erected in vain. All that is not love is not real, is only a bad puppet play.

I admit that such a life is not easy to shape. But at least there are some oases where we all can live for each other, for example, in our families, in our friendships, with relatives and neighbours. At least there it is not necessary to use power and oppression. At least there we do not need to keep up with the Joneses. This possibility is not a moral law, but a gift to us. It is a present that gives us a free and meaningful life, which God has shown us in Jesus. In this case we can play our own play, not the plays that are being played on us. The resurrection of the crucified Redeemer happens in our life.

We know about the deep relationship between our way of Gospel sharing and Christ's sharing himself in the Eucharist. In Christ we are invited to rest, to receive, to be receptive to his love. And this is possible because in Christ's path to the cross God has shared in our suffering, our anger, our hopes and our desperation. This is the trustful way God shares his love. If God hadn't suffered on this earth, there wouldn't be the slightest reason for us, fearful and suffering humankind, to believe God or in God.

But God lived a human life, serving humanity and risking danger and death. In such a way he proved his love and solidarity. We are celebrating this fact, that we are not alone, that we are not abandoned, because God is on our side, she walks with us like the risen Christ walked with the two disciples to Emmaus.

6. *One God as Trinity*

Human suffering sharpens the question of God. In the Bible we find no answer to explain this question. But what we find is a personal answer that opens a life-long relationship. Thus, Jesus in the Gospel of John says: "I am the way, the truth and the life." Jesus is the personal way to God, and at the same time he is God himself. Within this concrete truth he is God's son, who shows the *way* to our aim, to the Father. The connection of both, between the Father and the Son within God himself as well as between the Father and the Son incarnated is the Holy Spirit, by whom all baptised are connected, too. At first this sounds somehow abstract. And it is a "*mysterium stricte dictum*", which means a mystery we can never grasp. But nevertheless it has been revealed to us. And revelation means that God wants to come and comes into our experience. But how does this mystery come into our life? In the following I concentrate on the issue: What has God already done for us in her three-fold identity, which we know of by means of the revelation, of this encounter, which is not a mere mental one, but a holistic one. And how can we connect this grace with our life? Is it already connected? We try to detect this reality now.

Concerning God's revelation within human suffering: At first: On the one hand our life is beautiful; marvellous are the earth and the whole cosmos. On the other hand this world is not the best of all possible worlds: Too much suffering and agony; too much torture and cruelty, misery and injustice, violence and death. What sense does this creation have if it destroys its creatures, if it destroys people, even us ourselves? And it doesn't help if we justify God too quickly and proclaim God's innocence in this. In the Bible God is responsible for everything, and the Psalms express this fact intensively (according to Psalm 22:16). And it doesn't help to give the well-known explanation: suffering and evil are necessary because otherwise there would be no freedom to decide between evil and good so that there could not be a moral consciousness. The price is too high for such a freedom. You could expect that an almighty God could solve this problem by connecting freedom with liberation from pain and sin.

We have a certain spirituality that is not very helpful either: You have to submit yourself and carry the cross without any resistance. God knows why. It is God's will, and you have to obey. God has put, placed and fixed it this way. Then, even lamentation is not allowed, not to mention an accusation of God. To accuse God and to bring charges against her would be a sin and blasphemy. If this were right, then Jesus would sin on the cross; he would commit a godless blasphemy, because he cries his lament according to the beginning of the Psalm 22: "My God, my God, why have you abandoned me?" And this is not only a lament, but also an accusation. He, who has had a very intensive relationship with his father, a confidence like a child, addressing God as "Abba", which expresses his feeling of be deeply sheltered by his father—now he can only cry out the breach of this relationship. In Psalm 22 the whole history of pain and exile of the people of Israel finds their impressive expression. It is a prayer of resistance. It is the right of suffering people at least to stand in front of their creator to resist and to cry: why? It is the last right of the victim to save his or her dignity in such a lament. Forty per cent of the Psalms consist of lamentations!

Human suffering within God himself: Concerning our issue: Since the second divine person has come in contact with the history of humankind in such a substantial incarnated connection, he realises not only his being in God within the Trinity but also the lack of it, the desolation and the lament against his father. Even as the resurrected one after his return into the inner divine Trinity, Christ remains the incarnated Son of God who carries, by means of the remaining wound marks, the contradiction to God himself. The relationship to the outside has changed, has altered the inner Trinitarian relationship. The relationship between God the Father and the Son by means of the Holy Spirit is still an innermost bond of unending love, but because God loves humankind in such a deep way as he loves his son, this bond now includes—for the sake of suffering human beings—the contradiction in God himself. Christ still feels desolation as long as people feel desolation. The resurrected Christ sighs with us in the Holy Spirit (see Rom 8:26). Human suffering belongs now to his identity and becomes an innermost part of the Father-Son relationship. This is the bondage between the inner and outer Trinity: like God encounters us in Christ, the incarnated Christ encounters him in the Trinity. The outer relationship complies with his/her inner being. More we cannot know in our faith than what he has let us know in this revealing encounter, keeping in mind that even what we "know" remains a deep mystery in God.

So, the Trinitarian God shows us his suffering with the suffering, her lamenting with the lamenting, even his suffering for the sake of the sinners, the perpetrators and their reconciliation. Still there is no answer to why there is pain and evil. Accordingly, in Psalm 22 the why question is not answered. This question becomes increasingly irrelevant because this prayer leads to a new confidence: that God is not only near when we are well, but is also near, even nearer, when we are suffering. Anyway, an answer would not help if the pain remained and did not disappear simultaneously. The most important thing is that God does not leave us alone, not now, in being with and in us, and later, when God will rescue us forever.

Jesus also gave no explanations for why there is suffering and evil. He answered the suffering people and was in solidarity with those who needed consolation, justice and help, forgiveness and reconciliation. Doing this cost him his life. If we go to very ill people, we would not help them by explaining the medical reasons why he/she is sick. But if I sit very near and remain so that the suffering person can feel that I am not running away, then I at least can try to carry and bear the pain with him or her: only this is a helpful “answer”. Exactly this is the first characteristic feature of the Trinitarian God: that he sends us his son to be close to us in both our sorrow and our joy.

God’s desolation and powerless power: The second feature of the relationship of the Trinitarian God to us sounds paradoxical: the desolation of God. The Son of God has to experience that his father has abandoned him in this history. It is peculiarly strange and at the same time indicative that the pagan Roman centurion has a moment of realisation when Jesus is dying and cries out the lament: “My God, my God, why have you abandoned me!”; the truth of the Son of God. Therefore, the centurion says: “This war truly the Son of God!” It is not possible to express the fact more dramatically that suffering and the presence of God belong together in Jesus’ story, and therefore in our stories as well. God does not write the history of the winners and victorious ones but lives the life of a victim in history.

The Trinitarian truth of God is shown in the fact that Jesus not only endured a human life but also risked a life driven to the utmost suffering. He did not battle sin and violence by means of sin and violence and did not use earthly or even heavenly power to escape the pain (John 18:36). The father does not save his son from the cross. The son is entirely God on this earth as he is entirely human. The incarnation of God thus becomes the “in-suffering” of God.

This indicates the third characteristic feature of the relationship of the Trinitarian God with us, which is a specific lack of power, a specific powerlessness of God in our history. Jesus builds only on the power of love and freedom, of justice and mercifulness. Where and whenever these powers get powerless, when the experience of love and justice cannot have an effect in themselves, because destructive violence resists against them and destroys them, even God has no power to defeat them. Love cannot go with violence. The cross shows the power of love and reconciliation against the violence, the power of solidarity against the evil. There will be no final victory over violence and evil before Christ comes again.

We do not know why we have this kind of world, but we know in our faith that God is with us in this situation. Therefore, God will be with us in and beyond death and in and beyond of the end of this world, when God comes again.

In the power of the Holy Spirit: Therefore, we can summarise the connection between the Trinity in God and her relationship with us. If the spirit of the resurrected Christ suffers not only with but in us (according to Rom 8:19–26), then there is a correspondence for that in God too. Expressed in the picture of the resurrected Lord: When God the Father received the resurrected Christ with his wounds with his martyrdom, God received the passion of the whole humankind, the martyrdom of our history into the Trinitarian identity. The crucified Christ cries all lamentations of human beings against his father. If God did not have the endless divine power of love to bear this passion and his lamenting son in his Trinitarian life, he would fall apart or explode into pieces. Because all suffering of the world also takes place in God himself: through Christ our Lord. The Holy Spirit who holds together Father and Son is the same spirit who holds together Christ and the suffering of the world. Without his unending power of binding love both relationships, the inner and outer Trinitarian ones, could not exist. The Holy Spirit exists personally through this powerful connecting and unconditional love. The Passion in God is therefore not a weak thing but the proof of God's unending and inexhaustible power of love and life.

Twelve years ago in the Church Philip Neri in Soweto, I discovered the Stations of the Cross, created by a gifted artist: in this the second divine person experiences the suffering life of the people who live there. The pictures are drawn into the daily life of the people, into their experience of violence, suppression and hope. The Stations pick up these scenes and show in this way how Jesus identifies himself with the people, how he is present in the suffering, caring and hoping men and women. He experiences their fate and gives them hope by accompanying them. In this kind of "negative Christology" God hears the human cries, lamentations and accusations not only from outside but also in her innermost heart. This doesn't explain the dark mystery of human pain and evil (we have to wait till the last judgement for that), but our cries have been received in the realm of God himself. Thus, we are not alone. And this is the most important thing, more important than to know. Knowing without God's solidarity and without the simultaneous total liberation of the world from pain and evil would be hopeless and sarcastic.

If God shows his solidarity in such a way, if she is nearest to us when we are nearest to our deepest powerlessness, our death, where we have to let everything go, then God will save us as he has saved Jesus. The unending power of God to suffer in Christ with and for us will turn into the same inexhaustible power to give life forever. Because God is both together: unending love and life. And so he will bring a new world and creation without any pain and evil.

7. *Assumption of Mary*

Remembering the assumption of Mary into heaven, we think, like Paul in the reading today (August 15), 1 Cor 15:22–27, of our own life after death. Of course not in that extraordinary way that Mary was assumed but still with the same result: that we are allowed to live in heaven (whatever heaven may be) after death. In our Christian faith we believe in the resurrection of the dead and an eternal life hereafter. In this sermon I do not intend to explain what heaven or eternal life may be. Even in our faith we do not know much about it. We had better leave that to God in confidence and hope.

I'll confine myself to another point that often causes deep fears within our faith. I mean the question: everyone will be raised from the dead, but will everyone be saved? Isn't there a last judgement and the threat of hell?

I know from many talks and confessions how many anxieties are provoked by preaching unfounded fears to keep the believers obedient and in line. Therefore, I'd like to encourage you: wash all your fears away. God doesn't want to oppress us by threatening but wants to win us by a love that includes freedom as well as endless mercy.

Yes, there will be a last judgement; there will be the encounter with the coming Christ, in which all of us will regret our evil deeds, not because of fear, but because of the trusting love of God we have betrayed. Confronted with the revealed love of God (which we can realise in our present life only in an imperfect way; for many people this love of God has been hidden and destroyed by bad situations and relationships) every person will certainly know and deeply and painfully feel how she was and is loved by God and how he hasn't acted according to this love. The experience of this encounter will kindle a deep ardent fire within us, a fire of regret and sorrow, of remorse and pity. This fire within us will be judgement enough, because it goes right through our heart and mind and will change and renew us. Therefore, purgatory will be less a question of time and more one of intensity. Reaching this deepest root of the love that created and raised us, reaching this deepest divine source of our own existence and freedom, nobody will be able to decide nor act against it. I am certain of this in my belief.

St. Augustine said: *Deus semper maior*! God, God's love is always greater! Greater than we can imagine at all. This "always" has to be understood strictly: in an unending way, even and especially after the last judgement there will be mercy too. God's life-giving power has no end and has to be perceived as greater than any human sin and guilt can be. (This is not an attack on our freedom, because such a God proves to be the source of our freedom, because she dispenses with alienating pressure and fear.)

In the John Ryland's library in Manchester there is an old manuscript going back to the tenth century called the "*Exsultet roll*", which was read by the deacon on the Holy Saturday. Beside the letters of the text there you can see a simply made but very impressive and comforting drawing: After his death Jesus descends from his grave to the dead into hell and takes the first person he can reach by the hand. This person reaches with his free hand to take his neighbour by the hand, who does the same with his neighbour and so on. Therefore, Jesus is leading a long queue out of hell and nobody is left.

I think we have forgotten this message of Holy Saturday; we mostly only celebrate Good Friday and Easter Sunday, omitting and missing the Good News of Holy Saturday, which is also stated in the Apostle's Creed: he descended to the dead, which is a rather weak translation for what is meant in this original text: descended *ad inferos*, he descended into hell itself and emptied it. Of course, this was not a singular act at that time, but this is Christ's present and future continuing act as well. This is a promise like his own resurrection was a promise concerning our own resurrection.

Some weeks ago, I met an elderly priest; we were talking about what will be necessary in the future church and in the pastoral responsibility of the clergy. He especially stressed one thing: "In the past we emphasised the fear of hell too much. That was a big mistake on our part. We have to combine the word of God with his real love and the freedom he offers to humankind again." I totally agree with this statement.

Therefore, let us rejoice today. Of course, I would prefer to say there is no hell at all, but this would be against the dogma of the Church. But no dogma states that anyone will ever be punished with an eternal life sentence in hell. The Church has declared many people saints, which certainly means that they are in heaven. But the Church has never stated that anyone had been sent to hell. The great conservative Theologian Hans Urs von Balthasar said once: "Yes, there is a hell, but I am sure in my belief in our loving and eternally lifegiving God, that hell at last will be empty in the end."

Then, we do not have to be Christians because of our fear of God but because of our fear for God: that God's life and spirit of love and freedom will be fruitful and present among us now as it will be in the hereafter. Then, it will not be the fear of punishment that urges us to be good anymore, but the concern and care for all people who need our help and solidarity to be good for their own sake themselves.

8. *Which Picture of God?*

The German philosopher and poet Friedrich Nietzsche was the first to give the world the message that God is dead. Even if God lived, he said, then we would have to fight and kill him so that human beings can become free, can become God themselves. He thought that God always enslaves people and never allows them human freedom. He described the Church as God's own sword that he uses to tyrannise the so-called faithful. Such a God has destroyed the self-confidence of the creature; he has never loved his creature but plays with it for his own cruel pleasure.

If Nietzsche's picture of God were right, then I would agree with him and join his fight against such a cruel God. We human beings could never accept a God who has created and enslaved us for his own inhuman pleasure, for whom we are only toys, only puppets. This argument is still the most striking motivation for many atheists, also in our time, to hate the Christian God and Church.

But that is just the point, this is the crucial question: is Nietzsche's picture of God true? Or did he fight against his own illusion of God? If so, then he would have fought against his own idea of God, yes, against himself, but never against the true God.

Our Gospel of St. John gives us a different picture of God, and I think this is the only true one, because it can never be regarded as our own idea, but is given to us by the Son of God himself. For this picture of God is beyond the human mind, because in our text of St. John God is too good, too merciful for human invention (John 6:51–58, 20th Sunday, Year 2). God not only sends his only Son, but also suffers the life of a man who was entirely good in Jesus. And the risen Christ still feels the suffering of humankind in his own body. As such, he gives himself to us as the real food we need badly to overcome our distresses. Therefore, the belief in God's goodness is the only condition for experiencing his mercy. We should never be afraid of our God, but trust in her kindness, even though sometimes we have sinned so often or greatly that we believe God will not forgive us, if she is just. For this is the heart of the Good News: God's love for us is boundless if we only trust in his mercy. Therefore, all despair is contrary to the Christian virtue of hope.

This was different in the ancient Greek religions, for instance. There despair was part of the faith in the gods and goddesses. And why? Because these Gods were made according to our human image. In fact, people can never be inexhaustibly merciful. Nietzsche's idea of God is also made according to his image of humanity. Therefore, his beautiful poems are lost battles against despair.

Christian faith, however, is hope itself. And this is very important for our daily life as well. Even when we have failed again and again, despite our good resolutions, we still must never be without hope. Our offences do not burden us further; we are rather delivered and set free to start afresh, to look forward and to do good again. This process continues during our whole lifetime; yes, this process is life itself. God's Son welcomes sinners. He not only eats with them, but also gives himself to them by means of his own body. This means: God accepts every one of us as she or he is, without any conditions. Therefore, if God has accepted us unconditionally, then we have to do the same: Nobody is perfect; everyone has their weaknesses. Therefore, we should be very patient with ourselves and our neighbours.

Yes, we have to work hard in this world; we will sin and suffer, but we never have to be fearful, depressed or despairing, because we have a God, who is our father, who never abandons us. We are not God's slaves, but her free creatures.

Therefore, we shouldn't go through this world miserable and unhappy, but should live without fear, with joy and good humour, cheerfully and with patience. Then, we can become the witnesses of our loving and merciful God in this world. And nobody can say, as Nietzsche once did, "Maybe I could believe in the Christian God if the Christians themselves showed God's love in their behaviour."

9. *The First Will Be Last (Mt 19:23–30)*

"Many that are first will be last, and the last first!" (Mt 19:30). This well-known sentence was written not only for the Jews in Jesus's time, but for us as well. First, of course, it is a horrible criticism of the clergy, our priests and bishops, who are believed to be the first in Christ's company, to teach in his name. But do they really teach in his name? Or do they preach their own wisdom and mediocrity? Above all, in their own lives, do they practice what they preach? Then, it is a criticism of all who believe they are in the right church, being and living as Christians. Jesus criticises his own people; he does not spare them. He is always challenging us. He finally undertakes an overturning of all values and merits: "The last will be first and the first last" (Mt 20:16). Nothing is sure; nothing is guaranteed. The coming of the Lord will be an imposing surprise for every one of us. Jesus for example lived according to the will of God and became a victim in human history: therefore, in his resurrection he gained eternal life. The last in the eyes of the people became the first in the eyes of God. But Jesus never calculated according to merits. He lived this way for the sake of the people, not for the sake of reward.

Therefore, we should not be concerned about our merit, our reward, which the Lord has to give us. Merit is important in its time, in the time, when Christ will come again, but not yet. If we do good only for the sake of eternal reward, then we become to prize conscious, because then we want to become the winners, the first. For that reason, to be a real Christian it is not necessary to think about later rewards, but it is absolutely necessary to live as a real Christian now, in the present time. Our present life is substantial; the reward, everlasting life, can become a result of this life, but it should never be the first motivation of our deeds. When the New Testament tells us that somebody will be rewarded, that means: the life of this person is ratified as an everlasting example to us. Surely, he or she will get their reward, but not for the sake of an expectation of merit, but because they lived according to God's will. The will of God is the most important road sign for us, meaning that it itself has to be the deepest motivation for our deeds, not our secret wish to become rewarded. For the will of our creator is not our will, and often it goes against our purposes.

You may ask: what is the will of God? The answer is: God's will is personified and represented in Jesus of Nazareth forever. He was the first who entirely realised God's will through himself. In fact, this is the essential meaning of the resurrection: God raised this Jesus from the dead because he followed his will completely. Since that time, Jesus and his life have been the obligatory example for all who want to follow the will of their creator.

And what was Jesus's life like? It was a path to the cross, a passion to the death. But what made Jesus's life and love so decisive, so dangerous, a dangerous love leading to death? How can we understand this mystery? Let us look at the life of Jesus: he lived dangerously because he left himself open for every situation and person. That was his poorness and—at the same time—in the eyes of the Lord his richness, his humility and his greatness, his weakness and his strength, his humanity and his goodness. Continually Jesus ran a risk in presenting himself to the nearest, the next, who needed his help or criticism, his questions and answers, and above all his solidarity. Yes, solidarity: in Jesus's life and death God shows us his loving solidarity with the sinners and the poor, the living and the dying.

And this is important for us, too, if we truly call ourselves Christians: Our part in this life is not triumphalism, but to cope with daily life is not the resurrection but the cross, not the glory but the passion, not the glorious Christ, who is sitting at God's right hand—whom we never can imitate—but God's loving and suffering son Jesus of Nazareth. We have to realise that in this life the resurrection is hidden in its opposite. This means: only if we live in the imitation of the suffering servant of the Lord can we realise his resurrection through our deeds, because only then can we make an oasis of goodness and consolation around us. God does not want the crosses of human beings who are imprisoned, deprived of rights and despised, who are starving and bleeding to death. Therefore, he has erected a new cross through our Lord: the cross of kindness and unselfishness. By means of this now hopeful cross, the pain of humankind can be relieved and soothed. It is a strange law that God has made: the cross of hate and unkindness in this world can only be fought by the cross of love and patience. Jesus hat not abolished the cross; he has erected a new one, against ours that we create every day through our selfishness and malice. Since that time, hopeful pain has battled the hopeless pain of our earth.

Therefore, we do not suffer for the sake of suffering, but because in this life you have to expect to suffer if you are basically good. Many of us know this from own experiences. If you are good, then you lose power. But if we are willing to relieve the pain of humankind through our own suffering, as Jesus did, then we can bring a little peace and goodness to our neighbourhoods, because then God is able to work through us as she has worked through Jesus.

This is the will of God: let us live in the imitation of Jesus for the sake of our neighbours, entirely free, without any fear, whether we get a reward or not. Doing our creators will is our original duty, but reward is no business of ours. It is entirely up to God himself. Then, we will actualise the Lord's prayer: "Thy will be done!" We will discover a loving Father now, in the present time, and when Jesus comes again!

10. *Facilitating Grace*

Christ has the power to cure the sick, forgive sins and heal the body. This is how he encounters not only this man. His story is our reality, too. Christ actually wants to heal us, in our pains and sorrows. Every story in the Gospel first has this basic meaning: how Jesus forgives and heals the people in his time, in the same way the risen Christ forgives and heals us now in our time, and he does this permanently without end, saying: *ephata*, be opened to a new life, a new step and chance. Jesus did this in our baptism, in the ritual symbol of *ephata*, to open the child's senses to life, to communication, first for receiving and later for giving. In the last anointment, in the sacrament for the sick, the priest closes the person's eyes, ears and mouth, all the senses again, in the hope that God, the risen Lord, will open them again forever in the heavenly life.

Sometimes we are too quick to say: As Jesus did, so we must also do. But this strategy moralises God as if he were nothing else but a commander. For Jesus not only demands us; he also wants to facilitate, to enable, what he wishes. We are called to say: this story is my story. I am the one whom Jesus cures and liberates from evil. Then we accept being loved by God without any deeds, unconditionally, as sinners: this is the message of the first letter of St. John. We do not have not to show our achievements because Christ has already achieved everything.

For a long time, I couldn't understand, why Peter refused to get his feet washed during the last supper and why Jesus reacted so harshly. Peter hesitated because he didn't like being served by Christ, let's say by God himself. Therefore, before we tell each other to wash each others' feet, to serve one another, we are encouraged to believe, that God serves us and loves us radically unconditionally and forever. This communion with God is the deepest and unending source for our own good deeds, for serving humanity. We need this energy of grace badly, because serving our neighbours costs us a lot, as we all know by experience.

Community means both community of the faithful among themselves and community of the believers with God. We realise that God is the first facilitator of our life for the sake of others. The washing of feet is a symbol of this good will towards us.

11. *Ready for Rest (Mk 6:30–31)*

Jesus is ready for rest. With his disciples he goes to some lonely place, as he has done before many times. Yes, he allowed himself and his followers to rest to recover and pray. Quite a long time, four weeks, is recorded for when Jesus went into the desert. That is the first message of this Gospel: when you need rest, then allow yourself time to recover in spirit, mind and body. Do not hesitate. There is no reason to have a bad conscience about it. This is part of the fact that we are not God ourselves on this earth, even not in doing good deeds, because Christ himself will come again and establish the Kingdom of God entirely.

In my country the priests are often workaholics. They work too much and depend too much on mere effectiveness. Therefore, they are often not able to react according to their heart. They are too engaged in everything so that they have no time to take pity if it is required and necessary, if people are really suffering.

This is the second message of our Gospel: Jesus is able to dispense with a break if there are people who are longing for him, who need him badly.

Both are important: to rest for a while, to step away from one's current activity and to react spontaneously for the sake of others, if it is needed. The two messages are connected with each other.

12. *The Coincidence of the Opposites*

There is an extraordinary sentence in our second reading today: "Try then to imitate God as children of his that he loves." How can this be possible, to imitate God? St. Paul explained this imitating of God in the sentence before: "Never have grudges against others, or lose your temper, or raise your voice to anybody, or call each other names, or allow any sort of spitefulness. Be friends with one another, and kind, forgiving each other as readily as God forgave you in Christ" (Eph 4:30–5:2, 19th Sunday, Year 2).

There is quite a long list of ways we should deal with each other. It is not easy to fulfil all these commandments, which can be concentrated in two words: tolerance and plurality. These two words also express the characteristic essentials of God. Therefore, it is said that these virtues should be a realisation of the imitation of God, of God's multiplicity and tolerance in letting the being be.

From the beginning, God created a world of differences and opposites: as the result of God's own richness of vitality and creativity. Consequently, God created us as different and distinct people ourselves. We all have our own biography, experiences and talents, which are unique despite some their similarities. We are not only allowed, but also encouraged to foster our individualism, not to imitate others but to realise God's creative will by developing our own originality.

If this is true, how can there be communities among people who are allowed to be different and unique? The basic answer is: by tolerating and acknowledging this multiplicity and variety of people, their meanings and deeds, by learning that we only can enrich each other if we allow one another to be unique.

Especially in the church we are not together mainly because we should have the same meanings and beliefs about everything, but because we have the same God. And God has a unique interpersonal relationship with each of us. God is uniting us. Therefore, there is no need to enforce unity by uniformity. I am afraid to say that in our church different meanings are sometimes not very welcome. There is too much fear of losing the calmness, of forgoing law and order in the church. Exactly this is the reason why an increasing number of especially but not only young people find the church not very attractive and alive, not very vital and important for them, for their own different meanings and experiences.

In the imitation of the creative God we are bound to proclaim: a community (family or parish, etc.) in which you are only accepted if you consent, if you say always yes, destroys the living creativity of God in his creatures and is not a Christian community.

The foundation of our belief, which we call the revelation of God, the Bible shows us clearly enough how the church could and should be: The Bible is nothing more than a collection of different stories and authors, all of them unique in their different situations, reactions and beliefs. In addition, they are not only different from each other but in opposition to each other, too. You can't really compare the book of Kohelet, who is nearly an atheist (in the book of Ecclesiastes), with the book of Isaiah, who believes deeply. There are also important differences between the early letters of Paul and the late Pastoral letters in the New Testament.

The differences between the Catholic Church and Martin Luther, for example, were small compared with the oppositions in the Bible. So the revelation itself teaches us plurality and acceptance of plurality, which is tolerance, especially to learn in relation to our fellow Christians.

If we do not learn this lesson, the increasing fundamentalism within the Christian churches will split them right through the different denominations, will split the Catholic church as well as the Protestant churches including the Anglican church. The traditional borders between the confessional churches will become less important than the new borders between fundamentalism and plurality within all the churches.

The great medieval theologian Nikolas of Cues based his whole theology and faith on the sentence: "God is the coincidence of the opposites." Therefore, all who do not shelter those with ways different from their own, who do not protect people who are different, diminish God's life and spirit among us.

Let us therefore enjoy God's rich and exciting life among us by accepting and fostering our little and great differences. Then, the life in our church will never be as boring as it sometimes has been. Let us never punish other people by excluding them from our communities, parishes and families if they say no sometimes, if they oppose and object.

Appendix: Publication and Translation References

Chapter 1:

God's People: Instruments of Healing. The Diaconical Dimension of the Church, Bern/New York 1993, 27–44. 61–75. (translated by Kenneth Wynne)

God's People: Instruments of Healing. The Diaconical Dimension of the Church, Bern/New York 1993, 89–112. (translated by Kenneth Wynne)

Chapter 2:

Religious Identity as Gift and Task: A Christian Perspective, in: Mitri Raheb (Ed.), Palestinian Identity in relation to Time and Space, Bethlehem, Beit Jala (Diyar Publisher) 2014, 175–195. (translated by Jochen Scherer)

Church for Others. The Church's Identity through Service, in: Concilium 24 (1988) 4, 41–54. (translated by Margaret Kohl)

God's People: Instruments of Healing. The Diaconical Dimension of the Church, Bern/New York 1993, 45–60. (translated by Kenneth Wynne)

The Challenge of Contextuality in Europe: Destructing Exclusive Theologies, in: Bulletin ET 7 (1996) 2, 162–184 (translated by Jochen Scherer)

Suffering in the Practice of Christian Faith, in: Christoph Mandry (ed.), Suffering in Medicine, Theology and Medical Ethics, will be published 2019. (translated by Paul André Arend)

Chapter 3:

The Invention of History: A German Perspective, in: Mitri Raheb (ed.), A Century of Interplay between Theology and Politics in Palestine (Contextual Theology Series), Bethlehem 2011 (Diyar Publisher), 131–147. (translated by Jochen Scherer)

How to deal with Violence in Biblical Texts. Some Considerations towards Biblical Hermeneutics of Violence, in: Johannes Hunter, Joachim Kügler (Ed.), The Bible and Violence in Africa, (Bible in Africa Studies 20), Bamberg 2016, 11–34. (translated by Jochen Scherer)

How can Christian communities claim their "better truth" without violence against others, even more for the sake of solidarity with them? Some considerations reflected on Biblical traditions, in: Wilhelm Gräb, Lars Charbonnier (Eds.), Secularization Theories, Religious Identity and Practical Theology, Zürich, Berlin 2009, 308–315. (translated by Jochen Scherer)

Biblical Laments wherever People suffer. (translated by Bruce Allen)

The Unveiled View through the Tears of the Victims. (translated by World Day of Prayer, International Committee, New York)

Chapter 4:

Christian Mission in a Pluralistic, Unjust and Violent World, in: Elaine Graham/Anna Rowlands (eds.), Pathways to the Public Square. Practical Theology in an Age of Pluralism. International Academy of Practical Theology, Manchester 2003 (International Practical Theology 1), Münster 2005, 263–271. (translated by Jochen Scherer)

The Global Context: The Debate on the Role of Religion in the European Constitution, in: Mitri Raheb (Ed.), God's Reign and People's Rule. Constitution, Religion, and Identity in Palestine, Berlin 2009, 15–28. (translated by Jochen Scherer)

The Churches' Responsibility for the Media, in: Concilium 29 (1993) 6, 80–90. (translated by John Bowden)

Chapter 5:

Pope Benedict and the Perception of Reality (translated by Bruce Allen)

Heart to Heart. Pope Francis and the Grace of Preaching, in: Klaus Krämer, Klaus Vellguth (eds.), Evangelii Gaudium. Voices of the Universal Church (One World Theology Vol. 7), Freiburg i.B. 2015, 149–160. (translated by the team who compiled this volume, ibid. XVI).

Towards an Indicative Preaching, in: Praktise Teologie in Suid-Afrika 7 (1992) 2, 113–118. (translated by Kenneth Wynne)

Diaconate between Title and Implementation, in: Diaconia Christi 52 (2017) 1/2, 61–68. (translated by the International Diaconate Centre, Rottenburg, Germany)

Chapter 6:

"Priest-mothers" and "God-mothers". Qualitative Empirical Approaches to Research and the Human Image of God, in: H. Ziebertz/F. Schweitzer/H. Häring/D. Browning (ed.), The Human Image of God, Leiden 2001, 231–248. (translated by Barbara Schultz)

The Spiritual und Pastoral Meaning of the Marital Rite, in: INTAMS review (2009) 15, 44–50. (translated by Jochen Scherer)

New ways of pastoral eschatology, in: Jaco S. Dreyer/Johannes A. van der Ven (ed.), Divine Justice – Human Justice (Festschrift Hennie Pieterse), Pretoria (Unisa) 2002, 19–38. (translated by the team who edited this volume)

Christian Eschatology and Pastoral Care, in: Helmut Weiß, Klaus Temme (Eds.), Treasure in Earthen Vessels. Intercultural Perspectives on Pastoral Care Facing Fragility and Destruction (ContactZone. Explorations in Incultural Theology Vol 6), Berlin 2009, 107–125. (translated by Jochen Scherer)

Chapter 7:

Poetry as a Deep Emotional Experience of a Different World: The Example of Goethe's West-Eastern Divan, in: International Journal of Language and Linguistics Vol. 5 (2017) Numb. 6, 172–178. (translated by Jochen Scherer)

Sermons and Meditations. (corrected by Sr. Ignatius Thackaberry and Sr. Bernadette Doherty, PBVM)